THE BIBLE IN THE AMERICAN EXPERIENCE

BIBLE AND ITS RECEPTION

Rhonda Burnette-Bletsch, General Editor

Editorial Board:
Brennan Breed
Stephen R. Burge
Lesleigh Cushing
J. Cheryl Exum
Helen Leneman
Michael Rosenberg
Rodney S. Sadler Jr.
Robert Paul Seesengood

Number 2

THE BIBLE IN THE AMERICAN EXPERIENCE

Edited by
Claudia Setzer and David A. Shefferman

PRESS

Atlanta

Copyright © 2020 by SBL Press

All rights reserved. No part of this work may be reproduced or transmitted in any form or by any means, electronic or mechanical, including photocopying and recording, or by means of any information storage or retrieval system, except as may be expressly permitted by the 1976 Copyright Act or in writing from the publisher. Requests for permission should be addressed in writing to the Rights and Permissions Office, SBL Press, 825 Houston Mill Road, Atlanta, GA 30329 USA.

Library of Congress Cataloging-in-Publication Data

Names: Setzer, Claudia, editor. | Shefferman, David A., editor.
Title: The Bible in the American experience / edited by Claudia Setzer and David A. Shefferman.
Description: Atlanta : Atlanta : SBL Press, 2020. | Series: Bible and its reception; 2 | Includes bibliographical references and index.
Identifiers: LCCN 2019059628 (print) | LCCN 2019059629 (ebook) | ISBN 9781628372748 (paperback) | ISBN 9780884144373 (hardback) | ISBN 9780884144380 (ebook)
Subjects: LCSH: Bible—Influence. | United States—Civilization. | Popular culture—United States. | Religion and culture—United States.
Classification: LCC BS538.7 .B56 2020 (print) | LCC BS538.7 (ebook) | DDC 220.0973—dc23
LC record available at https://lccn.loc.gov/2019059628
LC ebook record available at https://lccn.loc.gov/2019059629

Contents

Abbreviations vii

Introduction
    Claudia Setzer and David Shefferman 1

1. The Bible and Bibles in America
    Lori Anne Ferrell 15

2. The Bible and Digital Media
    Jeffrey S. Siker 35

3. The Bible and Popular Culture
    Jason A. Wyman Jr. 69

4. The Bible in American Literature
    M. Cooper Harriss 93

5. The Bible and Visual Art in America
    Aaron Rosen 113

6. The Bible and American Music
    Joseph Orchard 133

7. The Bible, Law, and Political Rhetoric
    Steven K. Green 153

8. The Bible and the Curriculum of American Public Schools (K–12) in the Twenty-First Century
    Mark A. Chancey 189

9. But Is It Useful? The Perennial Problem of American Biblical
   Scholarship and Higher Education
   Davina C. Lopez 227

10. The Bible and Social Reform: Musings of a Biblical Scholar
    Emerson B. Powery 255

Contributors..287
Biblical Index 293
General Index...295

Abbreviations

AAR	American Academy of Religion
ARV	American Revised Version (1901)
BAGD	Bauer, Walter, William F. Arndt, F. Wilbur Gingrich, and Frederick W. Danker. *Greek-English Lexicon of the New Testament and Other Early Christian Literature.* 2nd ed. Chicago: University of Chicago Press, 1979.
BAL	*The Bible in American Life* (2017)
BibInt	*Biblical Interpretation*
DOMA	Defense of Marriage Act (1996)
ERV	English Revised Version (1885)
GPBS	Global Perspectives on Biblical Scholarship
JAAR	*Journal of the American Academy of Religion*
JBL	*Journal of Biblical Literature*
JNABI	*Journal of the National Association of Biblical Instructors*
JR	*Journal of Religion*
KJV	King James Version (1611)
MOBIA	Museum of Biblical Art (New York City, closed 2015)
MOTB	Museum of the Bible (Washington, D.C.)
NAB	New American Bible (1970)
NABRE	New American Bible Revised Edition (2011)
NCBCPS	National Council on Bible Curriculum in Public Schools
NCV	New Century Version (1987)
NIV	New International Version (1978)
NJB	New Jerusalem Bible (1985)
NKJV	New King James Version (1982)
NRSV	New Revised Standard Version (1989)
RBS	Resources for Biblical Studies
RSV	Revised Standard Version (1952)
SBL	Society of Biblical Literature
TED	Technology, Engineering, and Design

TTR   *Teaching Theology and Religion*

Introduction

CLAUDIA SETZER AND DAVID SHEFFERMAN

Before 1976, the state of scholarship on the Bible in America was, in Mark Noll's words, "decrepit." This Bible, it seemed, was everywhere and nowhere. It informed almost every historical period, social movement, and community identity. Yet its ubiquity made it hard to look at from a critical distance.[1] The Society of Biblical Literature responded with a publication effort to correspond with the centennial celebration of the founding of the Society in 1980, producing nineteen volumes by the end of 1986, with more to come. Central to that effort was the six-volume series The Bible in American Culture, edited by Edwin S. Gaustad and Walter Harrelson.[2] The volumes focused on American education; social reform; American arts and letters; law, politics, and rhetoric; popular culture; and Bible and Bibles (translations and versions).

This volume provides a one-volume update to the earlier series by Gaustad and Harrelson. Some of the original categories have changed, some have been added, and the definition of a specifically *American* expression of biblical ideas wavers in our global information age.[3] Given

---

1. Mark A. Noll, "Review Essay: The Bible in America," *JBL* 106 (1987): 493–509.
2. The series included David Barr and Nicholas Piediscalzi, eds., *The Bible in American Education* (Philadelphia: Fortress; Chico, CA: Scholars Press, 1982); Ernest Sandeen, ed., *The Bible and Social Reform* (Philadelphia: Fortress; Chico, CA: Scholars Press, 1982); Giles Gunn, ed., *The Bible and American Arts and Letters* (Philadelphia: Fortress; Chico, CA: Scholars Press, 1983); James Turner Johnson, ed., *The Bible in American Law, Politics, and Political Rhetoric* (Philadelphia: Fortress; Chico, CA: Scholars Press, 1985); Allene Stuart Phy, ed., *The Bible and Popular Culture in America* (Philadelphia: Fortress; Chico, CA: Scholars Press, 1985); Ernest Frerichs, ed., *The Bible and Bibles in America* (Minneapolis: Fortress; Atlanta: Scholars Press, 1988).
3. As a point of departure and in a manner consistent with the earlier volumes in the series, we begin here by using *America* and *American* to refer to the distinctive history of

the ubiquity of the biblical presence in our culture and the multiplicity of its expressions, our volume must be too brief and can merely point the way toward whole fields of research.

Noting the immensity of the subject in the 1980s, Noll called this effort only "the beginning of the beginning," and so it has been. Numerous edited volumes and sourcebooks on the general topic have appeared in the last decade alone.[4] Some works look at the Bible in the shaping of the historical and political narrative of the United States. No consensus emerges on the Founding Fathers' debt to biblical ideas in their thought and rhetoric.[5] Others consider the Bible's place in public debates over contemporary issues including immigration, poverty, and the teaching of evolution, with a look back at some historical debates over slavery and women's suffrage.[6]

Paralleling developments in the humanities as a whole, feminist and womanist interpretations of the Bible emerged as distinct fields in the late 1970s and 1980s, followed by the establishment of gender as a mode of analysis.[7] Recovery of historical feminist writings from the nineteenth century

---

the United States, recognizing it is one country within the larger Americas. We encourage readers to chart the destabilization of these terms across the essays in this volume.

4. Claudia Setzer and David A. Shefferman, eds., *The Bible in American Culture: A Sourcebook* (London: Routledge, 2011), Mark A. Chancey, Carol Meyers, and Eric M. Meyers, eds., *The Bible and the Public Square: Its Enduring Influence in American Life* (Atlanta: SBL Press, 2014); Paul Gutjahr, ed., *The Oxford Handbook of the Bible in America* (Oxford: Oxford University Press, 2017); and Philip Goff, Arthur E. Farnsley, and Peter Thuesen, eds., *The Bible in American Life* (Oxford: Oxford University Press, 2017), which includes a sociological approach, looking at who reads the Bible, how often, and which versions.

5. Mark A. Noll has completed *In the Beginning Was the Word: The Bible in American Public Life 1492–1783* (Oxford: Oxford University Press, 2016), the first in a multivolume work that will bring us to the present day. Daniel Dreisbach has focused on the biblical ideas that informed the Founding Fathers thought and rhetoric in his book, *Reading the Bible with the Founding Fathers* (New York: Oxford University Press, 2016). Continuing the examination of the interweaving of biblical principles and politics, Paul D. Hanson presents *A Political History of the Bible in America* (Louisville: Westminster John Knox, 2015). A shorter, popular version of the same broad-strokes approach is Jon Meacham's *American Gospel: God, the Founding Fathers, and the Making of a Nation* (New York: Random House, 2007).

6. See, for example, Frances Flannery and Rodney A. Werline, eds., *The Bible in Political Debate: What Does It Really Say?* (London: Bloomsbury T&T Clark, 2016).

7. Some general works include Julia O'Brien, ed., *The Oxford Encyclopedia of the Bible and Gender Studies* (New York: Oxford, 2014); and Marion Ann Taylor, ed., *Handbook of Women Biblical Interpreters* (Grand Rapids: Baker, 2012).

appear in general works and journals. The voices and stories of first-wave thinkers like Sarah Grimké, Sojourner Truth, Anna Julia Cooper, Frances Willard, Elizabeth Cady Stanton, and many others are regularly examined and contextualized. Second-wave feminist scholars have engaged the Bible to a degree that can hardly be summarized.[8] The fruits of such work are visible in the many feminist commentaries on the Bible.[9]

African American engagement is intertwined with the experience of slavery, where the Bible was used as a "poison book," in Allen Callahan's words, to justify the institution, but also as a font of liberation for African Americans who claimed the book as their story. Callahan chronicles the complex career of the biblical text in African American culture, while Emerson Powery and Rodney Sadler illustrate the favored texts and uses of the Bible among the enslaved in the antebellum period.[10]

An interdisciplinary effort headed by Vincent Wimbush resulted in a collection of essays on African Americans and the Bible, as well as the development of the Institute for Signifying Scriptures, a research center in California that considers the interplay of social and political factors in production and use of scriptures.[11] Several commentaries offer black perspectives, including the significance of Africa in the Bible, as well as the experience of the African diaspora.[12]

---

8. One attempt is Claudia Setzer, "Feminist Biblical Interpretation," in Gutjahr, *Oxford Handbook of the Bible in America*, 163–83.

9. See Carol A. Newsom, Sharon H. Ringe, and Jacqueline E. Lapsley, eds., *The Women's Bible Commentary*, 3rd ed. (Louisville: Westminster John Knox, 2012); the Wisdom Commentary Series, an ongoing project of feminist interpretation of every book of the Bible, published by Liturgical Press; and Tamara Cohn Eskenazi and Andrea L Weiss, eds., *The Torah: A Women's Commentary* (New York: URJ Press; Women of Reform Judaism, 2008).

10. Allen Callahan, *The Talking Book: African Americans and the Bible* (New Haven: Yale University Press, 2008); Emerson Powery and Rodney Sadler, *The Genesis of Liberation: Biblical Interpretation in the Antebellum Narratives of the Enslaved* (Louisville: Westminster John Knox, 2016).

11. Vincent L. Wimbush, ed., *African Americans and the Bible: Sacred Texts and Social Textures* (New York: Continuum, 2000).

12. Hugh R. Page Jr., Randall C. Bailey, and Valerie Bridgman, eds. *The Africana Bible: Reading Israel's Scriptures from Africa and the African Diaspora* (Minneapolis: Fortress, 2009); Brian K. Blount, Cain Hope Felder, Clarice J. Martin, and Emerson Powery, eds., *True to Our Native Land: An African American New Testament Commentary* (Minneapolis: Fortress, 2007).

Scholarship around different social concerns continues to percolate. The contemporary Black Lives Matter movement and its effect on biblical studies is the subject of a forum in a recent issue of the *Journal of Biblical Literature*.[13] The Museum of the Bible in Washington, DC, has provoked controversy as some question its neutrality and argue it privileges a Protestant Christian and evangelical stance.[14] Environmentalists both critique the Bible's role in climate degradation and harness its power to effect reform. *The Green Bible*, an NRSV that highlights verses relating to nature, God's creation, and stewardship, appeared in 2008. Projects of both biblical interpretation and advocacy have created a field called ecological hermeneutics.[15] The public interest in the history of Jewish-Christian relations and the role of New Testament interpretation in anti-Semitism partially explains the popularity of a commentary on the New Testament written entirely by Jewish scholars, now in its second edition.[16]

As this brief survey of the field suggests, scholarship on the Bible in America since 1976 has been much more robust than the previously decrepit state of the field that troubled Noll. Yet, the exponential expansion of perspectives and content in recent decades has only intensified one of the characteristics of the field that Noll identified. The Bible's presence in and influence on the so-called American experience is fraught with paradox. Scripture surfaces widely but inconsistently: in some cases, its role seems clear and profound, while, in others, the Bible appears to play no—or only a small and superficial—part.

The contributors here illuminate some common themes. First, a number of them call attention to a kind of biblical nostalgia, a longing for an earlier golden age of piety and biblical literacy that ostensibly contrasts with our more secular present. Second, several authors noted a similarly reverential attitude toward the Constitution as iconic and unchanging.

---

13. Wil Gafney et al., "JBL Forum: Black Lives Matter for Critical Biblical Scholarship," *JBL* 136 (2017): 203–44.

14. See Candida Moss and Joel S. Baden, *Bible Nation: The United States of Hobby Lobby* (Princeton: Princeton University Press, 2017); Jill Hicks-Keeton and Cavan Concannon, eds., *The Museum of the Bible: A Critical Introduction* (Minneapolis: Fortress Academic, 2019).

15. *The Green Bible* (San Francisco: Harper Collins, 2008); David G. Horrell, *The Bible and the Environment: Toward A Critical Ecological Biblical Theology* (London: Equinox, 2010).

16. Amy-Jill Levine and Marc Z. Brettler, eds., *The Jewish Annotated New Testament*, 2nd ed. (New York: Oxford University Press, 2017).

Third, the definition of an *American* biblical expression is murky. Authors and artists reflect distinctly American experiences, but their audiences are global. These questions about the fluidity of boundaries arise acutely in a world now structured by digital code. Fourth, the digital revolution has accelerated shifts in forms and formats. The Bible is no longer just a book. Finally, a stable *idea* of the Bible persists, with its attendant authority and singularity.

A Brief Overview

Lori Anne Ferrell notes a preservationist impulse in many of the new translations, combined with ingenuity and variety in format ("The Bible and Bibles in America"). The last half of the twentieth century brought the release of the New King James (1982), New Jerusalem Bible (1985), New Century Version (1987), New Revised Standard Version (1989), and Todays' New International Version (2005). She notes that the titles imply not radical revision but "mildly updated fidelity to what has always been." What has changed is the variety of formats and the carefully calibrated appeals to niche markets, driven by consumerism. Traditional texts are embedded in teen magazines like *Revolve*, which intersperse the material with make-ups tips and articles like "Are You Dating a Godly Guy?," or the *Journal the Word Bible*, with pages to write personal reflections, *Women of Color Study Bible*, *God's Little Princess Devotional Bible*, *The Green Bible* for environmentalists, and more. The expansive material universe of Bible production reflects an America in constant geographic and demographic flux, "a roving and restless nation of natives, nomads, exiles, and immigrants," but the American iterations of the Bible tend to support social stability over social reform.

Jeffrey S. Siker shows that the burgeoning of technology has changed the Bible experience itself ("The Bible and Digital Media"). Harnessing of digital forms has aided dissemination of the Bible in myriad ways. Biblical material is accessible via the digital app YouVersion, ebooks, Twitter, Facebook pages, and the like. He notes that these multiple forms have changed the shape and authority of the Bible itself. Now it is "a Bible that has in many ways lost its covers," softening notions of canon, authority, and fixed meanings. A reader (or listener) can compare translations, look up commentaries, watch videos, and generally choose what is congenial to her own world view. Siker calls the result a "stable instability." Siker notes that

American evangelical interests are prominent in the move to digital forms, ensuring that certain narratives take precedence. Accordingly, Ferrell's and Siker's analyses also trace the ongoing dynamic around the question of Americanness between shifting borders.

Biblical themes and American experience are most obvious—and especially fraught—in popular culture. Jason A. Wyman Jr. notes that the Bible itself *is* popular culture, a best-seller that appears in print, tablets, podcasts, teen magazines, and more ("The Bible and Popular Culture"). As Ferrell and Siker also suggest, that culture is increasingly global but develops with distinctly American characteristics in US contexts. Wyman's analysis goes beyond recognition of the ubiquitous popular presence of the Bible and its elements in American life. He focuses instead on multifaceted forms of engagement in popular culture. Not merely limited to occasional biblical phrases or verses, hip-hop lyrics amplify themes of liberation theology and prophetic critique. Exodus liberation, Deuteronomistic judgment, and the comfort of the psalms, become part of what Anthony Pinn calls "nitty-gritty hermeneutics" adapted to the streets.[17] These streets are the streets of major American cities, so reflect the experience of young people in a divided America. The American quality of the lyrics is not the scrubbed-clean version of exceptionalism but the protest against systemic racism.

In his essay on "The Bible in American Literature," M. Cooper Harriss digs even deeper into many of the same themes. Harriss establishes a clear link between forms of structural discrimination and enduring efforts to control meanings of *America* and *American* through entrenched notions regarding the Bible and its cultural influence. Specifically, Harriss delineates—and challenges—the idea that "biblical exceptionalism" pervades American literature and that we should interpret that pervasiveness as evidence of a self-conception that unites our culture. Harriss, directly engaging Giles Gunn's *The Bible and American Arts and Letters* (1983), notes that the volume unfolds around the proposition that the Bible is "America's Book." Harriss takes issue with a presumed *American* singularity (a "cheap *unum*") imposed on heterogeneous and contradictory actualities (a living *"pluribus"*). He illuminates another reality, that

---

17. Anthony Pinn, "Rap Music and Its Message: On Interpreting the Contact between Religion and Popular Culture," in *Religion and Popular Culture in America*, ed. Bruce David Forbes and Jeffrey H. Mahan, 3rd ed. (Oakland: University of California Press, 2017), 391.

recent American literature is *differently* biblical and "defies, takes exception to, the very property that makes it exceptional." As evidence of such developments in recent decades, Harriss offers analysis of novels by Toni Morrison and Octavia Butler as well as other exemplary works of fiction that break down reified conceptual boundaries (e.g., elite culture/popular culture, secular/religious, white/black, American/un-American). As Harriss concludes, "American literature has by no means abandoned the Bible. Instead, it no longer peddles such an historically narrow interpretation of the Bible's Americanness."

Aaron Rosen takes a similar tack to generate similar questions in "The Bible and Visual Art in America." Considering John Dixon's 1983 essay "The Bible in American Painting" as a helpful point of departure, Rosen shows how "the terrain looks dramatically different thirty-five years later." Rosen focuses first on the increasingly contested boundaries of art and argues for the expansion of the field beyond Dixon's focus on painting. Rosen also explores the hybridity and capaciousness of the Bible in visual art, which he notes is just one part of larger visual culture that includes nonrepresentational biblical art, comics (or comix), and digital media. Disputes over what gets to be called art are often ciphers for political and cultural positions. "*Art* is not the only thorny term in the search for the Bible in American art," Rosen notes. "*American* is also less self-evident than it might first appear." As he explains, scholars and more casual observers alike now wonder more openly and reflexively what counts as American. Does such an identity depend upon one or more locations (of the artist's birth, of her upbringing, of her production, of the art world that receives, reviews, and sells her work)? Does the classification arise from artistic responses to particular issues or experiences? Or does American designate a particular style or ethos?

In addressing the field of music (the boundaries of which, like art, continue to spawn vigorous debate), Joseph Orchard operates from the "safe" assumption that "the Bible maintains a presence in American music" ("The Bible and American Music"). But, like Rosen, Orchard asserts that, "beyond identifying works as being written by a composer of American heritage, or significantly exposed to American culture, defining a work as American is somewhat elusive." In Orchard's survey, the only discernible pattern in compositional music by Americans in recent decades is individualism. "One effect of individualism, or diversity," Orchard suggests, "is the undermining of any sense of a canonic repertoire. There is no typically American composer, except to the degree that they are unique." Orchard notes the weaving of contemporary contexts and biblical themes in works like *The Gospel according to the Other Mary*, *El Niño*, and Harbison's *Abraham*. He laments a loss of biblical awareness and would like to see more of a biblical presence in contemporary music. While biblical motifs are identifiable in compositions for Christmas and liturgy, he notes no particular musical identity for the Bible.

A more clearly American set of ideas appears in the areas of law and politics, as described by Steven K. Green in "The Bible, Law, and Political Rhetoric." Because of its grounding in the Constitution, American law is more clearly circumscribed and distinct from other nations. Our political rhetoric, flowing from particular issues and broadly differing understanding of our country's mission and meaning, has a uniquely American flavor. The paradoxes that emerge are rather about ideals versus realities. While references to the Founding Fathers as using biblical bases are common, one searches hard to find them. An idea that American law is based on the Bible, or at least on a higher law, derived from God, persists, despite limited evidence. Green identifies two versions of natural law that feed understandings. While John Locke and other Enlightenment thinkers developed a secular version of the idea that did not stress divine origins, British common law via William Blackstone made more of its higher origins. Both versions trade places over time in judicial and public understandings. Green notes recent surveys of the American public that show 63 percent think the Founders intended a Christian nation and 55 percent think the Constitution established it as such. Even the decision in the case of Glassroth v. Moore, which ordered the removal of a monument with the Ten Commandments from the Alabama state courthouse (put up by Judge Roy Moore), paid lip-service to the importance of the Ten Commandments as the basis of American law. Despite the popularity of ideas of religious foundation of law, Green notes the lack of evidence to support it in founding documents or legal decisions. When the occasional reference does appear, it is usually as an allegory or rhetorical flourish. It would seem the *idea* of biblical influence is more prevalent than the reality.

Other kinds of paradoxes emerge when one considers the Bible's appearance in political rhetoric and rhetorical statements about the law. Green shows no correspondence between politicians' use of the Bible and their own apparent piety. At times they seem inversely related. Green credits Franklin Roosevelt with ushering in a generalized rhetoric that cites the Bible as part of a civil religious discourse. With Ronald Reagan, references to God and the Bible in presidential rhetoric "skyrocketed," with presidents from both parties invoking the text. But no straight line links the apparent religious commitment of the speaker to use of the Bible. Jimmy Carter, one of the most religiously active presidents, was very cautious in his use of the Bible. Abraham Lincoln, on the other hand, was no church-goer or openly professing Christian but showed a deep and subtle use of the Bible in his writings. The Bible's place in political rhetoric is commonplace but correlates with neither the personal piety of the politician, nor with a particular vision of our nation's role in history.

In his examination of the role of the Bible in a narrower sector of public life and civic formation—namely, the sphere of K–12 education in the United States—Mark A. Chancey shows how the Bible always has been—and remains—a delimited influence and inconsistent presence in elementary and secondary education ("The Bible and the Curriculum of American Public School [K–12] in the Twenty-First Century"). As in the broader field of law and politics, the Constitution serves as the main factor for the Bible's circumscribed role. Chancey suggests that changing demographics, including waning attachments to religion, combined with the legal constraints create popular notions—and, in many cases, curricular practices—based on a presumed Bible ban in schools.

Despite a popular notion that the Bible is banned from public schools, the result of the decision in Abington v. Schempp (1963), only school-sponsored devotional reading of the Bible was judged a violation of the First Amendment. That ruling, as well as subsequent court rulings, affirmed the positive value of study of the Bible as central to American history and literature. This includes the influential Lemon v. Kurtzman (1971), which established the "Lemon test," declaring the intent of using the Bible for religious versus secular purposes as decisive in First Amendment cases.

Still, as Chancey delineates, the Schempp ruling shaped several competing trends. The 1980s and 1990s produced a range of active and visible campaigns for increased attention to the Bible in schools. Educators, civil liberties organizations, and religious groups devised curricula: The National Council on the Bible Curriculum in Public Schools, begun in 1993, leaned towards a conservative Christian view; the Biblical Literacy Project (2005) showed more recognition of diverse views; an in-progress curriculum associated with the Museum of the Bible in Washington, DC, has been criticized as promoting an uncritical understanding of the Bible. These efforts continue into the present. From his own professional perch, Chancey calls on biblical scholars to follow up on the call in Abington v. Schempp for more and better critical study of the Bible by helping to develop effective resources for use in elementary and secondary education.

In shifting the focus to higher education, Davina C. Lopez also calls attention to long-running debates around the role of biblical studies and to what such discussions reveal about the wider American culture ("But Is It Useful? The Perennial Problem of American Biblical Scholarship and Higher Education"). Lopez's discussion begins with the proposition that "the Bible has endured as a presence in American higher education not only because of its contents, but also because it functions as a lightning rod for curricular controversies, disciplinary and community identities, and institutional power relationships." More pointedly, Lopez sees American higher education and biblical studies as mutually constitutive. She situates biblical scholarship—and discussions of its value and role in higher education—within a broader rhetoric of utility in American culture: "Discourses about usefulness comprise a common defensive characterization of biblical scholarship—and the humanities as a whole—in the neoliberal, largely anti-intellectual, capitalist landscape that houses American higher education. The question 'but is it useful?' haunts many of us working in the humanities."

As Lopez also demonstrates, the rhetoric of usefulness—necessarily tied to conceptions of authority and power—has a long history that originates in the nineteenth century when biblical scholars and American universities sought to justify their value to each other and to the public. Past and present debates about the utility of biblical studies in/and American higher education are especially important now as a way of unsettling unifying myths that not only simplify and misrepresent the past but, in so doing, consolidate institutional and structural authority. Like other contributors, Lopez notes the persistence of an "alluring" narrative of "a golden age of true piety and biblical literacy" put forth to contrast with a decline in both.

Similarly, Lopez rejects a simple narrative of the history of biblical scholarship. Its image of biblical scholarship has often suffered in these discussions, as if it led to decline in attitudes towards biblical authority. Some have rejected the teaching of Bible as not serving the goal of usefulness, while others called to restore the teaching of more traditional attitudes of biblical authority. No homogenous narrative of biblical scholarship in America is evident, rather something more distinct and contentious.

In "The Bible and Social Reform: Musings of a Biblical Scholar," Emerson B. Powery also unsettles a whole series of homogenized narratives regarding the Bible's influence in American culture. Powery echoes Lopez and others by suggesting that the profound impact of scripture on developments in US history is less historical reality and more of a myth born of nostalgia or willful ignorance. He shows that, regardless of the Bible's role in the past, contemporary social-reform movements in the United States seek biblical endorsement far less often than movements like abolitionism and women's rights did in the nineteenth and early twentieth centuries. For instance, in contrast to the famous biblical imagery used by Dr. Martin Luther King and others to galvanize the Civil Rights movement in the 1950s and 1960s, the Bible appears infrequently (if at all) in the recent Black Lives Matter campaign. Powery argues that, in fact, the Bible now is folded into initiatives to maintain social control as often as it is to produce social change. For example, the dissenting opinion in the Supreme Court 5 to 4 decision to overturn the Defense of Marriage Act in 2015, Obergefell v. Hodges, contained some religious overtones, as well as a lament about the absence of an evangelical voice on the court. Biblical literalism and constitutional originalism often go together, or, as John Kutsko puts it, are "a match made in heaven."[18]

In light of these patterns, and with an eye to Ernest Sandeen's volume in the original series,[19] Powery shifts attention back to different corporeal realities. He addresses the Society of Biblical Literature's body of members (biblical scholars) and, at the same time, connects their work to living forms. Citing the work of scholar Richard Newton, Powery insists that "biblical interpretation matters because of its potential impacts on real bodies." Even if the Bible appears noticeably absent from current movements, Powery suggests that biblical scholarship *can*, *should be*, and in some cases *is* central to social reform in the United States. He discusses biblical scholars who promote more self-conscious and constructive use of their work to address problems of race, immigration, climate change, and more in the public square. Public conversations on social issues occur in radio programs like Rodney Sadler's in North Carolina, where he interviews biblical scholars (e.g., Brian Blount and Diana Swancutt), blogs by Wil Gafney and Bart Ehrman, and articles in *The Huffington Post* and *The Daily Beast* by Candida Moss, to name just a few. In a recent issue of the

---

18. John F. Kutsko, "The Curious Case of the Christian Bible and the U.S. Constitution: Challenges for Educators Teaching the Bible in a Multireligious Context," in Goff, Farnsley, and Thuesen, *The Bible in American Life*, 244.

19. Sandeen, *The Bible and Social Reform*.

Journal of Biblical Literature, for example, Gafney notes that "it cannot be said that that all lives matter in the Bible, nor can it be said that of those lives that do matter, they matter equally."[20] Ethnic conflict in the Bible provides an analogy to the race conflicts of today.

Still, Powery cites Sandeen's earlier insight to remind us that biblical scholarship—like the Bible itself—"cannot be defined simply as either a conservative or progressive force in social reform."[21] This claim holds true on a broader scale. The articles here show that the Bible belongs to no single group or political position. As Powery adds, "the Bible takes no sides, or, some may claim, the Bible seems to take both sides."

Bibliography

Barr, David, and Nicholas Piediscalzi, eds. *The Bible in American Education: From Source Book to Textbook*. Philadelphia: Fortress; Chico, CA: Scholars Press, 1982.

Blount, Brian K., Cain Hope Felder, Clarice J. Martin, and Emerson Powery, eds. *True to Our Native Land: An African American New Testament Commentary*. Minneapolis: Fortress, 2007.

Callahan, Allen. *The Talking Book: African Americans and the Bible*. New Haven: Yale University Press, 2008.

Chancey, Mark A., Carol Meyers, and Eric M. Meyers, eds. *The Bible and the Public Square: Its Enduring Influence in American Life*. Atlanta: SBL Press, 2014.

Dreisbach, Daniel. *Reading the Bible with the Founding Fathers*. New York: Oxford University Press, 2016.

Eskenazi, Tamara Cohn, and Andrea L Weiss, eds. *The Torah: A Women's Commentary*. New York: URJ Press; Women of Reform Judaism, 2008.

Flannery, Frances, and Rodney A. Werline, eds. *The Bible in Political Debate: What Does It Really Say?* London: Bloomsbury T&T Clark, 2016.

Frerichs, Ernest, ed. *The Bible and Bibles in America*. Minneapolis: Fortress; Atlanta: Scholars Press, 1988.

---

20. Wil Gafney, "A Reflection on the Black Lives Matter Movement and Its Impact on My Scholarship," *JBL* 136 (2017): 206.

21. Ernest Sandeen, "Introduction," in *The Bible and Social Reform*, ed. Ernest Sandeen (Philadelphia: Fortress, 1982), 7.

Gafney, Wil. "A Reflection on the Black Lives Matter Movement and Its Impact on My Scholarship." *JBL* 136 (2017): 204–7.

Gafney, Wil, Nyasha Junior, Kenneth Ngwa, Richard Newton, Bernadette J. Brooten, and Tat-siong Benny Liew. "JBL Forum: Black Lives Matter for Critical Biblical Scholarship." *JBL* 136 (2017): 203–44.

Goff, Philip, Arthur E. Farnsley II, and Peter Thuesen, eds. *The Bible in American Life*. Oxford: Oxford University Press, 2017.

The Green Bible. San Francisco: Harper Collins, 2008.

Gunn, Giles, ed. *The Bible and American Arts and Letters*. Philadelphia: Fortress; Chico, CA: Scholars Press, 1983.

Gutjahr, Paul, ed. *The Oxford Handbook of the Bible in America*. Oxford: Oxford University Press, 2017.

Hanson, Paul D. *A Political History of the Bible in America*. Louisville: Westminster John Knox, 2015.

Hicks-Keeton, Jill, and Cavan Concannon, eds. *The Museum of the Bible: A Critical Introduction*. Minneapolis: Fortress Academic, 2019.

Horrell, David G. *The Bible and the Environment: Toward A Critical Ecological Biblical Theology*. London: Equinox, 2010.

Johnson, James Turner, ed., *The Bible in American Law, Politics, and Political Rhetoric*. Philadelphia: Fortress; Chico, CA: Scholars Press, 1985.

Kutsko, John F. "The Curious Case of the Christian Bible and the U.S. Constitution: Challenges for Educators Teaching the Bible in a Multireligious Context." Pages 240–48 in *The Bible in American Life*. Edited by Philip Goff, Arthur E. Farnsley II, and Peter Thuesen. Oxford: Oxford University Press, 2017.

Levine, Amy-Jill, and Marc Z. Brettler, eds. *The Jewish Annotated New Testament*. 2nd ed. New York: Oxford University Press, 2017.

Meacham, Jon. *American Gospel: God, the Founding Fathers, and the Making of a Nation*. New York: Random House, 2007.

Moss, Candida, and Joel S. Baden. *Bible Nation: The United States of Hobby Lobby*. Princeton: Princeton University Press, 2017.

Newsom, Carol A., Sharon H. Ringe, and Jacqueline E. Lapsley, eds. *The Women's Bible Commentary*. 3rd ed. Louisville: Westminster John Knox, 2012.

Noll, Mark A. *In the Beginning Was the Word: The Bible in American Public Life 1492–1783*. Oxford: Oxford University Press, 2016.

———. "Review Essay: The Bible in America." *JBL* 106 (1987): 493–509.

O'Brien, Julia, ed. *The Oxford Encyclopedia of the Bible and Gender Studies*. New York: Oxford, 2014.

Page, Hugh R., Jr., Randall C. Bailey, and Valerie Bridgman, eds. *The Africana Bible: Reading Israel's Scriptures from Africa and the African Diaspora*. Minneapolis: Fortress, 2009.

Phy, Allene Stuart, ed. *The Bible and Popular Culture in America*. Philadelphia: Fortress; Chico, CA: Scholars Press, 1985.

Pinn, Anthony. "Rap Music and Its Message: On Interpreting the Contact between Religion and Popular Culture." Pages 390–412 in *Religion and Popular Culture in America*. Edited by Bruce David Forbes and Jeffrey H. Mahan. 3rd ed. Oakland: University of California Press, 2017.

Powery, Emerson, and Rodney Sadler. *The Genesis of Liberation: Biblical Interpretation in the Antebellum Narratives of the Enslaved*. Louisville: Westminster John Knox, 2016.

Sandeen, Ernest, ed. *The Bible and Social Reform*. Philadelphia: Fortress; Chico, CA: Scholars Press, 1982.

———. "Introduction." Pages 1–7 in *The Bible and Social Reform*. Edited by Ernest Sandeen. Philadelphia: Fortress, 1982.

Setzer, Claudia. "Feminist Biblical Interpretation." Pages 163–83 in *Oxford Handbook of the Bible in America*. Edited by Paul Gutjahr. Oxford: Oxford University Press, 2017.

Setzer, Claudia, and David A. Shefferman, eds. *The Bible in American Culture: A Sourcebook*. London: Routledge, 2011.

Taylor, Marion Ann, ed. *Handbook of Women Biblical Interpreters*. Grand Rapids: Baker, 2012.

Wimbush, Vincent L., ed. *African Americans and the Bible: Sacred Texts and Social Textures*. New York: Continuum, 2000.

1
THE BIBLE AND BIBLES IN AMERICA

LORI ANNE FERRELL

In the 1988 edition of the seminal textbook *The Bible and Bibles in America*, John Alden wrote, "of no nation can it be as aptly said as of the United States, that, in its settlement and development, the Bible has played a major role."[1] From sea to shining sea, the American Bible has been America's most portable and protean traveling companion since the first decades of the seventeenth century. In America, Bibles were testament not only to the material presence of the Word, but also to the longing for stability and identity that characterized a roving and restless nation of natives, nomads, exiles, and immigrants.

So there are many ways to tell the story of Bibles in America. This one will trace its progress over a restless continent and into the hands of an unprecedentedly diverse and sometimes surprising readership. Along the way we note the Bible's remarkable accessibility and its applicability to the lives of people who traveled distinct and different national byways. This was a matter, I will argue, of the Bible's superb *marginality*, by which I mean not only its lasting appeal to minority interests but also the capaciousness of its open pagescapes that could so easily be filled with commentary and opinions, family trees, and devotionals expressing the lives and interests of specific readerships. This long-standing capacity to speak to, and from, the in-between spaces thus led, ultimately, to a publication phenomenon of the twentieth century: the intentional tailoring of Bibles for *niche* markets served by specific content and packaging. So this essay will take a distinctly material turn, highlighting the versions—and styles—of Good

---

1. John Alden, "The Bible as Printed Word," *The Bible and Bibles in America*, ed. Ernest S. Frerichs (Atlanta: Society of Biblical Literature, 1988), 9.

Books conveyed by transatlantic schooner, preachers' saddle bags, and salesmen's "dummies," as well as on Victorian bookstands, in hotel bedside tables, and by way of the teen magazine trade.[2]

Coming to America, 1620 to 1800

The *Mayflower* landed on the northeastern shores of America in 1620, carrying 102 alienated English souls. Unable to stomach the moderate Protestantism reinstated in England by Queen Elizabeth I (r. 1558–1603), the people we call "Pilgrims" had originally sought refuge in Holland in 1608. The Bible they transported from the Old World to the New constituted a radical declaration of independence: not simply from England but also from England's church. The Pilgrims had come to America seeking religious liberty, if only for themselves. They would never have advocated the religious liberty of others, including—and especially—that of their former British neighbors.

The scripture they probably carried, *The Bible and Holy Scriptures Conteyned in the Olde and Newe Testament: Translated according to the Ebrue and Greeke, and Conferred with the Best Translations in Divers Languages*, was more popularly (and succinctly) identified with the Swiss city of its origin. In 1560 Anglophone exiles had produced this Geneva Bible for English-speaking congregations who, fleeing the reign of the Catholic monarch Mary Tudor (r. 1553–1558), were temporarily resident in the Protestant cities of sixteenth-century Europe. These translators followed William Tyndale (1494–1536) in working with earlier Hebrew and Greek sources rather than the Latin Vulgate Bible. The Geneva's compositors were also innovators in format, dividing and numbering verses for easier navigation and using clean-edged Roman type rather than the thick black letter script typically used in official texts like governmental proclamations (and, in England, Protestant Bibles printed by royal authority). This was a Bible befitting its radically reformed origins, designed for the instructing pastors of lay congregations.

---

2. As such, this chapter draws upon and pays admiring tribute to Alden's contribution to Frerichs's *The Bible and Bibles in America*: "The Bible as Printed Word," 9–29. Much of what follows, however, derives from my own work, *The Bible and the People* (New Haven: Yale University Press, 2008), especially chapters 4, 7, and 8. Many thanks to Yale University Press for allowing me to quote from this earlier published material.

Also as Tyndale had once done, but now even more exuberantly, the Geneva compilers inserted their candid political and doctrinal opinions into their Bible's margins. As befits a book originally designed for unhappy people on the run from hostile government surveillance, the Geneva's marginal notes treated the weak and willful monarchs who populate the pages of the Hebrew Bible as anti-Christian usurpers, wicked leaders ripe for divine comeuppance. A characteristic example can be found in the margins of 1 Kgs 12:27–28:

> If this people go up and do sacrifice in the house of the Lord at Jerusalem, then shall the hearts of this people turn again unto their lord, even to Rehoboam king of Judah: so shall they kill me, and go again to Rehoboam king of Judah.
> Whereupon the king took counsel, and made two calves of gold, and said unto them, It is too much for you to go up to Jerusalem: Behold, O Israel, thy gods which brought thee up out of the land of Egypt.

In the Geneva margins we find this pointed political gloss: "He feared lest his people should have by this means been enticed to rebel against him. So crafty are carnal persuasions of princes, when they will make a religion to serve to their appetite." Such explicit sideline instruction ensured that this Bible became a favorite of early modern English clergy and a thorn in the side of early modern English rulers. Later in the seventeenth century, few American settlers were as openly separatist as the Mayflower cohort. They did wish, however, to place an ocean's distance between themselves and the English bishops who had attempted to force them into more conformity with its liturgical practices and episcopal government than they could bear. Escaping the long reach of the state church, *these* Puritans were intent upon founding a church state, using their dashed hopes for England as a pattern and the Bible as a measuring tape.

The Bible they brought from England on their errand into the wilderness was no longer the Geneva Bible, which by the 1630s had been eclipsed by a new version: the 1611 Bible Americans still call, more or less correctly, the King James Version (KJV) and the British still call, more or less incorrectly, the "Authorized Version."[3] Unlike the Geneva, this *was* a public Bible, designed specifically to support the liturgical services of the Church of England and its Book of Common Prayer. Its margins wiped

---

3. This essay will use KJV throughout.

clean of anything but some few points of disputed translation, its locutions deliberately designed to be sonorous and mildly archaic, it was not as instructive a Bible as the Geneva, but it did sound more sweetly. Its scriptural contents, now unmoored from close association with the national church, went on to Christianize and, eventually, divide a continent into Protestant denominations.

The Massachusetts settlers' ambitions extended beyond transplanting their own religion onto foreign soil. They sought also to convert the native inhabitants of that soil, not to mere Christianity, but to *their* Christianity, at a time when Bible translation and distribution were the defining activities of new, and newly Protestant, missions. Notable in this effort was the Reverend John Eliot, who emigrated to Massachusetts in 1631 and became the leader of the church in Roxbury a year later. By 1647 he had become Massachusetts' best known (to quote the motto prominently featured on his portrait) "propagator of the gospel to the Indians," founding and printing a library for native Americans until 1689. Assisted by a British organization founded in 1649, the Society for the Promoting and Propagating the Gospel of Jesus Christ in New England, Eliot shipped a printing press, moveable type, and reams of paper from Britain to America. Aided by a Massachusetts native who took on the English name "John Printer," Eliot set about putting his Protestant and evangelistic values into action.

Thus it was that the first Bible to be printed by the staunchly Protestant Britons of Cambridge, Massachusetts was not in the English language. *Up-biblum GOD*, the first complete Bible printed in the Western hemisphere, was also the first of many Bible translations to invade North America. Written in the Natick dialect of the Algonquian inhabitants of Massachusetts, comprising 1,180 pages, and produced in 1663 in an unprecedentedly large initial print run of two thousand copies, most of "Eliot's Indian Bibles" would be destroyed in King Philip's War of 1675–1676. But Eliot's enterprise is evidence nonetheless of an early, pivotal, and most telling moment in the history of American Bible translation. By the end of the seventeenth century, Christians had become intent upon moving scriptures only very recently rendered familiar to European nations through their translation *out* of Latin into new and unfamiliar languages for the purposes of mission.

Early American Bibles thus reflect the fact that early America was a nation primarily made up of immigrants, strangers in a strange land. The next Bible to be printed on this continent was *Biblia, das ist: Die heilige Schrift Altes und Neues Testaments*. This American edition of the Bible first translated by Martin Luther was printed more than fifty years later, in 1743, by Christopher Saur. Despite the prohibitive costs of producing such a large text, Saur priced his Bible at a mere eighteen shillings and gave away free copies to the poor. With this, the age of the American Bible in Algonquian gave way to the age of the American Bible in German. Second and third editions of the Saur Bible were being printed in 1763 and 1776 when talk of producing an American Bible in English was still an inconclusive discussion about import costs and trade embargoes. English-speaking Americans dutifully purchased and shipped copies of the KJV from the Mother Country while American printers produced Bibles in foreign tongues.

The only thing unrevolutionary about Revolutionary-era America, then, may well have been its English-language Bible. However, the issues holding back the American production of Bibles in the English language were more legal and economic than political. Simply put, the 1611 Bible was protected by royal copyright. As relations broke down between the colonies and England, these British-made Bibles became increasingly difficult to transport and obtain. In 1775, the first continental Congress finally banned the importation of goods, including books and Bibles, from England. America had finally declared an economic separatism, challenging the British monarch's claim to have sole privilege of reproducing, printing, and selling the word of God.

Recalling, perhaps, the reasons for British emigration in the first place, the first continental Congresses also carefully kept religion and government separate even in this matter, extolling the benefits of but steadfastly refusing to finance the production of an American Bible in the English language—and in the version commissioned by King James (which steadfastly remained the Protestant scripture of choice for the next two centuries). Robert Aitken was the first from the private sector to rise to the financial challenge of underwriting the printing and distribution of the KJV in America. Aitken had already published several very popular New Testaments (as had a number of other enterprising printers in the late 1770s; the New Testament is a much shorter, and thus cheaper, book) before he personally raised the money to print both Testaments in 1781. The venture turned out to be a fiscal disaster, evidence of the still-prohibitive costs of producing an entire Bible in the last decades of the eighteenth century. At the end of the 1780s, £3,000 (approximately $600,000 today) in debt, his final request for Congress to allow him a patent to print the Bible refused, Aitken finally abandoned his project along with any notion of success as a Bible publisher.

He ought to have considered another business model. A smarter option in politically and economically uncertain times, with a government that both could not and would not publicly fund the printing and distribution of scripture, was to offer Bibles by subscription, pledges of start-up money by private individuals. In the end, the subscription model was best suited to the servicing of niche markets like Saur's: small but well-organized readerships bound together by specific languages, locations, and religious interests.

Another such case was the American Catholic Bible market, as motivated as it was miniscule in the early 1800s. The first Catholic Bible printed in the United States was published less than a decade after Aitken's venture aimed at Protestants came to naught. Its printer, Matthew Carey, refused to print this version of the English-language Douai-Rheims Bible—a Bible first translated by Catholic exiles from Protestant England at the beginning of the seventeenth century—until four hundred subscribers agreed to underwrite the cost. He collected 491 signatures and printed 491 copies. By 1825, Carey had parlayed this cautious success into a thriving business, publishing Protestant KJV's as well as Catholic Douai-Rheims Bibles. The success of the subscription method had taught him the importance of establishing a market before making a product, a lesson the unfortunate Aitken had learned the hard way.

The single, driving force behind the first English translation of the Hebrew Bible, Isaac Leeser (1806–1868), faced similarly hard lessons slightly later, in the nineteenth century when Jewish immigration from Central Europe was on the rise. Unfamiliar with Hebrew, struggling to learn the language of their new country, Jews made do at home, in synagogues, and in Sabbath schools with the KJV Old Testament. This recourse Leeser, himself a German immigrant to America, deplored as "a species of mental slavery" for its "[reliance] upon the arbitrary decree of a deceased King of England," thus anticipating the findings of Christian Bible revision committees by a half-century.[4]

A prolific author of commentaries; Hebrew spellers, grammars, and catechisms; sermons and religious tracts, Leeser produced a translation of the Pentateuch in 1845, *Biblia Hebraica* in 1848, and his magnum opus,

---

4. Isaac Leeser, preface to *The Twenty-Four Books of the Holy Scriptures*, 2nd ed. (Philadelphia: C. Sherman, 1856), iii–iv. Cited in Lance J. Sussman, "Another Look at Isaac Leeser and the First Jewish Translations of the Bible in their United States," *Modern Judaism* 5 (1985): 159–90.

Twenty-Four Books of the Holy Scriptures, in 1853–1854. He imported the Hebrew typefaces, oversaw printers unfamiliar with the language, and undertook the daunting task of proofreading without assistance, financial *or* human: like Saur and Carey, Leeser had to raise the front-money to print this American milestone of scriptural publishing himself. This he did in a four-month, whistle-stop, fundraising railroad tour of (as he wrote) "twenty-five settlements or congregations of Israelites, from the shores of Lake Erie to the Gulf of Mexico." Having thus thoroughly scoured the extent of his market, Leeser could then commence to serve it. Leeser's Bible—which, in the fashion of all American Bibles of the nineteenth century, featured footnotes, commentary, and well-designed inserts for family record keeping—remained the standard biblical text for American Jews until 1914, when the Jewish Publication Society commissioned a new English translation.[5]

New Economic Conditions, 1800–1900

In the Industrial Age, however, the cost of printing in America dropped precipitously. Improved print technologies made it possible for publishers to produce the scriptures at remarkably low cost. This abundance of cheap goods, along with an evangelical fervor for saving souls, inspired the American Bible Society, the American Tract Society, and the American Sunday School Union to join forces in the 1820s and announce a "general supply": a plan to distribute Bibles and other religious literature to every person in the United States, either gratis or priced on a sliding scale.[6] By the 1840s, a complete Bible could be purchased in America for a half-dollar; a New Testament cost a mere six cents.

This presented an entirely new fiscal challenge for Bible publishers now intent on profit. The Protestant Bible, once so difficult to ship and

---

5. Sussman, "Another Look at Isaac Leeser," 159, 163–68. For excerpts from the preface to that twentieth-century revision, including some pointed references to Leeser's earlier accomplishments, see Claudia Setzer and David Shefferman, eds., *The Bible and American Culture: A Sourcebook* (London: Routledge, 2011), 42–45.

6. According to Paul Gutjahr, by 1855 these three societies accounted for sixteen percent of all books printed in the United States: "Diversification in American Religious Publishing," in *The Industrial Book 1840–1880*, vol. 3 of *A History of the Book in America*, ed. Scott Casper, Jeffrey Groves, Stephen Nissenbaum, and Michael Winship (Chapel Hill: University of North Carolina Press, 2002), 194.

then so expensive to print, had suddenly become a cheap commodity: easy to produce in bulk and distributed in large numbers by both missionaries and Sunday school teachers to their equally captive audiences. Publishers who once scrambled for funds to print basic-fare Bibles now began searching for innovative means to make Bibles more alluring—and with that, more expensive—in a brand-new marketplace.

Luckily, the Bible's reputation as the one book no home could be without made it a perfect product upon which to base new and innovative schemes of presentation, production, distribution, and pricing. One colorful example, the astonishingly popular *Illuminated and New Pictorial Bible*, was sold by Harper and Brothers between 1843 and 1846 in fifty-four separate parts—each costing a quarter—at a total cost to the buyer of $13.50, which included complimentary binding. The prospectus advertisement promised, in addition to scriptural contents "drawn from the standard copy of the American Bible Society" (i.e., a KJV), sixteen hundred historical illustrations (the majority of these prints made from well-known scriptural engravings), as well as a customized presentation plate and ornamental borders.[7] At additional cost, the buyer's name and a picture of his or her church could even be stamped in gilt on the cover. This marketing strategy eventually garnered fifty *thousand* original subscribers, attracted no doubt both to the beauties of its pages, the thrill of having one's name in gold on the front cover, and the budgetary convenience of paying by installment.

Such useful and beautiful add-ons characterize all family Bibles of the nineteenth century, a book that in many American families remains a valued heirloom. True to its name, the Victorian family Bible makes a *familiar* impression: it is often the book we picture when we hear the word *Bible*. We think *old* and weighty (which they are) and, consequently, *valuable* (which they are not, except in that most precious and singular sense of any particular family's history). With their heavy, carved façades, and bright gilt edges, Victorian folio Bibles could easily be mistaken for ponderous pieces of Victorian furniture in themselves. The busy, lavish covers of these family Bibles were not designed to be hidden on the bookshelf. They were meant for special, singular view, left out and left open: displayed, like the great manuscript gift Bibles of medieval times, they

---

7. The 1843 frontispiece is reproduced in Gutjahr, "Diversification in American Religious Publishing," 202.

evoked so inexpertly, on specially designed lecterns or tables. Book and prop came together to form what the historian Colleen McDannell has termed a "Protestant altar."[8]

Such Bibles made sturdy cornerstones for the establishment of otherwise barely settled professions and households, offering publishers another new marketing opportunity. This one was embedded in a time-honored practice: using Bibles as places to record family history. In earlier printed Bibles we often find personal milestones handwritten into the one place, besides its flyleaves, that a Bible had always supplied chroniclers a decent expanse of blank space: the left-over page-and-a-half created between the end of the Old Testament and the beginning of the New. By the mid-nineteenth century, Bible publishers were providing specially designed pages for recordkeeping in this fortuitously found space: elaborately decorated sheets inserted between Testaments emblazoned with the words *Births*, *Marriages*, and *Deaths* with lines beneath to keep spidery handwriting on the straight and narrow. These insets were, as one supplier bragged, "very beautifully designed … affording ample space for a large number of names."[9] With these formal additions, the family Bible became a new kind of family artifact: uniformly custom-made, personal*ized* rather than personal. A substitute for the old parish registers of old and new England, it allowed families to turn their home Bibles into official record-keepers, something particularly important in this age of territorial expansion, wherein Bibles nearly always got to settlements before government did.

Traveling with the American Bible

In an age of westward expansion, American Bibles were daily leaving the comfortable environs of settled churches and homes to follow human migratory impulses both secular and sacred. By the early twentieth century, this American migratory impulse had become a thing of automobiles and better-paved, more extensive roadways. The Bible remained an integral part of the modern era of restlessness, perhaps the only thing one

---

8. Colleen McDannell, *The Christian Home in Victorian America, 1840–1900* (Bloomington: Indiana University Press, 1986), 83–84.

9. Alfred Nevin, *Salesman's Dummy for The Holy Bible [King James Version] … Together with a New and Improved Dictionary of the Bible* (Springfield, MA: W. J. Holland, [1879]).

could count on when on the road for evangelism, business, or pleasure. The most significant, most characteristic, and least-studied scriptural witness to a newly mobile modern age was the Gideon Bible.

The Gideons, a nondenominational group founded for the purposes of Christian evangelism in 1899, took their name from the victorious warrior of the book of Judges and their inspiration from an earlier, informal nineteenth-century drive to place wholesome literature in British hotel rooms. In 1908, they pledged to place the Bible in every hotel in America, initiating their resolve by stocking the rooms of the Superior Hotel in Superior, Wisconsin. By mid-century, their charitable reach had extended to other, less comfortable, homes away from home: schools, hospitals, the armed forces, and prisons.

Seemingly everywhere (in a hotel bedside drawer, in a line of a Beatles song) and nowhere (in academic essays, in the home), Gideon Bibles are instantly recognizable by their prefatory matter. The pages outline the portrait of a temporary reader, presently residing in an off-ramp counterculture: the motel bedroom. The transient state of a Gideon Bible reader is itself transient, of course: what has brought the traveler to this place will allow the traveler to depart. But Gideon Bibles treat brief stays in unfamiliar places as moments for brief biblical intervention for readers unfamiliar with the Bible, and so they are prefaced with efficient guides for easily looking up specific scriptural verses. The alluring dangers of being a stranger in a strange land seem most acute on the page entitled "Practical Precepts," which cites among the "Great Themes of Scripture" passages relating to "the sin of adultery," "the prodigal son," and the "consequences of forgetting God."

Bibles for a New Age of Biblical Ignorance

The Gideon Bible prefaces serve as reminders that, by the early twentieth century, and even in a Christianized nation, the Bible remained for many a stubbornly closed book, one that required special helps and cultural translation to find an audience. This makes the twentieth century seem uncannily akin to the mid-sixteenth: in both eras, new translations along with other, more material, forms of scriptural refashioning, were tailored to suit rapidly changing times and potentially—and then persistently—confused readers. Twentieth-century folk, however, were no longer the *readers* envisaged by ambitious early Protestant theologians and translators; they were thoroughly acclimated *consumers*, nudged into pluralistic being by enterprising publishers and the nascent field of market research. Once the driving force behind the printing press phenomenon, the Bible faced new challenges in the pluralistic and diversifying religious marketplace of a commercial and secular twentieth century.[10]

These challenges began with a change in scriptural content. Confronted with the combined forces of university biblical scholarship and the discovery of more, and more ancient, biblical texts than had been available to first-generation humanists and reformers, the once-hardy KJV was starting to look well past its intellectual sell-by date by the second half of the nineteenth century. Accordingly, the Church of England convened a committee to revise the only English-language version of the Bible in extensive use on both sides of the Atlantic since the early seventeenth century. They promised "as few alterations as possible" and to keep its modes of expression in "the language of the Arized and earlier English versions." The result of their labors was the English Revised Version (ERV), published by Oxford University Press in 1881: the first Bible in English to be extensively and definitively revised by authority since 1611.

Even the presence of a small cadre of American scholars on the ERV's revision committee could not rectify what had become striking differences between British and American speech. The rapid spread of American-English usage, a major transformation in the English-language world since the eighteenth century, had not figured in the new translation, despite the fact that by this time America had become by far the largest domestic market for the version of scripture it still called the "King James." At the urgent request of the American members of the revision committee, a substitute list of American words and phrases was hastily appended to the British version.

This inadequate fix haunted the American committee for over a decade. Finally, in 1901, the surviving American members of the original revision committee transferred these words and expressions, plus a significant number of other Americanisms the British committee had not considered worth considering at all, out of the ERV's back pages and into a text they now called the American Revised Version (ARV). What were these once-sidelined Yankee locutions? Some were innocuous examples of

---

10. This thesis has recently been persuasively advanced by David Paul Nord, *Faith in Reading: Religious Publishing and the Birth of Mass Media in America* (Oxford: Oxford University Press, 2004), 6–7 and passim.

Anglo-American differences in everyday usage: the American "wheat" for the British "corn," for example. Some gestured at nativist Protestantism, an attitude that continued to rear its ugly head with every influx of European Catholic immigrants into the United States: "love" for "charity" in 1 Corinthians, for example, may have downplayed the doctrines of good works and intercession that many Protestants thought defined Catholicism. Finally, some responded to the more lurid cultural obsessions of antebellum America: "Holy Spirit" instead of "Holy Ghost," for example. (The obsession with séances and spiritualism that flourished after the American Civil War perhaps had made people familiar with the unholy sort.)[11]

The publication of the ARV sparked a fervent half-century of scholarly translation and revision in the United States, with every foray into Holy Writ threatening not so much to sully the scripture's sacred nature as to alienate the sensibilities of the KJV's adherents. The sanctity often seemed to rest on old sound rather than new sense, a cultural predilection demonstrated once again in 1947 with the publication of the New Testament in the Revised Standard Version (RSV). Anticipating the usual resistance, the editors of the RSV wrote nearly as much about the things they had left undone than about the things they *had* done: "The Revised Standard Version is not a new translation in the language of today," they wrote in its preface. "It ... seeks to preserve all that is best in the English Bible as it has been known and used throughout the years," they continued, intent on being regarded as conservators rather than innovators.

To some readers, however, the RSV revisers' promise seemed to suggest that the preservation of the Bible's sacred status was a matter of remembering its emergence in English translation, rather than its origins in Greek and Hebrew texts. In America the RSV eventually became the most widely accepted and best known of the *twentieth-century* translations of the Bible, but that meant little: the RSV simply could not succeed in dethroning the KJV. In an age of dizzying change in morals and mores, the sound of "thee" and "begat" sounded ancient and timeless truths to those Christians whose notion of scriptural purity remained stubbornly fixed on 1611.

The revising committee had eliminated much of the KJV's archaic language from the RSV, a decision that seems simply to have etched the

---

11. John Stevens Kerr, *Ancient Texts Alive Today: The Story of the English Bible* (New York: American Bible Society, 1999), 149.

cadences of the KJV more deeply onto the hearts of Bible-loving evangelicals and, especially and more lastingly, biblical fundamentalists. America's enduring love of the KJV is a reminder that the language of Shakespeare and the sonorous liturgical rhythms of the Church of England had formed an essential building block of common speech in many parts of the United States. As late as the twentieth century, this version's elegant archaisms still resonated like a cradle language in regions lacking secular institutions of high culture or higher education: out-of-the-way places where even the poorest and most unworldly Christians held stately Elizabethan imagery by the very tips of their tongues.

Still the most frequently used translation in the United States today, the KJV reigns absolute in three very different settings: traditionalist American Episcopalian congregations, where it pairs perfectly with the 1662 (or 1928) Book of Common Prayer; African American congregations; and, seemingly far to the other side of the spectrum, the fundamentalist, independent, mostly Baptist congregations that call themselves "King James Only Churches." Adherents of this movement (there are hundreds of US churches listed in telephone and website directories as "King James Only"), claim the KJV is no *version*, liable to revision and retranslation, but, simply, a *Bible*—that is, the *only* Bible acceptable for Christian worship.[12]

This is not a matter of aurality. King James Only proponents do not simply prefer the authorized version's fluent cadences or its merrie olde locutions. They also do not, like the anti-immigrant and famously corrupt governor of 1940s Texas, "Ma" Ferguson, prefer the KJV because they think its English was good enough for Jesus Christ and thus suffices for young schoolchildren. The King James Only movement instead believes that the authorized version is the only scriptural text that can be considered inerrant *for English-speaking Christians.*

King James Only advocates claim the Bible commissioned by royal writ in the early seventeenth-century Britain has the same direct claim to divine inspiration as scripture's ancient originals. Promulgated in heated

---

12. Philip Goff, Arthur E. Farnsley II, and Peter Thuesen, "The Bible in American Life Today," in *The Bible in American Life*, ed. Philip Goff, Arthur E. Farnsley II, and Peter Thuesen (Oxford: Oxford University Press, 2017), 24. See also the 2014 online report from the University of Indiana at Purdue: "IUPUI Study, 'The Bible in American Life': King James Is Not Dead; African Americans Most Engaged." IUPUI Newsroom. 7 March 2014. https://tinyurl.com/SBL6704b.

website debates, unaccredited Bible colleges, and privately financed publications, the arguments forwarded by the King James Only Movement begin with a call to remember English-language textual origins that possesses a certain logic: the English translation *was* one of the first ones accessible to English speakers, and no one has yet located the Greek and Hebrew originals.

Given the fervor for translating and paraphrasing that has characterized the American Bible market for the past forty years, we might figure that the proponents of King James Only are merely reacting with bad grace to the spectacle of their once-familiar and nearly universal English scriptural world turned upside down. It is certainly true that the twenty-first-century future will most likely not favor the KJV, whose discernible decline in the past three decades is less attributable to disenchantment with its archaisms than it is to major changes in Christian worship patterns. According to a study by the American Bible Society, to be successful scripture translations must complement the sounds and cadences of congregational worship, and even Sunday mornings at church are finally beginning to look and sound a lot different than they did in the 1940s.

Once, the fiery preaching of men such as Jonathan Edwards (1703–1758) had led to an outpouring of public piety and private conversion experiences throughout the nineteenth century. The most notable effect of this religious fervor—there were, after all, many "awakenings" great and small—was the splintering of congregations of Protestants into hotly inspired individual sects. Professing, most often, only mild variations in doctrine, small groups of like-minded Protestants increasingly felt free to band together, put down new roots, and work out distinctive forms of governance, becoming in the process the subgroups we call *denominations*. Their Bibles were tabernacles carried into a new promised land, available whenever a preaching opportunity presented itself—and they were KJV's. By the end of the twentieth century, that was no longer the case: the Bibles, and the congregations, had changed.

This trend began with the vernacularization, in the directive promulgated by the Second Vatican Council (1962–1965), of the Latin mass, followed by a rise in alternative Protestant and, more recently, nondenominational services, all of which led to the publication of a myriad new translations of the Bible in the busy second half of the twentieth century: the New King James Version (NKJV, 1979), the New Jerusalem Bible (NJB, 1985), the New Revised Standard Edition (NRSV, 1989), and the Today's New International Version (2005). For all its claim of improvement, however, every title tells us as much about the preservation of traditional expectations: proclaiming not newness but, instead, a mildly updated fidelity to what has always been. Take away the *New*, after all, and we are left with the *old*: the King James Version, the Jerusalem Bible, and the Revised Standard Version.

What is new about the scriptural content of the new versions of the twentieth century is the size of their working vocabularies. "God never intended the Bible to be too difficult for his people," write the translators of *Revolve*, a magazine-format presentation of the New Testament in the New Century Version (NCV), itself a revision of the International Children's Bible originally designed for readers of English at a third-grade level; this revision, which dates from 2009, has raised the vocabulary to fifth-grade level. The verse on the title page offers an apt citation of Prov 31:30 in NCV: "Charm can fool you, and beauty can trick you, but a woman who respects the LORD should be praised." (The KJV is: "Favour is deceitful, and beauty is vain: but a woman that feareth the Lord, she shall be praised.")

The translators of the NCV claim the Bible is currently seen as irrelevant to everyday life, a problem they blame on difficult language rather than difficult tenets. In its original form, they write, the Bible was accessible: "the authors of the Bible recorded God's word in familiar, everyday language." They now offer a clearer version for the sake of recognition and familiarity:

> The *New Century Version* captures the clear and simple message that the very first readers understood. This version presents the Bible as God intended it.... A team of scholars from the World Bible Translation Center worked together with twenty-one other experienced Bible scholars from all over the world to translate the text directly from the best available Greek and Hebrew texts. You can trust that this Bible accurately presents God's Word as it came to us in the original languages. Translators kept sentences short and simple. They avoided difficult words and worked to make the text easier to read.[13]

This is, then, no translation but a paraphrase: "thought for thought" rather than "word for word." So the translators must tout their scholarly accuracy and the purity of their copy texts, while at the same time providing the

---

13. Translator's preface, *Revolve: The Complete New Testament* (NCV) (Australia: Nelson, 2003).

same reassurance offered by all revisers of translations. Where the Bible is concerned, to claim to be radically new is still, it seems, to commit a kind of heresy.

But in a world obsessed with *new and improved*, striking physical changes to the Bible are inevitable. Most of these serve to organize the internal contents of scripture to demonstrate its applicability to individual lives using a variety of editorial additions and study aids and commentaries precisely aimed and calibrated from extensive market research. The market now boasts an array of Bibles in which the same scriptural content can be tailored, with a set of interchangeable modules, to the many different needs of particular age and ethnic groups: the *Women of Color Study Bible* or *The Promise Keepers Men's Study Bible*, as well as Bibles designed for "special interest groups": recovering addicts (*The Life Recovery Bible*), prepubescent romantics (*God's Little Princess Devotional Bible*), hormonally addled teenagers (*The True Love Waits Bible*), and fans of the Marvel Universe (*The Super Heroes Bible*).[14] One currently popular version in a self-reflective age is called the *Journal the Word Bible*:[15] it contains specially designed pages for reflective reading, writing, and coloring. This catch-them-where-they-live approach defines the strategies of innovative Bible publishers whose market still overwhelmingly remains wedded to the physical book format.

Despite their diversity, the recent translations, paraphrases, and packaged versions of the Bible also seem tailored to meet the cultural expectations of a diverse pool of Bible readers living in a secular world: a world that can seem, to some passionate Christians, oppressively hostile, and, to others, worth learning from. Evangelical marketing makes good use of both these attitudes at the same time, producing a kind of counterculture of familiarity. Thus the hotter sort of today's Protestants can buy Bibles with eye-catching bindings that look like cheerful, ingratiating teen magazines and even Bibles in plain covers meant to prevent curious onlookers from discerning the Bible reader in their midst. Both are

---

14. *Women of Color Study Bible* (Nashville: Thomas Nelson, 1999); *The Promise Keepers Men's Study Bible* (Grand Rapids: Zondervan, 1997); *The Life Recovery Bible* (Carol Stream, IL: Tyndale House, 2017); *God's Little Princess Devotional Bible* (Nashville: Thomas Nelson, 2004); *The True Love Waits Bible* (Nashville: Holman Bible, 1996); *The Super Heroes Bible* (Grand Rapids: Zonderkidz, 2002).

15. *The Journal the Word Bible* (Nashville: Thomas Nelson, 2016). Available in multiple formats.

advertised as choices necessary to the public practice of piety in a hostile, secular world. The most talked-about Bible of the new millennium was a disposable, colorful teen magazine containing the full text of the New Testament. The product of extensive market analysis, *Revolve* (whose advent in 2003 was breathlessly covered in most sectors of the print media, including especially bemused commentary from *The New York Times* and *The New Yorker*) comes complete with scripturally informed tips for teenage girls seeking guidance on such timeless issues as dating, piercings, strict parents, and obnoxious little brothers. The editors describe the extrascriptural format:

> Each book [of the Gospels: Matthew, Mark, Luke, and John] has an Introduction written specifically to help answer these kinds of questions. There are other special features to help you get as deep inside the Bible as you can. Blabs are questions and answers with experts on a variety of topics important to you every day. Promises point out the commitments that God makes to us. Learn It and Live It give real-life application of tons of Bible verses. Bible Bios tell the stories of real-life girls who lived during the Bible times. Beauty Secrets show ways you can beautify your inner-self. There are notes on Relationships and Issues that you deal with daily. Guys Speak Out! gives you the opinion of real-life teen guys on questions you wonder about. There's just a ton of info for you to learn from. It's all here—truth, inspiration, bottom-line *actual* reality. Are you up for the challenge?[16]

These marginal conversations with "experts" and "real-life" girls and guys (there is no way of knowing exactly where, or from whom, the editors got their interlocutors) are not, as a skeptical observer might expect, relentlessly simplistic and oppressive, but nuanced: the only approach, if you think about it, that would satisfy teens faced with a book even less fallible and more authoritative than a parent.[17]

On the issue of body art, to cite one example, the girl who asks if it is okay to get a tattoo is told that, if she considers only the words of scripture, she will find none to help her: tattooing is not specifically banned in the Bible. Disobedience, on the other hand, *is*; parents are to be obeyed in all things not specifically prescribed or proscribed in Bible. The inquiring

---

16. Introduction to *Revolve*.
17. Daniel Rodosh, "Marketing the Good Book," *The New Yorker Magazine*, 18 December 2006.

girl is advised to ask her parents and to accept their decision, in a spot-on demonstration of scriptural exegesis.

Revolve sports a fashion-conscious yet wholesome look, spouts an affable and irreverent marginal tone, and offers a throwaway appeal along with its timeless message. The magazine format allows its publishers regularly to update and reset the commentary and blurbs, thus nimbly gauging the current teen-cultural scene and playing to it, while all the time keeping the words that run down the center of both pages sacrosanct. These Bibles are the direct descendants of the Geneva Bible of 1560, a translation also nearly overshadowed by *its* marginal notes, prefaces, charts, and adjunct material—and all designed to draw the portrait of a true Christian in the second half of the sixteenth century, a time of social and religious peril for the newly emergent evangelicals called Protestants. A teen-magazine Bible, remarkably innovative from the viewpoint of modern Bible publishing, employs its innovations to promote a traditional reading of the word.

Is nothing, then, sacred? This chapter has examined American Bibles both inside and out, tracing its producers'—and, eventually, revisers'—canny appraisal of the diverse and wide-flung American cultures they served. We find—to our surprise, perhaps—that the scriptural text—its content—has remained remarkably stable for a book with such diverse and contested origins. The social and cultural expectations of its readers, however, have not.

While the Bibles considered here sported new physical formats, came tailored for several enthusiastically developed niche markets, and were articulated in new versions—first, new translations for non-English speakers and then, after a long period of time, revisions and paraphrases of the long-lasting KJV—there are actually few significant differences between them. Wildly disparate in style and, finally, tone, none has in any significant sense transformed the general meaning of the scriptures, nor have any recast their basic narrative. From the Mayflower's Geneva Bible to the magazine rack's *Revolve*, the Bible's margins have always tailored the scriptures to far greater extents than new translations. These disparities merely point out the remarkable stability of the Christian Bible as a text—a collection of words that, more often than not, support social tradition rather than social change. (Or, for that matter, theological change: it is worth noting here that there is no liberal or mainstream equivalent to the inarguably vibrant and innovative evangelical Bible publishing market.)

This is not a matter of scriptural inviolability. It is a matter of a modern culture's expectations of a book—the only text in Western culture that projects an aura of both diversity and stability—and the powerfully conservative bent of a modern commercial culture intent, ultimately and always, upon profit. It remains to be seen whether the media revolutions of the past two decades will exert enough methodological force to significantly alter the biblical content of the future.

Bibliography

Alden, John. "The Bible as Printed Word." Pages 9–29 in *The Bible and Bibles in America*. Edited by Ernest S. Frerichs. Atlanta: Society of Biblical Literature, 1988.

Ferrell, Lori Anne. *The Bible and the People*. New Haven: Yale University Press, 2008.

God's Little Princess Devotional Bible. Nashville: Thomas Nelson, 2004.

Goff, Philip, Arthur E. Farnsley II, and Peter Thuesen. "The Bible in American Life Today." Pages 5–32 in *The Bible in American Life*. Edited by Philip Goff, Arthur E. Farnsley II, and Peter Thuesen. Oxford: Oxford University Press, 2017.

Gutjahr, Paul. "Diversification in American Religious Publishing." Page 194–278 in *The Industrial Book 1840–1880*. Vol. 3 of *A History of the Book in America*. Edited by Scott Casper, Jeffrey Groves, Stephen Nissenbaum, and Michael Winship. Chapel Hill: University of North Carolina Press, 2002.

"IUPUI Study, 'The Bible in American Life': King James Is Not Dead; African Americans Most Engaged." IUPUI Newsroom. 7 March 2014. https://tinyurl.com/SBL6704b.

Journal the Word Bible. Nashville: Thomas Nelson, 2016.

Kerr, John Stevens. *Ancient Texts Alive Today: The Story of the English Bible*. New York: American Bible Society, 1999.

Leeser, Isaac. Preface to *The Twenty-Four Books of the Holy Scriptures*. 2nd ed. Philadelphia: C. Sherman, 1856.

The Life Recovery Bible. Carol Stream, IL: Tyndale House, 2017.

McDannell, Colleen. *The Christian Home in Victorian America, 1840–1900*. Bloomington: Indiana University Press, 1986.

Nevin, Alfred. *Salesman's Dummy for The Holy Bible [King James Version] … Together with a New and Improved Dictionary of the Bible*. Springfield, MA: W. J. Holland, [1879].

Nord, David Paul. *Faith in Reading: Religious Publishing and the Birth of Mass Media in America*. Oxford: Oxford University Press, 2004.
The Promise Keepers Men's Study Bible. Grand Rapids: Zondervan, 1997.
Revolve: The Complete New Testament (NCV). Australia: Nelson, 2003.
Rodosh, Daniel. "Marketing the Good Book." *The New Yorker Magazine*. 18 December 2006.
Setzer, Claudia, and David A. Shefferman, eds. *The Bible and American Culture: A Sourcebook*. New York: Routledge, 2011.
The Super Heroes Bible. Grand Rapids: Zonderkidz, 2002.
Sussman, Lance. "Another Look at Isaac Leeser and the First Jewish Translation of the Bible in the United States." *Modern Judaism* 5 (1985): 159–90.
The True Love Waits Bible. Nashville: Holman, 1996.
Women of Color Study Bible. Nashville: Thomas Nelson, 1999.

2
THE BIBLE AND DIGITAL MEDIA

JEFFREY S. SIKER

Introduction

Over the last generation nothing has had a greater impact on the way Americans relate to the Bible than the seismic shift from print Bibles to digital Bibles across a variety of digital media. Perhaps the best indicator of this shift to the use of the Bible in digital form is the smartphone app YouVersion, a digital app that is well-known in the church community but relatively unknown in academic circles.[1] YouVersion has been downloaded over three hundred million times since its first appearance in 2007 on the iPhone app store. It provides free access to over 1,400 different versions of the Bible in over 1,100 languages. YouVersion is sponsored by LifeChurch, a large church that started in Oklahoma and that now has multiple satellite campuses around the country. It is affiliated with the Evangelical Covenant Church denomination, a conservative Protestant denomination with a very high view of the Bible as "the only perfect rule for faith, doctrine, and conduct."[2] The slogan for YouVersion is that "the Bible is Everywhere," meaning that anyone with a smartphone can now have instant access to the Bible whenever they want. Not only can people read the text; they can listen to it or even watch videos about it. Multiple reading plans are offered through the app, with the idea that people can more readily integrate the Bible and its content into their daily lives with the kind of immediate access that the app allows. While there are any

---

1. This observation speaks to the gap between the academy and the church when it comes to the Bible.

2. See Evangelical Covenant Church, "Beliefs," Covchurch.org, https://tinyurl.com/SBL6704d.

number of apps in the digital realm, YouVersion has really taken the largest share of the smartphone digital Bible market, both because it is very functional and because is it free.

Even before the advent of the iPhone, the Bible was available in digital form on an array of platforms ranging from computers and dedicated Bible programs such as Bible Gateway (1993) to early handheld devices such as the PalmPilot with its BibleReader software (1998). But these early versions of digital Bibles did not really compete with traditional print Bibles, in part because they operated on relatively expensive devices and in part because they were not nearly as user friendly as the iPhone and its successive versions would prove to be.

The revolutionary year for digital Bibles was 2007, and not only because of the iPhone. The year 2007 also marked the introduction of Amazon's Kindle e-reader to the marketplace. This dedicated e-reader was a game changer in the digital market for books of all kinds, including Bibles. Its screen was much larger than the iPhone's screen, and its price was much lower than the multipurpose iPhone. While the iPhone's app store allowed the user to manage a great variety of programs on the same device, the Kindle had the advantage of one primary purpose—reading. Successive versions of the iPhone (and other smartphones) and the Kindle (and other e-readers) resulted in a dramatic increase in digital reading of all kinds. Prognosticators started a radically premature discussion about the end of print books, "the late age of print," as though the revolution introduced by Gutenberg had now run its course. These predictions have so far proved to be wrong. Print Bibles still far outpace the sale and use of digital Bibles, and the print-book market continues to be strong.

Another significant development was the introduction of the iPad in 2010, with its larger touch screen. This had a particularly important impact on making e-books more reader-friendly, especially with the Kindle app becoming available free of charge to be downloaded onto iPads, as it had already become available as a program for larger computer formats and laptops. Now users could access the Bible in more readable form on larger, very portable screens. Many digital Bible publishers entered the marketplace, including the copyright holders of traditional major print Bible translations. Zondervan, the copyright owner of the New International Version (NIV) of the Bible, acquired the web-based Bible Gateway in 2008. Zondervan itself had already been acquired by the publishing giant HarperCollins as its Christian publishing arm twenty years earlier in 1988. In 2011 HarperCollins purchased another major Bible-publisher, Thomas

Nelson, the copyright holder of the New King James Version (NKJV), and so cornered the market on the two most popular translations of the Bible, the NIV and the NKJV. (The traditional King James Version [KJV] of the Bible, produced in 1611, remains the most widely used version, though it has long been in public domain without a particular copyright holder.)

One of the most important developments in how we read the Bible in digital form has to do with the relatively fluid forms of orality, what Walter Ong has termed a kind of "secondary orality,"[3] that digital media have introduced. Digital culture in the popular form we know it today was in its infancy when Ong was writing *Orality and Literacy*, but his observations about the fluidity of this new orality were prescient.

Before Johannes Gutenberg's invention of the printing press with movable type in the 1450s, most people were illiterate. Reading was reserved for the educated, for the ruling class, and for clergy. Before Gutenberg invented movable type, individuals who occupied a lower place on the economic ladder could listen to scripture being read (initially mostly in Latin, then sometimes glossed in the vernacular) or see the stories of scripture unfold on stained glass windows. Thus one accessed the Bible by listening to readings and by seeing the depictions of Bible stories in the windows of churches. But the facility to read did not grow rapidly until there was a means by which to have books and pamphlets copied quickly and distributed widely, which Gutenberg's invention made possible.

With the printing press it became possible to print and disseminate the Bible quickly and relatively inexpensively. The printed page quickly took hold and became the primary vehicle that an increasingly literate populace purchased and treasured as the most important book of the home. But with the advent of digital media in the late twentieth century, once again one could listen with ease to scripture being read out loud through digital audio. Once again one could watch the stories of scripture unfold with images to amplify the meaning of the words. With digital media the Bible is no longer bound to a physical and printed text. The digital Bible is

---

3. Walter Ong, *Orality and Literacy: The Technologizing of the Word* (New York: Methuen, 1982). See now *Orality and Literacy*, 30th anniversary ed. (New York: Routledge, 2012), with additional chapters by John Hartley (a professor of Cultural Science at Curtin University, Western Australia), esp. 133–34. Already in 1982 Ong could refer to "secondary orality" as "present-day high technology culture, in which a new orality is sustained by telephone, radio, television, and other electronic devices that depend for their existence and functioning on writing and print" (11).

a Bible that has in many ways lost its covers. This chapter will explore how the Bible and our understanding of the Bible as text have morphed in light of digital culture.

My goal in this chapter is to trace in broad outline some of the most important developments related to the Bible and digital media in American culture. To organize this chapter I have divided it into six sections: (1) an overview of statistics about usage of digital Bibles; (2) the impact of reading the Bible on screens rather than in print form; (3) the different forms of digital media on which the Bible has been used; (4) the use of computer programs for Bible study; (5) the Bible and digital social media; and, finally, (6) some of the strengths and weaknesses associated with the use of the Bible in digital media.[4]

1. Surveys of Digital Bible Usage

The use of digital Bibles must be framed within the larger context of the shift from print to digital in more general terms. A September 2016 Pew Research report showed that between 2011 and 2016 e-book reading rose from 17 percent to 28 percent overall, while print-book reading held relatively steady at 65 percent (down from a high of 71 percent in 2011). About 14 percent of individuals polled for 2016 indicated they had listened to an audio book in the previous year.[5] The report concludes that while most Americans are reading digital books on smartphones and tablets, the use of dedicated e-readers lagged behind. Overall, though, people still preferred paper books to digital screens by a wide margin, over two to one. The significance of this data is certainly subject to debate, but it does appear to show that the anticipation that print would shift almost completely to digital was overstated in the extreme. Print has bounced back, even as digital continues to occupy an important place in the overall market. Rüdiger Wishenbart, the Director of International Affairs for the BookExpoAmerica (BEA) tradegroup, put it well in his 2016 Global E-book Report:

---

4. For a more thorough examination of all these topics and more, see my book *Liquid Scripture: The Bible in a Digital World* (Minneapolis: Fortress, 2017).

5. Andrew Perrin, "Book Reading 2016," Pew Research Center: Internet and Technology, https://tinyurl.com/SBL6704g.

Altogether, what we currently see is most probably the "end of the digital beginning" and the beginning transition into the next, perhaps even more challenging phase, where writing, publishing, and reading morph in fluid settings; where any content, in any format, is available for almost any user—yet without much stability both with regard to who is offering what, as well as how that offer is taken in by the many fickle audiences around the world.[6]

In the last couple of years the sale of e-books has slowed considerably, with print books continuing to show strong support among readers.

This general summary applies to digital Bibles as well. Between 2011 and 2017 the American Bible Society commissioned an annual "State of the Bible" report from the Barna Group, an evangelical Christian research and polling firm. They surveyed about two thousand people nationwide, one thousand in telephone interviews, and another one thousand people via online surveys of a representative group of people. The survey asked about frequency of reading the Bible, which version people used, whether they used digital or print Bibles, and other questions about relating the Bible to current events. The 2011 report indicated that roughly 18 percent of individuals stated that they used their smartphones to search for a verse in the Bible and that 90 percent still used a print Bible. Another 37 percent stated that they had used the internet or a computer to access the biblical text.[7] Clearly, people are using multiple formats. By 2015, the American Bible Society report indicated that while people continued to prefer the print bible over digital Bibles, in point of fact, over half of the people had made use of a digital Bible in the previous year. Slightly over half of the population also now owned smartphones or personal computers, making it increasingly easy to access the Bible in digital form.

In addition to the American Bible Society surveys, the Center for the Study of Religion and American Culture at Indiana University/Purdue University in Indianapolis (IUPUI) released a report in 2014 that included information about use of digital Bibles. Their survey found that 31 percent of Bible readers used the Internet to read the Bible, and 22 percent used e-devices (smartphones, tablets) to read the Bible. It is important to note

---

6. Porter Anderson, "As BEA Opens: A New Global Ebook Report on a Mercurial World Market," PublishingPerspectives.com, https://tinyurl.com/SBL6704c.

7. American Bible Society, "State of the Bible, 2011," https://tinyurl.com/SBL6704k.

that most individuals used multiple forms of media (print/digital) to read the Bible. Not surprisingly, younger users more familiar with digital technology tended to use digital Bibles more than those over the age of sixty. Lower-income and less well-educated individuals also typically made greater use of print than digital Bibles. Given the cost of digital devices this finding is also to be expected.

A conference on "The Bible in America," held in conjunction with the IUPUI study, resulted in the 2017 publication of *The Bible in American Life*. A number of chapters in this book also address the use of digital Bibles. John Weaver's "Transforming Practice: American Bible Reading in Digital Culture" confirmed that people who use digital Bibles also use print Bibles, with a preference for print Bibles when it comes to devotional reading.[8] Bryan Bibb's essay on "Readers and Their E-Bibles" shows how the use of digital Bibles has led to an increase in readers having multiple translations open in parallel windows. He also sees the use of digital Bibles leading to an increased transformation of the canon to a narrow focus on particular verses rather than paying attention to the larger whole, thus shrinking the canon. In addition, there is a tendency to expand the canon by drawing on larger extracanonical literary and historical contexts in such a way that the canonical text can be watered down.[9]

Surveys also indicate that, whereas in 2007 a certain stigma was attached to using the iPhone to read the Bible during worship services, a decade later there is no such stigma. It is seen as simply another way to read the Bible, no different really than projecting the biblical text on a large screen during a worship service.[10] The utter ubiquity of iPhones and other smartphones across the American landscape has rendered those without such devices as the odd ones out. Indeed, Apple Computers announced in summer of 2016 that they had sold their billionth iPhone worldwide.[11]

---

8. John Weaver, "Transforming Practice: American Bible Reading in Digital Culture," in *The Bible in American Life*, ed. Philip Goff, Arthur E. Farnsley, and Peter J. Thuesen (New York: Oxford University Press), 249–55.

9. Bryan Bibb, "Readers and Their E-Bibles," in Goff, Farnsley, and Thuesen, *The Bible in American Life*, 256–65.

10. See Bobby Ross Jr., "Texting during Worship? No, Just Reading the Text," *The Christian Chronicle*, 1 September 2009; https://tinyurl.com/SBL6704h; and Ross, "Digital vs. Print: Readers Weigh in on Bible Choices," *The Christian Chronicle*, 1 October 2012, https://tinyurl.com/SBL6704i.

11. See Kia Kokalitcheva, "Apple Has Sold Its Billionth iPhone." *Fortune*, 27 July 2016.

2. The Impact of Reading the Bible on Screens Rather Than in Print Form

So what difference does it really make to read the Bible on a digital screen rather than in a bound print version of the Bible? What is the difference between reading pixels versus paper? This question has occupied researchers over the last generation as students in particular are reading more and more on screens than in traditional print books. Professors are also assigning more and more articles and books that are accessed via digital screens. It is much less expensive, and students do not have to lug around the traditional backpacks full of heavy books and heavy Bibles! So what have researchers found, and how might their findings apply to reading digital Bibles?

In order to appreciate what difference it might make to read print versus screens, it is important at the outset to understand that reading in general is not something that comes to us naturally. Unlike acquiring spoken language, acquiring the ability to read is a relatively recent phenomenon in human evolution. Although something like modern humans have been around for about fifty thousand years, writing and reading have only been a human activity for the past six thousand years, and alphabets for only the last thirty-eight hundred years. Two studies in particular have been seminal in helping us to understand how it is that we developed the capacity to read and write. Maryanne Wolf's *Proust and the Squid: The Story and Science of the Reading* and Stanislas Dehaene's *Reading in the Brain: The Science and Evolution of a Human Invention* both demonstrate how the human brain has made use of neural plasticity to develop the ability to read.[12] Neural plasticity refers to a small "fringe of variability" in brain architecture that allows for the formation of new neuronal connections and structures.[13] Apparently, as Wolf explains it:

> the reading brain exploited older neuronal pathways originally designed not only for vision but for connecting vision to conceptual and linguistic functions.... Our brain had at its disposal three ingenious design principles: the capacity to make new connections among older struc-

---

12. Maryanne Wolf's *Proust and the Squid: The Story and Science of the Reading Brain* (New York: Harper Perennial, 2007); Stanislas Dehaene's *Reading in the Brain: The Science and Evolution of a Human Invention* (New York: Viking, 2009).

13. Dehaene, *Reading in the Brain*, 6.

tures; the capacity to form areas of exquisitely precise specialization for recognizing patterns in information; and the ability to learn to recruit and connect information from these areas automatically.... These three principles of brain organization are the foundation for all of reading's evolution, development, and failure.[14]

Reading is a difficult skill to acquire because it involves the coordination of three different parts of the brain to pull it off. Functional magnetic resonance imaging (fMRI) has shown the three areas of the brain that light up when we read. The temporal lobe decodes and discriminates sounds; the frontal lobe comprehends the grammar of language and speech that we have learned; and the angular gyrus in the parietal lobe links these brain functions together, allowing reading to take place. A further indication of how reading is an adapted rather than a natural brain process can be seen in the very mechanics of how our eyes read. As Dehaene points out, our eyes do not move smoothly across a sentence on a page (either printed or screen); rather they jerk along in what are called saccades, the rapid shifting of our eyes from one fixed point to another.[15] We only read a few letters at a time, which our brains then combine to form words and sense units that are then processed into meaning.

But more than our eyes are involved, and this is where it does make a difference whether we are reading a physical page or a digital screen. When we hold a book in our hands, our brains get far more information than our mere eyes can communicate. The very physicality of holding the book communicates via haptic senses. Haptics refers to the sense of touch. Our hands communicate information to our brains that supplements what our eyes perceive—the thickness of a page, the location of particular words on a printed page, where we are in the book. This is anything but minor information. We all, I think, have had the experience of trying to find a passage in a book we have read, and we can often remember where the passage occurred on a printed page. This is because of haptic memory. This is why I sometimes lose my place when the physical print layout of my Greek-English diglot New Testament changes from one edition to another.

---

14. Wolf, *Proust and the Squid*, 12. See now also Wolf's *Tales of Literacy for the Twenty-First Century* (New York: Oxford University Press, 2016), especially chapter 7 on an important initiative teaching nonliterate children to read only through the use of digital screens.

15. Dehaene, *Reading in the Brain*, 17.

I am used to the physicality of the page and the words on it. A new edition means I have to relearn where a passage is on the page.

But with digital screens all bets are off in terms of haptic memory. Words on digital screens are slippery at best. Since we can resize the words and change the font style at will, let alone the spacing, a virtual page is never particularly stable. Haptic memory in reading print books allows us to flip through a book and keep our place, to turn a few pages back and relocate a passage, or to flip ahead to see how much further we might have to read to complete a chapter or a section. Our brains perceive a frame of reference that associates printed words and sentences on a page with spatial locations.

Haptic memory is enhanced by the physicality of the printed page. The more sensory input our brains receive over a longer period of time, the more readily such input gets stored in long-term memory. Because digital screens can prove somewhat slippery for our brains, research has shown that we do not retain information as well from screens as we do from print.[16] This is why manufacturers of e-readers do their best to approximate the experience of reading a physical book by adding virtual physicality—the page turn mimics turning a page in a print book (sometimes even with the sound of a turning page); there is a virtual thickness to the pages showing how much we have read and how much farther we have to go. These virtual approximations certainly can help, but they are, after all, only virtual.

Further, when it comes to the Bible, there is another downside to reading on digital screens rather than in print form, and this has to do with knowing the Bible as a book. When we read on digital screens we are only reading one screen, and the words change as we "turn pages," but there is never a real sense of the Bible as a whole book. Rather, the Bible becomes a fragmented text at best. Unless they knew it beforehand by becoming familiar with the lay of the land of the Bible, students have no real sense of the canonical shape of the Bible—that the Jewish scriptures, for example, have different sections of Torah, Prophets, and Writings. Similarly with the writings of the New Testament, students are unaware of the location of the Gospel of Matthew relative to Paul's Letter to the Galatians. Moreover, they do not particularly need to know since all they have to do is to do a search for Matthew or Galatians, and, voilà, there they are! But something is lost in this process. While the canonical shape of the Bible may

---

16. See, e.g., Anne Mangen, "Hypertext Fiction Reading: Haptics and Immersion," *Journal of Research in Reading* 31 (2008): 404–19.

not matter much for doing historical reconstruction of ancient Israel or the development of early Christianity, it does make a difference if one is concerned with the history of biblical interpretation or with how people read the Bible theologically by seeking to understand one part of the Bible in light of another. Reading the Bible on digital screens can thus result in a somewhat fragmented perception of the biblical text, just as reading the Bible as a bound volume can result in a kind of homogenization of the different books of the Bible. Both the function of the individual writings in their own contexts and the function of the collective amalgamation of the Bible are important in their own right.

Another issue that some have raised with using the Bible in digital form, especially on smartphones, in contrast to print Bibles, is the observation that print Bibles have but one function—to be read. The Bible on a smartphone is but one small function of the many things one can do with this device—calling, texting, surfing the web, taking pictures, posting pictures, playing games, and so much more. The monofunctionality of the Bible in print form suggests to some people a certain sacred character to the text itself, as opposed to the multifunctionality of a device that is first and foremost a phone that can also do any number of other things, including serving as a device with a screen on which one can read the Bible.

For others, however, it makes no real difference whether one is reading the Bible in print form versus on digital screens.[17] It is the text that is sacred, not the form that the text takes—whether on a printed page, on a digital screen, in spoken word, or even in a stained glass window or a children's cartoon. A good illustration of this point has been observed by Katja Rakow, a professor of religious studies at Utrecht University. She was studying pastor Joel Osteen's megachurch (Lakewood Church) in Houston, and she was struck by a ritual that recurred each Sunday in worship. At the beginning of the service Pastor Osteen invited the congregation to hold up their Bibles and then in unison recite the following declaration:

> This is my Bible. I am what it says I am. I can do what it says I can do. Today, I will be taught the Word of God. I boldly confess, my mind is alert, my heart is receptive. I will never be the same. I am about to receive

---

17. See, e.g., Michael Gryboski, "Are Digital Bibles as Holy as Paper Bibles?" *The Christian Post*, 15 July 2014, https://tinyurl.com/SBL6704e.

the incorruptible, indestructible ever-living seed of the Word of God. I will never be the same.[18]

What Rakow noticed was that while most individuals held up their print Bibles, there were also a number of individuals who held up their digital Bibles on smartphones, tablets, or e-readers. Over the course of a year (2011–2012), she noticed more and more such digital Bibles being held up over the weeks. Her conclusion is important:

> In that moment of declaration, these electronic devices became the Bible. They were not just a technology that enabled its users to read the digital version of the Word of God. For this short moment, the fact became irrelevant that the same device could be used in very different ways besides providing Bible verses.[19]

Of course, this very moment of transfiguration, in which the digital device becomes the sacred text, can be shattered in an instant with a text message, a tweet, a phone call, a calendar reminder, or any number of other interruptions that break the scripture spell. But not all digital devices are created equal in terms of their suitability for reading text uninterrupted, which leads to a discussion about the relationship between form and function in digital design. As we will see, the digital interface can both facilitate and complicate how we access and navigate the biblical text.

3. The Changing Shape of the Bible in Digital Media

There are a variety of issues to be discussed under the general category of how digital media can change the shape of the Bible, both physically and metaphorically. Here we will focus on the issues of: (1) digital screens, (2) translations, (3) paratexts, (4) children's Bibles, and (5) audio Bibles.

---

18. To watch a video of this ritual, see DWARF202, "This Is My Bible," YouTube, https://www.youtube.com/watch?v=ncxlkokN-6Q.

19. Katja Rakow, "The Bible in the Digital Age: Negotiating the Limits of 'Bibleness' of Different Bible Media," in *Christianity and the Limits of Materiality*, ed. Minaa Opas and Anna Haapalainen (London: Bloomsbury, 2017), 101–2.

3.1. Digital Screens

We encounter many choices when it comes to the functionality and usability of digital screens for accessing and displaying the biblical text. The last generation has seen one technological advancement after another in the readability of screens. The monochrome heavily pixelated cathode-ray tube screens of the 1960s and 1970s gave way to color screens in the 1980s, then to the incorporation of light-emitting diodes (LED), organic light-emitting diodes (OLED), plasma, and liquid crystal displays (LCD) in the 1990s and early 2000s. Since then we have witnessed the invention of gorilla glass, touch-screens, electronic paper, and retina display. Smartphones, tablets, and computers (both laptop and desktop) have all been outfitted with more readable screens with each successive generation.

But readability is only one factor in the functionality of the screens that display the biblical text. There is a hierarchy of digital devices for displaying digital Bibles, and it has less to do with the screens per se and more to do with how multifunctional a digital device is. The rule of thumb is that the greater the multifunctionality, the more awkward a digital device is for reading the Bible. Why? Distractions and multitasking.[20]

At the top of the digital reading hierarchy are dedicated e-readers, such as the Kindle Paperwhite, the Kindle Voyage, or the newer Kindle Oasis. These devices excel at doing one thing—seeking to emulate the experience of reading a physical book, with as few distractions as possible. They come with added bonuses that in many ways surpass physical books: they can hold thousands of digital books; they can be adjusted in terms of lighting, letter size, and font; one can highlight or mark text and take (relatively primitive) notes. Slightly below the dedicated e-readers are tablets, which function much like e-readers because they support e-reader software (e.g., the Kindle app), but which also have many more functions (web access, messaging, photos, music, games) and many more distractions as a result. Then come computers of all kinds, laptops and desktops with their much larger screens and much greater power to have multiple windows open at once and even more ways to be distracted by one thing after another popping up on the screen.

---

20. See, e.g., Adam Gazzaley and Larry D. Rosen, *The Distracted Mind: Ancient Brains in a High-Tech World* (Boston: MIT Press, 2016); Dave Crenshaw, *The Myth of Multitasking: How "Doing It All" Gets Nothing Done* (San Francisco: Jossey-Bass, 2008).

Smartphones typically have the most functionality: talking, texting, web surfing, shooting photos and videos, calendaring, getting traffic directions, and the thousand other things that smartphone apps allow the user to explore. This abundant functionality limits their usefulness as devices for digital reading. One can certainly read on smartphones, but their screen size is typically much smaller than a book page, providing relative snippets of text at a time. Though screen sizes of smartphones have grown larger over the last decade, smartphones remain the champion distractors. If reading, at least deep reading, is best served by sitting still and concentrating on the text, then smartphones do not lend themselves to this kind of concentration since by definition they are *mobile* devices intended to allow for multiple forms of interaction with the user.

3.2. Translations

One of the great strengths of digital Bibles is how easily one can toggle among a whole panoply of translations. This feature is also one of the great ironies of the Bible in the digital age. There is a kind of stable instability in the tremendous variety of translations. Whereas the original language texts underlying the Bible have remained mostly unchanged for several generations (especially the Hebrew Bible, but also the Greek Septuagint and New Testament), the last fifty years have seen the appearance of dozens of new translations, a veritable Babel of Bibles! In English alone the YouVersion app offers the user forty-eight different versions of the Bible. While, on the one hand, the many translations serve to highlight that translation is really the first step of interpretation, on the other hand, the sheer multitude of translations raises important questions about the stability of the biblical text itself. With so many translations, one may reasonably ask if there is anything *standard* about the New Revised Standard Version or *international* about the New International Version or *common* about the Common English Bible. The great variety of translations creates a very broad field of possible readings of contested biblical passages.

Take, for example, the myriad translations of the Greek *malakoi* and *arsenokoitai* from 1 Cor 6:9–10. An aspiring leader in a group Bible study utilizing the wonders of digital technology might decide to share several parallel translations with the group:

    KJV (1611)   "nor effeminate nor abusers of themselves with mankind"
    RSV (1947)   "nor sexual perverts"

NIV (1978) "nor male prostitutes, nor homosexual offenders"
NKJV (1982) "nor homosexuals, nor sodomites"
NRSV (1989) "male prostitutes, sodomites"
NABRE (2002) "nor boy prostitutes, nor practicing homosexuals"

Confusion will surely abound when it is revealed that the original Greek terms literally mean "soft ones" and "men-bedders," and even these translations (my own) could be contested.

To be sure, the multiplicity of translations could be evident simply by comparing different *print* versions of the Bible, but it is far easier to line up parallel translations via digital media, leading to a kind of hyper-awareness of the fluidity of translations as well as a kind of democratization of translations, even when such equivalencies are not warranted. Some translations actually are better than others,[21] and this can get lost in the flurry of different translations, to such a degree that people might actually be misled into thinking that one translation (or paraphrase) is just as good or just the same as another, that it is all a matter of personal taste. It is not uncommon to hear someone declare their preference for this flavor or that flavor of Bible translation, with the result that all seem equally legitimate, especially when facilitated by digital ease of access. While in general the wide dissemination and democratization of different translations of the Bible is a good thing, it is far too easy for readers of the Bible to presume that the Living Bible or The Message (both paraphrases, not translations) are somehow the equivalent of the NRSV, the NIV, or the NABRE (all good translations, by and large).[22] They are not.

3.3. Paratexts

Paratext refers to all the things that accompany the text but are not actually part of the text itself.[23] Such features as chapter headings and the

---

21. For example, to translate either *malakoi* or *arsenokoitai* with the English word "homosexual" is anachronistic in the extreme. Even to use the word "sodomite" is tendentious at best.

22. My standard line about any translation is that to read anything in the original is to read it in "color," while reading a translation is reading the text in "black and white." The basic meaning comes through, but the nuances are often lost.

23. See the fundamental study by Gerard Genette, *Paratexts: Thresholds of Interpretation* (Cambridge: Cambridge University Press, 1997).

numbering of the Bible into chapters and verses are the most common paratexts. They are so common, in fact, as to having almost blended with the text itself. Paratexts are typically intended to serve as helps for the reader, and such helps can indeed be very useful for those reading the Bible. In print form we are perhaps most familiar with the paratexts associated with study Bibles—all the editorial notes and references at the bottom of the page to help the reader understand the text.[24] Such paratexts help to frame the biblical text and provide contextual explanations.

In print form the paratexts are typically easy to separate out from the biblical text itself, though there are Bibles that are amplified with additional words added in brackets or italics to the actual text for clarification.[25] The paratextual content of print Bibles is delimited and demarcated by physical print. There are relatively clear boundaries. But in the digital realm paratexts take on a different aspect. Through the use of hyperlinks, digital paratexts may *initially* be programmed by a Bible publisher such as YouVersion or any digital Bible or Bible app. But once a user (a better term than *reader* here) plugs and plunges into the hypertextual world of the Bible, all bets are off. Each user ends up creating their own hypertextual journey, their own set of individual paratextual rabbit holes beyond the text. Some will hypertext from a biblical text to a map, others to a Bible dictionary, others to a concordance or to a Greek or Hebrew lexicon. Rather than serving as communal paratexts for the print reader of the Bible, the hyperlinked realm of digital Bibles offers individual users an endless array of paratexts from which to choose. As Wido van Peursen has observed, in the digital realm the Bible is "losing its covers."[26] As a result, the boundaries between text and paratext can get blurred.

3.4. Children's Bibles

Children's Bibles have long been a staple of Bible publishing.[27] Typically, such Bibles are storybook Bibles that retell classic Bible stories in language

---

24. The *HarperCollins Study Bible* (Student Edition, NRSV), the *New Oxford Annotated Bible* (NRSV), *The Catholic Bible: Personal Study Edition* (NABRE), the *Jewish Study Bible*, and any number of NIV study Bibles come to mind.

25. See, e.g., Zondervan's *Amplified Study Bible*, clearly designed for evangelical Christian audiences.

26. Wido van Peursen, "Is the Bible Losing Its Covers? Conceptualization and Use of the Bible on the Threshold of the Digital Order," *HIPHIL Novum* 1 (2014): 44–58.

27. See Ruth Bottigheimer, *The Bible for Children: From the Age of Gutenberg to*

that is simplified for the comprehension level of children. The younger the child, the simpler and shorter the story. Almost all children's Bibles come replete with pictures to illustrate the story that is being told.

The emergence of the digital era has seen an important shift in children's Bibles, as children of all ages have increasingly become quite tech-savvy—digital natives. They are used to navigating digital devices of all kinds, and although they may still be novices at reading, they are sophisticated consumers of digital screens. Publishers of digital Bible apps have not been slow to respond to the growing demand for children's Bibles that are attentive to this unique demographic. YouVersion, for example, has published a now widely downloaded children's Bible, *The Bible App for Kids Storybook Bible*. The ad for this kids' Bible states that it is "everything kids need to fall in love with God's Word."[28] The app includes simple animated characters (people and animals who move when touched on the screen), videos, a companion curriculum for parents to use with their children, and the storybook Bible (in twenty-six languages), among other resources. It contains forty-one Bible stories evenly divided between Old and New Testament stories. For anyone familiar with childrens' Bibles, the stories are very familiar: Adam and Eve, Noah's ark, Abraham and Isaac, Moses, the exodus; and from the New Testament various gospel stories about Jesus and a few stories about Paul from the Acts of the Apostles. The app concludes with "God's Good News" about how kids can be part of the story themselves. The app has a decidedly evangelical Protestant flavor with a traditional atonement theology stressing Jesus as God's perfect sacrifice on behalf of sinful humanity. Whereas more typically we see print books being digitized, in this case the digital app has now been published as a print book![29]

Another widely downloaded children's Bible app is the *Superbook Kids Bible, Videos and Games*, published by the Christian Broadcasting Network (CBN). This kid's Bible has the full biblical text (in dozens of languages) that is interspersed with hyperlinks to questions and answers, profiles of biblical figures, pictures, and games. The app began life as a

---

the Present (New Haven: Yale University Press, 1986); and Caroline Vander Stichele and Hugh S. Pyper, eds, *Text, Image, and Otherness in Children's Bibles: What Is in the Picture?*, SemeiaSt 56 (Atlanta: Society of Biblical Literature, 2012).

28. Youversion, *The Bible App for Kids Storybook Bible*, Multiplatform app, https://bibleappforkids.com/storybook.

29. *The Bible App for Kids Storybook Bible* (Pompano Beach, FL: OneHope, 2015).

1980s evangelical television cartoon in Japan that grew to have fifty-two animated episodes of Bible stories.

There are many other Bible apps that are geared to children and youth of all ages, ranging from Bible Trivia games, Bible Scrabble, Bible Hangman, Bible Bingo, Park the Ark, and hundreds upon hundreds more. Zondervan's *The Beginner's Bible* provides a website designed for children, with a similar collection of games, coloring sheets, mazes, and other ways to interact with the biblical stories. Significantly, even with the increasing presence of digital children's Bibles, the popularity of children's Bibles in print form (from comic book Bibles, to Manga Bibles, and more traditional versions) has continued to be a growing market.[30] Parents appear to be interested in having children relate to the Bible as a physical book, especially for reading together at bedtime. It is easier to communicate that the Bible is a special book when it has all the tangibility of a print Bible, and one that is especially designed for children.

3.5. Audio Bibles

The advent of digital audio books has been another important development in the realm of digital books. Audio books, of course, are not to be found on screens but make use of digital audio as a book is read out loud to the user. Sales of audio books have increased over the last several years, utilizing such applications as Audible, Audiobooks, Bookmobile, and Nook audiobooks, among others.[31] It is somewhat ironic that over the last two thousand years the Bible has surely been heard read aloud in a communal context (most often a worship setting) far more often than it has been read silently in print by individuals. The advent of the printing press and the marked increase in reading resulted in many more people reading a physical print Bible. But the oral proclamation of the Bible never ceased. Now the digital audio version of the Bible has expanded still further the reach of the Bible especially in mobile contexts. This most modern form of digital audio is often used to relay the least modern translation of the Bible, the KJV, though other versions

---

30. The Manga Bible first appeared in 2007. See Robert Hutchinson, "The Bible as a Comic Book," *Our Sunday Visitor Newsweekly*, 30 May 2012.

31. In 2015 alone, sales of audiobooks jumped 38 percent according to the Association of American Publishers.

are available, with the NIV a popular choice as well.[32] Amazon lists *The Complete Audio King James Bible*, as read by James Earl Jones, among its bestsellers. It is striking that the famous voice for the evil character Darth Vader in the Star Wars trilogy should be the same voice that reads the sacred biblical text!

People are certainly used to hearing sacred texts read out loud, as it happens all over the world in worship services every day, be they Jewish, Christian, or Muslim. So the digital form of the Bible as an audiobook is not such a change from what people are accustomed to hearing, even though the context of listening to the Bible in a car, while working out, or at home as an individual is different from the more communal setting of a worship service. Audiobooks in general tend to personalize the experience of reading through listening, and this is certainly the case for audio Bibles as well.

The CEO of audiobooks.com, Ian Small, has argued that audiobooks have three advantages over print books.[33] First, a book "read" with one's ears is open to the narrative performance that has the potential to create a world that takes advantage of an expansive auditory experience (e.g., sound effects, excellent narration). Second, according to Small, several studies show that retention is as good or better with listening when compared to reading. He argues that this is because audio books lend themselves to more focused listening as one consumes a book. Third, audiobooks allow one to multitask, as long as the tasks are not too distracting. Thus one can listen while driving or doing chores. One might well ask if listening to the Bible functions in the same way as listening to any other book. A person could certainly be engaged in devotional listening to the reading of a biblical passage, a kind of *lectio divina*, but such meditative listening typically only accommodates small portions of the biblical text upon which one reflects, rather than the more typical extended narrative reading of a novel.

---

32. The Barna Group reported that 28 percent of those surveyed in 2016 used audio versions of the Bible. See Barna Group, *The Bible in America: The Changing Landscape of Bible Perceptions and Engagement* (Ventura, CA: Barna Group, 2016), 148.

33. Brian Feinblum, "Interview with Audiobooks.com Ian Small," Digitalbookworld.com, https://tinyurl.com/SBL6704j.

4. Computer Programs and Bible Study

One of the most significant advances in the study of the Bible, both in more academic and ecclesial settings, has been the growing importance of quite sophisticated computer programs dedicated to detailed Bible study. Equally important have been the ways in which the developers and publishers of these programs have managed to make them work across different digital platforms, from traditional desktop computers, to laptops, tablets, and especially smartphones.

The story of digital Bible software for personal use dates to the rise of personal computers in the 1980s. Early software already had the capacity to do relatively quick concordance searches of words in various languages, including Hebrew and Greek. It was also possible to arrange multiple translations in parallel columns for easy comparison. Among the earliest of such programs was *CD Word: The Interactive Bible Library*, developed at Dallas Theological Seminary in the late 1980s. In addition to four English translations of the Bible, this computer program also offered the Greek New Testament (the Nestle-Aland 26th edition), Rahlfs Septuagint, two Greek lexicons (BAGD and the intermediate Liddell and Scott), three one-volume biblical commentaries, two one-volume Bible dictionaries, and the advent of hyper-texted links between all of these resources, available on CD-ROMs. The program was relatively expensive, and eventually Dallas Theological Seminary decided to sell it in 1991 to Logos Research Systems, the precursor of Logos Bible Software, now a branch of Faithlife.com.

At present three powerful and sophisticated Bible computer programs dominate the market: Logos, Accordance Bible Software, and Olive Tree Bible Software. Each program offers very deep and ever-evolving resources in software packages that can be customized in a variety of ways and that are offered at a variety of price points. Each resource provides the Bible in dozens of languages, along with a great many primary and secondary tools, many of which come with the basic programs and many others that can be purchased as additional modules. They all work on both the PC and Mac platforms, though Logos was originally a dedicated program for the PC, and Accordance and Olive Tree were originally dedicated for the Mac. Further, Logos, Accordance, and Olive Tree all can be operated on tablets and smartphones with iOS.

An indication of how quickly the world of digital Bibles changes can be seen from the fate of the program BibleWorks, which began in 1992 as a program for the PC but which ceased operation in June of 2018. Several factors led to the demise of BibleWorks, even though it enjoyed initial great success: (1) it was unable to keep up with the increasing emphasis on iOS software for portable devices; (2) it was the most complicated Bible software on the market as it relied extensively on hard-to-remember search codes; (3) and it did not offer any extensive library of secondary resources for Bible study that has been the hallmark of Logos and Accordance in particular. Still, BibleWorks was purchased by thousands of people and is still being used (if no longer supported). The ever-morphing world of digital Bible software has increasingly stressed user-friendly and on-the-go apps to deliver the scriptures in multiple forms. BibleWorks simply got left in the dust of programs that have slightly different strengths, many of them overlapping.

Logos prides itself on having a massive library of quite literally thousands of primary and secondary materials that users can access if they have purchased the relevant package. (The Collector's Edition of Logos comes with a staggering five thousand digital books, all intended to enhance the study of the Bible.) Between the exegetical guide and the passage guide that opens with each search, Logos offers so many avenues of research and study that the program can be a bit overwhelming at times. The software is designed to aid both the scholar and the preacher with resources ranging from highly technical lexicography to sermon helps and outlines. One can even take virtual online courses through the Logos program that features scholarly lectures, syllabi with reading assignments, and in general the kind of coursework one would find in a seminary curriculum.

The goal of Logos Bible Software is to be as comprehensive as possible and as integrated as possible with resources beyond the study of the Bible. The change in name from "Logos Bible Software" to "Faithlife" in 2014 speaks directly to the all-encompassing framework that the software seeks to provide for everything from Bible study to sermon preparation to integrated worship helps. As their website states, "Faithlife Platform unites our family of resources and streamlines local church communication and ministry."[34] This integration of resources supports such programs in the Faithlife Network as Faithlife Groups, Logos Mobile Ed, Proclaim, Bible Study Magazine, and more. Logos Bible Software remains at the core of Faithlife's network of programs, but it is only one component part of the much larger whole. Faithlife.com and its flagship Logos Bible Software is

---

34. https://www.logos.com/faithlife.

also the largest digital Bible program and the most aggressive in terms of marketing its software.

The only real downside of all that Logos offers (and this applies to most of the other programs as well) is the significant use of public domain resources, which are essentially free to the publisher and user alike. While many of these represent ancient texts (e.g., the Ante-Nicene and Post-Nicene Fathers), many others come from popular eighteenth- and nineteenth-century writings, and as such they represent the theological ideas and debates of their time, many of which could be considered antiquated and out of date by today's standards. There are certainly valuable insights in many of these older, now public, resources, but unless the user happens to be aware that they are reading very old material in modern digital garb, there is little to inform the user that, for example, Matthew Henry's commentary on the Bible was first published in the early eighteenth century. This is particularly a problem in student use of these materials, as they often tend to make use of online materials indiscriminately and without sufficient critical awareness about the context of these secondary sources. It is helpful, for instance, to be aware of the fundamentalist movement or the modernist controversy at the beginning of the twentieth century that shaped much of the theological debate about the Bible at that time. The contextualization of the commentaries on the Bible is arguably as important as the contextualization of the biblical writings themselves.

Accordance Bible Software markets itself as "simple, lightning fast, easy to use … Simply Brilliant."[35] The program emphasizes getting into the biblical text quickly with as many resources as one may need. The conviction of the developers of Accordance is that "Bible study software shouldn't be cumbersome or complicated."[36] If Logos tends to overwhelm the user with an overabundance of tools and resources, the approach of Accordance stresses building a configuration of resources suited to one's needs. Accordance has a much simpler interface than Logos, though both programs can be adapted in a great variety of ways.

The heart of the Accordance program is the biblical text itself. One can choose to emphasize a focus on English studies, Greek studies, or Hebrew studies, each replete with a set of tools and modules that the user can

---

35. accordancebible.com.
36. "Why Accordance," Accordance.com, https://tinyurl.com/SBL6704m.

configure to their own particular needs. Beyond this the user can access graphic resources and a variety of academic bundles. There are also different levels of users that Accordance seeks to target. The Lite version is free, followed by Starter, and then a progressive approach to Bible study for those who identify as Learners, followed by Discoverers, with special focus on study of the English, Greek, or Hebrew biblical texts. This, in turn, leads to Pro, Master, and Expert levels of users. Each step involves more sophisticated tools and modules.

Like Logos, Accordance also offers plenty of basically free public-domain resources from the eighteenth and nineteenth centuries. Users need to be aware of the theological contexts out of which these materials arose. If Logos seeks to be comprehensive and all-inclusive in providing resources for Bible study and worship alike, Accordance really hones in on the biblical text proper and has a slightly more academic feel to it. One can stack resources together, which creates a cluster of reference materials tailored to any kind of study the user pursues. Similarly, one can call up the "paper" mode, which facilitates the development of outlines for writing research papers, lectures, or sermons, depending on the paper template one chooses.

Since its beginning in 1992 BibleWorks stressed deep engagement with the original languages of the biblical text, in Hebrew and Greek. The slogan for BibleWorks was "Focus on the Text," and it marketed itself as "Software for Biblical Exegesis and Research." In addition to the standard multiple languages, both ancient and modern, for reading the Bible, the program boasted sophisticated capabilities for detailed analysis of grammar, morphology, and syntax, all to aid translation. Because BibleWorks could really drill down to fine points of word study in the original languages, it also tended to be the most complex of the programs in terms of its interface with users. Further, BibleWorks focused so much on the biblical text proper that it did not really have anything like the huge library of secondary sources offered by Logos or the somewhat smaller library of resources offered by Accordance. But it was also much less expensive than these larger programs.

Olive Tree Bible Software began life in 1998 as BibleReader, a program for the handheld Palm OS device. It continued to specialize in the market for mobile digital devices, culminating in its applications for the once popular Blackberry, the iPhone (2007), and the iPad (2010), as well as Android versions of the program. It eventually released a desktop version of its software, but its real strength has also been found in the mobile digital device products. In 2014 it was acquired by the Christian Publishing arm of the HarperCollins group (which also owns the copyright to Zondervan). Of the stand-alone software programs presented here, Olive Tree has the simplest interface, perhaps in part because it began as a program for mobile devices. It is a very intuitive program to use. One can purchase various additional secondary resources for Bible study with Olive Tree, as with the other programs.

Beyond these dedicated computer-based programs, each of which also has a web-based version, there are many other programs that are dedicated to study of the Bible in the digital domain. These include such programs as BibleGateway.com (also owned by Zondervan/HarperCollins), eSword, BibleStudyTools, WordSearchBible, The Word, and many others. All of them offer multiple versions of the Bible in various languages, and they each have the capacity to search the biblical text. Many also come with daily reading programs and such features as a "verse of the day." They tend to be more popular in orientation and are not geared towards more academic study of the Bible in the same way that the four programs surveyed above are.

5. The Bible and Digital Social Media

The explosion of digital social media over the last ten to fifteen years has been nothing short of breathtaking. First there was blogging that developed in the late 1990s and early 2000s on personal computers, eventually settling into blogging apps such as Tumblr and WordPress. In 2005 a different kind of social media took off—YouTube, a digital video-sharing program that swept the web with everything from endless cat videos to TED Talks to concert excerpts, Bible studies, and everything in between. The advent of the iPhone in 2007 brought with it an avalanche of apps that pivoted around Facebook, Instagram, Snapchat, Twitter, and other social media programs. It also became a platform for blogging and YouTube, which only expanded further with the advent of the iPad and other digital tablets.

For the purposes of exploring the function of social media in relation to the Bible, four forms of social media clearly stand out: blogging, twitter, YouTube, and Facebook. As we will see, blogging and YouTube have proven to be much more impactful for the place of the Bible in social media than have Twitter and Facebook. We begin with the blogging Bible.

5.1. Blogging

Blogs are relatively text heavy, and as such they have been a good match for discussions about the biblical text. A quick search for "Bible Blogs" on the Google search engine yields over twenty-one million hits! Among the sites is the Bible Gateway Blogger Grid, an international network of hundreds of independent bloggers who blog about a wide variety of issues related to the study of the Bible.[37] Long-form blogs tend to be more suited to larger screens that can better accommodate the more extended form of text than is comfortable for the smaller screen sizes of smartphones. The shift to more mobile forms of social media over the last several years has meant a slight move away from blogs as the most common way of engaging the biblical text via social media. Yet, as noted by social media critic Dylan Kissane, blogging will continue to develop and will "draw together text, images, online video, knowledge of pop culture and trends ... to bring all of this to bear in a dynamic zeitgeist."[38] As forms of digital media becomes increasingly blurred between different platforms, text/image/video/audio will continue to get mashed and remixed in endless ways, sometimes in short forms and sometimes in much longer forms.

A good example of how Bible blogging has morphed can be seen in the *Blue Letter Bible Blog*.[39] This site began in 1996 by offering an online version of the KJV of the Bible, along with a concordance, a lexicon, and various evangelical commentaries. It was called the "Blue Letter Bible" by way of referring to the blue color of hyperlinks that provided an expansive set of cross-references for Bible study. At present the site boasts of a ten-million member user base and over five hundred million views per year.[40] With over 3.5 million hyperlinks and links to over twelve thousand different websites, the *Blue Letter Bible Blog* has developed into a complex web presence for interacting with a variety of approaches to the study of the Bible. Not all blogs are created equal, of course, and they range from relatively crudely constructed single-author blogs to highly sophisticated sites that will take the user on virtually endless explorations of the Bible.

---

37. https://www.biblegateway.com/blog/bloggergrid/.

38. Dylan Kissane, "5 Most Important Trends for Blogging in 2016," Doz.com, https://tinyurl.com/SBL6704f.

39. http://blogs.blueletterbible.org/bib/.

40. "History of Blue Letter Bible," *Blue Letter Bible Blog*, https://tinyurl.com/SBL6704n.

5.2. YouTube

In addition to blogs about the Bible, the ubiquitous digital video web site YouTube has become an important resource for Bible study. A search for "Bible" in the YouTube search window garners nearly twelve million hits, with over half a million YouTube channels dedicated to study of the Bible. Televangelists such as Beth Moore, Joel Osteen, and Joyce Meyer (among many others) make significant use of YouTube as a way of spreading their particular approaches to the Bible and its message. There are also many YouTube channels geared towards children's engagement with the Bible. "The Beginner's Bible" on YouTube, for example, which offers a series of twenty-five-minute animated Bible stores has been viewed over a million times.

In addition to more evangelical approaches to the Bible on YouTube, one can also find more cynical and critical approaches to the Bible. "The Bible Reloaded: The Atheist Bible Study" offers Bible studies that seek to criticize traditional understandings of the Bible. Indeed, the two irreverent hosts, Hugo and Jake, offer a not so tongue-in-cheek trigger warning at the beginning of their first episode about what the viewer/reader of the Bible might expect: "This video may contain one or more references to the following: rape, incest, misogyny, murder, genocide, ghosts, talking animals, prostitutes, slavery, impalement, bear mauling, or tree cursing."[41] From this perspective the Bible is fraught with problems. The difficulty with almost all social media as it relates to the Bible is that users can find themselves fairly well insulated in one silo or another. One can readily find YouTube videos with which one is sympathetic, as well as videos that one can simply turn off.

5.3. Twitter

In 2012 Claire Diaz-Ortiz, a Senior Executive in charge of Twitter for Non-profits, commented: "Pastors tell me, Twitter is just made for the Bible."[42] At 140 characters per tweet (recently increased to 280 for some users), it does seem to be the ideal length of digital text to tweet as a favorite verse

---

41. Hannah and Jake, "The Bible Reloaded: The Atheist Bible Study," YouTube, https://www.youtube.com/watch?v=3TDrtuGIHrs&list=PLCgW8bgP5lDHK8WhWIlFRzyGE_vZbAyH.

42. See Pauline Cheong, "Tweet the Message? Religious Authority and Social Media Innovation," *Journal of Religion, Media and Digital Culture* 3.3 (2014): 1–19.

or to follow a Twitter account that sends out daily Bible verses. In many respects the Bible has long been "tweeted," even before the age of electricity, let alone digital media. Such pretweets appeared, for example, already as prooftexts lifted out of context to serve as a slogan or as a focal passage that might invoke further reflection upon the part of the reader or hearer. I think of the apostle Paul's appeal to Gen 15:6 ("Abram believed God, and God reckoned it to him as righteousness") in his letter to the Romans (4:3) and the linkage there between Abraham's faith with righteousness that was so important to Paul's theological vision. The New Testament is, of course, replete with all kinds of brief citations (tweets, if you will) from the Jewish scriptures. Throughout Christian history, the Bible has been essentialized into tweetable nuggets of inspiration or truth not unlike how the twittering of the Bible has come to function in the digital age.

Tweets do tend to be inherently reductionistic. Unless one already knows the larger context of a biblical passage, such a context will be lost in the tweet. Tweets do not function particularly well as stand-ins for a larger narrative. Tweets are intentionally minimalist transmissions of text intended to give a nutshell of an idea or thought. Context is typically provided by a frame of reference that is presumed to be understood between the person tweeting and the people reading the tweet. But verses from the Bible often get tweeted as disembodied texts of wisdom that are presumed to be self-explanatory, most often devoid of context that would provide a framework for interpreting meaning.

5.4. Facebook

The digital footprint of Facebook is nothing short of mind-boggling. With over two billion monthly active users, it is the most pervasive social media app on the planet (perhaps in the universe). Over three hundred million photos are uploaded daily. Every minute over half a million comments are posted.[43] Launched in 2004 as an app to link university students, Facebook exploded with the advent of the iPhone and mobile social media in 2007. Given the ubiquity of Facebook it comes as no surprise that individuals make significant use of Facebook as a venue for posting things from and about the Bible. There is a great variety of dedicated Facebook pages to

---

43. Dan Noyes, "The Top Twenty Valuable Facebook Statistics—Updated January 2020," Zephoria.com, https://tinyurl.com/SBL6704o.

the Bible, for example, the King James Bible Facebook page or the Bible Verses, Encouragements and Thoughts Facebook page.[44]

As pervasive as Facebook is on social media, however, it functions more like Twitter in providing quotations from the Bible without much, if any, reflection. It is a shallow resource when compared to blogs about the Bible or the millions of videos on YouTube dealing with the Bible. Perhaps this should not come as a particular surprise given the way that people interact with others on Facebook. People glance and surf on Facebook, posting a comment or a "like" here and there, so it is a way of keeping in touch—but it is a light touch.

This leads us, finally, to an important observation about social media in general, with apps like Facebook particularly in view. In 2010 Fr. Adolfo Nicolás, then the Superior General of the Society of Jesus, coined a memorable expression to describe much of the impact of social media: "the globalization of superficiality." Nicolás warned that the modern age of digital screens would lead to a certain shallowness in relationships, in imagination, and in reflection:

> When one can access so much information so quickly and so painlessly; when one can express and publish to the world one's reactions so immediately and so unthinkingly in one's blogs or micro-blogs; when the latest opinion column from the *New York Times* or *El Pais*, or the newest viral video can be spread so quickly to people half a world away, shaping their perceptions and feelings, then the laborious painstaking work of serious, critical thinking often gets short-circuited.[45]

What does it mean for someone to have eight hundred Facebook friends and have friendship mean very much more than superficial acquaintance? What happens when that superficial friendship extends to the Bible? To be sure, more meaningful exchanges about the Bible on social media can take place in the blogosphere than on twitter. While YouTube can present developed understandings of the Bible, it tends to be a one-way street from uploader to viewer. Nicolás suggests that the most meaningful and deep

---

44. King James Bible—Facebook page, https://www.facebook.com/KingJamesBibleOnline/; Bible Verses, Encouragements and Thoughts Facebook page, https://www.facebook.com/BibleVersesEncouragementsAndThoughts/

45. See Fr. Adolfo Nicolás, S. J., "Challenges to Jesuit Higher Education Today," *Conversations on Jesuit Higher Education* 40.1 (2011): art. 5. Nicolás was Superior General from 2008–2016.

relationships are formed through "communities of dialogue in the search of truth and understanding." Such communities of dialogue about the Bible can, indeed, be quite profound. But they typically happen in smaller conversational communities, most often in person as groups of individuals gather around a biblical text and sometimes in virtual communities of online conversation partners. Such groups are certainly commonplace in Christian and Jewish groups around the country. (The Jewish tradition of *hevruta* comes especially to mind—literally, "friends" gathering to discuss sacred texts.)[46]

Benefits and Limitations of Digital Bibles

In drawing this chapter to a close, it is appropriate to offer some summary comments regarding the benefits as well as the limitations of digital Bibles that have emerged even in this relatively early stage of the use of digital Bibles. First, there is clearly no turning back from the growth and usage of digital Bibles on every sort of screen. Mobile screens will continue to experience the most growth and development, and touch screens in general will become the standard for all screen interfaces. The touchability of screens is also an important consideration, as one of the downsides of digital media to date has been its lack of tangibility in comparison to print books. The tangibility of screens remains two-dimensional, but the ability to turn a digital page or to scan a cluster of pages (e.g., with Kindle's 2016 Page Flip navigation) marks a significant development in the usability of digital screens. In short, digital Bibles will benefit from any advancement in making the digital reading experience more fluid. The Bible remains without covers in the digital realm, but the capacity to frame larger sections of the Bible will give increased integrity to the different books of the Bible.

Second, the digital experience is one that is highly adaptable to individual preference. This is especially the case in the world of hypertext and links, obviously not available for print Bibles but a key feature of Bible software programs. This adaptability further breaks open the covers of the Bible, since one can go down any digital rabbit hole one may want to

---

46. See, e.g., Orit Kent, "Interactive Text Study: A Case of *Hevruta* Learning," *Journal of Jewish Education* 72.3 (2006): 205–32.

explore; and even with the back button, there are not enough bread crumbs to always find one's way back to where one started in the digital domain.

This highly individualized aspect of digital Bibles raises a third issue, about the function of the Bible as a communal text in contrast to its use in personal study. Digital screens are really designed for personal rather than communal use. Computers can certainly be linked together, but there is an iconic function to the physicality of the Bible as a singular book that a digital screen simply does not carry. The physical Bible has long served as a talisman for the divine. It is a sacred book with a sacred text. A digital Bible may well contain sacred text, but the delivery system, the device itself, is really quite devoid of any sacred character. Further, digital Bibles are not self-contained in any real way. There's nothing about a digital Bible that defines canonical boundaries or contours. If anything, digital Bibles mask the canonical shape of the Bible simply by virtue of only being able to display one screen of text at a time. There is no boundness to a digital screen. For some this makes no difference, but for others it is an important consideration.

A fourth issue involves the very nature of reading on a screen when compared to reading a physical print book. As we have seen, not all screens are created equal, and some screens are far more friendly for reading than others. Dedicated e-readers such as Amazon's Kindle or Barnes and Noble's Nook are effective e-readers. The iPads and other tablets using Kindle software are a close second, though even there the problem of distraction begins to enter into the equation. But when we move to online Bibles read on smartphones or on laptop or desktop computers, things start to change significantly. Both the small smartphone screens and the larger computer screens can interrupt the reading process at any time with myriad distractions popping up on the screen, from a phone call or tweet to an incoming instant message or a pop-up ad, a new email, a Snapchat message, and so much more. Beyond the issue of distraction, it appears that screens are simply more slippery for the eyes than print text. We tend to scan digital screens, but we tend to read print text. It is typically slower to read print, but precisely because it is slower we tend to retain more of what we have read. Reading digital screens simply does not allow our brains enough time to really hold on to whatever it is that we just read, whereas reading print text gives our brains enough time to shift short-term memory into longer-term memory.

But digital screens also have certain advantages over traditional print Bibles. First, the most obvious advantage is the convenience factor. One can elect to carry a very portable smartphone that contains the whole Bible rather than lug the cumbersome physical book around. As YouVersion Bible advertises, the Bible is always with you, and you can read it whenever/wherever you are.

Second, with digital Bibles it is very easy to compare a multitude of translations. This feature reminds the reader that we are all, in fact, reading the Bible in translation. In addition to being able to read a variety of versions of a biblical passage, one also becomes aware that no one translation solves all the difficulties of the translation process. Translation is simply the first step in interpretation.

Third, the availability of sophisticated computer-based and online Bible study programs allows people to engage easily in relatively comprehensive study of the Bible, whether by accessing a multitude of commentaries, looking at maps, using a Bible dictionary, a concordance, et cetera. There are so many resources and tools for studying the Bible that it can often be difficult to see the biblical text through the thick forest of resources at hand.

Fourth, and perhaps most significant, the digital world allows the Bible to be experienced in a multidimensional framework that print Bibles simply do not have. In the digital realm you can certainly read the Bible on screen, but you can also listen to digital audio being read to you. Or you can watch a YouTube video cartoon reenacting a parable from the Bible. The Bible can thus be accessed in multimedia form, and typically multimedia tends to reinforce and create thick understandings of a topic. The more our different senses have an opportunity to interact with the Bible, even in digital form, the more readily we will appreciate the layers of a biblical story or passage. The print Bible can be read, but not much more (although it can certainly also be preached!). But the Bible in digital form can present the print text and display artistic depictions of biblical scenes, as well be read out loud, heard in digital song, viewed by children in cartoon form, and the like. Certainly many of these forms of display can happen in the analog world as well, but the digital realm is designed to shift with relative ease from one mode of interaction to another—a multimedia approach to the Bible. In the middle ages it was possible for those who could not read the Bible in written form to read stained glass windows instead. When Gutenberg invented movable type for the printing press it became possible for the dissemination of the Bible, which in turn fostered more widespread literacy. Now in the digital age it is possible for people to access the Bible in a variety of forms. Print Bibles, and print publishing in general, will surely continue along with the digital revolution. But digital Bibles are here to stay, and only time can tell how they will continue to develop and grow.

Bibliography

American Bible Society. "State of the Bible, 2011." https://tinyurl.com/SBL6704k.

Anderson, Porter. "As BEA Opens: A New Global Ebook Report on a Mercurial World Market." PublishingPerspectives.com. https://tinyurl.com/SBL6704c.

Barna Group. *The Bible in America: The Changing Landscape of Bible Perceptions and Engagement*. Ventura, CA: Barna Group, 2016.

Bibb, Bryan. "Readers and Their E-Bibles." Pages 256–65 in *The Bible in American Life*. Edited by Philip Goff, Arthur E. Farnsley, and Peter J. Thuesen. New York: Oxford University Press.

The Bible App for Kids Storybook Bible. Pompano Beach, FL: OneHope, 2015.

Bottigheimer, Ruth. *The Bible for Children: From the Age of Gutenberg to the Present*. New Haven: Yale University Press, 1986.

Cheong, Pauline. "Tweet the Message? Religious Authority and Social Media Innovation." *Journal of Religion, Media and Digital Culture* 3.3 (2014): 1–19.

Crenshaw, Dave. *The Myth of Multitasking: How "Doing It All" Gets Nothing Done*. San Francisco: Jossey-Bass, 2008.

Dehaene, Stanislas. *Reading in the Brain: The Science and Evolution of a Human Invention*. New York: Viking, 2009.

DWARF202. "This Is My Bible." YouTube. https://www.youtube.com/watch?v=ncxlkokN-6Q.

Evangelical Covenant Church. "Beliefs." Covchurch.org. https://tinyurl.com/SBL6704d.

Feinblum, Brian. "Interview with Audiobooks.com Ian Small." Digitalbookworld.com. https://tinyurl.com/SBL6704j.

Gazzaley, Adam, and Larry D. Rosen. *The Distracted Mind: Ancient Brains in a High-Tech World*. Boston: MIT Press, 2016.

Genette, Gerard. *Paratexts: Thresholds of Interpretation*. Cambridge: Cambridge University Press, 1997.

Gryboski, Michael. "Are Digital Bibles as Holy as Paper Bibles?" *The Christian Post*. 15 July 2014. https://tinyurl.com/SBL6704e.

Hannah and Jake. "The Bible Reloaded: The Atheist Bible Study." YouTube. https://www.youtube.com/watch?v=3TDrtuGIHrs&list=PLCgW8bgP5lDHK8WhWIlFRzyGE_vZbAyH.

"History of Blue Letter Bible." *Blue Letter Bible Blog.* https://tinyurl.com/SBL6704n.

Hutchinson, Robert. "The Bible as a Comic Book." *Our Sunday Visitor Newsweekly.* 30 May 2012.

Kent, Orit. "Interactive Text Study: A Case of *Hevruta* Learning." *Journal of Jewish Education* 72.3 (2006): 205–32.

Kissane, Dylan. "5 Most Important Trends for Blogging in 2016." Doz.com. https://tinyurl.com/SBL6704f.

Kokalitcheva, Kia. "Apple Has Sold Its Billionth iPhone." *Fortune.* 27 July 2016.

Mangen, Anne. "Hypertext Fiction Reading: Haptics and Immersion." *Journal of Research in Reading* 31 (2008): 404–19.

Nicolás, Fr. Adolfo, S. J. "Challenges to Jesuit Higher Education Today." *Conversations on Jesuit Higher Education* 40.1 (2011): art. 5.

Noyes, Dan. "The Top Twenty Valuable Facebook Statistics—Updated January 2020." Zephoria.com. https://tinyurl.com/SBL6704o.

Ong, Walter. *Orality and Literacy: The Technologizing of the Word.* New York: Methuen, 1982.

Ong, Walter, and John Hartley, *Orality and Literacy: The Technologizing of the Word.* 30th anniv. ed. New York: Routledge, 2012.

Perrin, Andrew. "Book Reading 2016." Pew Research Center: Internet and Technology. https://tinyurl.com/SBL6704g.

Rakow, Katja. "The Bible in the Digital Age: Negotiating the Limits of 'Bibleness' of Different Bible Media." Pages 101–21 in *Christianity and the Limits of Materiality.* Edited by Minaa Opas and Anna Haapalainen. London: Bloomsbury, 2017.

Ross, Bobby, Jr. "Digital vs. Print: Readers Weigh in on Bible Choices." *The Christian Chronicle.* 1 October 2012. https://tinyurl.com/SBL6704i.

———. "Texting during Worship? No, Just Reading the Text." *The Christian Chronicle.* 1 September 2009. https://tinyurl.com/SBL6704h.

Siker, Jeffrey S. *Liquid Scripture: The Bible in a Digital World.* Minneapolis: Fortress, 2017.

van Peursen, Wido. "Is the Bible Losing Its Covers? Conceptualization and Use of the Bible on the Threshold of the Digital Order." *HIPHIL Novum* 1 (2014): 44–58.

Vander Stichele, Caroline, and Hugh S. Pyper, eds. *Text, Image, and Otherness in Children's Bibles: What Is in the Picture?* SemeiaSt 56. Atlanta: Society of Biblical Literature, 2012.

Weaver, John. "Transforming Practice: American Bible Reading in Digital Culture." Pages 249–255 in *The Bible in American Life*. Edited by Philip Goff, Arthur E. Farnsley, and Peter J. Thuesen. New York: Oxford University Press.

"Why Accordance." Accordance.com. https://tinyurl.com/SBL6704m.

Wolf, Maryanne. *Proust and the Squid: The Story and Science of the Reading Brain*. New York: Harper Perennial, 2007.

———. *Tales of Literacy for the Twenty-First Century*. New York: Oxford University Press, 2016.

Youversion. *The Bible App for Kids Storybook Bible*. Multiplatform app. https://bibleappforkids.com/storybook.

3
THE BIBLE AND POPULAR CULTURE

JASON A. WYMAN JR.

Popular culture is frequently referenced but not often indicated with much precision. Analyses of what makes popular culture distinct have zeroed in on a few characteristics that make popular culture a phenomenon to be engaged with on its own terms. It is often contrasted with high culture and folk culture. The borders between all three are porous, and things can shift from case to case. But the overall idea is that high culture is that which has an element of intentional exclusivity, whether due to financial resources, the need for taste/education/refinement in order to appreciate it, and its limited accessibility.[1] Again, keeping in mind that the borders are porous, things like opera or ballet or cutting-edge art may be considered high culture. Such things are not meant for mass consumption, either intentionally or by practical concerns of the medium itself. High culture has a very long history. While high culture may, and does, frequently draw upon the Bible, those allusions are not likely to affect culture at large in any significant way, except, perhaps, by way of influencing popular culture.

Folk culture, on the other end of the spectrum, has likewise been around for a very long time. Everyone has a folk culture: it is the culture of families and localities. Even as mass culture increasingly homogenizes what sorts of cultural experiences are available to people in the United States, every person has unique practices and things that make their intensely local communities unique. The most common example comes from food. More or less everyone has a visceral memory of a food—or

---

1. Bruce David Forbes, "Introduction: Finding Religion in Unexpected Places," in *Religion and Popular Culture in America*, ed. Bruce David Forbes and Jeffrey H. Mahan, 3rd ed. (Oakland: University of California Press, 2017), 7.

many foods—that is brought to family gatherings like holidays. There is usually not anything objectively aesthetically special about these foods, but they hold a special place in our smaller communities. They will never be mass produced, and, unless one receives an invitation to another family's holiday gathering, these foods tend to be eaten only in their particular forms by a small group of people and passed down for replication by a small group of people by tradition, often oral or handwritten.

Popular culture is widespread. It is easily accessible and everywhere, and typically the costs to consume it are within reason for the great majority of people. The possibility of popular culture really arises with the advent of mass production. For example, high-culture music has always existed, the domain of those who had access to and could afford performances of sophisticated pieces of music. Likewise, folk-culture music has always been around, the localized songs and the way they are performed that are unique to any given locale. Music as popular culture, however, awaited the easy and affordable reproduction of recordings. With phonographs and records, specific songs, artists, and styles of music were able to be embraced and shared across greater areas and by more and greater varieties of people. Popular culture appeals to the tastes and preferences of people at large and does not require any targeted education to appreciate, although, like any culture, deeper appreciation may arise with deeper engagement and understanding of the culture being consumed. Popular culture is not, however, necessarily lowest-common-denominator entertainment, despite its widespread acceptance. Instead, it reflects and is shaped by the people which it forms, as the people are in turn reflected and shaped by it. There is no value judgment intended or inherent in dividing culture between high, folk, and popular culture, although ideological or critical stances may give a person a preference or suspicion of one or another. Instead, the demarcations indicate spheres of influence and ultimately an appreciation of each for the role it plays in society generally. Ultimately, no hard and fast distinctions can be made between the three. High culture can be embraced more popularly; folk-art forms can reach wider audiences, either by intention or not. Folk music itself has become a genre, taking what was once the purview of music in folk culture—specifically rural, often Southern or Appalachian US folk culture—and made it, through its widespread embrace and mass reproduction, a cornerstone of contemporary popular culture. But popular culture as a category, despite its ambiguities, speaks to a set of texts, objects, songs, practices, attitudes, et cetera that are widely shared and widely accessible by a culture at any given moment. It is tied in with consumer culture, has been driven by consumerism and advertising, and yet also offers important sites of rebellion against and critique of the status quo and even injustice itself in certain instances.

The Bible itself *is* part of popular culture. Hard numbers are difficult to parse, but it is something of a truism that the Bible is perennially a best seller. Its sales numbers, across the many versions and editions, are always near the top of book sales every year, if not number one. As an object itself, the Bible was one of the first books to be produced quickly and distributed widely, which contributed to the Protestant Reformation. The King James (KJV) translation of the Bible helped to standardize English, as other translations did with other vernacular languages throughout Europe. The famous nonprofit organization Gideons International alone distributes more than two million free copies each year and celebrated handing out its two billionth free Bible in 2015.[2] According to the Barna Group, an evangelical polling organization in California that studies trends in the relationship between Christianity and culture from a conservative Christian point of view and conducts polls and surveys regarding the intersection of faith and culture in people's lives in the United States, 50 percent of people in the United States consider themselves Bible users, defined as engaging the Bible on one's own outside of the context of church on a regular basis.[3] That is to say, as an object, the Bible itself fits the criteria for being considered part of popular culture. It is ubiquitous, inexpensive, accessible, and widely consumed. It is no wonder, really, that the Bible shows up as often as it does in other arenas of popular culture. Sheer numbers and accessibility alone make its incorporation into popular culture expressions of all kinds more or less inevitable.

Furthermore, many of what might be considered the sacred texts of our civil religion in the United States are often read *into* the Bible. According to the Barna Group, in 2017, 52 percent of practicing Christians strongly believed the Bible teaches that "God helps those who help themselves,"[4]

---

2. Gideons International, "Gideons Distribute Historic Two Billionth Scripture," Gideons International Blog, https://tinyurl.com/SBL6704s.

3. Barna Group, "State of the Bible 2018: Seven Top Findings," Barna.com, https://tinyurl.com/SBL6704q.

4. Barna Group, "Competing Worldviews Influence Today's Christians," Barna.com, https://tinyurl.com/SBL6704r.

despite the phrase not appearing anywhere therein; many have pointed out that the Bible seems to teach the exact opposite, that God's intervention is not premised on one's ability to help oneself, theologically captured in the concept of God's preferential option for the poor. The phrase in the contemporary US context is usually taken from Benjamin Franklin's *Poor Richard's Almanac*. The sentiment, of course, reflects the idealized rugged individualism that is an integral part of the civic religion and national mythos of the United States. Anecdotally, I have students routinely report that the Bible teaches that "all men [sic] are created equal." Of course, while that may be an admirable sentiment and important to multiple religions, it is in the Declaration of Independence. The Bible that is floating around in popular culture often is not the Bible as text, word for word, steeped in history, at all. It is the sense of authority, ethics, even divine legitimacy the Bible gives to sentiments that makes these nonbiblical ideas and phrases work their way back into the Bible that many in the United States are carrying around in their minds. If the Bible says something is so, the thinking goes, then there must be something worthwhile about what is being said ... even if the Bible does not *actually* say it. It lends legitimacy, even when it is not being legitimately engaged. Therefore, it is crucial that we mind how the Bible is being used in our popular culture, as well as how popular culture is influencing the understanding and usage of the Bible.

What follows is a theological exposition on uses of the Bible in contemporary popular culture. Two phenomenological instances from two different types of contemporary popular culture of the Bible will be examined and the theological argument arising therein made explicit and evaluated. Contrasting examples will also be included to make explicit how the importance and meaning of the Bible is being interrogated and negotiated by different people and their communities from different perspectives and for different meanings.

The first section engages hip hop, one of today's most popular—if not currently the most popular—music genres. The content and messages of hip hop are widespread and never monolithic, of course, but it is nearly impossible to ignore, when one has a sensitivity for it, the prevalence of religion in hip hop, especially Christianity and the Bible.[5] The Bible is often

---

5. Full monographs have been done on this topic because of its prevalence, as well as a group formed in the American Academy of Religion. See Monica R. Miller, *Religion and Hip Hop* (New York: Routledge, 2013); Miller, Anthony B. Pinn, and Bernard "Bun B" Freeman, eds., *Religion in Hip Hop: Mapping the New Terrain in the US* (New

seamlessly woven into hip-hop music through lyrics and background support in such a way that it almost becomes naturally part of the idiom of the music itself—and therefore often goes unnoticed. Theologically speaking, this section draws out instances in hip hop that articulate an understanding of the Bible that closely aligns with black liberationist understandings of the biblical narrative—especially the exodus from the Old Testament and Jesus in the New—and its significance for oppressed minority communities in the United States.

The second section looks at uses of the Bible in film, in particular exploring the environmental activism that has been given embodiment in different realizations of the story of the flood of Noah. It gives two very different examples, *Evan Almighty* and *Noah*, one comedic and one terrifically violent, to show how different but connected retellings and reusings of a familiar narrative can make a theological claim about God, the destruction of the environment by human beings, and the judgment they may deserve for their unscrupulous exploitation of the land, animals, and the world at large.

Many other instances of popular culture could be used. The Bible has been represented in many different ways in film, from the very earliest days of cinematography and film making. Either by implication or explicitly, the Bible has served as a source for silent films, films during Hollywood's golden age, animated films, including through the present moment. It has served as the basis for drama, action, and comedy. The remarkable development of special effects has in particular made the production of epic biblical tales a resurgent interest. Notable recent examples of biblical films include *The Passion of the Christ*, which caused significant controversy in Christianity and with respect to interreligious engagement between Christianity and Judaism; *The Prince of Egypt*, an animated film that tells the story of the exodus and underwent scrutiny by leaders in all three Abrahamic religions before its release; and even *Paul, Apostle of Christ*, based on the implied life of Paul as found in the New Testament.

In popular literature, as well, the Bible has been immensely influential. Using just the most popular example, of the Harry Potter series, J. K. Rowling has pointed to the narrative and thematic connections between

---

York: Bloomsbury, 2015); Daniel White Hodge, *Hip Hop's Hostile Gospel: A Post-soul Theological Exploration* (Leiden: Brill, 2017); Hodge, *The Soul of Hip Hop: Rims, Timbs and a Cultural Theology* (Downers Grove, IL: InterVarsity Press, 2010).

the protagonist's life and the story of Christ.[6] The Bible is rehashed on social media, is a frequent referent on television, shows up on and has been a marketing tool for clothing (as an example, Forever 21, a popular fast-fashion clothing brand, prints Bible verses on its shopping bags), has inspired popular diets and trendy weight-loss schemes (see the Maker's Diet, among others), and, of course, serves as the foundation for Christmas, Easter, and Hanukkah (when including Maccabees), holidays that have become part of popular culture themselves and ramp up popular consumerism in the United States. In any conceivable aspect of popular cultural life in the United States, the Bible shows up. In short, the Bible is ubiquitous in US popular culture.

Overall, this chapter argues that many instances of the appearance of the Bible in popular culture reflect what Sallie McFague calls metaphorical or parabolic theology. By using symbols, stories, and narratives from the Bible to carry theological meaning without resorting to conceptual analysis or taking the meaning out of those narratives entirely, popular culture uses of the Bible keep religious messages "in solution."[7] They are both more accessible and more complex. I suggest, however, that in looking at nonspecialists' theological constructions from the biblical text, one does not necessarily look for theological truths, but simply theological claims being conveyed through the uses of the Bible in popular culture contexts. My approach tracks such uses and looks to evaluate them based on their theological content, whom the claims are being made for, and whether they are instrumental, interpretive, intentionally theological, or incidentally biblical. What remains consistent is that biblical language, biblical allusion, and the wide-ranging interpretation of the Bible continue to be foundational for the United States, and its popular culture is shot through with influence from the Bible. The Bible and its understanding in the United States is, in turn, being changed and shifted by popular culture. Ultimately, perhaps what is most important to notice is that whatever specialist academic theologians make of the Bible today, either in practical theology or in systematic/constructive theologies, the contours of the Bible as refracted and understood through popular culture must be contended with, as an ally or as something to be contested.

---

6. Jonathan Petre, "J. K. Rowling; 'Christianity Inspired Harry Potter,'" https://tinyurl.com/SBL6704u.

7. Sallie McFague, *Speaking in Parables: A Study in Metaphor and Theology* (Minneapolis: Fortress, 1975), 2.

The Bible, Liberation, and Hip Hop

Anyone with a sensitive ear for the biblical text who listens closely to hip hop will notice the frequent references to the Bible that have been present throughout the history of the genre. This may seem surprising given the standard view that hip hop, and for that matter other genres of popular music, promotes values that run counter to what may popularly be considered traditional Christian morality. Anthony Pinn, who considers the intersection of hip hop and Christianity, notes that "media sources tend to highlight the negative and reactionary interaction between religious ideologies and popular culture.... The former argues that this form of musical production erodes moral values and religious sensibilities; the artists respond that they are speaking of reality and are misunderstood and disrespected."[8] Pinn proposes what he calls "nitty-gritty hermeneutics." The nitty-gritty,

> seeks a clear and unromanticized understanding of a hostile world, and entails "telling it like it is" and taking risks. Embedded in this method of interpretation is a sense that paradox and tension are not necessarily problems but rather can serve as opportunities to explore dimensions of cultural life that we might otherwise overlook or downplay. This way of approaching cultural life begins with an understanding that human life is messy, complex, and layered.[9]

Upon closer inspection, the Bible plays into and reinforces the morally and culturally complicated narratives and themes that play out in hip hop. Indeed, perhaps one of the reasons the Bible is so prevalent in hip hop is because its own moral and cultural world is so ambiguous, ethically, morally, relationally, and in terms of its legacy, from the narrative within to its lasting effects in the world today.

When speaking of the nitty-gritty, the discomfort that many encounter with hip hop emerges with gangsta' rap and its description and frequent glorification of violence, drugs, and misogyny. At the same time, it contains within it a critique of life in poor, violent, ghettoized inner cities.

---

8. Anthony Pinn, "Rap Music and Its Message: On Interpreting the Contact between Religion and Popular Culture," in Forbes and Mahan, *Religion and Popular Culture in America*, 390.

9. Pinn, "Rap Music and Its Message," 391.

Pinn points out that, while these descriptions may be hyperbolic and often defined by fantasy, they also point to underlying truths about black urban experience of systemic injustice in the United States.[10] Perhaps what scares listeners unfamiliar with the tropes being used or the experiences being described is the confrontation with the reality that those lyrics speak to. Hip hop from its inception has focused intently on the realities, positive and negative, of black experiences of both joy and marginalization in the contemporary United States. It has been consistent in naming, even while seemingly glorifying, the trenchant problems of drugs in poor areas of color, gang violence, police antagonism, and the daily vicissitudes of impoverished inner-city life for black people.

Hip hop can at the same time certainly be criticized for its misogyny, its obsession with guns and violence, and its idolization of money and status. In recent years, since Pinn's article, a number of higher profile women rappers have challenged the male status quo of hip hop. They have participated in and challenged the tropes and idioms of the misogynistic traditions of hip hop. Throughout, hip hop, in many different places (the Bronx and New York City, Compton and Los Angeles, Chicago, Atlanta, and others), has maintained an unflinching variety of honesty that often speaks in metaphor and hyperbole but always reflects an understanding of the situation as it exists for young people of color in the projects and poor inner-city ghettos. Its discourse on religion, in this regard, has been prophetic, unique, and impossible for culture at large to ignore.

Christianity in hip hop exhibits, for Pinn, "usable religion," which

> must not place abstraction and neat theological categories above human experience: only that which is proven by experience holds value. Religious expression is here defined by its commitment to human accountability, and responsibility for human occurrences. to a large extent, productive religiosity is fluid, in that its dynamics alter with the existential situation; thus it avoids dilemmas of applicability resulting from the rigid demands and dictates of religion.[11]

With respect to the Bible, this means the easy weaving of biblical phrases and passages into rap stanzas and verses that otherwise may not naturally appear to be particularly religious at all. The messiness of lived experience

---

10. Pinn, "Rap Music and Its Message," 391.
11. Pinn, "Rap Music and Its Message," 392.

often mixes uncomfortably with what may be seen as the pristine theological categories of Christianity. Where expressions in church or from Christian institutions may separate the biblical world and the concepts to be drawn from the nitty-gritty realities of life, hip hop brings the Bible and its world firmly into that space.

The late James Cone, founder of black liberation theology, argued that "there can be no Christian theology that is not identified unreservedly with those who are humiliated and abused. In fact, theology ceases to be theology of the gospel when it fails to arise out of the community of the oppressed."[12] For all the messiness and profanity of hip hop and its lyrics, there is no question that it comes out of the circumstances of the oppressed, those who are often "humiliated and abused." In a very real sense, hip hop that names, criticizes, and condemns the circumstances of being black and oppressed in the United States is itself Christian theology, in particular black liberation theology. As Cone goes on to argue, "what is important [about scripture] is whether it can serve as a weapon against the oppressors." He concludes, "The God who is present today in our midst is the same God who was revealed in Jesus Christ as witnessed in the scriptures.... The meaning of scripture is not to be found in the words of scripture as such but only in its power to point beyond itself to the reality of God's revelation—and in America, that means black liberation."[13] Cone founds his black theology of liberation in the exodus, making a direct comparison between the Israelites and black people in the United States; "God's call of [the Israelites] is related to its oppressed condition and to God's own liberating activity already seen in the exodus. *You have seen what I did!* By delivering this people from Egyptian bondage and inaugurating the covenant on the basis of that historical event, God is revealed as the God of the oppressed, involved in their history, liberating them from human bondage."[14] The foundational Bible story for black liberation is the exodus. Christ identifies with the poor, disenfranchised, and oppressed, in the United States, the black community. From a black liberation perspec-

---

12. Recent commentators have pointed out that Albert Cleage Jr.'s *Black Messiah* predates Cone's *A Black Theology of Liberation* by two years. Both are important. The black liberation tradition in theology, however, to this point at least, is much more foundationally built upon Cone's work.

13. James H. Cone, *A Black Theology of Liberation*, 40th anniv. ed. (Maryknoll: Orbis, 2010), 34.

14. Cone, *Black Theology of Liberation*, 2.

tive, God's work in the world is exhibited through God's inbreaking and liberating activity in history. For Cone, from a Christian perspective, the Bible serves as a witness to the liberating work God did with the Israelites and through Jesus, as one who identifies with, dies as one of, and is resurrected for the oppressed.

Many examples point to the dialogic exchange between the Bible and hip hop. Daniel White Hodge, who has written several books on the relationship between religion, theology, and hip hop, has noted in particular the work of luminaries such as A Tribe Called Quest, Digable Planets, Nas, Bone Thugs-N-Harmony, Kanye West, Ice Cube, Kendrick Lamar, Lauryn Hill, Tupac, and others.[15] Coolio's "Gangster's Paradise" leaps to mind, which directly quotes Ps 23, one of the most famous and widely memorized passages in the Bible, to draw parallels between the experiences, metaphorical or otherwise, of death and oppression—walking through the valley of the shadow of death—in marginalized black communities in the United States: "As I walk through the Valley of the Shadow of Death / I take a look at my life and realize there's nothin' left. / 'Cause I've been blastin' and laughin' so long / That even my mama think that my mind is gone." Juxtaposing the peaceful, comforting image of the Lord as a shepherd in the psalm, Coolio casts a sharp relief of a desperate and alienated experience seemingly bereft of the Lord's presence because of the realities of poor black urban life, especially for those caught up in gangs.

Kanye West, one of the most popular musical artists in the world, hip hop or otherwise, gained a new level of fame with his hit "Jesus Walks" in 2001. The lyrics of the song reference the unjust treatment of black people by police officers and the systemic injustices of poverty as they affect black people in the United States. The music video for the song helps to draw out the analogy between Jesus and the injustices suffered by black people in the United States; as a gospel choir sings "Jesus walks," images of black prisoners on a chain gang being harassed by white guards play. West asserts that his choice of Christian themes, talking about Jesus in a positive manner, would be a roadblock to achieving commercial success and fame. He, of course, turned out to be wrong. His much later "Life of Pablo" means to draw comparisons between himself and the apostle Paul. West, one of the most popular musicians in the world and a figurehead for hip hop, has

---

15. Hodge, *Hip Hop's Hostile Gospel*.

maintained a sustained, if episodic and oftentimes opaque, conversation with the biblical text as he has received it. It has ranged from humility to brash egotism. But all the while, it shows a sophisticated engagement with the Bible as a cultural touchstone. West is far from alone.

A particularly noteworthy exemplar of the sophisticated use of religion, including the Bible, in hip hop, geared toward liberation, is hip-hop phenomenon Kendrick Lamar. Hodge has characterized Lamar as "a sort of secular, profane, and sacred Hip Hop icon who is taking up the mantle that Tupac left."[16] Examination of Lamar's uses of the Bible, explicitly or implicitly, can help to illuminate some of the ways hip hop can and does propose a popular black theology of liberation through its storytelling, imagery, and verse. Lamar uses Christian imagery, taken from the Bible and black church tradition, throughout all of his albums. *Good Kid m.A.A.d. City*, which marked his breakthrough to a larger audience, starts with a prayer of commitment and asking for forgiveness of sins. His 2018 album *DAMN.* is a full-blown meditation on Christian themes, US culture, and the pressures of fame, with frequent allusions to racial injustices in the United States. The album reflects the circumstances in which Lamar came to be associated with the #BlackLivesMatter movement with his song "Alright," which unabashedly proclaimed that God would take care of those struck down by unfairness in the world. In the song "YAH" from *DAMN.*, Lamar explores the theological implications of the exodus and Deuteronomic theology, as well as a movement called the Hebrew Israelites. Bracketing the question of the Hebrew Israelites—not because it is not an interesting and perhaps important phenomenon in some contemporary black communities, but because Lamar's references equally stand on their own—Lamar claims a direct connection between the narrative of the Israelites and that of black people in the contemporary United States: "I'm a Israelite, don't call me black no mo' / That word is only a color, it ain't facts no mo' / My cousin called, my cousin Carl Duckworth / Said know my worth/ And Deuteronomy say that we all been cursed." Referring to the curses of Deuteronomy, an ironic take on the Deuteronomic theology of the Bible as it applies to black experience in the United States. As he seems to reject the reality of race, he points to a transcendent place, a closer identification between black experience and God in the United States. Echoing black religious movements and Cone's liberationist strand

---

16. Hodge, *Hip Hop's Hostile Gospel*, 86.

of biblical engagement, Lamar finds identification with the Israelites and their covenant with God. The title itself, "YAH," though said in a laid back, nondescript manner that conveys the sense of "yeah," connects with the shortened version of the name of God, the Tetragrammaton, that shows up throughout the Bible and has been used by various traditions throughout the history for Judaism and Christianity, in particular those in the African diaspora. The song "YAH" is a complicated exploration of black experience in US culture, the connections between Israelite experience as conveyed through the Bible, and the potential for liberation and transcendence in the current United States, especially against the backdrop of continued police violence against people of color as protested by #BlackLivesMatter.

Lamar has explored specific biblical motifs elsewhere. In the music video for "HUMBLE." from *DAMN.*, Lamar depicts an image of the Last Supper that defies its historical whitewashing. The song and video, together, intentionally contrast and invert the perceived humility of Jesus. Lamar sits at the center in the parody of Da Vinci's depiction of Jesus's last meal on the eve of his crucifixion, boasting and acting notably unhumble. The image challenges received notions about the story itself and resists the Eurocentric mythologization of the narrative. It also, in its irony, provides a critique of church attitudes of piety and grandiosity. A connection is made between Lamar and his entourage in the video and Jesus and his twelve disciples. If Lamar and the meal they consume seems like an unlikely embodiment of Christ and the Last Supper, that is exactly the point. It resists the masquerading piety of whitewashing, providing an alternative image of who Christ might be and look like. The effect, again in the vein of Cone or Albert Cleage, is a confrontation with a literal black Christ, though parodically. Further, as the message of the song, in its brash (though self-awarely ironic) rejection of self-humility by encouraging others to be humble—in a dominating tone—seems against what may be considered Jesus's apparent humility in the gospels, it nonetheless once again reflects liberation theology. Cone contended,

> To be human in a condition of social oppression involves affirming that which the oppressor regards as degrading. In a world in which the oppressor defines right in terms of whiteness, humanity means an unqualified identification with blackness. Black therefore, is beautiful; oppressors have made it ugly. We glorify it because they despise it; we love it because they hate it. It is the black way of saying, "To hell with

your stinking white society and its middle-class ideas about the world. I will have no part in it."[17]

The video is a forceful rejection of the overlaying of white interests, white history, and white oppression onto the biblical text. It forces at the very least a reckoning with the veiled normatizations that have come to seem so natural in whitewashed Bible narratives and historical representations of them.

The overall effect of uses of the Bible in Kendrick Lamar and in many other instances of popular hip hop is both to use the Bible and its narratives and to construct with them. Narratives and sentiments from the Bible are linked up with, compared to, and employed as representative of contemporary experience, in particular black experience in the contemporary United States in hip hop. The powerful effect is to confront US society, in particular in its racist white forms, with a rereading of Jesus's life, of the gospels, of the stories of the Israelites found in the Tanak. Hip hop has many problems throughout its history. It can be misogynistic, heteronormative, glorifying money and conspicuous consumption. But it also has a strong thread of resisting, dramatically and narratively, white conceptions of Christianity and theology. Hip hop is often an organic black liberation theology which uses the Bible as a primary source, alongside black experience and the black church. Hip hop makes the Bible itself counter-culture, counter-hegemonic, even while participating in those systems. It condemns racism, and in some way recovers a historical, radical tradition in the Bible, embodied in the prophets, Jesus, and others.

Other varieties of popular music in the United States also draw on the Bible for source material or to give voice to perspectives and experience. The Bible is pervasive in popular music, providing storylines and religious themes, things for critique or things with which to build. Some songs are explicitly appreciative of the Bible, some are negative, while some are more complicated (Leonard Cohen's "Hallelujah," which weaves biblical heroes and stories into a melancholy hymn comes to mind). Hodge argues that "hip hop his about liberation, authenticity, and freedom from the shackles of modernity."[18] Hip hop is in many ways distinctive because of the prevalence of the Bible, quoting it, referencing it, alluding to it, in such an

---

17. Cone, *Black Theology of Liberation*, 16.
18. Hodge, *Hip Hop's Hostile Gospel*, 21.

immensely popular variety of music, in such a sustained way, and with the overarching overall effect of drawing direct parallels between the narratives found therein with the experience of being black in the United States today. From prophetic fire and rage to alienation to joy and salvation—thinking specifically of Chance the Rapper, a protege of Kanye West's who has made a heavily gospel-imbued style of hip hop popular and has also spoken publicly about his faith on big stages like *Saturday Night Live*—hip hop constructs meaning out of the linking up of experience and the narratives and expressions of the Bible.

The Bible and Popular Film: Noah's Flood Two Ways

The story of Noah and the flood God sent to the world has become an especially pertinent, and depictable, story from the Bible. With the advances in special effects and computer-generated effects in cinema, it has become possible to create realistic portrayals of catastrophic worldwide flooding. Further, the current state of the world, especially with respect to the climate and human hubris, has made the story a particularly apropos one. Two recent movies, *Noah* and *Evan Almighty*, with very different takes on the worldwide flood found in Gen 6–9, serve to show how popular culture works to construct theological, political, and ideological meaning with the narratives encountered in the Bible. On one level, the story provides fodder for an epic movie, especially as it has become possible to depict an event of such magnitude. It is a familiar story with familiar names and, most importantly, the pedigree of the Bible behind it. Naturally, religious communities and culture at large weighed in on its alternative variations in recent film history.

Evan Almighty, released in 2007, is a comedic spin off of *Bruce Almighty*, a movie starring Jim Carrey that gave a humorous look at the potential pitfalls of omnipotence being given to a human being. While *Bruce Almighty* did not draw on any specific biblical stories, it touched on theological themes such as omnipotence, omnibenevolence, the fallibility of human beings, and theodicy. The overall message is one of a generally folksy, but blandly Christian admonition to respect mystery and uncertainty, even in the face of challenges and setbacks in life. It is a movie with religious themes but is not particularly biblical in any sense. *Evan Almighty* builds on the themes of human fallibility and hubris but does so by creatively repurposing the flood narrative found in Genesis.

In the movie, Evan Baxter (Steve Carrell), who was Bruce's work rival in television reporting in *Bruce Almighty*, is a newly elected congressperson. Almost immediately upon assuming his position, Evan is presented job perks and a cushy office when a senior congressperson (John Goodman) in his party presents him with a bill to cosponsor the obscurely named the Citizens' Integration of Public Lands Act. Evan's political career is quickly derailed, however, when unexplainable events start intruding upon his daily life: he finds himself the owner of a large plot of empty land; he starts to grow a long beard which cannot be removed; animals begin to follow him everywhere he goes; and the number 614 starts to appear in strange places. He eventually ascertains that the number is a reference to the scriptural verse Gen 6:14, "Make yourself an ark of cypress wood; make rooms in the ark, and cover it inside and out with pitch" (NRSV), and interprets this to mean that God is calling him to build an ark like the one Noah did. Evan starts building, to the confusion and consternation of his friends, family, and coworkers. Eventually, however, his spouse and children join him in the building, and animals begin to arrive and board the ark.

When the fateful day arrives—revealed to be September 22—a gathering of people from the town and local authorities come to watch. At the appointed time, when it had previously been sunny, a storm blows in, briefly causing a wave of anxiety among the people. It quickly passes, however, leaving Evan feeling humiliated, until he realizes that the coming flood is not from the sky but rather from a dam built above. The ark has been built in the middle of a housing development called Prestige Crest, which was made possible by the damming of a river, the dam having been pushed through by the same congressman who had enlisted Evan's cosponsorship on the Citizens' Integration of Public Lands Act. The dam was built without proper oversight and regulation, and with the small amount of rain from the storm that blew through, it fails, flooding the development beneath it in a sudden deluge that would have hurt or killed many had it not been for Evan's ark, which he convinces all present to board just before the dam breaks. Unsubtly, the movie ends with the ark washing up on the shores of the Capitol in Washington DC, interrupting the vote over the similarly foolhardy and corrupt Citizens' Integration of Public Lands Act and leading to the corrupt congressperson's indictment. Evan retakes his position as a congressperson and spends his career passing positive and responsible legislation.

Evan Almighty was widely panned by critics despite its all-star cast and big budget and fell short of box office expectations. It was heavily marketed to Christians[19] but ultimately never garnered the attention of *Bruce Almighty* or became the summer box office hit it was expected to be. Indeed, the plot is full of holes and gimmicks—*Los Angeles Times* reviewer Carina Chocono notes that it seems a little over the top to require huge African mammals to show up to an ark that would not have affected them in the first place—and the mood is ultimately saccharine. But granting its indulgences, the movie does offer a look at an attempt to make a biblical story into a contemporary parable.

The film reveals itself to be an employment of the Noah story in order to indict greed, degradation of the environment for the sake of profit alone, and political corruption. This indictment carried into the production of the movie itself, beyond the plot or performance. In the production, Tom Shadyac offset production of carbon emissions and encouraged crew and cast to ride bicycles to the set, reused wood from the set to build new houses in the area, and required those who worked on it to plant trees. The movie itself takes a starkly serious story—after all, in the original everything on earth except that which has the fortune to board the ark dies a horrific death—and makes it lighthearted and silly. The only destruction is material, and the implication is that we can all agree the corrupt politicians and developers deserved it and that the message needed to reach those who were not listening in government. The movie, while coming up short of pointing directly to climate change, points to the need for owning up to the responsibility humans bear when it comes to its their interactions with the natural world. *Evan Almighty* was the most expensive comedy ever made at the time, much of that budget being for the special effects, the huge model ark that was actually built, and the animals brought on set. Its statement seems to be that the story of Noah has a warning for people today and that comedy can have a serious, even religiously sincere, message. Once again, echoing the ability of biblical stories to keep important ethical and theological ideas "in solution," *Evan Almighty* explicitly draws a connection between the wickedness of human beings in the flood narrative and the corrupt, profit-driven commodification and exploitation of the land and earth in the contemporary United States. Its attention to the details of the narrative is surprisingly thorough: the dimensions of the ark, the materials from which the ark is made, the composition of

---

19. Mark Moring, "Make 'Em Laugh," *Christianity Today*, https://tinyurl.com/SBL6704t.

Noah's family. A PG-rated family movie, *Evan Almighty* dispenses with the more difficult themes of the flood narrative in Genesis—a nicety Darren Aronofsky's *Noah* does not do—to offer an accessible biblical touchstone for giving attention to the consequences of human perfidy with respect to God's creation. Against the familiar, often flattened narrative presented in Sunday school, *Evan Almighty* makes the argument that God's judgment of human disregard for creation, for human wickedness, remains to be reckoned with, especially with respect to affluent US citizens' ongoing cavalier mistreatment of the natural world.

In short, *Evan Almighty* presents, in the form of a modern retelling of a well-known biblical story, a version of theology "in solution." It presents a theology in which God cares about the earth writ large and in which judgment for greed, corruption, and degrading the environment is a real threat. It is neither the deepest theology nor the greatest art. But as popular culture—the movie remains relatively popular even after its box office disappointments—it makes the unexpected, for many, claim that God is interested in and engaged with the protection of the environment and with a sense of environmental justice.

Darren Aronofsky's *Noah* takes a very different tack, though it begins from much the same starting place. *Evan Almighty* was the most expensive comedy production at its time in large part because of the special effects involved. Likewise, *Noah* is heavily special-effects driven. It is, however, epic in its presentation. The narrative portrayed is much closer to the one found in the book of Genesis. As promised by God, in this version of the story, everything but Noah and those close to him is destroyed. There is much that could be discussed, criticized, or praised about the movie when considering its critical lens and how religion plays into its recapitulation of a biblical story. Here, it will serve to focus on one aspect, to show how disperse theological meaning is carried from the Bible to this popular retelling and, further, to show how ecological/environmental arguments are made through such an ancient and potent mythological narrative.

One thing that is difficult to miss in the movie, if one watches critically, is Noah's concern for animals. Noah, the character in the movie, provides healing for injured animals, stresses closeness with the earth, and departs from his contemporaries, it is implied, by respecting the creation around him. In the original Genesis narrative, whatever "the earth was corrupt in God's sight, and the earth was filled with violence" (Gen 6:9, NRSV) may mean, for the Noah in the movie, it means having lost a connection with and respect for the natural world. Tubal-Cain, who in the creative adaptation serves as the villain, proposes turning a hill into a mine—an obvious connection with the frequently damaging practices of extraction in juxtaposition to Noah's own simpler, less industrialized way of living. Further, part of how we know Tubal-Cain is the villain in the movie is his and his followers' propensity for eating flesh, animal and human. Tubal-Cain sets traps for animals, and as a verboten stowaway aboard the ark—he rushes on just as the gates of heaven open and the flood begins—he eats the flesh of animals in the hull of the ark.

Noah, the movie, draws on an oft overlooked detail in the primordial narrative of Genesis that, if one takes the stories at face value, human beings did not eat meat before the end of the flood. Indeed, it seems that eating anything other than plants was forbidden by God. Only after the floodwaters recede and Noah and his family are left in a vastly changed world does God give permission to eat the flesh of animals and only under certain conditions:

> The fear and dread of you shall rest on every animal of the earth, and on every bird of the air, on everything that creeps on the ground, and on all the fish of the sea; into your hand they are delivered. Every moving thing that lives shall be food for you; and just as I gave you the green plants, I give you everything. Only, you shall not eat flesh with its life, that is, its blood. (Gen 9:2–4, NRSV)

Animals before the flood, in the actual biblical text, are used for clothing and as a sacrifice, but the eating of animals is not sanctioned until after the worldwide flood, an indication of the lostness, the destruction, and the wickedness of human beings. It is seen as something of a concession to a fallen world. Similarly, in the movie, the ongoing symbol of Tubal-Cain's and others' wickedness and disregard for God's creation is their malevolent attitude toward the natural world and especially toward animals.

Aronofsky, the director of *Noah*, is a famous vegan. Further, he has been an activist for environmental concerns throughout his career, using his platform to press for specific aspects of environmental activism he cares about. Aronofsky has commented that, drawing on his Jewish background, he intended *Noah* to be a type of midrash on the biblical narrative, drawing from extrabiblical sources to flesh out and deepen the bare bones narrative offered in Genesis. *Noah* takes the widely known narrative from Genesis and makes it a parable of environmental activism. It asserts environmental degradation of God's creation and disregard for land as the primary wickedness of human beings. Like *Evan Almighty*, *Noah* included its environmentalism in the production of the movie. Aronofsky used digitally created animals rather than real ones and spoke widely about his refusal to subject animals to the conditions necessary to use them in such a production.

Popular reactions to the movie included both those that were inspired by the latent promotion of vegetarian or vegan diets, as well as environmentalism more generally, and those who were breathlessly incensed by it. Of course, because it was a biblical story being told, the debate took on a theological veneer. Joel S. Baden, a professor of Hebrew Bible at Yale Divinity School, published an article in *Politico* titled "Sorry, Darren Aronofsky: God is Not a Vegan," in which he asserts, "it is the movie's green message that has most rankled its critics, especially those on the religious-political right, who have been quick to dismiss the film…. In this case, though, the religious right is unmistakably correct: Of all the stories in the Bible, the flood narrative is perhaps the *least* environmentally friendly."[20] The critique somewhat misses the point. After all, against what the title of the article says, the movie does not actually make the claim that *God* was vegan. Hardly at issue is anything about God's gustatory choices. Even if animal sacrifices please God in Genesis, there are things in the earth given to and withheld from human beings. What the movie *Noah* does argue about God's flood in Genesis is that the degradation and mistreatment of the earth, and in particular animals, may be a transgression worthy of the judgment of God, up to and including destruction. It also suggests that the current damage from environmental crises may be worthy of prompting human beings to look to their own behavior and contributions rather than wondering about why God would allow such things to happen.

Ultimately, Baden comes to something similar to such a conclusion, even if he disagrees with Aronofsky's comprehension of the Bible:

> At the risk of stating the obvious, if the Bible does not have a green message, it is because it didn't need one. Ancient Israelites were already "green" by our standards. They didn't have the technological capacity to inflict any substantial damage on the environment. We, on the other hand, have that power almost beyond measure. Aronofsky has given us a version of the flood that recognizes the contemporary human condition.

---

20. Joel S. Baden, "Sorry Darren Aronofsky: God Is Not a Vegan," *Politico*, https://tinyurl.com/SBL6704p.

His *Noah* speaks to the present political and social climate, as have 4,000 years of authors and interpreters before him. Every generation gets the flood story it deserves.[21]

Of course, this brings the discussion of the Bible and popular culture, here encountered in the movie *Noah*, full circle. Aronofsky uses a received story, in this case a well-known one, to make theological points about the significance of human beings' actions with respect to the earth, giving the sense of God's judgment hanging over the continued destruction humans continue to reap upon the world. Whether one agrees or not, Aronofsky indicts the use and treatment of animals, as livestock, as foodstuffs, without regard to their suffering or their place in God's creation. He uses a subtle point in the biblical narrative to construct a theological point for the contemporary world in which he lives. Aronofsky was celebrated in corners where such an attitude would, of course, be welcome: PETA and other animal-rights groups heralded the movie, in its message and in its treatment, or avoidance thereof, of animals.

Both *Evan Almighty* and *Noah* use one of the most well-known, one of the most popular, stories in the Bible to make contemporary theological meaning. They make claims about the relationship between human beings, God, and God's creation through the spectacle of contemporary cinema. In turn, by encountering these movies, audiences are invited into considering unknown, if not exactly novel, meanings and insights to be drawn from the Bible. In essence, these two movies serve as examples for the way the Bible is used as a source for contemporary cinema in order to make theological assertions in a way that speaks to a greater swath of people and in ways that carry greater and deeper meaning than simply arguing that the earth is important to God. Such an abstract claim is given real flesh, drama, and spectacle in order to carry greater and noncontainable meanings with respect to the Bible's relevance for the world as it is today. It means something very different to be told that God cares about creation and the earth, a claim by no means accepted by the full range of people who take the Bible seriously as a religious text versus seeing, in dramatic and fine detail, the repercussions of a wrathful God being manifest on a giant screen in a creative engagement with what may incur such judgment in some humans' actions today.

---

21. Baden, "Sorry Darren Aronofsky."

Analysis and Conclusions

The Bible helps to tell stories and provide ad hoc bases for reasoning in everyday life. It provides a narrative and sense of justification in popular culture, connecting with traditions, imagined or real, that make sense of experiences and beliefs in the contemporary world. In the case of hip hop, it offers a religiously authoritative narrative to which to connect contemporary black experiences of oppression and disenfranchisement in the United States. In its best forms it develops, organically, something that resembles black liberation theology: radical, gritty, truthful, unashamed to proclaim love of oneself and one's people despite hostility from culture at large. It gives expression, in conversation with biblical texts and other popular culture, to anger and joy, from the melancholy protest of "Gangster's Paradise" to the self-affirming anthem of Kendrick Lamar's *I*.

Sallie McFague, a constructive theologian who pioneered creative ways of working with the Bible theologically, argues that the Bible offers parabolic theology, that metaphor is a means of keeping religious truths in solution. She argues that for the contemporary world, new theologies and new models must be offered to make biblical truths continue to speak in a relevant way. The parables as primary theological discourse show how theological metaphors must work. They make a claim that the truth of the narrative of the parable reveals a truth about God in a way that cannot be extracted from the story itself. To try to describe the truth is to lose important elements of the truth. At the same time, parables, in their great diversity, never pretend to ever fully encapsulate God or the Kingdom of God. Our approach to the Bible must highlight the continued vivaciousness and vigor of the Bible in our current context, still able to speak to people in their contemporary contexts, and the innumerous interpretations that can be created and held of the Bible that help to affirm the existence and experience of the multiplicitous diversity of humanity. Uses of the Bible in popular culture do similar work, on a less academic level. Referencing the Bible in popular culture discourse allows for a metaphorical engagement with an authoritative text and also allows for a theological reflection on one's own place in the world and the meaning thereof.

The Bible in popular culture is not primarily an academic book or even a historical one. It is a metaphorical one, one out of which people make meaningful models of their own lived lives. References to the Bible in hip hop and in film provide quotidian modes of theological reflection. The Bible serves as the basic starting point and common source for publicly constructed popular theology. Hip hop at its best offers a kind of organic parabolic theology from below, making sense of the challenges of contemporary black life using vignettes, short stories, and references, not least to the Bible. The episodic use of the Bible put in conversation with the nitty-gritty, as Pinn calls it, of life gives it an authentically parabolic character. Uses of the Bible in hip hop, and other types of music for that matter, can be to good or bad ends. At its best, though, it speaks to, calls for, and enacts liberation. In film, likewise, uses of the Bible can be for good or ill. Regardless, it provides models for understanding the crises faced by human beings in the present and relating them to mythological narratives that echo from deep within a religious understanding of the world. Film provides an accessible and spectacular way to show the relevance of biblical narratives for the state of the world as it is encountered today, in all its beauty and destruction.

Whether this, in popular culture, is responsible exegesis or not is an important and serious question. But it also, at scale, does not seem to matter to those who are doing it. The Bible provides a text for organic theological construction. It can be a tool of help or harm. It is mutually constructive and mutually critical with US popular culture. As the Bible is used in popular culture, it critiques who we are and holds our contemporary ways of life responsible to tradition and, for some, even revelation. At the same time, uses of the Bible in popular culture shape what it is and what it means for people today. A genuine challenge arises with regard to what responsibility academic biblical scholars and theologians have to engage with the ways that culture at large is working with and interpreting the Bible. How can biblical studies insights be more widely acknowledged and used outside of the academy and the church? How can more responsible theological norms be promoted in a culture that will be proposing theological norms whether those proposals are rooted in any solid ground or not? The Bible is never a self-evident thing. It has been shaped historically by interests, ideologies, and histories, and it continues to be today. It is a popular culture object even as it is a religious one. It is a text that cannot help but be confronted theologically in each new encounter, exegesis, or artistic representation. It is both a thoroughly historical text and a thoroughly modern one. Its rhythms and vocabulary are echoed in some corners almost effortlessly. It is a book that *is* popular, that has shaped and is shaping our popular culture today and is itself continuing to be shaped by it.

Bibliography

Baden, Joel S. "Sorry Darren Aronofsky: God Is Not a Vegan." *Politico*. https://tinyurl.com/SBL6704p.

Barna Group. "Competing Worldviews Influence Today's Christians." Barna.com. https://tinyurl.com/SBL6704r.

———. "State of the Bible 2018: Seven Top Findings." Barna.com. https://tinyurl.com/SBL6704q.

Cone, James H. *A Black Theology of Liberation*. 40th anniv. ed. Maryknoll: Orbis, 2010.

Forbes, Bruce David. "Introduction: Finding Religion in Unexpected Places." Pages 1–24 in *Religion and Popular Culture in America*. Edited by Bruce David Forbes and Jeffrey H. Mahan. 3rd ed. Oakland: University of California Press, 2017.

Gideons International. "Gideons Distribute Historic Two Billionth Scripture." Gideons International Blog. https://tinyurl.com/SBL6704s.

Hodge, Daniel White. *Hip Hop's Hostile Gospel: A Post-soul Theological Exploration*. Leiden: Brill, 2017.

———. *The Soul of Hip Hop: Rims, Timbs and a Cultural Theology*. Downers Grove, IL: InterVarsity Press, 2010.

McFague, Sallie. *Speaking in Parables: A Study in Metaphor and Theology*. Minneapolis: Fortress, 1975.

Miller, Monica R. *Religion and Hip Hop*. New York: Routledge, 2013.

Miller, Monica R., Anthony B. Pinn, and Bernard "Bun B" Freeman, eds. *Religion in Hip Hop: Mapping the New Terrain in the US*. New York: Bloomsbury, 2015.

Moring, Mark. "Make 'Em Laugh." *Christianity Today*. https://tinyurl.com/SBL6704t.

Petre, Jonathan. "J. K. Rowling: 'Christianity Inspired Harry Potter.'" https://tinyurl.com/SBL6704u.

Pinn, Anthony. "Rap Music and Its Message: On Interpreting the Contact between Religion and Popular Culture." Pages 390–412 in *Religion and Popular Culture in America*. Edited by Bruce David Forbes and Jeffrey H. Mahan. 3rd ed. Oakland: University of California Press, 2017.

4
THE BIBLE IN AMERICAN LITERATURE

M. COOPER HARRISS

The Word

In his introduction to *The Bible and American Arts and Letters* (1983)—one volume that this book updates—Giles Gunn calls the Bible "America's Book." This proves true, he writes, "not only because Americans like to think that they have read it more assiduously than other people but also because Americans like to think that the Bible is the book that they, more than any other people, have been assiduously read by."[1] Summarizing his contributors' arguments, Gunn details Cotton Mather's model of American exceptionalism, asking, in paraphrase: "If the Bible could be used to determine America's exceptionality, might not America be used to demonstrate the Bible's?"[2] Later he notes certain "disturbing dimensions" that extend from Mather's exceptionalist mode—a mode that qualifies as *both* exegetical *and* eisegetical:

> The Bible ... belong[ed] to America because America, it could be assumed, already belonged to the Bible, because America *was* the Bible or, better, the realization of its promises. The result ... was to reduce the Old and New Testaments to a kind of National Testament and to convert the biblical *Heilsgeschichte*, or history of salvation, into the American salvation of history.[3]

---

1. Giles Gunn, introduction to *The Bible and American Arts and Letters*, ed. Giles Gunn (Philadelphia: Fortress, 1983), 1.
2. Gunn, introduction, 1.
3. Gunn, introduction, 1–2.

Gunn highlights a centuries-long trajectory of US exceptionalism as biblical in character, authorized by and authoring its unique cultural authority in American national contexts.

This chapter updates Gunn's description by identifying significant challenges to biblical exceptionalism in American literature that have emerged since the final quarter of the twentieth century (when Gunn's volume was published). Things have changed during this period. One may follow anxious trends in the assessment of American religiosity—the secularization thesis, the rise of religious pluralism especially since the 1965 Hart-Cellar Act, and most recently the emergence of "nones" who claim no specific religious affiliation. Given that many understand these changes to offer evidence of religious decline (and by *religion* they often mean *Christianity*), commentators also point to broader biblical illiteracy among nonevangelicals that erodes the foundations of this exceptionalist mode.[4] This is not to deny that Americans may be less proficient in Bible than earlier generations. But it does question the degree to which such shifts foreclose the non- or counterexceptional ways the Bible participates in American literary expression.

Consider the category of *none*. Often misconstrued (or misrepresented) as the disappearance of religiosity, more appropriately its appeal as a category to twenty-first-century scholars points to the insufficiency of how surveys (and the societies that they reflect) categorize religious identity in the first place. Nones are *differently* religious. Similarly, I want to argue here that recent American literature is *differently* biblical from what it has largely been before, that changing dynamics over the past several decades owe considerably less to trends of growing biblical illiteracy than they do the critical failure to imagine and recognize alternative biblical modes. The kind of exceptionalism that Gunn charts, while culturally evident, may no longer be presumed to characterize the best recent literary contentions with the Bible. Indeed, the past several decades reflect a broader tendency to take exception to such exceptionalism and the cultural legacy it encapsulates.

This chapter traces the terms of this shift away from the US and biblical exceptionalism Gunn describes in three ways. First, it tracks changing cultural dynamics of America and the Bible running parallel to one another

---

4. Lesleigh Cushing Stahlberg and Peter S. Hawkins, *The Bible in the American Short Story* (New York: Bloomsbury, 2018), 15.

since the 1970s. New literary and intellectual voices complicate the conflation of biblical and national authority as a form of political and social oppression (especially in terms of race and gender). Second, and along these lines, this chapter offers close readings of biblical dimensions in so-called secular novels by two black women American authors working around the turn of the twenty-first century: Toni Morrison and Octavia Butler. Both Morrison and Butler submit an interrogative position toward formerly stable assertions: What is the Bible? Who are Americans? Whose Bible? Which Americans? As black women, Morrison and Butler defy and reorganize the historically colonized biblical exceptionalism that Gunn profiles. A coda to this chapter frames a wider range of recent authors and works, demonstrating that American literature has by no means abandoned the Bible. Instead, it no longer peddles such an historically narrow interpretation of the Bible's Americanness.

The Word and the Contradiction of the Word

What, precisely, do Gunn's authors assume the Bible and America share in common? One way to answer this question suggests that both terms represent singular properties that hold a myriad of pluralities in productive tension. Paradox, simultaneity, irresolution, even contradiction and hypocrisy emerge as ironic characteristics registered by a diversity of ideas, traditions, identities, characters—even as they change over time—marshaled by stable conceptions of both nation and text. In the process they manage and even discipline parallel categories of America and Bible. A *pluribus*, in this way, submits to the *unum*. America and the Bible, then, historically emphasize the need for cooperative antagonism between contradictory cultural and political impulses. Consider the novelist and critic Ralph Ellison's riff on the Fourth Gospel to discuss the Declaration of Independence and US Constitution (both of which he considered, though not without complication, sacred documents): "In the beginning was not only the word but the contradiction of the word."[5] For Ellison this coupling holds *word* and *contradiction* to be partners in crime—approximate equals in the negotiation of American pluralism that characterizes the whole. It privileges the word but acknowledges the related necessity of the

---

5. Ralph Ellison, "Society, Morality, and the Novel," in *The Collected Essays of Ralph Ellison*, ed. John F. Callahan, (New York: Modern Library, 1995), 698.

contradiction, even as the word manages contradictory impulses as part and parcel of its overriding identity. In this way we may recognize a model for and, indeed, a conceptual parallel to the relationship between Bible and America depicted by Gunn's contributors.

This historical assumption of balance between word and contradiction in American identity resembles a postwar movement (itself roughly coterminous with Gunn's volume) that established a cohesive Christian biblical theology by inflecting the Bible's historical-critical pluralities through the stabilizing influence of its reception as Christian scripture. Brevard Childs, for instance, sought a "theologically normative" Christian interpretation of a canon he recognized to bear "enormous variety and multilayered growth."[6] He did so with an appeal to equilibrium between its constituent parts (here, the Old Testament or Hebrew Bible and New Testament) that holds together in a manner reminiscent of *pluribus* and *unum* in conceptions of America:

> The problem for Christian theology in delineating the relation of its Bible to the Hebrew canon can perhaps best be summarized in terms of a delicate balance between the elements of continuity and discontinuity, which both unite and separate. The point is ... to establish the proper theological dialectic between the Old and the New [Testaments].[7]

In the process Childs warns against overemphasizing either continuity or discontinuity, sounding a great deal like Gunn's historical overview: "The Old Testament is interpreted by the New, and the New Testament is understood through the Old, but the unity of its witness is grounded in the One Lord."[8] Whatever contradictions or discontinuities may pertain—and Childs, like Gunn, acknowledges that they do—function in service of a canonical Christian *unum* just as "America," à la Gunn's contributors, "was the Bible."

The past several decades have witnessed a shift in political and intellectual assumptions away from such cohesion. US founding documents have emphasized more historically overlooked identities affected by the

---

6. Brevard S. Childs, *Old Testament Theology in a Canonical Context* (Philadelphia: Fortress, 1985), 5.

7. Brevard S. Childs, *Introduction to the Old Testament as Scripture* (Philadelphia: Fortress, 1979), 670–71.

8. Childs, *Introduction to the Old Testament as Scripture*, 671.

whitewashing of the exceptionalist synthesis. Indeed, even as it prescribed freedom for white men, the US Constitution also enslaved Ellison's own grandparents; the very tenets of US constitutional freedom have necessarily derived from the unfreedom of others. In this context the vagaries of cooperative antagonism become a trickier prospect. Speaking particularly for enslaved people and their descendants, the notion of being "assiduously read by" the Bible (which, of course, served as a primary textual and religious authority for the justification of US slavery) takes on a far more sinister valence for those who lacked the power of negotiation.[9] As Malcolm X put it: "We didn't land on Plymouth Rock. The Rock landed on us!"[10]

Biblical studies rooted in identity and social categories emerged in response to such perspicuity. Most germane to this present discussion is African-American biblical criticism, which evolved alongside black and womanist theological movements that still were relatively nascent in the early 1980s.[11] These movements have sought to correct Eurocentric readings, practices, and interpretive schematics, which constituted, in the words of Vincent Wimbush, "one larger empire of willful, playful readers, little involved in the dynamics and griminess always played out on the (colonial/racialized) fringes."[12] Such innovations directly challenge the presumptions of Gunn's authors surrounding the centrality of the Bible to the singular word of so-called American culture by

---

9. See especially Mark A. Noll, *The Civil War as Theological Crisis* (Chapel Hill: University of North Carolina Press, 2006), 31–50.

10. Malcolm X with Alex Haley, *The Autobiography of Malcolm X* (New York: Ballantine, 1965), 232.

11. Cain Hope Felder's volume *Stony the Road We Trod: African American Biblical Interpretation* (Minneapolis: Fortress, 1991) represents a deliberate programmatic shift toward the codification of a uniquely African-American biblical interpretation. Felder writes that "much of what is regarded as legitimate and objective biblical analysis (exegesis) and interpretation (hermeneutics) has been done for the distinct purpose of maintaining Eurocentrism. The biblical role of non-Europeans in general and blacks in particular has thereby been trivialized and left in the margins" (ix). African-American biblical criticism does not represent the only shift, of course, but it coheres especially well with my examples—Butler and Morrison—highlighted in the next section.

12. Vincent L. Wimbush, "Knowing Ex-centrics/Ex-centric Knowing," in *MisReading America: Scriptures and Difference*, ed. Vincent L. Wimbush (New York: Oxford University Press, 2013), 2.

emphasizing a sense of contradiction: "African Americans have held fast to the Bible by holding fast to its contradictions," writes Allen Dwight Callahan. "Indeed, the contradictions suited their condition, for African Americans themselves incarnated America's greatest contradiction. They were slaves in the land of the free."[13] Thus, as black Americans have been assiduously read by the Bible, the terms of such a reading do not accord with the agency and self-determination of the assiduous dominant reading that Gunn's authors presume.

Within the domain of Callahan's contradiction, then, one may take exception to the word that Gunn's authors presume—offering an assiduous counterreading, as it were. Wimbush perceives that "the Bible became a 'world' into which African Americans could retreat, a 'world' they could identify with, draw strength from, and in fact manipulate for self-affirmation."[14] The very terms of existence for such a world, however, demand that such a space remain contested, not contained. Callahan notes that at the heart of the black contradiction must reside an understanding of the Bible not only as Good Book—akin to Wimbush's affirming organizing principle—but also a Poison Book. *Poison* marks the complicity of biblical narrative with hegemonic traditions (consider the racial legacies of the Curse of Ham, for instance, derived from Gen 9:20–27 or Col 3:22's injunction "Slaves, obey your earthly masters"[15]) and recognizes biblical significance in historical oppression, even in the face of something like Jesus's statement in Luke 4:18 (citing Isa 61:1)—

> The Spirit of the Lord is upon me,
>   because he has anointed me
>   to bring good news to the poor.
> He has sent me to proclaim release to the captives
>   and recovery of sight to the blind,
>   to let the oppressed go free[16]

---

13. Allen Dwight Calhahan, *The Talking Book: African Americans and the Bible* (New Haven: Yale University Press, 2006), 25.

14. Vincent L. Wimbush, "The Bible and African Americans: An Outline of an Interpretive History," in Felder, *Stony the Road We Trod*, 83.

15. For delineation and analysis of this passage's influence, see Sylvester A. Johnson, *The Myth of Ham in Nineteenth-Century American Christianity: Race, Heathens, and the People of God* (New York: Palgrave Macmillan, 2004).

16. Unless otherwise stated, biblical citations follow the NRSV.

—a specific passage that inspires the drive for black liberation among Christian theologians such as James Cone.[17] This critical mode from within the contradiction has also fostered creative responses to the Bible as text and legacy, leading writers, religious leaders, and political figures to revise or innovate its stories and characters to offer new visions and possibilities. Consider, for instance, the Nation of Islam's Myth of Yakub, expanding upon—even as it derives from—the biblical Jacob and certain dispensational attributes of the book of Revelation.

An indispensable figure representing this in-dwelling of biblical contradiction is Hagar—maidservant of Sarai and mother of Ishmael, whose conception (by Abram) leads to Sarai's wrath, Abram's indifference, and Hagar's escape into exile. Delores Williams frames Hagar's story as representative of black women's womanist experience within this contradictory frame, an existence ever suspended within the questions posed to Hagar by the angel of the Lord: "Where have you come from and where are you going?" (Gen 16:8).[18] By working through a tradition of Hagar-appropriation that formulates the biblical worldview of black women marginalized by Hebrew patriarchs *and* matriarchs, translated to the present day (and in such a present context implicating even black patriarchy), the example of Hagar establishes the ambivalence of the Bible as a source of both orientation and disorientation, both good and poison to deploy Callahan's categories. Both coming and going, existence always registers somewhere in between—yet not in an exceptionalist way. Instead she represents the *exception* to such exceptionalism.

The following section deploys this same question asked to Hagar to characterize the appropriation of biblical narrative in the work of two (black women) American authors working near the turn of the twenty-first century: Morrison (particularly through her novel *Beloved* [1987]) and Butler (especially through two sequential novels from the 1990s: *Parable of the Sower* [1993] and *Parable of the Talents* [1998]). Both instances complicate the exceptionalism of Gunn's America and the Bible by challenging the biblical perspective that informs their literary production.

---

17. Cone posits this verse as central to the content of generative work in his black theology of liberation. See James H. Cone, *A Black Theology of Liberation* (Maryknoll, NY: Orbis, 2010), 3.

18. Delores S. Williams, *Sisters in the Wilderness: The Challenge of Womanist God-Talk* (Maryknoll, NY: Orbis, 2013). For womanists, of course, such a contradictory frame is always complicated by a second, gendered contradiction.

Broadly speaking, as black women writers, heirs of a sort to Hagar's question, they take exception to the exceptionalist pose, bearing witness to the risks of cheap *unum*'s easy grace.

At the same time, Morrison and Butler represent exemplars of a post-Christian (and thus a postbiblical-theological) America that contends with inescapable biblical echoes and legacies (for good *and* ill) while simultaneously striving to reimagine its certain textual futures that respond to and move beyond these legacies and their innovations. Morrison recasts this biblical mode by looking backwards and renovating the terms of its contribution to American literary expression. Butler looks ahead, innovating not only the meaning of the Bible but its canonical possibilities for the future tense. While these examples do not represent the only transformations in play in recent decades, they do afford deep engagement that a brief coda seeks to expand. Nevertheless, Morrison and Butler as examples prove uniquely situated for tracking a number of important emerging developments along the way.

Where Have You Come From? Morrison's *Beloved*

Morrison's use of the Bible primarily qualifies as retrospective, a mode of ancestry shorn of nostalgia. Such a mode offers, at turns, a repository for character names (literally so in her earlier novel *Song of Solomon*[19]), a source for collective and personal memory, and a lexicon that imperfectly accounts for the discomfiting violence and regulatory intimacies that characterize black life in America (and beyond)—particularly the lives of black women. In *Beloved* such retrospection takes the form of hauntedness, a "mystification" that Amy Hungerford argues "seeks to replace white possession of the Bible, and its cultural and spiritual authority, with an authority based in the illiterate's possession of that sacred book, in the process maintaining—and, more importantly, deploying—the ultimate privilege accorded to the Bible in Western culture."[20] For a people strategically stripped of authoritative genealogies, the Bible (complicit, of course, in such a theft of ancestry) supplies a surrogate, subverting the exceptionalist myths.

---

19. Toni Morrison, *Song of Solomon* (New York: Vintage, 2004). Orig. 1977.

20. Amy Hungerford, *Postmodern Belief: American Literature and Religion since 1960* (Princeton: Princeton University Press, 2010), 96.

This subversion of American biblical exceptionalism comes about in two ways. First, it deemphasizes the Bible's written, and therefore archival, authority, pushing instead an immediate and irruptive power from its oral interpretation, from its role as what Hungerford calls "illiterature."[21] In this way biblical words, forms, characters, and sensibilities no longer offer the kind of seamless currents of meaning or resolution that contribute to the stability necessary for a cohesive biblical theology. It also destabilizes the comfort or consolation of biblical perspicuity that enables certain providential readings. "Replac[ing] white possession" of the Bible, then, takes place within multiple meanings of *possession* as signifying both ownership and spiritual intrusion. *Beloved*'s biblical hermeneutics repossess the Bible from canonical assumptions native to whiteness and also possess the biblical text in a way that alters it, estranging it from these oppressive legacies that nevertheless give it definition.

Central to *Beloved*'s hauntedness is its narration of the unaccountable return (as a highly embodied ghost) of Sethe's slain daughter—the "crawling already?" baby that, not quite two decades earlier she succeeded in killing rather than allowing slave patrollers to return her to bondage. This is Beloved—resurrected, excavated, avenging angel of destruction for any sense of progress or redemption that may have crossed the characters' minds. Her irruptive capacity cannot be stressed enough. Beloved, whose name bears biblical significance, does not represent the reunion of families or the triumph of domestic order. She augurs the repossession of these stable modes as something far less stable—indeed, something intrinsically destructive. One way Morrison works to achieve this effect is through the strategic conflation of biblical antecedents for this titular word *beloved* throughout the narrative.

The novel's epigraph cites Rom 9:25: "I will call them my people, which were not my people; and her beloved, which was not beloved," signaling a Pauline valence that touches again on questions of possession and otherness. Elsewhere, a series of voices speak in stream-of-conscious cadences that echo Song 2:16—"My beloved is mine and I am his"—in the opening lines of four consecutive chapters. The first comes from Sethe: "Beloved, she my daughter. She mine.... And when I tell you you mine, I

---

21. Hungerford, *Postmodern Belief*, 96. US slavery prevented literacy among the enslaved precisely in order that they could not read the Bible, pointing to a kind of biblical illiteracy by design. See Callahan, *Talking Book*, 10.

also mean I'm yours."[22] The following chapter begins with a parallel opening statement from Denver—"Beloved is my sister"[23]—followed by two more disjointed chapters probably spoken by Beloved, the ghost, herself, both of which begin with this statement: "I am Beloved and she is mine."[24] Within these allusive echoes we might recognize preoccupation with possession—of ownership in love and duty but also through the corruption of these relational properties, introducing dynamics of power over or even the possession and thus the enslavement of another. Note, too, the instability of pronouns. Who is the second *she* in Beloved's statements? Sethe? Beloved herself? Indeed, what ought we to make of Sethe's excess of *you* in the second clause cited above? Morrison's narrative seeks biblical stability yet comes to embody its notable internal fractiousness and instability. In this way the Bible bears a significant role in the novel's hauntedness.

At the same time, despite the myriad biblical associations we may ascribe to Morrison's use of the word *beloved*, the character name itself is not strictly biblical. Indeed, it is only implicitly so, meaning that its most direct origin in the novel is in fact liturgical (and thus performative instead of textual—a function, perhaps, of its role as illiterature). Sethe recalls being released specifically to attend her child's burial ("not the funeral, just the burial"):

> The sheriff came with me.... I believe a lot of folks were there, but I just saw the box. Reverend Pike spoke in a real loud voice, but I didn't catch a word—except the first two, and three months later ... I went and got you a gravestone, but I didn't have money enough for the carving so I exchanged (bartered, you might say) what I did have and I'm sorry to this day I never thought to ask him for the whole thing: all I heard of what Reverend Pike said. Dearly Beloved, which is what you are to me and I don't have to be sorry about getting only one word.[25]

Beloved's name, then, connects her liturgical identity (the one that is performed and overheard) with the biblical antecedents to which it points, from which it derives. There remains, however, no stable biblical correspondence in any textual sense. Reverend Pike speaks "beloved" as a matter of course—both derived from and sanctioned by the Bible's textual

---

22. Toni Morrison, *Beloved* (New York: Vintage, 2004), 237, 239.
23. Morrison, *Beloved*, 242.
24. Morrison, *Beloved*, 248, 253.
25. Morrison, *Beloved*, 216–17.

authority, yet Beloved herself represents no ordered continuum of influence, *tupos*, or allusion. She *possesses* the novel's action, its title, its epigraph, and as a consequence this possession generates the desire for biblical connection that always turns away from itself. Morrison illuminates a sense of the Bible not as helper, partner, or any other stable relational participant with or through its text. Instead, the Bible disrupts, enslaving even as it liberates. It names an agenda and a trajectory yet defies any sense of a way forward that does not lead back somehow to the devastation of this point. "This is not a story to pass on," says Morrison's implied narrator in closing, speaking of a *possession* no one should wish to inherit.[26]

Where Are You Going? Butler's Parables

Butler's fiction is associated with the literary and cultural movement known as Afrofuturism—offering direct correlation to the angel's question to Hagar, "Where are you going?" Such futurity contrasts Morrison's retrospection, though it also emerges as a mode of resistance to certain overdeterminations of American biblicism in the broader legacies (such as that described by Gunn) to which it responds. In this way, while Butler shares Morrison's awareness of the Bible's potential as Poison Book, this sense of futurity offers a different orientation to it. Instead of drawing on the many traces of biblical legacy that continue to constrain black characters—especially black women—as Morrison does, Butler points to the possibility for change. Significantly, such change requires the destruction of most canonical understandings of the Bible, both as category and content. At the same time, such rewriting also provides a way forward that pushes beyond older biblical-theological conceptions of the Bible and American literature.

Parable of the Sower and its sequel, *Parable of the Talents*, are set between the years 2024 and 2036 (with some leaps ahead to 2090).[27] They largely take place against the backdrop of a recognizably dystopic United States, narrating the struggles and legacy of Lauren Oya Olamina and, in the second novel, her daughter Larkin Olamina. These narratives derive from Lauren's journals and Larkin's observations pertaining to the creation and survival of a new religion that Lauren creates, known as

---

26. Morrison, *Beloved*, 324.
27. Butler never completed a planned third volume, *Parable of the Trickster*.

Earthseed, named for the text that Lauren writes (*Earthseed: The Books of the Living*) as a guide to this new religious movement. Earthseed's central theological tenet holds that "God is change"—indeed, "the only lasting truth is change."[28] Such openness to change serves a practical purpose for Butler's biblicism: it fractures the canon, opening the Bible (and especially the Christian dimensions that it helps structure in the novel) to new developments.

Such new developments mold Lauren's character and the religion she writes into existence (paraphrasing Kimberly Ruffin).[29] On the one hand, they help her break from a past represented by her father, a sympathetic figure whose ways no longer pertain (though certainly one may read a kind of toppling of patriarchy in this dismissal of her father's Bible). To explain the clear and present failures of the US system that we first encounter in *Sower*, for instance, he argues that the Deist founding fathers should have "had more faith in what their Bibles told them."[30] At the same time, she clearly draws influence from his example. His facility with parables and their significance for Lauren's own teaching and writing figure prominently in Lauren's memories and resurface over and again across the saga.[31]

What becomes clear is that Butler wishes to characterize *Earthseed* as scripture—biblical with a signal difference—especially as Lauren becomes a political prisoner and, later, a martyr for her cause. In *Talents*, Lauren uses a Bible issued to her in captivity as a desk in order to compose *Earthseed*, suggesting superscription if not supersession—*Earthseed* as palimpsest.[32] When teaching others to read she uses passages from *Earthseed* that "some people even seemed to think ... was from the Bible" (though she still draws a sharp distinction): "I couldn't bring myself to let them go on thinking that."[33] The character of change that takes place in *Earthseed* reflects, among other things, an openness to science. As one character puts it, "'God is Change' she [writes in *Earthseed*] and means it. Some of the faces of her God are biological evolution, chaos theory, relativity theory,

---

28. Octavia E. Butler, *Parable of the Sower* (New York: Grand Central, 1993), 17, 3.
29. Kimberly J. Ruffin, "Parable of a Twenty-First Century Religion: Octavia Butler's Afrofuturistic Bridge between Science and Religion," *Obsidian III* 6.2–7.1 (2005–2006): 88.
30. Butler, *Parable of the Sower*, 15.
31. Octavia E. Butler, *Parable of the Talents* (New York: Grand Central, 1998), 15.
32. Butler, *Parable of the Talents*, 15.
33. Butler, *Parable of the Talents*, 296.

the uncertainty principle, and, of course, the second law of thermodynamics. 'God is Change, and, in the end, God prevails.'"[34]

Such openness to a world of possibilities functions to counter a retrospective problem in *Talents*. If Lauren sees one contemporary problem for the Bible in its insufficiency to contend with modern times, an even more harrowing example proves its simultaneous *hyper*-sufficiency. In the midst of profound financial and environmental crisis the United States has elected, as president, Steele Jarret of the hard-right Christian America Party (their motto: "Make America Great Again").[35] By linking the party (and its eerily prescient slogan) to a violent conflation of Christian and US identities, Butler invokes shades of Gunn's assiduous reading. Indeed, it points specifically to the retrospection that occupies Morrison. Lauren describes Jarret and his followers as "a revival of something nasty out of the past.... He wants to take us all back to some magical time when everyone believed in the same God, [and] worshipped him on the same way.... There was never such a time in this country. But these days when more than half the people in the country can't read at all, history is just one more vast unknown to them."[36] Butler recognizes the opening of scripture, via *Earthseed*, as a way of inaugurating a future that disentangles itself from the noxious political complicity of Bible and America.

Whereas Morrison deploys retrospection to challenge a sense of historical inevitability at play in the hegemonic conflation of Bible and America, Butler sees a similar project in the adaptation of the biblical modes to establish through futurity a line of demarcation from the Christian American past. In both cases the idea of the Bible as America remains untenable. Also, in both cases, something biblical can and must trigger the attempt to resolve this issue. Accordingly we arrive at what we might call a biblicism situated within the contradiction of the word, one that emphasizes the contradiction as a productive space for reorienting America (which is unabashedly black woman America) outside of older presumptions of perspicuity and the seamless readings (of self and other) that they afford. "Where did you come from and where are you going?" Morrison and Butler, among other things, offer the affirmation that "we're still right here." Their broader taking of exception to older exceptionalist

---

34. Butler, *Parable of the Talents*, 46.
35. Butler, *Parable of the Talents*, 20.
36. Butler, *Parable of the Talents*, 19.

biblical modes offers a template for identifying other exemplars of this transition concerning the Bible and American literature.

Further Legacies

Beyond the specific legacies that Morrison and Butler permit us to observe at close range, other American literary writers continue to draw on biblical significance that emerges from the contradictory space. James McBride, for instance, relies on biblical misprecision to emphasize certain weird qualities of the US abolitionist John Brown in his novel *The Good Lord Bird* (2013), toying at the same time with conceptions of history and the politics of representation.[37] McBride's characters, for instance, cite what they claim to be biblical quotations, though in fact they are vague slogans rendered in Bible-ese that may seem to address a given situation but prove misheard, poorly rendered, or even fabricated:

> "Tell me," [John Brown said,] "Which books in the Bible do you favor?"
> "Oh, I favors 'em all," Pa said. "But I mostly like Hezekiel, Ahab, Trotter, and Pontiff the Emporer."
> [John Brown] frowned. "I don't recollect I have read these ... and I have read the Bible through and through."

Brown's interlocutor asks him to share some of his own favorite verses, and Brown supplies them: "Whosoever stoppeth his ear at the cry of the Lord, he also shall cry himself." "Put a Christian in the presence of sin and he will spring at its throat." "Free the slave from the tyranny of sin ... so that the slave *shall ever be free*."[38]

McBride's examples, which contradict exceptionalist authority by, for instance, being wrong, nevertheless reflect the abiding political power of the biblical category even when rendered as something like Hungerford's illiterature. Certain cadences of King James English frame the political escalation of the Civil War as biblical, even sacred, and thus even more exceptionally fraught. (Note, too, that the book of "Ahab," denotes Moby Dick as a biblical book that pushes beyond biblical allusion to, in fact, a kind of canonical inclusion in McBride's depictions of Brown's exception-taking).

---

37. See also Ted A. Smith, *Weird John Brown: Divine Violence and the Limits of Ethics* (Stanford, CA: Stanford University Press, 2014).

38. James McBride, *The Good Lord Bird* (New York: Riverhead, 2014), 12.

Hungerford elaborates on correspondences between Bible and literature in Cormac McCarthy's *Blood Meridian* (1985) by noting first that despite the ubiquity of the comparison—the popular sense that McCarthy's novel offers biblical style or cadence—to think of *Blood Meridian* as somehow biblically "authoritative" proves "counterintuitive."[39] This quality owes to a sense of contradiction, as one of Judge Holden's sermonic reflections on the Bible and war elicits this observation from a listener: "The good book does indeed count war an evil.... Yet there's many a bloody tale of war inside it."[40] In this contradiction resides a complicating factor—an exception—that becomes generated by the biblical cadences of Judge Holden's words and, indeed, of the narrator's broader relation of the story through rich vernacular derived from canonical sources. In this way language itself defies, takes exception to, the very property that makes it exceptional as literature in the first place. Similarly, the postapocalyptic setting and landscape of *The Road* (2006) calls a kind of bluff for the millennial orientation often associated with US exceptionalism. In defiance of certain rapturous expectations that attend the common dispensational assumptions grounded in the book of Revelation, *The Road* enervates the harrowing implications that have been deemphasized in John of Patmos's account by familiarity, by biblical literacy in this way, among those who believe themselves soteriologically exceptional.[41]

Marilynne Robinson's deeply theological fiction bears a particularly defensive posture when considered in light of her essays' arguments for the abiding significance of Calvinism for contemporary political and cultural debates (as in her 2015 essay "Fear," on US gun violence).[42] The Calvinistic notion of *Sola Scriptura* (discernment of God through the authority of scripture alone) provides conceptual and organizational background for novels, including *Gilead* (2006), *Home* (2009), and *Lila* (2015).[43] Yet it is her broader reflections on literature that afford a more specific worldview. In an essay titled "The Book of Books," Robinson speaks broadly of great literary texts as "Socratic dialogues" with biblical legacies and antecedents: "each venture presupposes that meaning can indeed be addressed within

---

39. Hungerford, *Postmodern Belief*, 90.
40. Cormac McCarthy, *Blood Meridian* (New York: Vintage, 1992), 259.
41. Cormac McCarthy, *The Road* (New York: Knopf, 2006).
42. Marilynne Robinson, "Fear," *New York Review of Books*, 24 September 2015.
43. Marilynne Robinson, *Gilead* (New York: Picador, 2006); Robinson, *Home* (New York: Farrar, Straus & Giroux, 2009); Robinson, *Lila* (New York: Picador, 2015).

the constraints of the form and in its language, while the meaning to be discovered through this argument cannot be presupposed."[44] Socratic dialogues are, of course, interrogative—even as the interrogator drives the conversation. In this way we may understand Robinson's biblical mode to resemble the questions demanded by Morrison and Butler—not exceptionalist assertions but tempered and chastening subversions of certainty. Robinson's Calvinism does not draw on this theological legacy to reinforce the exceptional properties of American life. She plies it as a mode of exception-taking, a deliberate anachronism that chips away at presumptions of US progress and virtue.

C. E. Morgan in *All the Living* (2010) and *The Sport of Kings* (2016) draws on different biblical modes, ranging from the quieter meditations of her first novel to the sprawling generational sagas of her second.[45] Like Robinson she reappropriates a relic of US exceptionalism—in this case the Great American Novel—in the attempt to undo contemporary implications of US exceptionalism. The Bible resembles a great novel, she suggests, in that it "relentlessly explores the full complexity of the human and plunges us into the tangled thick of the language, both without regard for consequences."[46] Addressing the cultural milieu that produced the candidacy and election of Donald Trump as US president, replete with his slogan "Make America Great Again," Morgan refuses to concede the category of greatness to such aggressive indecency. She advocates for the resurrection of the Great American Novel as a genre she admits has been abandoned for several decades. She does so not as an expression of US exceptionalism but as its antidote—a kind of left-hand greatness that qualifies as a contradiction of that word. In this way Morgan's reappropriation of the exceptionalist biblical mode inoculates against its grotesque present-tense contexts, tracing a line as she does from Melville to Faulkner to Ellison to Morrison.

What all of this biblical and American literary evidence adds up to is the sense of a prominent shift in recent decades. Much as singular understandings of cultural or religious identity have been shorn from creative

---

44. Marilynne Robinson, "The Book of Books: What Literature Owes the Bible," *New York Times Book Review*, 22 December 2011.

45. C. E. Morgan, *All the Living* (New York: Picador, 2010); Morgan, *The Sport of Kings* (New York: Farrar, Straus & Giroux, 2016).

46. C. E. Morgan, forward to *Light in August*, by William Faulkner (New York: Modern Library, 2012), xix.

expression, so have certain dualisms of race, gender, and sexuality. Whatever these nuances may draw from the diversity of voices and perspectives contained within the Bible, they do so primarily because (at least for readers and writers of literary fiction) no singular biblical center can be said to hold. While such developments surely prove disappointing to some, the sense that these pluralities challenge and work around the older singularities offers hope for richer and more robust literary expression that surely draws from or responds to biblical dimensions no less than earlier examples have done, but also (and no less certainly) does so in different and improved ways.

To denominate writing as literature is to set it apart and, thus, to render it sacred after a fashion. Broadly speaking, American literature—even (or especially) secular American literature—has historically maintained a strong biblical aspect, drawing from both familiarity with and the authority derived from this ancient canon. Likewise, this biblical orientation sets America and its literature apart, marking it as exceptional. While this has never been a fully uncritical enterprise, such critical intent is often regulated in order to maintain a certain exceptionalism at the heart of American identity at home and abroad. This chapter has charted a shift in the past few decades, certainly since the publication of Gunn's 1983 volume, in the literary reception and replication of such exceptionalism. Indeed, the hallmark of this more recent literature is its pronounced willingness to take exception to such biblical exceptionalism by rendering it deeply problematic or even branding it playfully as a kind of biblical illiteracy. As black women, Morrison and Butler overtly challenge (in their respective ways) the historical power of such exceptionalism as it often manifests in racial and gendered terms. Yet the broader survey provided by this coda suggests that such exception-taking has proliferated and that the implications for biblical illiteracy continue apace not as the supplanting of the Bible in American literature but in the Bible's literary reconfiguration. No longer content to remain merely exceptional, it dismantles former legacies even as it reinscribes them for a future age.

Bibliography

Butler, Octavia E. *Parable of the Sower*. New York: Grand Central, 1993.
———. *Parable of the Talents*. New York: Grand Central, 1998.

Callahan, Allen Dwight. *The Talking Book: African Americans and the Bible*. New Haven: Yale University Press, 2006.
Childs, Brevard S. *Introduction to the Old Testament as Scripture*. Philadelphia: Fortress, 1979.
———. *Old Testament Theology in a Canonical Context*. Philadelphia: Fortress, 1985.
Cone, James H. *A Black Theology of Liberation*. Maryknoll, NY: Orbis, 2010.
Ellison, Ralph. "Society, Morality, and the Novel." Pages 698–729 in *The Collected Essays of Ralph Ellison*. Edited by John F. Callahan. New York: Modern Library, 1995.
Felder, Cain Hope, ed. *Stony the Road We Trod: African American Biblical Interpretation*. Minneapolis: Fortress, 1991.
Gunn, Giles. Introduction to *The Bible and American Arts and Letters*. Edited by Giles Gunn. Philadelphia: Fortress; Chico, CA: Scholars Press, 1983.
Hungerford, Amy. *Postmodern Belief: American Literature and Religion since 1960*. Princeton: Princeton University Press, 2010.
Johnson, Sylvester. *The Myth of Ham in Nineteenth-Century American Christianity: Race, Heathens, and the People of God*. New York: Palgrave, 2004.
Malcolm X with Alex Haley. *The Autobiography of Malcolm X*. New York: Ballantine, 1965.
McBride, James. *The Good Lord Bird*. New York: Riverhead, 2014.
McCarthy, Cormac. *Blood Meridian*. New York: Vintage, 1992.
———. *The Road*. New York: Knopf, 2006.
Morgan, C. E. *All the Living*. New York: Picador, 2010.
———. Forward to *Light in August*. By William Faulkner. New York: Modern Library, 2012.
———. *The Sport of Kings*. New York: Farrar, Straus & Giroux, 2016.
Morrison, Toni. *Beloved*. New York: Vintage, 2004.
———. *Song of Solomon*. New York: Vintage, 2004.
Noll, Mark A. *The Civil War as Theological Crisis*. Chapel Hill: University of North Carolina Press, 2006.
Robinson, Marilynne. "The Book of Books: What Literature Owes the Bible." *New York Times Book Review*. 22 December 2011.
———. "Fear." *New York Review of Books*. 24 September, 2015.
———. *Home*. New York: Farrar, Straus & Giroux, 2009.
———. *Gilead*. New York: Picador, 2006.

———. *Lila*. New York: Picador, 2015.
Ruffin, Kimberly J. "Parable of a Twenty-First Century Religion: Octavia Butler's Afrofuturistic Bridge between Science and Religion." *Obsidian III* 6.2–7.1 (2005–2006): 87–104.
Smith, Ted A. *Weird John Brown: Divine Violence and the Limits of Ethics*. Stanford, CA: Stanford University Press, 2014.
Stahlberg, Lesleigh Cushing, and Peter S. Hawkins. *The Bible in the American Short Story*. New York: Bloomsbury, 2018.
Williams, Delores S. *Sisters in the Wilderness: The Challenge of Womanist God-Talk*. Maryknoll, NY: Orbis, 2013.
Wimbush, Vincent L. "The Bible and African Americans: An Outline of an Interpretive History." Pages 81–97 in *Stony the Road We Trod: African American Biblical Interpretation*. Edited by Cain Hope Felder. Minneapolis: Fortress, 1991.
———. "Knowing Ex-centrics/Ex-centric Knowking." Pages 1–22 in *MisReading America: Scriptures and Difference*. Edited by Vincent L. Wimbush. New York: Oxford University Press, 2013.

5
THE BIBLE AND VISUAL ART IN AMERICA

AARON ROSEN

Writing in 1983, in the precursor to the present volume, the esteemed theologian John W. Dixon Jr. set some parameters for his inquiry:

> The problem of "The Bible in American Art" must be distinguished carefully from the larger problem of "religion in American art." They are not the same thing nor is the smaller question rightly understood as a special case of the larger; they are in some degree different problems, however much the areas overlap.[1]

While visual art, and the way we study it, has changed dramatically in the intervening decades, Dixon's intuition remains helpful. Given the multiplicity of ways in which religious themes and questions surface in contemporary art—even just within America—exploring religion writ large would quickly exceed the constraints of this chapter. For those interested in exploring such wider concerns, ranging from the experience of the sublime to civic rituals, my volume *Art and Religion in the Twenty-First Century* might prove a helpful point of entry.[2] For its part, this essay will restrict itself to identifying some primary, hopefully illuminating, ways in which the Bible appears in recent American art.

While it is helpful to set similar boundaries to Dixon's, within these guideposts the terrain looks dramatically different thirty-five years

---

1. John W. Dixon Jr., "The Bible in American Painting," in *The Bible and American Arts and Letters*, ed. Giles Gunn (Philadelphia: Fortress; Chico, CA: Scholars Press, 1983), 157.
2. Aaron Rosen, *Art and Religion in the Twenty-First Century* (London: Thames & Hudson, 2015).

later. To begin with, the question of what should count as art is highly tendentious. While Dixon was writing at a time of burgeoning experimentation in fields such as performance, installation, and video art, his essay ignores such developments. Tellingly, while he begins his essay by identifying the Bible in American art as his subject, he almost exclusively discusses painting, without ever pausing to justify this move. In doing so, Dixon was clearly a product of his times. While artists in this period strained against and often successfully dismantled traditional boundaries, academics often struggled to catch up. This was doubly true of religious scholars, whose definitions of art tended to lag behind the evolving categories of art historians and critics. Dixon concludes his 1983 essay with an extensive discussion of the works of two great titans of abstract expressionism, Mark Rothko and Barnett Newman, who both died in 1970.[3] Well after Dixon's essay, scholars of art and religion continued to treat abstract expressionism as the apotheosis of modern art. While this would have delighted Rothko, who famously predicted a thousand-year reign for abstraction in the visual arts,[4] the truth is that even when Rothko made these remarks a generation of younger artists was already scrambling to dethrone the orthodoxy he promulgated. An updated assessment of the place of the Bible in American art must, first of all, attempt to do justice to the multifarious practice of contemporary artists. In this essay, I will attempt to give an indication of this variety by analyzing examples from three fields that have seen tremendous growth in recent decades: graphic novels, digital art, and environmental art.

Art is not the only thorny term in the search for the Bible in American art. *American* is also less self-evident than it might first appear. Dixon seeks to identify an authentically American spirit in the visual arts, capable of standing alongside what he views as the more coherent categories of say French or Chinese art. It is no mistake that he concludes his survey with a paean to the abstract expressionists who—despite the inspiration they drew from various sources, including European surrealists—believed they had pioneered the first truly American school of painting, a claim trumpeted by the critic Clement Greenberg, who famously termed these works "American-Type Painting."[5] While subse-

---

3. Dixon, "Bible in American Painting," 174–80.

4. James Breslin, *Mark Rothko: A Biography* (Chicago: University of Chicago Press, 1993), 431.

5. Clement Greenberg, *Art and Culture* (Boston: Beacon, 1989), 208.

quent generations of American artists have continued to play a leading role in the art world, it is increasingly difficult to make claims for any dominant or distinctly American school or style of art. The art world might have epicenters in New York and Los Angeles, but it is now indisputably global, with major art schools, museums, biennials, and fairs from London to Berlin, São Paolo, and Dubai. In this global context, the most important dialogues between artists, curators, dealers, critics, and academics are less nationally determined than ever. *American art* is a useful descriptor to frame broad inquiries or to discuss artistic responses to specific issues, such as the terrorist attacks of September 11 or police violence towards African Americans. But in many cases it can be either too small or too big a category to do much conceptual work. When it comes to assessing the role of the Bible in contemporary American art, we must be cognizant, on the one hand, of the way in which artists today continually look outwards, beyond their country of origin. At the same time, we must pay attention to artists' hybrid identities, considering how their religious, ethnic, and sexual self-definitions shape their sense of what it means to be an American. In the section that follows, I will attempt to break down some basic preconceptions about artists who address biblical themes.

There is one more important piece of the puzzle missing from Dixon's analysis: context. Dixon offers sensitive reflections on key works, especially by Thomas Eakins, Albert Pinkham Ryder, and Barnett Newman, and he is well aware of how individual spectators might devise different interpretations of such works. However, like many scholars of his era, he pays hardly any attention to the material conditions in which such encounters occur. One of the most promising developments of twenty-first century scholarship has been a widening of scholars' fields of vision to encompass varied dimensions of visual and material experience and the discourses that shape and structure these encounters. One of the key figures in this material turn is David Morgan, who helpfully coins the term "sacred gaze" to describe how images *become* religious in our eyes. He writes:

> *Sacred gaze* is a term that designates the particular configuration of ideas, attitudes, and customs that informs a religious act of seeing as it occurs within a given cultural and historical setting. A sacred gaze is the manner in which a way of seeing invests an image, a viewer, or an act of viewing with spiritual significance. The study of religious visual culture is therefore the study of images, but also the practices and habits that rely

on images as well as the attitudes and preconceptions that inform vision as a cultural act.[6]

As we recall from Dixon's remarks at the outset, we should be careful not to treat biblical and religious resonances as simply interchangeable. Yet, as Morgan would remind us, even the ostensibly self-evident problem of the "Bible in American Art" is implicated by the complexities of the sacred gaze. Categorizing an artistic subject as biblical is not only conditioned by multiple material, cultural, and ideological factors; it structures and conditions religious possibilities. With this in mind, I will offer some reflections in this chapter about how biblical references are activated differently within disparate spaces from religious institutions to museums. In brief, then, this essay will revolve around three basic questions about contemporary American art: *Who* engages with biblical subjects? *What* methods and media do they use? And *where*, *when*, and *how* are biblical references rendered visible?

Piety and Impropriety

The mere mention of a contemporary artist engaging with biblical subject matter summons competing stereotypes. On the one hand stands the artist as purveyor of pious kitsch; on the other the talented but godless iconoclast. Both stereotypes are problematic in their own right, and it is important to clear away some of the presumptions they entail. Taking the former stereotype first, we might turn our attention to Thomas Kinkade, the artist behind such ubiquitous works as *The Cross* (2010), which depicts Calvary glistening amidst candy-floss colored clouds. While such works may well be considered kitsch, this makes them no less interesting when it comes to assessing the place of the Bible in American culture. As many as one in twenty American homes owns a print or other object produced by Kinkade, the self-anointed "painter of light."[7] I can report anecdotally that every time I visited the local framer in my former home of Billings, Montana, I seemed to spot a new Kinkade image being fastened into a

---

6. David Morgan, *The Sacred Gaze: Religious Visual Culture in Theory and Practice* (Berkeley: University of California Press, 2005), 3.

7. Alexis Boylan, introduction to *Thomas Kinkade: The Painter in the Mall*, ed. Alexis Boylan (Durham, NC: Duke University Press, 2011), 1.

gilded frame! Kinkade might lack the brooding Romanticism of Caspar David Friedrich, but for many contemporary Americans his insertion of Christian symbols into a proudly unfurling vista appears to be no less religiously charged than the works of his German precursor. Similarly, Jon McNaughton's *One Nation under God* (2009)—in which Jesus clasps the US Constitution surrounded by the founding fathers—might rankle contemporary critics with its strongly didactic content. However, it sits within a tradition of last judgment paintings that have referenced the perceived heroes and villains of their own day.[8] Both Kinkade and McNaughton muster historically effective strategies from the art of the past to convey an image of the United States as it should be, whether conjuring images of a halcyon, biblically anchored past or preparing for an apocalyptically tinged struggle to "make America great again." As Morgan notes, "simply scorning [such works] misses the opportunity to understand something powerful moving through many religious sub-cultures in the United States today."[9]

On the opposite side of the spectrum stands the image of artists as cynical unbelievers, scorning the Bible to the cackling applause of intellectuals. A string of well-publicized controversies from the mid-1980s to the present have tended to reinforce a predictable pattern. Various artists have found themselves at the center of conflagrations over biblical imagery, including Renee Cox, Chris Ofili, and Cosimo Cavallaro. But the reception of two works from the late 1980s demonstrates this trend particularly well: Andres Serrano's photograph *Piss Christ* (1987) and David Wojnarowicz's unfinished short film, *A Fire in My Belly* (1986–1987). *Piss Christ*—which shows a crucifixion suspended in urine—first came to national attention when US Senator Jesse Helms used an exhibition of it in 1989 as a pretext to call for severe funding cuts to the National Endowment for the Arts, part of a larger assault on what the senator considered the propagation of anti-Christian values.[10] When the work was exhibited in New York in 2012, Republican lawmakers, the Catholic League, and conservative pundits demanded unsuccessfully that President Barack Obama denounce the work, repeating the same charges of

---

8. David Morgan, "The Art of Jon McNaughton, the Tea Party's Painter," *Religion & Politics*, 25 July 2012, https://tinyurl.com/SBL6704y.

9. Morgan, "Art of Jon McNaughton."

10. "National Endowment for the Arts: Controversies in Free Speech," NCAC.org, https://tinyurl.com/SBL6704r1.

blasphemy that had been leveled against the piece a generation earlier.[11] For its part, Wojnarowicz's video exploring suffering and myth became a lightning rod for controversy during the 2010–2011 exhibition *Hide/Seek: Difference and Desire in American Portraiture* at the Smithsonian's National Portrait Gallery.[12] Labeled anti-Christian hate speech by the Catholic League and key Republican congressmen who threatened to withhold federal funding for the Smithsonian, the work was pulled from the exhibition.

These recent controversies expose what could almost be termed nostalgia for the culture wars of a bygone era, those good old days when threatening public funding for the arts and bemoaning assaults on traditional values felt fresh and invigorating! Digging beneath the surface, these recycled jeremiads have very little to do with either protecting the Bible or Christianity. As confrontational as its title may sound, *Piss Christ* can be read more coherently as a devotional image, produced by an artist born and bred in a Brooklyn neighborhood steeped in Catholicism. What better way to meditate on the torments and degradation of Christ—both in his time and ours—than to see his form submerged in urine? At the same time, the resplendence of the image, suffused in golden light like a Byzantine icon, also seems to signal Christ's capacity to triumph over ignominy. Likewise, the controversy over a mere three-second section in Wojnarowicz's thirteen-minute video—in which ants crawl over a crucifix—ignores ample art historical precedents for a flayed and even putrefying Savior. We need only think of Jesus's gangrenous, weeping wounds in Matthias Gruenewald's *Isenheim Altarpiece* (1515) to make a case for Wojnarowicz's *restraint* while confronting a world ravaged by HIV/AIDS, the disease that would later take his life. Ironically, reproaches of Serrano and Wojnarowicz—much like denigrations of Kinkade and McNaughton—fail to contextualize these works within the wider tradition of Christian art and spirituality. Disputes over *how* the Bible is depicted often turn out to be fights about *who* is doing the depicting.

---

11. Colin Campbell, "Congressman Calls Obama Out for Defending Muhammad, But Not Jesus," *The Observer*, 21 September 2012, https://tinyurl.com/SBL6704q1.

12. Catholic League for Religious and Civil Rights, "The Arts," https://tinyurl.com/SBL6704v; cf. Christopher Knight, "Gay Art: The Catholic League Responds to Commentary on 'Anti-Gay Bullying,'" *Los Angeles Times*, 22 January 2011, https://tinyurl.com/SBL6704x.

Medium and Message

In recent decades, art has become increasingly difficult to pigeonhole into traditional categories such as painting, sculpture, printmaking, and photography. Not only do artists specialize in fields ranging from performance to video to installation art, many have refused to define themselves by a single medium, preferring to move fluidly between different modes of expression. Rather than attempt a comprehensive overview of how the Bible has surfaced in various art forms, I want to focus instead on a few select media—namely, graphic novels, digital art, and environmental art—that signal the sheer breadth of recent work engaging biblical subjects. These new works do more than simply illustrate or represent the Bible. They change how we read it, disclosing tantalizing horizons for future artists.

Comics may seem at first like an unlikely, irreverent, even offensive medium through which to explore scripture. Yet, since the 1960s the medium of comics has increasingly evolved, tackling serious themes whilst developing complex representational and narrative strategies. To many practitioners, critics, and readers, the term *comix* is preferable to comics, denoting the art form's underground roots and its complicated blend (or co-mix-ing) of image and text. The media theorist and graphic novelist Douglas Rushkoff is not merely puckish when he suggests that the "Bible may have actually been better off as a comic book."[13] Comix present the opportunity to draw out dimensions of the text that other art forms struggle to capture. R. Crumb uses his signature smutty style to disclose the bodily, even crude dimensions of the original text of Genesis, to which most translations apply a fig leaf.[14] But comix can do more than sensitize us to salacious subtexts. Through their highly adaptable structure they can also suggest new hermeneutic possibilities. In *Megillat Esther* (2005), J. T. Waldman draws upon the haptic experience of reading the scroll of Esther to create a work in which words and images unfurl across the page.[15] In the comic book *Testament: Akedah* (2006), Douglas Rushkoff and illustrator Liam Sharp interweave the story of the binding of Isaac (Gen 22) with a dystopian narrative set in the near future, and mythic tales

---

13. Douglas Rushkoff and Liam Sharp, *Testament: Akedah* (Vertigo, 2006), n.p.
14. R. Crumb, *Genesis* (New York: Norton, 2009).
15. J. T. Waldman, *Megillat Esther* (Philadelphia: Jewish Publication Society, 2005).

from ancient cultures.[16] The result emphasizes the palimpsestic nature of the Bible itself, composed of different authorial and editorial layers, each pointing toward different interpretive possibilities. For Rushkoff, comics is better positioned than any other medium to reveal and extend the process of the text's creation, which he compares to open-source collaboration in computer programming.[17] While rewriting and reimaging the Bible in this way might discomfit literalists, the intrinsically democratic spirit of such an endeavor might feel quintessentially American to others.[18]

Digital technology not only provides a powerful metaphor for understanding interpretive possibilities; it is already a key part of how many people engage with the Bible today. Bespoke software allows new methods of searching texts, comparing translations, and accessing commentaries; apps can deliver daily devotions, converting phones into Books of Hours; and social media spawns new communities of interpreters. While a number of artists have touched upon such intersections between digital technology and the Bible, no one has probed this interface in greater depth than the American artist Michael Takeo Magruder. Magruder takes Rushkoff's parallel between computer coding and biblical composition a step further, recognizing the theological implications of the coder *qua* creator. In *Visions of Our Communal Dreams v2.0* (2012), Magruder provides an apparatus for gallery visitors to help shape a shared, virtual Eden (fig. 1).

"I sought to adopt God's position as creator and instigator by constructing a beautiful realm of open possibilities that others could inhabit as they desired," he explains.[19] Magruder imagines "the world's first rays of virtual sunlight illuminat[ing] a newly rendered synthetic landscape made from data and code—the fundamental building blocks of creation in the Information Age."[20] Rather than retreating from reality, this simulation models a process of collaborative world-building that can be downloaded, so to speak, into the real world. Of course, just as easily, the same technology can also generate communal nightmares, as Magruder explores

---

16. Rushkoff and Sharp, *Testament: Akedah*.
17. Rushkoff and Sharp, *Testament: Akedah*.
18. Other recent works laced with biblical references include Craig Thompson, *Blankets* (Marietta, GA: Top Shelf, 2003); Craig Thompson, *Habibi* (New York: Faber & Faber, 2011); Steve Ross, *Marked* (New York: Seabury, 2005); and Gary Panter, *Songy of Paradise* (Seattle: Fantagraphics, 2017).
19. Personal Communication with Michael Takeo Magruder, 14 May 2014.
20. Personal Communication with Michael Takeo Magruder, 14 May 2014.

Fig. 1 Michael Takeo Magruder with Drew Baker, Erik Fleming, and David Steele, *Visions of Our Communal Dreams* (2012). Image copyright and courtesy of the artist.

in his 2014 exhibition *De/coding the Apocalypse*, which grew out of close readings of the book of Revelation. Ultimately, Magruder leaves it open to interpretation whether our ever-evolving technology will help us realize prophetic possibilities or force open the seals of our destruction.

Our potential for self-destruction is nowhere more evident than in the rapidly accelerating effects of manmade climate change. In the United States, the political debate over climate change has been increasingly framed in terms of faith, with a sizeable number of evangelical Christians denying or expressing strong doubts about global warming in the face of overwhelming scientific evidence. At the root of this reluctance seems to be a general anxiety about scientific discourse—especially its ability to challenge biblical accounts of creation—as well as a reflexive rejection of causes associated with the political left, seen as opponents of traditional values. The irony is that refusing to acknowledge this manmade catastrophe actually runs counter to a key point of scripture, which emphasizes human responsibility for the environment. In the garden of Eden, for instance, humanity is entrusted with the stewardship of nature (Gen 1:28–30), while Noah is charged with preserving the planet's biodiversity (Gen 6:19–7:3). Building on such examples, there is a tremendous opportunity—as an increasing number of American artists have recognized—to reclaim environmental concern as a religious imperative.

One of the most innovative artists addressing this topic at the moment is Sam Van Aken. For his living sculpture, *Tree of 40 Fruits* (2008–2013), he spent years painstakingly grafting branches of assorted stone fruits—including plums, apricots, peaches, and nectarines—onto a single trunk, so that all these different species might blossom and fructify together (fig. 2).

As he notes, the number forty is frequently used in the Bible to symbolize a boundless multitude.[21] In this case, the number evokes the story of the flood, which according to Genesis lasted forty days and forty nights (Gen 7:4). When the floodwaters receded and Noah finally set foot on dry land, the Bible informs us that he immediately did two things: he offered thanksgiving to the Lord (Gen 8:20) and planted a vineyard (Gen 9:20). This second act was just as important as the first. It confirmed that Noah not only feared the Lord but believed God's promise never again to destroy the earth. Today, it is we who must promise that "as long as the earth endures,

---

21. Sam Van Aken, "The Tree of Forty Fruit Is Exactly as Awesome as It Sounds," interview by Lauren Salkeld, *Epicurious*, https://tinyurl.com/SBL6704z.

Fig. 2. Sam Van Aken, *Tree of 40 Fruits* (2008–2013). Image courtesy of the artist.

seedtime and harvest, cold and heat, summer and winter, day and night, shall not cease" (Gen 8:22, NRSV). But while our roles may be reversed, we can still seal this covenant with the same simple act of faith: planting fruit. In an age of environmental catastrophe, Van Aken's *Tree of 40 Fruits* provides a hopeful symbol of blessing and abundance. For the great American landscape painters of the nineteenth century, the land that stretched before them was imbued with biblical majesty. Today, that promise must be carefully regrown, and artists amongst others must sow the seeds.

Places and Spaces

After considering the motivations and materials of contemporary artists, it is time to look at questions of context a bit more closely. Where is it today that we might expect to find art that deals with Bible? The most straightforward answer, of course, is religious institutions. While religious patronage is certainly not like it was in centuries past, when it provided the main source of employment for Western artists, many American churches today have robust programs of visual art. To name just a few in New York City, we might think of the Cathedral of Saint John the Divine, Trinity Church Wall Street, and Saint Peter's Lutheran Church, which each have a reputation for innovative permanent installations and temporary exhibitions. The art displayed in churches often broadly follows the prevailing artistic tastes in the surrounding area, and it is not surprising that a city like New York boasts some of the more adventurous ecclesial art. Still, it is important not to make regional presumptions, and there is strong contemporary work being produced for institutions across the country. To note but one example, the Catholic painter Alfonse Borysewicz—who often takes inspiration from specific biblical passages and liturgical rites—has created an impressive body of work that hangs in churches, monasteries and seminaries from Brooklyn to Grand Rapids (fig. 3).

Fig. 3. Alfonse Borysewicz, *Cor Unum* (2004). The Oratory Church of Saint Boniface, Brooklyn, NY. Courtesy of artist.

Whether urban, suburban, or rural, congregations often struggle to find a balance between accessibility and innovation. This can be thrown into especially sharp relief when commissioning works on biblical subjects, which activate strong preconceptions. The process surrounding the construction and decoration of the Cathedral of Our Lady of the Angels (2002) in Los Angeles encapsulates this tension. After commissioning a daring architectural design from Rafael Moneo, the cathedral moved in a different direction for its interior, opting for explicit representations of holy personages, with clear references to the local community. From the architect's perspective, the cathedral's fear of art that might be labelled "in any way elitist" led to a missed spiritual and aesthetic opportunity.[22] For

---

22. Rafael Moneo, "Architecture as a Vehicle for Religious Experience: The Los Angeles Cathedral," in *Constructing the Ineffable: Contemporary Sacred Architecture*, ed. Karla Britton (New Haven: Yale University Press, 2010), 168.

others, its conscious embrace of traditional Hispanic visual culture made the cathedral more, not less, modern. Ultimately, of course, each community must decide for itself how far to press its tastes and where the greatest benefit lies.

This tug-of-war between innovation and accessibility applies to synagogues as well, which must manage the same risk that art might be deemed elitist, on the one hand, or banal, on the other. But there are additional complications that Jews confront when creating works of art for sacred spaces. A key concern is how to interpret the second commandment, the so-called prohibition against graven images (Exod 20:4; Deut 5:8). While it is a still a common misconception that the commandment prohibits visual art *in toto*, there is little basis for this in Jewish history or tradition, as scholars have demonstrated convincingly in recent years.[23] In practice, Jews have usually interpreted the second commandment permissively, and excavations of late antique synagogues at Beth Alpha and Sepphoris have even revealed lavish depictions of pagan gods. When it comes to synagogue art, one might even argue that modern designers have been more cautious than their ancient precursors!

While there are differences across denominations, contemporary Orthodox and Conservative congregations tend to shy away from human figures in synagogue art and certainly anything that might risk anthropomorphizing the Divine. Still, this reticence should not be confused with a lack of creativity. Indeed, such restrictions have at times yielded extraordinary results, such as Archie Rand's murals for the Orthodox B'nai Yosef Synagogue in Brooklyn and Adolph Gottlieb's stained glass windows for the Conservative Park Avenue Synagogue in Manhattan. Reform congregations have taken the most widely varied approach to visual art among these denominations. In 2010, Temple Emanu-El B'ne Jeshurun in Milwaukee, Wisconsin unveiled an entire interior—from wall paintings to liturgical implements—created by the Orthodox artist Tobi Kahn (fig. 4).

To Dixon's question whether there exists "a nonrepresentational art that is biblical,"[24] Kahn presents a compelling argument in the affirmative, conjuring mysterious forms—by turns cellular, geological, and

---

23. See, e.g., Kalman Bland, *The Artless Jew: Medieval and Modern Affirmations and Denials of the Visual* (Princeton: Princeton University Press, 2000); Margaret Olin, *The Nation without Art: Examining Modern Discourses on Jewish Art* (Lincoln: University of Nebraska Press, 2001).

24. Dixon, "Bible in American Painting," 175.

Fig. 4. Tobi Kahn, Interior (2010). Temple Emanu-El B'ne Jeshurun in Milwaukee, WI. Courtesy of artist.

Fig. 5. Siona Benjamin, *Zodiac Floor* (2015). Central Reform Congregation in Saint Louis, MO. Courtesy of artist.

cosmic—which channel the dynamic energy of creation (Gen 1:1–3). On the opposite end of the formal spectrum stands the tiled floor that Siona Benjamin designed for Central Reform Congregation in Saint Louis, Missouri (2015) (fig. 5).

Inspired by the zodiac mosaics of Beth Alpha and Sepphoris, the Indian-born artist created concentric blue circles that seem to oscillate like a whirlpool, swirling together biblical iconography with images from other faiths, including Hinduism and Islam. Rather than making the work less Jewish, this exuberant hybridity expresses a cultural openness that has become a defining emphasis of Reform Judaism in the United States.

After looking at the place of biblical motifs in religious institutions, it is time to turn now to a more ambivalent category: museums. The great museum collections of the United States, from the Metropolitan Museum in New York City to the National Gallery of Art in Washington, DC are replete with works on biblical themes, mostly from premodern periods, when scriptural imagery was ubiquitous. Whilst major national collections like the National Gallery do feature select modern works with biblical connections—such as Barnett Newman's magisterial *Stations of the Cross: Lema Sabachthani* (1958–1965)—the Bible is rarely an emphasis in their modern holdings. There are, however, a number of smaller museums that have sprung up in recent decades that have bridged this gap. On the campus of Saint Louis University, for instance, Terrence Dempsey, S.J., developed the Museum of Contemporary Religious Art in the 1990s by repurposing a Jesuit chapel. Meanwhile, on the West Coast, two seminal scholars of religion and visual art, Jane Dillenberger and Doug Adams, built up the Center for the Arts and Religion at Graduate Theological Union in Berkeley, which dedicated a gallery in Adams's memory in 2009.

Several museums specifically focus on the Bible and visual culture. The Museum of Biblical Art in Dallas was founded in 1966 but was reconstructed and expanded in 2010. On the one hand, the museum explicitly seeks to engage Christian visitors looking for a devotional experience, as in its Via Dolorosa Sculpture Garden. On the other hand, it endeavors to engage in interfaith dialogue through its National Center for Jewish Art, which collects works by contemporary Jewish artists including Kahn. It is especially revealing to contrast the fates of two other biblical museums: the Museum of Biblical Art in New York City (MOBIA), which closed its doors in 2015, and the Museum of the Bible in Washington, DC, which opened in 2017. The curator Ena Heller opened a gallery space in the headquarters of the American Bible Society in 1997, which became MOBIA in 2005. As Heller explained in 2009, "to me the importance of the Bible is cultural and historic [and] the point that we're trying to make is that there's this one book that has influenced Western civilization more than any other book."[25] Despite this scholarly insistence on exploring the Bible's reception history, MOBIA still struggled—as Heller noted—under the assumption that it had "some sort of hidden agenda."[26] If, on the one hand, MOBIA wanted to reassure secular audiences that it had no desire to proselytize, it also had to tread lightly concerning the missional work of its host organization, the American Bible Society, and appeal to visitors and donors who wanted to see the museum embrace a more confessional approach to biblical subject matter.[27] Treading this delicate line ultimately proved too difficult as the museum sought to establish secure financial footing to move into a new space.

At the same time that MOBIA was struggling, the Museum of the Bible was consolidating its plans by actively embracing an evangelical agenda, spearheaded by its chairman and chief donor, Steve Green. Green is the founder of the Hobby Lobby supply chain, which in 2014 won the right to discriminate against female employees' healthcare based on the religious beliefs of the corporation's owners.[28] Issues surrounding the Green family's religious and political agenda have been compounded recently by revelations about Hobby Lobby's illegal acquisition of artifacts from the Middle East.[29] Given this backdrop, it is an open question whether the Museum of the Bible can deliver on its stated educational and research aims[30] in a way that is consistent with the standards of other museums in the capital. It is also unclear to what extent the most adventurous contemporary artists, and those who own their work, will lend or sell to the

---

25. Cited in Aaron Rosen, "Unpacking the Bible: The Museum of Biblical Art," *Art & Christianity* 59 (2009): n.p.

26. Rosen, "Unpacking the Bible."

27. Randy Kennedy, "Museum of Biblical Art to Close, Despite Recent Crowds," *New York Times*, 28 April 2015, https://tinyurl.com/SBL6704w.

28. Adam Liptak, "Supreme Court Rejects Contraceptives Mandate for Some Corporations," *The New York Times*, June 30, 2014, https://tinyurl.com/SBL6704p1.

29. Julie Zauzmer, and Sarah Pulliam Bailey, "Hobby Lobby's $3 Million Smuggling Case Casts a Cloud over the Museum of the Bible," *The Washington Post*, 6 July 2017, https://tinyurl.com/SBL6704a1.

30. "Scholars Initiative," Museum of the Bible, https://www.museumofthebible.org/research.

museum and, if so, whether the museum will have the stomach to display works that question the ideological commitments of the museum's leadership. While religious *criticism* has sometimes successfully threatened museums—as we observed in the first section of this chapter—it remains to be seen whether religious *support* is enough to overcome educational and curatorial concerns about a museum.

Conclusion

This chapter has surveyed some key ways in which the Bible appears in contemporary American art. While focusing on visual art has allowed us to contain an otherwise sprawling inquiry, it is important—in parting—that we do not ring-fence this category too closely. Visual art is but one dimension of the wider field of visual culture, and the Bible surfaces in every facet of this domain, from the content we browse on the internet to the television we binge watch to the leaflets we discover crammed into our mailboxes. Indeed, had this chapter been longer, I would have sampled the vast trove of memes that have recently populated the internet, reimagining Donald Trump into biblical paintings (e.g., "Blessed are the poor.... Wrong!").[31] Art does not exist in some sacrosanct realm, safe from the swells of everyday concerns. It bobs within the frothy, chaotic currents of visual culture. W. J. T. Mitchell asked in the title of a recent volume, *What Do Pictures Want?*[32] The question is deceptively simple, inviting us to consider not only the demands we make of images but the demands we allow them to make of us through the culturally constructed act of seeing. In the context of the current inquiry, we might also formulate a follow-up: what does the Bible want? Many Americans—too many, I would argue—think they know the answer to this question. Taken together, the first question helps destabilize the second. When the Bible becomes an image, it should give us pause. Even the most seemingly straightforward illustration makes additional demands of us. The best art today wants to interrogate our religious certainties, not confirm them.

---

31. "Blessed Are the Poor, Wrong. Donald Trump Jesus Meme," Starecat.com, https://tinyurl.com/SBL6704s1.

32. W. J. T. Mitchell, *What Do Pictures Want?* (Chicago: University of Chicago Press, 2005).

Bibliography

Bland, Kalman. *The Artless Jew: Medieval and Modern Affirmations and Denials of the Visual*. Princeton: Princeton University Press, 2000.

"Blessed Are the Poor, Wrong. Donald Trump Jesus Meme." Starecat.com. https://tinyurl.com/SBL6704s1.

Boylan, Alexis. Introduction to *Thomas Kinkade: The Painter in the Mall*. Edited by Alexis Boylan. Durham, NC: Duke University Press, 2011.

Breslin, James. *Mark Rothko: A Biography*. Chicago: University of Chicago Press, 1993.

Campbell, Colin. "Congressman Calls Obama out for Defending Muhammad, But Not Jesus," *The Observer*. 21 September 2012. https://tinyurl.com/SBL6704q1.

Catholic League for Religious and Civil Rights. "The Arts." Catholicleague.org. https://tinyurl.com/SBL6704v.

Crumb, R. *Genesis*. New York: Norton, 2009.

Dixon, John W., Jr. "The Bible in American Painting." Pages 159–85 in *The Bible and American Arts and Letters*. Edited by Giles Gunn. Philadelphia: Fortress; Chico, CA: Scholars Press, 1983.

Greenberg, Clement. *Art and Culture*. Boston: Beacon, 1989.

Kennedy, Randy. "Museum of Biblical Art to Close, Despite Recent Crowds." *New York Times*. 28 April 2015. https://tinyurl.com/SBL6704w.

Knight, Christopher. "Gay Art: The Catholic League Responds to Commentary on 'Anti-Gay Bullying.'" *Los Angeles Times*. 22 January 2011. https://tinyurl.com/SBL6704x.

Liptak, Adam. "Supreme Court Rejects Contraceptives Mandate for Some Corporations." *The New York Times*. 30 June 2014. https://tinyurl.com/SBL6704p1.

Mitchell, W. J. T. *What Do Pictures Want?* Chicago: University of Chicago Press, 2005.

Moneo, Rafael. "Architecture as a Vehicle for Religious Experience: The Los Angeles Cathedral." Pages 158–69 in *Constructing the Ineffable: Contemporary Sacred Architecture*. Edited by Karla Britton. New Haven: Yale University Press, 2010.

Morgan, David. "The Art of Jon McNaughton, the Tea Party's Painter." *Religion & Politics*. 25 July 2012. https://tinyurl.com/SBL6704y.

———. *The Sacred Gaze: Religious Visual Culture in Theory and Practice*. Berkeley: University of California Press, 2005.

"National Endowment for the Arts: Controversies in Free Speech." NCAC.org. https://tinyurl.com/SBL6704r1.

Olin, Margaret. *The Nation without Art: Examining Modern Discourses on Jewish Art*. Lincoln: University of Nebraska Press, 2001.

Panter, Gary. *Songy of Paradise*. Seattle: Fantagraphics, 2017.

Rosen, Aaron. *Art and Religion in the Twenty-First Century*. London: Thames & Hudson, 2015.

———. "Unpacking the Bible: The Museum of Biblical Art." *Art & Christianity* 59 (2009): n.p.

Ross, Steve. *Marked*. New York: Seabury, 2005.

Rushkoff, Douglas, and Liam Sharp. *Testament: Akedah*. Vertigo, 2006.

"Scholars Initiative." Museum of the Bible. https://www.museumofthebible.org/research.

Thompson, Craig. *Blankets*. Marietta, GA: Top Shelf, 2003.

———. *Habibi*. New York: Faber & Faber, 2011.

Waldman, J. T. *Megillat Esther*. Philadelphia: Jewish Publication Society, 2005.

Van Aken, Sam. "The Tree of Forty Fruit Is Exactly as Awesome as It Sounds." Interview by Lauren Salkeld. *Epicurious*. https://tinyurl.com/SBL6704z.

Zauzmer, Julie, and Sarah Pulliam Bailey. "Hobby Lobby's $3 Million Smuggling Case Casts a Cloud over the Museum of the Bible." *The Washington Post*. 6 July 2017. https://tinyurl.com/SBL6704a1.

6
THE BIBLE AND AMERICAN MUSIC

JOSEPH ORCHARD

This chapter discusses the Bible and American musical culture since 1980, beginning with a brief summary of the dominating trends in American music since that time and then giving an overview of specific compositions by an array of composers, many of whom are well known. This latter discussion will mostly be broken down by biblically related themes and by selected books of the Bible.

Over the span of the thirty-five-year period since the article by Edwin Good was written,[1] the terrain of American art music has shifted. In the 1980s, the American art music scene was dominated by the spirit or presence of groups of American composers, which were distinguished by certain stylistic traits. Probably the most influential style was that of serialism.[2] Serialists dominated music composition in academia and included composers such as Milton Babbitt, George Perle, Elliott Carter, and Charles Wuorinen. But there were other styles as well: Howard Hanson and Samuel Barber wrote in a romantic style called the Rochester school; Leonard Bernstein and Aaron Copland both embraced popular culture (musical theater, jazz idioms, American hymns) in similar ways;

---

1. Edwin M. Good, "The Bible and American Music," in *The Bible and American Arts and Letters*, ed. Giles Gunn (Philadelphia: Fortress; Chico, CA: Scholars Press, 1983), 131–58.

2. Serialism is a sophisticated and rigorous method of composition in which musical elements such as pitch, dynamics, rhythm, etc. are each organized into a series; the series, in turn, governs the ordering of those individual elements in a composition. It found particular favor in American academia because of the intellectual demands of the technique, together with its strong links to the Western music tradition. The technique was employed by a broad spectrum of composers.

the minimalists, such as Philip Glass, John Adams, and Steve Reich, were young but well known; experimentalism had waned since the 1960s but remained a factor. One additional element, cultural or ethnic identity, though not a technique, often dominated music in which it was present. The music of William Grant Still is one outstanding example. These are some of the styles and trends that could be found in American classical music around 1980, and each was an element in the American sound.

Mixed in with these styles and approaches were elements of individualism, distinguished by composers using various combinations of these stylistic traits but not specifically identified by one in particular. There was a reactionary element to several of these individualists, primarily a reaction to hegemonic academic intellectualism. In the music of many of these individualists, such as David Diamond and Morton Gould, sentiment is expressed unapologetically, with arching romantic melodies and measured chromaticism. This last group has gained significant ground in the last thirty-five years, and their stylistic palette has expanded.

Since the early 1980s, the American sound has splintered into innumerable bits, and the specific stylistic labels have largely succumbed to individualism. While composers may still be identified with their teachers and with a predominant style or technique, their individualism and independence is the most prominent element. Each composer defines themselves with their music and can be associated with a multitude of styles, embracing different levels of their own cultural experience and different types of formal education in composition. One effect of individualism, or diversity, is the undermining of any sense of a canonic repertoire. There is no typically American composer, except to the degree that they are unique. There may come a time when hindsight will reveal a coherent view of the current musical terrain, but for now, it remains fragmentary. One result of these developments is that any discussion of American music is something of a free-for-all as critics and historians struggle to discern trends. Thus, beyond identifying works as being written by a composer of American heritage or significantly exposed to American culture, defining a work as American is somewhat elusive. Consequently, this discussion is also fragmentary, and similar to Paul Griffith's 1995 survey of modern music, weighted by personal experience.[3]

---

3. Paul Griffiths, *Modern Music and After: Directions since 1945* (Oxford: Oxford University Press, 1995), xiii–xv; Richard Taruskin and Christopher Gibbs echo this

It is safe to say that the Bible maintains a presence in American music. In some ways, this presence is predictable, because as long as there are churches and synagogues with any sort of music program, the Bible, which contains the central texts for these religious institutions, will be subject to fresh musical treatments. Also, while the music of these spaces may not strongly influence the culture in which they exist, it does give life to the Jewish and Christian beliefs they preach and nurtures the sense that the Bible continues to be relevant to Americans' lives. Also, sociologists tell us that those who worship regularly make the best citizens: more law abiding, more generous, more socially active, and with more stable families and more regular jobs. These civic virtues can be found in scripture, and it is not surprising that they thrive in members of institutions guided, in various degrees, by this book.[4]

That being said, it must be admitted that the Bible presently has almost no specific musical identity in American culture, with the exception, perhaps, of music for Christmas. Even in largely secularized form, Christmas songs with direct and indirect references to the nativity remain a part of the standard repertoire. From a biblical perspective, one reason Christmas, in itself, is so significant is because it is foreshadowed by the Hebrew Bible, and its implications are played out in the New Testament, even if another event, the resurrection, looms larger theologically in the latter. Thus, Christmas embraces large swaths of scripture. As shall be seen, American composers have been expanding the repertoire touching on this singular biblical event.

Christmas

It will readily be seen that there are strong efforts to explore the event and its implications more deeply. New Jersey composer John Harbison (b. 1938) has frequently turned to scriptural texts, even winning a Pulit-

---

sentiment in the final chapter of *The History of Western Music*, college ed. (New York: Oxford University Press, 2013), 1088.

4. There are studies that have shown how individuals, families, and their environments benefit from religious practice, among them: John P. Bartkowski, Xiaohe Xu, and Martin Levin, "Religion and Child Development: Evidence from the Early Childhood Longitudinal Study," *Social Science Research* 37 (2008): 18–36. Sociologist Robert D. Putnam treats the topic in his *American Grace: How Religion Divides and Unites Us* (New York: Simon & Schuster, 2010).

zer Prize for a work based on Matt 3:13–23, *The Flight into Egypt* (1986). While a Christmas story, the work was inspired by the holiday's darker side, particularly for those enduring hardship, for whom it is "a time when need, isolation, and anxiety increases."[5] The text is treated in a straightforward fashion, and the work is intensely canonic, bearing the subtitle *Sacred Ricercar*. The term *ricercar* (or *ricercare*) was applied to many compositions of the fifteenth and sixteenth centuries. Many of these pieces featured imitative texture (similar to later fugues), but the term captures the process of composition. Through this subtitle Harbison is invoking this older tradition.

A different kind of probing, contemplative by nature, is found in other repertoire. While Morten Lauridsen (b. 1943) is not the most well-known composer, he is very highly regarded by those who know his music. His output is entirely voice-centered, primarily choral. His few instrumental works are arrangements of vocal works. Few of his vocal works are actually based on biblical texts, though the texts he uses in sacred works, often traditional, are all inspired by scripture. His most widely-performed work, *O magnum mysterium* (1994), is a case in point: a meditation on the nativity of Jesus. The text, however, is from a responsorial chant from Christmas, borrowing an image from Isa 1:3. It has been set by many composers.

El Niño by John Adams (b. 1947) is a retelling of the infancy narrative of Jesus, centered on the story of a young Hispanic girl giving birth in Los Angeles. It is called an oratorio, implying that it is not staged, though it often is, with film and dancers. The text was compiled by Adams's colleague Peter Sellars, who also staged the premiere in Paris. Texts include the nativity narratives from the gospels. The oldest texts are the prophetic utterances of Haggai and Isaiah. The newest are by the Mexican poet and novelist Rosario Castellanos, four of whose poems stand at the psychological and emotional center of *El Niño*. Among the other sources are Juana Inés de la Cruz, Gabriela Mistral, Rubén Dario, the Wakefield Mystery Play, Martin Luther's Christmas sermon, and passages from Luke and several gnostic gospels. In the finale of part 1, Mistral's *The Christmas Star* is woven into a choral setting of the Latin chant *O quam preciosa* by Hildegard von Bingen.[6]

---

5. John Harbison, "Programme Note: *The Flight into Egypt* (1986)," Wise Music Classical, https://tinyurl.com/SBL6704e1.

6. John Adams, "Works: El Niño," Earbox.com, https://tinyurl.com/SBL6704b1.

The Pulitzer award-winning Brooklyn-born composer Jennifer Higdon (b. 1962) composed a handful of choral works inspired by the scriptures, including a setting of Christina Rossetti's *Love Came down for Christmas* (2015) and the Christmas response, *O magnum mysterium* (2002). Both borrow imagery from scripture and fragments of text, focusing on the nativity of Jesus. The latter work, which includes two flutes and two bells, aims at the transcendental aspects of the text.

Mary Magdalen

One of the frequent themes of music of the past thirty-five years is the topic of Mary Magdalen, who is first identified as one of the women ministering to Jesus and as having been freed from seven demons (Luke 8:2). In all the gospels, she is prominent in the crucifixion and resurrection narratives. But like other biblical figures, she has taken on a life of her own, particularly in artistic representations. Two of the more common, even traditional, misappropriations of Mary Magdalen, are those in which she is associated with the unnamed woman caught in adultery (John 8:2–11) and with the unnamed woman who washes the feet of Jesus with oil. While the circumstances vary in each gospel, Luke (7:36–50) calls this woman "sinful" but also a "woman who loved much." Despite the lack of scriptural evidence for connections between these different figures, this reception history has made her into something of a lightning rod for controversial treatments.

Adams's interest in Mary Magdalen is articulated in *The Gospel according to the Other Mary* (2012), which won a Pulitzer Prize. The opera/oratorio relates the final weeks of Jesus's life and uses texts from the Hebrew Bible and New Testament but also poetry by Louise Erdrich, Primo Levi, Rosario Castellanos, June Jordan, Hildegard von Bingen, and Rubén Darío, and excerpts from the autobiography of the Catholic activist Dorothy Day. The New Testament passages are primarily from the gospels relating to the passion narrative, with Jesus's movements centered on the family of Mary, Martha, and Lazarus. Parallels are drawn between the trauma of the crucifixion, particularly for the community surrounding Jesus, and the trauma of the spectrum of abuses suffered by underprivileged women, especially those who protest their dismal state. While the narrative is from the perspective of Mary, Jesus as God-man remains the central figure, and the crucifixion remains a point of liberation for Christian believers—its traumatic elements all point to our own culpability and how humanity has been freed from that culpability. The parallel is potent and does not rely on a distortion of the scriptural Mary Magdalen but more of a possible repositioning of the woman "who loved much" into a contemporary passion.[7]

Adams's treatment bears comparison with an opera that appeared about the same time, *The Gospel of Mary Magdalene* by Mark Adamo (b. 1962). Adamo's version presents a major departure, not only in the figure of Mary Magdalen, but of Jesus and Peter, as well. Among the new elements, Jesus, a bastard son of Miriam (Mary of Nazareth), is married to Mary Magdalen, and Peter does not much care for her. Mary Magdalen, meanwhile, emerges as a copreacher together with her husband. Like Adams, the author takes advantage of reception history of the Magdalen and, further, draws on noncanonical narratives of the gnostic gospels, with which the libretto is heavily footnoted. Since its discovery in 1945, the gnostic literature has stood in contrast to scripture's authoritative position. Gnostics have an unorthodox theology, identifying the physical world—the one in which we daily move—as evil and the spiritual world as good. The only way to perfectly attain the good is to avoid all contact with the physical world. Adams's work also draws on the gnostic gospels; they function there more as an elaboration. For Adamo, they serve a substantial role, defining major portions of his plot.

The music itself is romantic in style, and there are a number of touching moments. But the opera at its premiere in San Francisco in June 2013 was not well received, even by critics unoffended by the distortions in the biblical narrative. Still, the work belongs in this discussion because of its inclusion of prominent persons from the gospels, and it casts some light on trends that seek a redefinition of those persons.[8]

---

7. David Mermelstein, "The Gospel of Adams," *Wall Street Journal*, https://www.wsj.com/articles/SB10001424052702304840904577426022341798112. Also, Thomas May, "Like a Bird Crucified in Flight," in *The Gospel according to the Other Mary*, by John Adams, mp3 booklet (Deutsche Grammaphon, 2014), 5–10. Available at https://tinyurl.com/SBL6704j1.

8. Admittedly, it is difficult to understand this controversial work, not having actually seen it nor being able to watch or listen to a performance. My grasping of the work largely relies on reviews of the performance and comments by Adamo. See Jeffrey S. McMillan, "World Première of Mark Adamo's *The Gospel of Mary Magdalene* in San Francisco," Backtrack Review, 24 June 2013, https://tinyurl.com/SBL6704f1; Georgia Rowe, *Opera News* 78.3 (2013): https://www.operanews.com/Opera_News_Magazine/2013/9/Reviews/SAN_FRANCISCO__Gospel_of_Mary_Magdalene.html;

Chicago composer Sidney Corbett (b. 1960) moved to Germany when he was twenty-five. He studied with György Ligeti and taught in Hamburg until his retirement. He wrote a number of choral works featuring biblical texts, usually from the Hebrew Bible. He also wrote an oratorio entitled *Maria Magdalena* (2005–2007) for three female voices, choir, and orchestra. The texts come from the Hebrew Bible in the original, the Vulgate (Latin), and other sources compiled by the composer and the Jewish philosopher Almut Shulamit Bruckstein Çoruh. The work begins at the tomb and juxtaposes sundry texts from the various sources. Corbett has also written instrumental pieces with suggestive titles, such as *Lamentations of the Prophet Micah* (1998) and *Variations (l'annunziazione)* (2002).[9]

Genesis

Among American composers who have treated subject matter from the first book of the Bible, four will serve as examples, each representing different perspectives. Steve Reich (b. 1936) casts a wide net for material from which to compile his music. In *The Cave*, premiered in 1993 in Vienna, he employed a technique of using recorded speech as a basis for melodic writing. The work makes extensive use of recorded interviews, from which Reich derives melodic writing. The technique was first used in *Different Trains* (1988), a piece for the Kronos Quartet. These interviews are carried out by Reich and his wife Beryl Korot, who ask Israeli, Palestinian, and American persons a series of questions: "Who is Abraham?," "Who is Sarah?," and "Who is Ishmael?" The cave referred to in the title is the Cave of the Patriarchs located in Hebron, where Abraham and Sarah (and others) are buried. It is thus a place of great reverence to Christians, Jews, and Muslims. Thus, the text is not scriptural and the content is not controlled by a biblical understanding of the patriarchs in question. Nevertheless, the tensions between Hagar and Sarah and between Isaac and Ishmael are central to the work, and Reich uses these to reflect the sustained tensions between Israel and Muslim states. The opera also uses modern cultural contexts to elucidate these historical and political issues. These contexts are largely manifested in the responses to the questions. The

---

Sidney Chen, "Mark Adamo's *The Gospel of Mary* Magdalene," Newmusicboxusa, 15 July 2013, https://tinyurl.com/SBL6704c1.

9. Sidney Corbett, "Works," sidneycorbett.com, https://tinyurl.com/SBL6704d1.

American portion reveals a spectrum of ignorance and knowledge, particularly revealing as it follows the Israeli and Palestinian portions. Reich's piece implies that Genesis continues to have a broad cultural impact no matter what the actual level of awareness of that impact might be.

Among settings of texts from Genesis, mention can be made of the composer Charles Wuorinen (1938–2020), who long identified himself with the serialist tradition of composition in Western music, closely associated with Milton Babbitt. Wuorinen is prolific and speaks often of tradition—he is well read in the Western culture and sees his music as solidly in line with the Western musical tradition. He is a deeply thoughtful composer who studies his material intimately, applying an expansive knowledge and appreciation of the Western intellectual tradition. The surface impression of his music is an acquired taste, owing to the dissonance and the intensity of the rhetoric. When he uses a text, it is with clear intentions. Yet his use of the Bible is rare, a significant exception being *Genesis* (1989), a cantata composed in response to a suggestion from conductor Harold Blomstedt and a commission from the Honolulu Symphony, the Minnesota Orchestra, and the San Francisco Symphony. The work probes its subject in five movements, Invocation, Meditation, Creation History, Cosmology, and Doxology. Three of the five sections are sung, all in Latin, with the central movement quoting the creation narrative of Gen 1. As for the outer movements, the first draws on the titles and music of seven chant settings of the Mass while the Doxology randomly draws on canticles found in the *Liber Usualis*, a monastic prayer book. While the music, which employs a wide range of styles from Gregorian chant to serialism, is not openly appealing, it is unrelentingly rich, wrapping the work in a cerebral timelessness.[10]

Laurie Anderson (b. 1947) is a performance artist whose work has found wide appeal among audiences ranging from bohemian intellectuals to pseudo-bohemian pseudo-intellectuals. Anderson's *United States: Parts I–IV* was performed as a seven-hour work at the Brooklyn Academy of Music in 1983 and released as a sound recording in a five-hour version in 1985. The work is a meditation and commentary on what the United States is, how the desires expressed by Americans contrast with what they

---

10. See Charles Wuorinen, "Genesis," charleswuorinen.com, https://www.charleswuorinen.com/compositions/genesis/ for links to documentation, which includes critic Michael Steinberg's notes for the premiere.

want and what they do.[11] *United States* is thematically divided into four sections—transportation, politics, money, and love. The final section, *Hothead*, invokes the Genesis story of the creation, with the man and the woman alone on an island. The woman engages with a snake, who tempts her with an alternate version of the way things are. She is presented with an image that causes her to fall in love and to turn against Adam's apparently naïve vision. The music itself is minimalist: engaging in simple harmonies and extensive repetitions of text, much of which is in French.

Abraham by Harbison was another high-profile composition, having been commissioned for a 2004 performance at the Vatican in the presence of Pope Saint John Paul II with other leaders of the Christian, Jewish, and Islamic faiths. The text came from Ps 17 and depicts Abraham as the father of all nations. The concert, organized by conductor Gilbert Levine, was to urge reconciliation between these three faiths and included a performance of Gustav Mahler's second symphony.

King David

Eric Whitacre (b. 1970) is from Reno, Nevada, where he studied composition with Ukrainian composer Virko Baley. At Juilliard he worked with John Corigliano and David Diamond. He has written a good number of choral works, but only one is clearly biblical: *When David Heard That Absalom Was Dead* (1999), based on 2 Sam 18:33, is a meditation on the king's reaction upon hearing of the death of his beloved and rebellious son Absalom. Whitacre's choice of text was inspired by the wrenching silence it implies, which is a significant part of the work. Whitacre exploits music's ability to expand time, suspending the listener within David's profound loss.

Psalms

Because so many works are settings of the psalms for their own sake, they deserve to be treated as a separate topic. The psalms have continued to be of interest to composers, evidence of the universal human expression exhibited by these sacred poems. Returning to Reich, in 1981 he wrote

---

11. See Susan McClary, "'This Is Not a Story My People Tell': Musical Time and Space according to Laurie Anderson," *Discourse: Journal for Theoretical Studies in Media and Culture*, 12.1 (1989–1990): 104–28.

Tehillim, a Hebrew word for "psalms" or "praise." It was a breakaway piece for the composer and emerged indirectly from Reich's encounters with African traditions. As he was pondering music from Ghana, he began to wonder about his own tradition. This train of thought led him to consider more deeply his own Jewish traditions; he began studying Hebrew, the Torah, and cantillation, and he visited Israel. Yet in *Tehillim* he explores only the textual heritage, not a musical heritage. He sets excerpts of four psalms (Pss 19; 34; 18; 150). The usual performance forces for this piece are four women's voices and a chamber ensemble of winds, strings, and percussion. It is the first major piece in which he incorporated voices. The composer points out that the contrapuntal and variation techniques he uses in the work are more reminiscent of pre-1750 Western music than either his own usual techniques or cantillation, but the rhythms are derived from the Hebrew texts. The overall impression is ebullient, full of energy and overflowing with counterpoint and unpredictable rhythms that are derived from the text.

Philip Glass's (b. 1937) *Psalm 126* was commissioned by the American Symphony Orchestra in 1998 to mark the fiftieth anniversary of the founding of the modern state of Israel. It is set for a narrator (who recites the psalm), a wordless chorus, and orchestra. Psalm 126, like the psalms around it, is associated with ascent. The music, with its repeating harmonic sequences and pulsating rhythms, is consistent with Glass's style.

The acclaimed composer Richard Danielpour (b. 1956) has written only a handful of pieces with biblical references, including a work for baritone and string quartet (no. 3; *Psalms of Sorrow*; 1994). The texts come from an adaptation of Pss 39 and 17. The piece marked the fiftieth anniversary of the liberation of Auschwitz. He complemented this work with his seventh quartet, *Psalms of Solace*, which included portions of Pss 40 and 96, in Hebrew, in the finale, as well as single verses from *Isaiah* and *Luke*.[12] He has also written *Oratio Pauli* (an intercessory prayer from Eph 3) for chorus and string orchestra. It was commissioned in 1983 by the Paulist Fathers in New York City.

Minnesota-born Libby Larsen (b. 1950) has written a number of works invoking scripture, and several of those are based on the psalms. Perhaps the largest of such works is *Praise One*, commissioned on the

---

12. Richard Danielpour, *String Quartets nos. 5–7*, Hila Pittmann and Delray String Quartet, Naxos 8.559845, 2018, mp3. Available at https://tinyurl.com/SBL6704k1.

one hundredth anniversary of Baylor University's first awarding of music degrees. The work draws on the last five psalms to convey the unity, the oneness of God. The four movements are played without break. The composer writes of the last movement, which brings together the preceding parts, "I set the music of the texts to echo two musical styles of Christian worship—four-part hymn tradition and gospel tradition—combining them to create music which, as a whole, suggests a unified prayer."[13]

Albany, New York, composer Adolphus Hailstork (b. 1941) has written in a wide array of genres, but only his choral music is peppered with texts stemming directly from scripture. He also sets texts inspired by scripture, such as spirituals and hymns. His *The God of Glory Thunders* (1999) for chorus is inspired by the repeated scriptural theme mentioned in the title that is specifically referenced in the psalms.

Nico Muhly (b. 1981), a native of Vermont, grew up singing in the choir at Grace Episcopal Church in Providence and completed his bachelor's degree at Columbia University in English before doing a Masters in composition at Juilliard. He studied with Corigliano and Christopher Rouse. A good portion of his music is texted. Among the most well known of the young composers, Muhly has written several works for choir. *Set Me as a Seal* (2003) is based on Song 8:6–7. *Like as the Hart* (2004) is a setting of Ps 42 and a response to English composer Herbert Howells's well-known setting. It is scored for SATB chorus, violin, and percussion. The score manifests some influence of Glass, for whom he had worked. In contrast to Howells's setting, Muhly elongates harmonies, which "drag" melodic fragments behind them.[14]

Proverbs

While the psalms have garnered musical settings through the ages, it has not been the case for the biblical proverbs, which are primarily didactic but clever and insightful. Michael Torke (b. 1961) has written two works using these texts, *Proverbs: Four Proverbs* (1993) and *The Book of Proverbs* (1996). In both works, the texts are brief and are repeated extensively. The earlier work is for soprano and eleven musicians; the latter is for larger

---

13. Libby Larsen, "Praise One," libbylarsen.com, https://tinyurl.com/SBL6704m1.
14. Nico Muhly, "Like as the Hart," The Website of Nico Muhly, https://tinyurl.com/SBL6704n1.

forces: soprano and baritone, full choir, and orchestra. Both works are refreshingly sanguine. Using a minimalist technique of text repetition, bright harmonic colors, angular themes, and vibrant rhythms, Torke delivers these life lessons with simultaneous joy and firmness. In the later work, Torke establishes a poignant sense of wonder in "The Way of an Eagle," based on Prov 30:18–19.

The Prophets: Jeremiah and Micah

The charismatic and vibrant Alabama native Rosephayne Powell (b. 1962) has found much inspiration in the work of Still and dedicated much of her performance and academic career to promoting his music. As a composer, she has embraced his ideas of integrating the black voice into American mainstream music. Her *Cry of Jeremiah* (Jer 20; 2012) is a large-scale example of this, written for four-part choir, organ, and orchestra, with narration. It renders the joys and sorrows of the life of a prophet, a life of abandonment to the will of God. African drumming, call-and-response, jazz harmonies, and gospel sounds are among the most pronounced black musical style traits exhibited in this work.[15]

Michigan composer Edward Knight (b. 1961) studied with the distinguished composers Anthony Iannaccone and Corigliano and now teaches in Oklahoma. He has composed a variety of instrumental works but also songs, showing both a convincing pliability and a striking affinity with narrative. That is, each work has its own personality, and, when there is a text, his settings are impressively responsive to it. His early choral work *O vos omnes* (1988) is a setting of Lam 1:12.

Song of Songs

John Zorn (b. 1953) who made a splash as a postmodern composer, has more recently emerged in the field of Jewish music. Despite this identity, little of his music is clearly biblically inspired with the exception of the

---

15. Powell provides extensive performance notes, along with recordings of the premiere by the Nashville Chamber Singers and Orchestra at her website: Rosephanye Powell, "SATB Sacred," http://rosephanyepowell.com/compositions/sacred-compositions/.

album *Shir Hashirim* (2013; *Song of Songs*), with a heavy emphasis on the text's erotic aspects.[16]

Buffalo, New York, composer Paul Moravec (b. 1957) seems to have raised eyebrows because of the muscular nature of his music. Perhaps his best-known work using scriptural texts is his choral piece that began as *Four Transcendent Love Songs* in 1983, taking texts from 1 Corinthians, Song of Songs, and the Gospel of John. In 2011, the songs were revamped and reproduced in *Sacred Love Songs*, with the addition of a text by Francis of Assisi and an instrumental interlude. This version originally had recorder accompaniment but was arranged for string quintet in 2012.[17]

René Clausen's (b. 1953) *Set Me as a Seal* (Song 8:6–7, recorded 1990) is easily his best-known work. Written for four voices, it is part of a sacred cantata *New Creation*. The excerpt seems to celebrate a romantic notion of love ("love strong as death"), until the listener understands that these were the actual circumstances under which it was composed: in the midst of a time of great hope, intimacy, and joy, death visited Clausen and his wife. The ensuing loss generated this touching work.[18]

Other Works

Saint Louis composer Douglas Knehans (b. 1957) was educated in Australia but did graduate work in the United States and worked at several academic institutions here, including a stint as dean of the University of Cincinnati College-Conservatory of Music. Biblical references have been limited to choral works, including a piece on the Shoah (2001–2010) and the setting of three psalms (2010), together with a Magnificat (1986) and a planned setting of the last words of Jesus Christ from the cross. This last set of texts, which are drawn from the passion narratives of all four gospels, has received little attention from American composers. Exceptions include the choral composer Michael J. Trotta (b. 1978; *Seven Last Words/ Septum ultima verba*, 2016) and Korean-American composer Byong-

---

16. John Zorn, *Shir Ha-Shirim*, Tzadik 8310, 2013, compact disc.

17. Based on composer Paul Moravec's homepage, www.paulmoravec.com, and *Amorisms: Music of Paul Moravec* Sonoma: Delos Productions DE3470, 2016, liner notes.

18. Clausen's own testimony can be heard in an interview with Tesfa Wondemagenehu, "Sing to Inspire: Clausen's Courage," ClassicalMPR, 11 January 2016, https://tinyurl.com/SBL6704o1.

kon Kim (b. 1929; *The Seven Last Words of Christ*, 1986). The latter is for organ and percussion—an inspired combination for a meditation that digs deeply into the "sign of contradiction"[19] embodied in the suffering and death of Jesus of Nazareth.

Linguistic approaches to the Bible have surfaced in this repertoire. One of the biblical events in which language is central to the narrative, Pentecost, unfolds in Acts 2. Harvey J. Stokes (b. 1957), who teaches at Hampton University, composed *The Second Act* (published 1988), based on this episode in which early Christians, inspired by the Holy Spirit, were speaking in tongues ("glossolalia") and in a manner in which each person, believer and nonbeliever alike, no matter what language they were speaking, could understand what was being said. It is the linguistic element that is most central to Stokes's work.[20]

David Lang (b. 1957) won a Pulitzer for *The Little Match Girl Passion* in 2008, a work he translated from Hans Christian Anderson's tale into a passion story, incorporating texts from the psalms and Matthew. The focus is Anderson's story rather than the one found in the gospels. Lang is also quite taken by the psalms, in part because of the range of experiences expressed therein, as well as the language. Like the scriptural passion, the misery and suffering of the little girl are trumped by transcendent elements. In other works, he has also taken topics raised by Song of Songs (*for love is strong*, 2008), Ecclesiastes (*again [after Ecclesiastes]*, 2005), and Genesis (*evening morning day*, 2007).[21] His *How to Pray* (2002) is an orchestral piece with no text but is inspired by the psalms. It explores the process of prayer exhibited in the psalms: the speaking and the waiting. Musically, the work draws on Stravinsky's *Symphony of Psalms* and Lang's own incomplete set of piano works that render each of the 150 psalms.[22]

The avant-garde, multimedia band The Residents's concept album, *Wormwood: Curious Stories from the Bible* (1998), takes a look at the many

---

19. In Luke 2:34, the prophet Simeon refers to the child Jesus as "a sign that will be contradicted," a phrase rich in meaning. It is an image that was often referenced by Pope Saint John Paul II.

20. Harvey J. Stokes, *Compositional Language in the Oratorio* The Second Act: *The Composer as Analyst* (Lewiston: Mellon, 1992).

21. All but the piano works based on the psalms are included on 2009 Harmonia Mundi recording *The Little Matchgirl Passion*.

22. Ample notes to David Lang's works are available at his website https://davidlangmusic.com/music.

darker stories of the holy book. The interests of The Residents are broad, and this is but one of their many projects. The work is performed as a series of stories in a kind of operatic narrative and includes alternating solo performances by the band's male and female lead singers. The musical styles vary, but the backup consists mostly of electronics, electric guitar, and percussion. The focus on these stories, it is claimed, is not intended as a criticism of the Bible as much as an exploration of some of its more difficult content. The stated targets, however, are "zealous, self-appointed arbiters of morality" who use the Bible as a moral stick to beat those with whom they disagree.[23] With its simultaneously provocative, insightful, cynical, satirical, hyperbolic narrative, *Wormwood* is a bitter reminder that scripture is not short on scandalous actions and decisions by its protagonists, including God. It is not clear that this approach, in which the songs often rely on added material while taking liberties with the biblical text, can really have the intended effect. But the project resonates with a widening cultural skepticism towards religion, if only because it draws attention to less attractive facets of scripture.

Catholic Church

One category I will speak of only broadly as a positive and significant trend, not just for Catholicism but also for religious practice in general. It is in reference to the Mass, large portions of which are scriptural or directly derived from scripture.

In the years following Vatican Council II, in the mid-1960s, efforts were made to adopt the principles laid down by the council in music composition. A great deal of music was composed, primarily with the aim of drawing the congregation into a musical participation in the liturgy and of strengthening the communal aspect of the Mass, the summit of Catholic life. What resulted from this effort, for the most part, was not impressive on a musical level. Since that time, into the twenty-first century, Catholic liturgy in the United States has been in the grip of an oppressive sentimentality and a "chic amateurism," according to one observer.[24] Serious efforts at impressive church music by Catholic musicians were spotty. That

---

23. "Wormwood." Residents.com. https://tinyurl.com/SBL6704g1.

24. Based on Jeffrey Tucker, "The Revival of Catholic Musical Creativity," *Sacred Music* 138.3 (2011): 54–55.

situation has shifted in the last decade, part of what could be attributed to the "Benedict effect," after the liturgical perspectives of Pope Benedict XVI. Jeffrey Tucker noted that 2011 marked a major turnaround, with the palpable coalescence of beautiful compositions for the liturgy. The movement is the result of a number of church musicians deciding they could have a direct impact on the music in the churches where they worked and, through existing communities on the internet, shared these pieces with their colleagues, who were not only composing their own music but were hungry for more pieces.

Responses to 9/11

Surprisingly, few prominent works written in response to 9/11 seemed to use the Bible.[25] One exception is the prolific and highly acclaimed Minnesota composer Stephen Paulus (1949–2014), who released a great deal of music with scriptural texts, some of it religious, some of it not. His more immediate response to the catastrophe was the choral work *All Things New*, for chorus and organ, which uses Rev 21:1–5. The second, the Grammy Award–winning *Prayers and Remembrances*, appeared a decade later, having been partly commissioned by Dorothy Vanek in memory of her husband and of her friends, lost on 9/11. It is a multimovement work and includes soloists and orchestra with only minimal reference to scripture, Lev 19:18, in the movement *Grant That We May Love*, bound with a prayer Muhammed taught to his followers.

Memorials

Beyond 9/11 memorials, there are others that have provided opportunities for composers to turn to Scripture. *To Be Certain of the Dawn* (2005), another work by Paulus, is a large choral piece using a spectrum of texts, all fulfilling a commission from the Basilica of Saint Mary in Minneapolis. The idea originated from Fr. Michael O'Connell, inspired by the well-considered conviction that Christians should be concerned with teaching about the Holocaust as much as, if not more than, Jewish people. The work intermingles traditional Jewish prayers (including the blowing of a shofar)

---

25. René Clausen's large-scale *Memorial* (2003) also includes biblical texts.

and Hebrew Bible and New Testament texts, underlining the depth of this crime against humanity. The main and repeated theme of the work is, "you shall love your neighbor as yourself," which is not only biblical but was also written on the only stone left standing after the Nazis destroyed the Berlin synagogue.

The German-born Herman Berlinski (1910–2001) came to the United States in 1941, fleeing the Nazis. He was raised in Łódź and Leipzig in the Ashkenazi tradition of Orthodox Judaism. He eventually moved to Paris and served honorably in the French military before leaving for New York City, where he quickly became part of the music-making Jewish community. Two important influences on his music were Olivier Messiaen in 1948 and his study of the origins and practices of ancient Jewish music, complemented by studies with Hugo Weisgall. His career continued to flourish, but the works from his retirement years are of most interest to this study, including his oratorio *Hiob*, a reworked version of an earlier oratorio (*Job*[26]), commissioned in 1993 for the opening of the Neue Synagoge in Dresden and performed in conjunction with a commemoration of Kristallnacht.

The highly acclaimed composer Dominick Argento (1927–2019) incorporated liturgical prayer, which included scripture, into a memorial for his wife in *Evensong: Of Love and Angels* (2008). The work had been requested as part of a centennial anniversary of the National Cathedral in Washington, DC. The commission coincided with the illness and death of Carolyn Bailey Argento, and the composer was hesitant to accept it. J. Reilly Lewis, who spearheaded the commission, encouraged Argento to write a work for Carolyn, to which the composer finally agreed. The piece contains passages based on Ps 102, John 5 (the original inspiration of the piece: the hospital Argento visited for 180 consecutive days was called "Bethesda," also the site of the pool where Jesus of Nazareth heals the paralytic), and Luke 2 (Nunc Dimittis).

Dale (Jack) Grotenhuis (1931–2012) spent his life in the Midwest, building the choral program at Dordt College. He set Rev 15:3–4 in *Song of Triumph* (1985) as a memorial to his immensely gifted son, who died in an auto accident. The text is the Song of the Lamb and parallels the Song of Moses (Exod 15), sung after the deliverance of Israel from enslavement

---

26. Originally commissioned in 1968 by the widow of Rabbi Norman Gerstenfeld, of the Washington Hebrew Congregation, for her husband.

at the hand of the Egyptians. The brief work remains a staple of the choral repertoire.[27]

As I surveyed the works of American composers, it was apparent that, while many of these composers, and others, have been writing musical works probing ultimate questions (origins, death, life, love), surprisingly few resorted to scripture for inspiration, relying on an assortment of nonbiblical texts or texts that were not evidently related to a biblical perspective, including those of other religions and poems by a spectrum of authors. This state of affairs may stand in stark contrast to, say, the Renaissance and the Baroque, when many composers held positions at churches. But it is consistent with the recent past, when secularism, as a worldview, has typically encouraged artists to look elsewhere for insights into the human condition. At least some of the composers discussed here would urge artists to do otherwise and to allow the rich and beautiful content of the Bible to inspire them further.

Bibliography

Adams, John. "Works: El Niño." Earbox.com. https://tinyurl.com/SBL6704b1.

Amorisms: Music of Paul Moravec. Sonoma: Delos Productions DE3470, 2016, liner notes.

Bartkowski, John P., Xiaohe Xu, and Martin Levin. "Religion and Child Development: Evidence from the Early Childhood Longitudinal Study." *Social Science Research* 37 (2008): 18–36.

Chen, Sidney. "Mark Adamo's *The Gospel of Mary* Magdalene." Newmusicboxusa. 15 July 2013. https://tinyurl.com/SBL6704c1.

Corbett, Sidney. "Works." sidneycorbett.com. https://tinyurl.com/SBL6704d1.

Danielpour, Richard. *String Quartets nos. 5–7*. Hila Pittmann and Delray String Quartet. Naxos 8.559845, 2018, mp3.

Good, Edwin M. "The Bible and American Music." Pages 131–56 in *The Bible and American Arts and Letters*. Edited by Giles Gunn. Philadelphia: Fortress; Chico, CA: Scholars Press, 1983.

Griffiths, Paul. *Modern Music and After: Directions since 1945*. Oxford: Oxford University Press, 1995.

---

27. "In Memoriam: Jack Grotenhuis 1931–2012," *Choral Journal* 53.6 (2013): 85.

Harbison, John. "Programme Note: *The Flight into Egypt* (1986)." Wise Music Classical. https://tinyurl.com/SBL6704e1.

"In Memoriam: Jack Grotenhuis 1931–2012." *Choral Journal* 53.6 (2013): 85.

Lang, David. "David Lang." https://davidlangmusic.com/music.

Larsen, Libby. "Praise One." libbylarsen.com. https://tinyurl.com/SBL6704m1.

May, Thomas. "Like a Bird Crucified in Flight." Pages 5–10 in *The Gospel according to the Other Mary*. By John Adams. mp3 booklet. Berlin: Deutsche Grammaphon, 2014.

McClary, Susan. "'This Is Not a Story My People Tell': Musical Time and Space according to Laurie Anderson." *Discourse: Journal for Theoretical Studies in Media and Culture* 12.1 (1989–1990): 104–28.

McMillan, Jeffrey S. "World Première of Mark Adamo's *The Gospel of Mary Magdalene* in San Francisco." Backtrack Review. 24 June 2013. https://tinyurl.com/SBL6704f1.

Mermelstein, David. "The Gospel of Adams." *Wall Street Journal*. https://www.wsj.com/articles/SB10001424052702304840904577426022341798112.

Moravec, Paul. Homepage. www.paulmoravec.com.

Muhly, Nico. "Like as the Hart." The Website of Nico Muhly. https://tinyurl.com/SBL6704n1.

Powell, Rosephanye. "SATB Sacred." http://rosephanyepowell.com/compositions/sacred-compositions/

Putnam, Robert D. *American Grace: How Religion Divides and Unites Us*. New York: Simon & Schuster, 2010.

Rowe, Georgia. "The Gospel of Mary Magdalene." *Opera News* 78.3 (2013): https://www.operanews.com/Opera_News_Magazine/2013/9/Reviews/SAN_FRANCISCO__Gospel_of_Mary_Magdalene.html.

Stokes, Harvey J. *Compositional Language in the Oratorio* The Second Act: *The Composer as Analyst*. Lewiston: Mellon, 1992.

Taruskin, Richard, and Christopher Gibbs. *The History of Western Music*. College ed. New York: Oxford University Press, 2013.

Tucker, Jeffrey. "The Revival of Catholic Musical Creativity." *Sacred Music* 138.3 (2011): 54–55.

"Wormwood." Residents.com. https://tinyurl.com/SBL6704g1.

Wondemagegnehu, Tesfa. "Sing to Inspire: Clausen's Courage." ClassicalMPR. 11 January 2016. https://tinyurl.com/SBL6704o1.

Wuorinen, Charles. "Genesis." charleswuorinen.com. https://www.charleswuorinen.com/compositions/genesis/.

Zorn, John. *Shir Ha-Shirim*. Tzadik 8310, 2013, compact disc.

7
THE BIBLE, LAW, AND POLITICAL RHETORIC

STEVEN K. GREEN

Including a chapter in this anthology about the relationship of the Bible to American law and political rhetoric may strike some people as odd. After all, the United States purportedly operates under a regime of separation of church and state. At least in theory, legal and governmental policies and functions should be insulated from religion, and, conversely, the government should abstain from interfering with the operations of religious institutions or seeking to influence the religious choices of individuals. Those principles are represented by the complementary provisions contained in the First Amendment to the Constitution: the nonestablishment and free exercise clauses. As Supreme Court Justice Hugo Black famously wrote in a 1948 case, "the First Amendment rests upon the premise that both religion and government can best work to achieve their lofty aims if each is left free from the other within its respective sphere."[1]

Still, considerable anecdotal evidence refutes the idea that there is no overlap between the respective spheres that Justice Black declared. Even a casual observer of the nation's political culture will note the frequent references to faith, religion, and the Bible by public officials. The ability to master "God talk" has become essential for successful politicians, and a frequent theme in political rhetoric is America's special or chosen status in God's plan for humankind. Such rhetoric is reinforced by popular books touting America as a Christian nation, all of which impacts popular attitudes. A 2008 public opinion survey and study indicated that 63 percent of Americans believed the Founders intended the United States to be a Christian nation, while 55 percent believed the Constitution actually establishes

---
1. McCollum v. Board of Education, 333 U.S. 203, 212 (1948).

a Christian nation, notwithstanding the nonestablishment clause.[2] When one also considers the innumerable scholarly works about civil religion and religion and politics, it suggests that things are not as one would expect under a regime of church-state separation.[3]

Accordingly, this chapter explores the paradox of the long-standing coexistence of a *formal*, constitutionally entrenched partition between religion and government and a deep but *informal* influence of religion in American public life. These two seemingly contradictory realities remain competing touchstones in public discourse.[4] Disputes over the Bible not only reflect but also serve as a central staging ground in American legal and political traditions. What follows, then, is an *essay* rather than an exhaustive account of the past and ongoing relationship between the Bible and American law and government. This chapter will first consider the historical and ongoing relationship between the Bible and the nation's law and legal establishment and then do the same with the Bible and political culture and rhetoric. In both areas, the formal separation but enduring presence of religion in general and of the Bible in particular become evident.

The Bible and American Law

Undoubtedly, the emergence of American ideals of nonengagement between religion and the government and law was a unique historical development. Even in the European traditions of political philosophy and practice in which the principle of disestablishment ostensibly has its roots, state-sanctioned religious establishments and monarchs have long claimed authority to rule by divine right. To this day, the queen of Great Britain is the head of the established Church of England. In Western Europe, the Roman Catholic Church asserted its independence from temporal authority in 1075, yet church and state were hardly separated, as civil authorities enforced religious norms through the law. Church officials prosecuted

---

2. First Amendment Center, *State of the First Amendment 2008* (Arlington, VA: Freedom Forum, 2008), 3.

3. David Barton, *The Myth of Separation* (Aledo, TX: Wallbuilder, 1992); John Eidsmoe, *Christianity and the Constitution* (Grand Rapid: Baker Book House, 1987).

4. For more on this theme, see Ira C. Lupu and Robert W. Tuttle, *Secular Government, Religious People* (Grand Rapids: Eerdmans, 2014).

violations of church doctrine, whether scripturally based or not, but then often turned to civil authorities to impose punishment. Beyond that reciprocal and reinforcing relationship, church canon law strongly influenced the development of civil legal systems throughout Medieval Europe (in no small part because clerics constituted the bulk of educated jurists). Legal historian Harold J. Berman wrote that "as the Papal Revolution gave birth to the modern Western state, so it gave birth to modern Western legal systems, the first of which was the modern system of canon law."[5] Berman claimed, in fact, that the Western legal tradition is derived directly from canon law and religious customs, and he titled his major work on the subject *Law and Revolution: The Formation of the Western Legal Tradition*, the revolution being the Papal Revolution of 1075. The biblical or religious foundation for the Western legal tradition can be overstated, however. Berman acknowledged that the same medieval church clerics also rediscovered Emperor Justinian's code (*Corpus Juris Civilis*), which had revised the civil Roman law, and that this latter body of law strongly influenced the development of the Western legal tradition, as well.[6]

In light of the foundational role of these European traditions on American government, it would be easy to assume that those same religious codes, especially those of Christianity and the Bible, had a profound impact as a new, postcolonial nation took shape across the Atlantic at the end of the eighteenth century. Yet one still may question whether the Bible had any role in the development of the United States' legal and political systems. The United States has a "godless Constitution," as scholars Isaac Kramnick and R. Laurence Moore reminded us a generation ago,[7] and that governing document is bereft of any mention of the Bible, Christianity, or religion generally, other than to prohibit a religious test for public office holding, hardly a rousing affirmation of religion's political value. The Constitution does not include the words "so help me God" in the required oath of office for the president or suggest that oath be taken with one's hand on a Bible, both traditions being established *sua sponte* by George Washington. Certainly, one may question the current relevance of any

---

5. Harold J. Berman, *Law and Revolution: The Formation of the Western Legal Tradition* (Cambridge: Harvard University Press, 1983), 115.

6. Berman, *Law and Revolution*, 127–28. See also Kermit L. Hall, *The Magic Mirror: Law in American History* (New York: Oxford University Press, 1989), 9–10.

7. Isaac Kramnick and R. Laurence Moore, *The Godless Constitution: The Case against Religious Correctness* (New York: Norton, 1996).

such inquiry, considering the secular nature of our legal and governmental establishments today.[8] In fact, in 2003 Alabama Chief Justice Roy Moore was unceremoniously dismissed from office for refusing to remove a Ten Commandments monument from the rotunda of the state supreme court building, despite Moore's insistence that the Ten Commandments was the basis of American law.[9]

For centuries, philosophers, jurists, and theologians have postulated about the law's religious origins or a connection between the law and God's revelation. At times, such theories have involved nonspecific claims of a higher natural law—commonly acquired through human reason—that was eternal, universal, and superior to all other law. At other times, such claims have contained a stronger deific element. During the Middle Ages, Catholic scholars rediscovered the classical natural law strain advanced by figures such as Aristotle and Cicero, with Thomas Aquinas reclassifying much of it as divine law, which was acquired through revelation and scripture.[10] In still other instances, religious communities, such as the New England Puritans, have attempted to operate legal systems based directly on biblical dictates. Even in modern times, people have asserted a direct connection between scripture and civil law. Writing in 1986, Berman insisted that "two generations ago, if one had asked Americans where our Constitution—or indeed, our whole concept of law—came from, on what it is ultimately based, the overwhelming majority would have said, 'the Ten Commandments,' or 'the Bible,' or perhaps 'the law of God.'"[11] This idea of a connection between the law and the Bible—or at least particular biblical mandates like the Ten Commandments—remains popular to this day.[12]

---

8. Forrest Church, *So Help Me God* (New York: Harcourt, 2007), 445–49; John Meacham, *American Gospel: God, the Founding Fathers, and the Making of a Nation* (New York: Random House, 2006), 14–15.

9. Moore v. Judicial Inquiry Commission, 891 So.2d 848 (AL 2004); Joseph L. Conn, "Down for the Count," *Church & State* (2003): 2–4.

10. Edward S. Corwin, *The "Higher Law" Background of American Constitutional Law* (Ithaca, NY: Cornell University Press, 1955), 7–18; Cornelia Geer Le Boutillier, *American Democracy and Natural Law* (New York: Columbia University Press, 1950), 59–60, 68–69.

11. Harold J. Berman, "Religion and Law: The First Amendment in Historical Perspective," *Emory Law Journal* 35 (1986): 788–89.

12. See American Legion v. American Humanist Association, 139 S.Ct. 2067, 2083 (2019) ("The Ten Commandments ... have significance as one of the foundations of our legal system").

American law developed chiefly out of the British common law. British-American colonialists brought the common law with them to their new settlements and used it to govern legal transactions and disputes; its rules also set the foundation for the operations of civil society, determining such crucial matters as property ownership, inheritance, and marital and familial relationships. American colonialists also adapted the common law to meet their own conditions. By the seventeenth century, the common law had evolved as a secular institution, distinct from the ecclesiastical law administered by the Church of England or royal law, the latter now in decline.[13]

Even though the common law arose chiefly out of customary relationships, early British jurists debated the extent to which it was infused with and subjected to higher law principles. Writing in 1610, Sir Edward Coke asserted that the "law of nature is that which God at the time of creation of the nature of man infused into his heart (which is also the moral law)." This higher/natural law, Coke asserted, was prior and superior to "any judicial or municipal law in the world," "immutable," and "part of the laws of England."[14] By the time William Blackstone published his *Commentaries on the Laws of England* in 1765, the idea that a higher law, derived from revelation and scripture, informed and ultimately controlled the common law was well established. In his *Commentaries*, Blackstone reaffirmed the idea of a preeminent higher law. Blackstone asserted that natural law was "dictated by God himself" and was "of course superior in obligation to any other [law]." At the same time, Blackstone distinguished natural law, which was discoverable through reason, from divine or revealed law, which "are found only in the holy scriptures." Yet both forms emanated from the will of God and were "part of the original law of nature."[15] Blackstone's *Commentaries* was first published in the American colonies in 1772, and it quickly became the most influential legal treatise

---

13. Hall, *Magic Mirror*, 10–26; Morton J. Horwitz, *The Transformation of American Law, 1780–1860* (Cambridge: Harvard University Press, 1977), 4–7.

14. Calvin's Case, 7 Co. 4b, 12a–12b (1610), quoted in Steven K. Green, *The Second Disestablishment: Church and State in Nineteenth-Century America* (New York: Oxford University Press, 2010), 151–52.

15. William Blackstone, *Commentaries on the Laws of England—Book the First: Of the Rights of Persons*, ed. Stanley N. Katz (Chicago: University of Chicago Press, 1979), 40–42.

among colonial lawyers, selling approximately 2500 copies by the time of the American Revolution.[16]

During the seventeenth and eighteenth centuries, Enlightenment theorists began to articulate a distinctly secular version of natural law, one that was based on reason and immutable laws of nature devoid of any divine influence. One of the more influential Enlightenment writers for the founding generation was John Locke, who wrote extensively about natural law. Locke asserted that law generally was not traceable to divine standards of right and wrong: "laws are not concerned with the truth of opinion, but with the security and safety of the commonwealth and of each man's goods and person. The truth is not taught by law, nor has she any need of force to procure her entrance into the minds of men."[17] Like other Enlightenment theorists, Locke occasionally spoke about "Eternal Law" and used terms such as "Law of Nature" and "Law of God" interchangeably. He wrote in his *Second Treatise on Government* (1690) that the "Word of God" (scripture) acted as "fundamental law" and served as "a rule of righteousness to influence our lives."[18] But Locke's approach was common for the time. Enlightenment writers generally distinguished natural law from higher law, yet they viewed the concepts as compatible. Most significant, Enlightenment writers grounded natural law on natural rights based on reason rather than relying on revelation or scripture. This alternative, secular notion of natural law meant that lawyers and other leaders of the revolutionary era could affirm the verity of natural law without accepting its religious origins. The Enlightenment notion of natural law influenced not only understandings of the law but also of principles of government, as well.[19]

In the years following the Revolution, American lawyers sought to reconcile this secular basis for law and government with Blackstonian understandings of higher/natural law. This tension is seen in writings of legal theorists during the early national period. One such figure was James Wilson (1742–1798), a leading drafter of the Constitution (along with

---

16. Corwin, *"Higher Law" Background*, 84–85.

17. John Locke, *Second Treatise of Government*, ed. Mentor Book (New York: Cambridge University Press 1963), §135.

18. Locke, *Second Treatise of Government*, §195

19. Benjamin F. Wright, *American Interpretations of Natural Law* (New York: Russell & Russell, 1962), 7–10; Richard B. Morris, *Studies in the History of American Law*, 2nd ed. (New York: Octagon Books, 1974), 23.

James Madison) and later Supreme Court justice. In his published law lectures at the College of Philadelphia (University of Pennsylvania), Wilson struggled to integrate republican principles into the common law. Initially, Wilson advanced the traditional view of higher/natural law: "The great Creator ... has established general and fixed rules, according to which all the phenomena of the material universe are produced and regulated. These are usually denominated natural law." "Human law must rest its authority, ultimately, upon the authority of that law, which is divine."[20] But Wilson then distinguished the functions of divine law, natural law, and human (positive) law. While "God ... is the promulgator as well as author of natural law," he wrote, "as promulgated by reason and moral sense, it has been called natural; as promulgated by the holy scriptures, it has been called revealed law." In essence, scripture was a means for identifying these eternal legal principles but was not essential; lawyers could also do so by using reason and moral sense. For Wilson, considerations of revealed law were not directly applicable for the day-to-day practice of law; they "are the more peculiar objects of the profession of divinity."[21] Thus the Bible was a means of understanding those ultimate laws of nature to which all the law was subject, but it was not applicable to the general practice of human law.

Likely the strongest advocate for a religiously based natural law was Supreme Court Justice Joseph Story (1779–1845), who considered it integrated into the common law. An intellectual giant and conservative Unitarian (and apologist for the Unitarian church establishment in Massachusetts), Story staunchly defended the common law against efforts by liberal jurists to replace it with system of codification. Story was also a leading proponent of the maxim that Christian principles underlay the common law, such that judges were obligated to punish public affronts to Christianity. Story advanced an undeniably theistic conception of natural law, writing that the "obligatory force of the law of nature upon man is derived from its presumed coincidence with the will of the Creator... as he is our Lawgiver and Judge, we owe an unreserved obedience to his commands."[22] Story believed that natural law did more than pronounce universal and immutable principles; it directed how the law applied to matters such as marriage, fornication, adultery, lewdness, and, as shall be

---

20. James Wilson, "Lectures on Law" (1804), in *The Works of James Wilson*, ed. James G. McCloskey (Cambridge: Harvard University Press, 1967), 1:102.

21. Wilson, "Lectures on Law," 1:124–25.

22. Joseph Story, "Natural Law," *Encyclopedia Americana* 9:150.

seen, blasphemy. "There never has been a period in which the common law did not recognize Christianity as lying at its foundations," he asserted.[23] "Thus, Christianity becomes, not merely an auxiliary, but a guide, to the law of nature, establishing its conclusions."[24] Like most natural law proponents, Story did not emphasize the role of the Bible in his schema, other than to specify that scriptural revelation was a chief source for discovering God's natural laws.

Despite political disestablishment in the United States, during the first half of the nineteenth century conservative judges occasionally enforced Christian precepts through the law. Between 1810 and 1837, state appellate judges upheld a handful of criminal convictions for blasphemy, punishing individuals for reviling Christianity, Jesus Christ, the Virgin Mary, or for "speaking loosely of the Scriptures of Truth."[25] (While only six reported blasphemy cases exist, the number of prosecutions was likely much greater because they would have taken place in justice-of-the-peace courts and most would never have been appealed and reported.) In an 1824 case, a member of a Pittsburgh debating society was convicted of blasphemy after making the innocuous remark during a debate that "the Holy Scriptures were a mere fable." The Pennsylvania Supreme Court upheld his conviction under the state blasphemy law, asserting that "Christianity is part of the common law of this state," such that to revile scripture undermined the law and the society it protected.[26] Prosecutions for blasphemy died out in mid-century, replaced by charges of disorderly conduct or creating a public nuisance, but they were a stark example of the law protecting Christianity and the Bible.

Another area of the law where courts applied biblical principles was in the enforcement of Sunday laws. Sunday or Sabbath laws had existed in all of the British colonies, even those without established churches, and they

---

23. Joseph Story, "Value and Importance of Legal Studies" (1829), in *The Miscellaneous Writings of Joseph Story*, ed. William W. Story (Boston: Little & Brown, 1852), 517.

24. Story, "Value and Importance of Legal Studies," 535.

25. People v. Ruggles, 8 Johns. 290 (NY 1811); Bell's Case, 6 N.Y. City Hall Rec. 38, 3 Am. St. Tr. 558 (NY Ct. Gen. Sess. 1821); People v. Porter, 2 Parker's Crim. Rep. 14 (NY Oyer & Term. 1823); Updegraph v. Commonwealth, 11 Serg. & Rawl. 394, 407 (PA 1824); Commonwealth v. Kneeland, 20 Pick. 37 Mass. 206 (MA 1836); State v. Chandler, 2 Harr. 553 (DE 1837). For more information on these cases, see Green, *Second Disestablishment*, 162–78.

26. Updegraph v. Commonwealth, 11 Serg. & Rawl. 394, 407 (PA 1824).

prohibited profaning the Lord's Day by working, engaging in sports or other recreations, consuming alcohol, and disturbing any worship service. After the Revolution all of the new states carried over aspects of their colonial Sunday laws, and later admitted states enacted similar measures.[27] For at least the first half of the nineteenth century, judges regularly justified Sunday law enforcement based on Christian practice and biblical mandate. Some judges found authority in the New Testament's account of the resurrection, while others, ironically, cited the Ten Commandments—ironic in that a handful of such cases involved Jewish merchants who asserted their right to follow the Jewish Sabbath as affirmed in the biblical commandments and not to be forced to observe the Christian Sabbath.[28] Gradually, the stated justification for Sunday laws evolved, with judges embracing worker health and safety rationales supporting a uniform day of rest rather than relying on religious ones. By the last third of the century, religious or biblical justifications for Sunday laws had all but disappeared.[29] Finally, judges occasionally cited to scripture in cases involving moral obligations, such as in the areas of oath requirement, domestic relations, and wills and estates law, although such reliance declined in the latter part of the century. By the end of the century, the Bible had all but disappeared as a resource for legal decision making.[30]

In addition to this secularizing trend in the law, the popularity of natural law theories declined in the mid-nineteenth century, supplanted initially by legal positivism—which taught the law was nothing more than positive enactments by the sovereign—and then legal realism—which insisted the law reflected social trends—both jurisprudential schools taking an amoral approach to the substance and function of the law. Today, these jurisprudential schools and their progeny dominate legal theory.[31] Resistance to an amoral basis for the law has come from Catholic legal scholars who promote a neo-Thomist version of natural law and from other conservative jurists who bemoan the rise of indeterminacy within the law and the secularizing tendency of the Supreme Court's church-state decisions. Berman was one of the leading critics of modern law's amoral nature, decrying what he called the "radical separation of law and religion

---

27. Green, *Second Disestablishment*, 182–83.
28. Green, *Second Disestablishment*, 170–72, 184–87.
29. Green, *Second Disestablishment*, 231–47.
30. Green, *Second Disestablishment*, 214–21.
31. Hall, *Magic Mirror*, 221–24, 269–71.

in the twentieth century."[32] Such critiques, however, could not stop the secularizing trend within the law.

As noted, likely the most popular belief about the Bible's influence on the law centers on the idea that the Ten Commandments, rather than the Bible writ large, has strongly influenced the development of American law. This is evinced in the multitude of legal cases involving official displays of the Ten Commandment on public property, monuments that are frequently justified on the ground that the Commandments represent one of the foundations of American law and government. Supreme Court justices have given lip-service to this claim, with the Court in 2005 declaring that it was "not [prepared] to deny that the Commandments have had influence on civil or secular law."[33] Despite the popularity of this axiom, even within the legal community, there is little historical support for the proposition. References to the Ten Commandments in the speeches, writings, and public documents of the founding period are rare, particularly those involving claims that the Commandments served as a basis for republican government or American law. Assertions that the Ten Commandments influenced the development of the law are also absent in the legal decisions and treatises of the early nineteenth century. Those references to the Ten Commandments that do exist are allegorical or in the form of rhetorical flourishes; as mentioned, the only area where the Ten Commandments appears with regularity is in early Sunday law cases. Even then, those references were used to demonstrate the basis for Sunday observance, not for Sabbath laws generally. Nonetheless, the idea of a connection between the Ten Commandments and the law remains popular to this day, even though there is a lack of documentary evidence to support that claim.[34]

Today, the law and the legal system are overwhelmingly considered to be secular institutions. Legal education is a secular enterprise, though a handful of law schools at conservative religious colleges teach courses

---

32. Harold J. Berman, "The Interaction of Law and Religion," *Capital University Law Review* 8 (1979): 345–55; Berman, "Religion and Law," 788–89.

33. McCreary County v. ACLU of Kentucky, 545 U.S. 844, 869 (KY 2005). See William J. Federer, *The Ten Commandments and Their Influence on American Law* (St. Louis: Amerisearch, 2003).

34. Steven K. Green, "The Fount of Everything Just and Right? The Ten Commandments as a Source of American Law," *Journal of Law and Religion* 14 (1999–2000): 525–58; Paul Finkelman, "The Ten Commandments on the Courthouse Lawn and Elsewhere," *Fordham Law Review* 73 (2005): 1477–1520.

from a Christian perspective, and some, but not all, law schools at Catholic institutions offer courses in natural law (e.g., Georgetown University Law Center, a Jesuit-affiliated institution, does not offer a course in natural law, though it does have courses in religion and the law).[35] Laws must rest on secular rationales and promote secular goals, though judges have recognized that some laws—such as murder prohibitions—may parallel religious teachings. In 1961, the Supreme Court upheld the constitutionality of Sunday law restrictions; while acknowledging the laws' religious origins, the justices found that the laws were now based on secular rationales. The Court has also ruled that state laws restricting access to abortions are not unconstitutional merely because they may conform to doctrines of the Catholic church. But if a law fails to have a dominant secular purpose, then courts will strike it down.[36]

Likely the most famous legal case involving the Bible was the Supreme Court's 1963 decision striking the practice of Bible reading in the public schools.[37] Devotional religious exercises—Bible readings, prayers, hymn singing—were common in schools from the earliest days of public education. Initially, school authorities used religious exercises to instill religious fealty and promote moral character; in many instances, the practices were sectarian in orientation in that children were taught about human sinfulness and redemption through Jesus Christ.[38] During the mid-nineteenth century, education reformer Horace Mann advocated a nonsectarian approach to the exercises—for schools to emphasize the universal moral principles in the Bible by reading scripture without note or comment—in Mann's words, to allow the Bible "to speak for itself."[39] Mann believed that this approach would make the Bible accessible to children of all denominations, including Catholics. "In every course of studies, all the practical and perceptive parts of the Gospel should have been sacredly included; and all the dogmatical theology and sectarianism sacredly excluded."[40] Mann's

---

35. See Georgetown Law, "J.D. Program," Georgetown.edu, https://www.law.georgetown.edu/academics/jd-program/

36. McGowan v. Maryland, 366 U.S. 420 (1961); Webster v. Reproductive Services, 492 U.S. 490 (1988).

37. Abington School District v. Schempp, 374 U.S. 203 (1963).

38. Bruce J. Dierenfield, *The Battle over School Prayer* (Lawrence: University Press of Kansas, 2007), 13–14.

39. Horace Mann, *Twelfth Annual Report to the Board of Education* (Boston: Dutton & Wentworth, 1849), 117.

40. Horace Mann, *Go Forth and Teach: An Oration Delivered before the Authori-*

goal of identifying a universal Christian norm was undermined by the fact that public schools used the Protestant King James Version (KJV) of the Bible, which Catholic leaders considered to be sectarian. Despite Catholic opposition, Mann's nonsectarian approach to Bible reading became the prevailing model by the latter third of the century.[41]

Over time, nonsectarian Bible reading became a rote exercise in many schools. Evangelicals often complained that the exercises were devoid of religious meaning whereas Catholics insisted the practices still promoted Protestantism. Catholics, Jews and freethinkers mounted approximately twenty legal challenges to Bible reading during in the late nineteenth and early twentieth centuries, with courts striking down the practices in about one-third of the cases.[42] One of the more famous challenges arose in Cincinnati in the early 1870s, where Judge Alphonso Taft (father of the future president and chief justice) wrote that to hold that Protestants "are entitled to have their mode of worship and their bible used in the common schools is to hold to the union of Church and State."[43] By the time that the US Supreme Court finally considered the issue in 1963, daily Bible reading occurred in less than half of the nation's public schools, a victim of dissatisfaction with the practices, negative judicial rulings, and a growing sensitivity to religious pluralism. (Bible reading still remained common in the South and in rural areas throughout the Northeast and Midwest, however.)[44]

In Abington School District v. Schempp, the justices ruled eight-to-one that Bible reading in the public schools violated the Establishment Clause. The Court held that the readings were inherently religious, such that the practices amounted to government promotion of religion. Responding to the claim that the Bible was being used solely to promote moral values, Justice Tom Clark wrote that "even if its purpose is not strictly religious, it is sought to be accomplished through readings, without comment, from

---

ties of the City of Boston, 4 July 1842 (repr. Washington, DC: Committee on the Horace Mann Centennial, National Education, 1937), 44.

41. Steven K. Green, *The Bible, the School, and the Constitution* (New York: Oxford University Press, 2012), 16–36.

42. Green, *Bible, the School, and the Constitution*, 236–43.

43. Green, *Bible, the School, and the Constitution*, 93–135; Board of Education v. Minor, 23 Ohio St. 211 (1873).

44. Steven K. Green, *The Third Disestablishment: Church, State, and American Culture, 1940–1975* (New York: Oxford University Press, 2019), 276.

the Bible. Surely the place of the Bible as an instrument of religion cannot be gainsaid." Anticipating the potentially hostile reaction to the Court's holding, Clark attempted to assuage concerns that the justices were hostile to religion or sought to "establish a 'religion of secularism.'"

> It might well be said that one's education is not complete without a study of comparative religion or the history of religion and its relationship to the advancement of civilization. It certainly may be said that the Bible is worthy of study for its literary and historic qualities. Nothing we have said here indicates that such study of the Bible or of religion, when presented objectively as part of a secular program of education, may not be effected consistently with the First Amendment.[45]

Justice Clark's nod to the Bible's pedagogical value and his affirmation of its permissible uses in public schooling did little to blunt the public outcry over the holding. (A year earlier, the Court had struck down the practice of students reciting a prayer composed by school officials.) In response to the decisions, the Senate and House of Representatives held hearings on proposed amendments to the Constitution to allow prayer and Bible reading in the nation's schools. Although the proposals initially had wide bipartisan support, they all came to naught, either dying in committee or failing to garner the necessary two-thirds majority necessary to pass a constitutional amendment. The last serious effort to enact a prayer and Bible reading amendment, promoted by President Ronald Reagan, failed in 1984. The Court's prayer and Bible reading decisions would remain controversial, however, and they are partially responsible for the rise of the conservative Religious Right in the 1980s and the ensuing culture wars.[46]

While the principle of church-state separation has limited the Bible's impact on the law considerably, some scholars have asserted a striking parallel between the Bible and one significant aspect of the law, that being the Constitution. The parallel does not concern the content of the two documents or even one directly influencing the other. Rather, the parallel involves the similarity in the way in which people sometimes approach and interpret the two texts. The operative hermeneutic approaches are biblical literalism, with its insistence on inerrancy of the scriptures, and the concept of constitutional originalism. A belief in the inerrancy of

---

45. Abington School District v. Schempp, 374 U.S. 203, 224–225 (1963).
46. Dierenfield, *Battle over School Prayer*, 179–212.

the Bible likely needs no explanation; originalism, on the other hand, advocates an interpretive method of the Constitution that seeks out the original meaning of a particular provision or the drafters' original understanding of that text. Originalism promotes fealty to that original understanding as a means of imposing restraint on judicial decision making while ensuring the consistency and legitimacy of constitutional rule. Originalism eschews the notion of an evolving or living Constitution. Even though all judges consider the text and likely purposes of a provision when interpreting the Constitution, originalist-leaning jurists—like Justices Antonin Scalia and Clarence Thomas—elevated originalism to a determinative level, such that, for example, one might consider the types of accepted criminal punishments in 1789—branding, whipping, ear splicing—for determining today what constitutes cruel or unusual punishment under the Eighth Amendment.[47]

With the rise of modern originalism in the 1980s, legal critics began drawing parallels between proponents of biblical literalism and constitutional originalism. Both biblical literalists and constitutional originalists believe that their respective texts are fixed, authoritative, and readily ascertainable by anyone willing to approach them with an open mind. As two scholars of the topic have written:

> The similarities extend beyond the obvious shared presuppositions that the relevant texts have a timeless, fixed meaning that is readily ascertainable. The modern movements to which literalism and originalism are central both arose in large part as reactions to competing approaches, and both movements are in significant part projects of restoration-of both the proper approach to interpretation and a particular set of values that have been under siege. Literalists and originalists alike contend that the text itself is available to control those who claim to be authoritative interpreters, and they are deeply concerned about the loss of constraint that results from interpretation that is untethered to text.... Literalists and originalists defend their approaches with an air of absolute certainty about their approaches' legitimacy and correctness.[48]

---

47. H. Jefferson Powell, "Rules for Originalists," *Virginia Law Review* 73 (1987): 659–99; Antonin Scalia, "Originalism: The Lesser Evil," *University of Cincinnati Law Review* 57 (1989): 849–66.

48. Peter J. Smith and Robert W. Tuttle, "Biblical Literalism and Constitutional Originalism," *Notre Dame Law Review* 86 (2011): 693–763.

As a result, critics of originalism have labeled its proponents "legal fundamentalists" for their efforts "to restore literal meaning of a sacred text."[49] Other scholars have noted additional similarities between the strict constructionists of both texts. According to one study, 57 percent of Americans believe the Bible is inspired and inerrant, with an additional 16 percent believing it is inspired.[50] Despite 73 percent of Americans believing that the Bible is at least inspired, less than 50 percent state they have read the Bible during the previous year, and studies reveal a higher than expected degree of illiteracy over core biblical facts. On the other side, a similar disconnect exists among proponents of constitutional originalism. Legal scholar Jack Balkin has observed that most Americans possess a high degree of fealty to the Constitution and desire to follow the wisdom of its drafters; at the same time, Balkin continues, there is an appalling degree of ignorance about the Constitution's content and coverage (at least among non-jurists): "Most Americans know comparatively little about what the framers and adopters actually wanted or sought to achieve in the creating the Constitution."[51] This commonality has led to an interesting, though not surprising, cross-over. According to a 2010 analysis of survey data, one of the leading determinants of a constitutional originalist is not her political affiliation, education, or race but her religiosity. Fifty-two percent of originalists consider themselves to be evangelical or born-again, compared to only 17 percent of nonoriginalists. Even starker, 76 percent of constitutional originalists believe in the literal truth of the Bible, whereas only 35 percent of nonoriginalists are biblical literalists.[52] These commonalities have led one scholar to quip that "popular biblical and constitutional hermeneutics are a match made in heaven."[53]

---

49. Cass R. Sunstein, *Radicals in Robes* (New York: Basic Books, 2005), xiii; Morton J. Horwitz, "The Meaning of the Bork Nomination in American Constitutional History," *University of Pittsburg Law Review* 50 (1989): 655.

50. Barna Group, *State of the Bible 2017* (Philadelphia: American Bible Society, 2017), 32.

51. Jack M. Balkin, "Why Are Americans Originalists?," Yale Law School, Public Law Research Paper 492.

52. Jamal Greene, Nathaniel Persily, and Stephen Ansolabehere, "Profiling Originalism," *Columbia Law Review* 111 (2011): 356–418.

53. John F. Kutsko, "The Curious Case of the Christian Bible and the U.S. Constitution," in *The Bible in American Life*, ed. Philip Goff, Arthur E. Farnsley, and Peter J. Thuesen (New York: Oxford University Press, 2017), 244.

The similarities between the two interpretive approaches, while striking, can be overstated, as they involve two vastly different documents with different claims of authorship. Nonetheless, this may be a chief area in which the Bible continues to impact modern American law. In other words, the confluence between constitutional and biblical hermeneutics points to political *rhetoric* as the sphere where the enduring presence of the Bible in American politics most visibly surfaces.

The Bible and American Political Rhetoric

Related to the preceding discussion about the contestable (and oft-contested) influence of the Bible on the American legal system is consideration of the role the Bible played in the founding of the nation's political system and its continuing impact on that system today. The Bible and biblical language have always played some part in political rhetoric, but almost never have its use and frequency corresponded directly with the religious commitment or biblical literacy of the individual politicians who use it.

The initial question—whether the Bible influenced the ideology behind the American Revolution and informed the Founders' ideas of republican government—exists on two related levels. The first level is an inquiry involving intellectual history—of seeking to establish the various strains of thought that informed the Founders' worldviews and of how they synthesized those sometimes discordant strains into a cohesive ideology of revolution and republicanism.[54] The second level, while not devoid of historical analysis, is more ideologically driven, using the Founders' religious or deistic bona-fides to establish whether they intended to create a Christian nation or secular regime of church-state separation, a controversy that then governs the modern debate about the role of religion in American public life. Overlaying both levels is the irrefutable historical fact that the political leaders of the founding—not to mention the leading clergy of the time—regularly used religious rhetoric and biblical symbolism to justify the patriot and republican causes.[55]

---

54. Bernard Bailyn, *The Ideological Origins of the American Revolution* (Cambridge: Harvard University Press, 1967), passim.

55. Mark David Hall, *Did America Have a Christian Founding?* (Nashville, TN: Nelson Books, 2019); Thomas Kidd, *God of Liberty: A Religious History of the American Revolution* (New York: Basic Books, 2010); Vincent Philip Munoz, *God and the*

With the outbreak of the American Revolution, religious rhetoric became a powerful political tool for sanctifying the patriot cause and demonizing Great Britain. Unquestionably, the most popular scriptural allusion, used by clergy and politicians alike, was the Exodus story. First and foremost, it was a story of war and of a victory by a chosen people over a superior military force. Clergyman Nicholas Street declared in 1777 that "the British tyrant is only acting over the same wicked and cruel part, that Pharaoh king of Egypt acted towards the children of Israel about 3000 years ago."[56] Exodus was also a story of redemption, both politically and spiritually. As Street continued, "We in this land are, as it were, led out of Egypt by the hand of Moses," the current Mosaic savior being George Washington.[57] These parallels resonated with a scripturally literate public. Political figures also made analogies to the Exodus story. In a 1776 letter to his wife Abigail, John Adams commended a sermon that had made "a Parallel between the Case of Israel and that of America, and between the Conduct of Pharaoh and that of [King] George."[58] Not only did latent Puritans like Adams draw such parallels but also religious dilettantes, including Benjamin Franklin, Thomas Jefferson and Tom Paine. In *Common Sense*, Paine referred to the King as "the hardened, sullen-tempered Pharaoh of England."[59] Then, in his tenth *American Crisis*, Paine again described King George III as "Pharaoh on the edge of the Red Sea" who "sees not the plunge he is making" in opposing American independence.[60] Such imagery was immensely popular, in no small part because it was familiar and resonated in peoples' imaginations. Franklin

---

Founders (New York: Cambridge University Press, 2009); Derek H. Davis, *Religion and the Continental Congress, 1774–1789* (New York: Oxford University Press, 2002); Steven K. Green, *Inventing a Christian America: The Myth of the Religious Founding* (New York: Oxford University Press, 2015), 1–14.

56. Nicholas Street, "The American States Acting over the Part of the Children of Israel in the Wilderness and Thereby Impeding their Entrance into Canaan's Rest" (1777), in *God's New Israel: Religious Interpretations of American Destiny*, ed. Conrad Cherry (Englewood Cliffs, NJ: Prentice-Hall, 1971), 70.

57. Street, "American States Acting over the Part of the Children of Israel," 78.

58. John Adams to Abigail Adams, 17 May 1776, Adams Family Papers, Massachusetts Historical Society, www.masshist.org/digitaladame/archive.

59. Thomas Paine, "Common Sense," in *The Life and Major Writings of Thomas Paine*, ed. Philip S. Foner (New York: Citadel Press Book, 1993), 10–11.

60. Thomas Paine, "American Crisis X," in Foner, *Life and Major Writings of Thomas Paine*, 193.

and Jefferson even recommended that the Great Seal of the new nation feature an image of Moses leading the Israelites to the promised land.[61]

As noted, the ubiquity of biblical and providential discourse during the revolutionary era is indisputable. Deciphering the purposes and meanings of this religious-political rhetoric, however, is a more difficult task. In one review of original documents from the period—pamphlets, letters, speeches, debates, and sermons—Donald Lutz determined that the Bible was cited more frequently than any other source or ideological tradition, appearing in approximately one-third of the documents (the other traditions being Enlightenment and Whig sources, the common law, and classical writings). Lutz acknowledged, however, that "about three-quarters of all references to the Bible came from reprinted sermons," a fact that possibly limits the scope of the Bible's influence.[62] Scholarly and popular writers have disagreed over how much significance to attribute to the prominence of religious rhetoric; in essence, were the Founders more religiously devout than they traditionally have been portrayed and did their beliefs inform their understanding of republican principles, or were the Founders simply employing familiar and powerful idioms to inspire and motivate people in the patriot cause? For example, after retiring from public life, John Adams told Thomas Jefferson that "the Bible is the best book in the World. It contains more of my little Philosophy than all the Libraries I have seen."[63] In another letter, this one to Benjamin Rush, Adams affirmed that "[t]e Bible contains the most profound Philosophy, the most perfect Morality, and the most refined Policy, that was ever conceived upon earth. It is the most Republican Book in the World, and therefore I will still revere it."[64] How is one to evaluate such affirmations—and dozens of similar statements by other Founders—particularly those contained in private correspondence not intended to inspire the greater populace? Does the fact that Adams and others venerated the Bible mean

---

61. James P. Byrd, *Sacred Scripture, Sacred War: The Bible and the American Revolution* (New York: Oxford University Press, 2013), 45–47, 63–70; Irving L. Thompson, "Great Seal of the United States," *Encyclopedia Americana* 13:362.

62. Donald S. Lutz, *The Origins of American Constitutionalism* (Baton Rouge: Louisiana State University Press, 1988), 140–42.

63. Adams to Jefferson, 25 December 1813, in *The Adams-Jefferson Letters*, ed. Lester J. Cappon (Chapel Hill: University of Chapel Hill Press, 1987), 412.

64. Adams to Rush, 2 February 1807, in *The Founders on Religion: A Book of Quotations*, ed. James H. Huston (Princeton: Princeton University Press, 2005), 23.

that they intended to integrate biblical values into principles of republican governance? How does one reconcile such affirmations against other seemingly contradictory statements? In another letter to Jefferson written within months of the aforementioned letter, Adams extolled the contributions of deist and skeptic writers Voltaire, Bolingbroke, Gibbon and Hume, all critics of the Bible.[65] A few years later Adams commented caustically on the founding of the American Bible Society with its goal "to propagate King James' Bible, through all Nations." "Would it not be better to apply these pious Subscriptions, to purify Christendom from the Corruptions of Christianity, than to propagate those Corruptions in Europe, Asia, Africa and America!" Adams exclaimed.[66] Depending on which sources are examined, Adams can be classified as an admirer of the Bible or a critic of its common uses.

This debate will likely never be resolved. Mark Noll has noted that "even the least orthodox of the Founders of the nation paid some attention to scripture," such that, for that time, "to be an educated member of the Atlantic community was to know the Bible."[67] With scripture providing a common language and source of wisdom—and with the Bible being the most familiar and widely read book at the time—it would have been unusual if scriptural language had not played a prominent role in the revolutionary discourse. In all likelihood, even committed deists such as Benjamin Franklin and Tom Paine were sincere in their use of religious imagery; Franklin (and likely George Washington, as well) had little trouble disputing the authenticity of many Christian doctrines contained in the Bible (e.g., the virgin birth) while believing in forms of interposing providence.[68] As one scholar has concluded, "the mere fact that the founding generation frequently quoted from and alluded to the Bible reveals little about the American founding or the Bible's influence on late eighteenth-century political thought, except that the Bible was a familiar and useful literary source."[69]

---

65. Adams to Jefferson, 18 July 1813, in Huston, *Founders on Religion*, 361–62.
66. Adams to Jefferson, 4 November 1816, in Huston, *Founders on Religion*, 493–94.
67. Mark A. Noll, "The Bible in Revolutionary America," in *The Bible in American Law, Politics, and Political Rhetoric*, ed. James Turner Johnson (Philadelphia: Fortress, 1985), 39–40.
68. Green, *Inventing a Christian America*, 110–53.
69. Daniel L. Dreisbach, *Reading the Bible with the Founding Fathers* (New York: Oxford University Press, 2016), 7.

Although the literature on this subject is exceedingly rich, three recent books have expanded understandings about *how* members of the founding generation used the Bible, opting for qualitative rather than quantitative approaches. In *Sacred Scripture, Sacred War: The Bible and the American Revolution* (2013), James P. Byrd examined sermons, pamphlets, and speeches to see how clergy and politicians plumbed the Bible for authority to prosecute the war against a king with claims of divine authority.[70] Daniel L. Dreisbach's *Reading the Bible with the Founding Fathers* (2016), examined those popular and recurring scriptural passages found in many writings to discover how particular religious themes—righteousness, exaltedness, and resistance to tyranny—influenced the political thinking of the Founders.[71] Finally, Noll, the putative dean of scholarship about the subject, combined more than three decades of work into *In the Beginning Was the Word*, which separates the rhetorical uses of the Bible from the important political themes that the Founders saw reinforced in scripture.[72] Noll concludes that "the founders may have read the Bible, but themes from scripture are conspicuously absent in the political discussions of the nation's early history."[73] One could add that themes from scripture are conspicuously absent in the important political documents of the day, as well. The "Bible's direct political influence was extremely limited, the occasions when the leaders turned to it for assistance in political reasoning extremely rare," Noll asserts. "The Bible was everywhere (in the national consciousness) and nowhere (in explicit political theory)."[74]

The political use of scripture evolved in the nineteenth century. As is well known, the nation experienced a series of evangelical revivals during the nineteenth century, the leading event being the Second Great Awakening, which lasted upward of forty years and was followed by additional spiritual outbursts before and after the Civil War. Evangelical Protestant bodies grew exponentially while new denominations sprung up in the spiritual hothouse that extended from upstate New York, through the Midwest, and into the South. By mid-century, evangelical Protestantism was a

---

70. Byrd, *Sacred Scripture, Sacred War*.
71. Dreisbach, *Reading the Bible with the Founding Fathers*.
72. Mark A. Noll, *In the Beginning Was the Word: The Bible in American Public Life, 1492–1783* (New York: Oxford University Press, 2016), 271.
73. Noll, "Bible in Revolutionary America," 43.
74. Noll, "Bible in Revolutionary America," 52–53.

7. THE BIBLE, LAW, AND POLITICAL RHETORIC 173

dominant force in culture, commandeering the nation's private and public institutions—in particular, the emerging common schools—and securing adherents at the highest levels of business and government. Whereas the first five presidents professed varying degrees of religious skepticism, a majority of the next twenty chief executives had evangelical backgrounds or leanings. For evangelicals, the notion of sola scriptura took on greater meaning than before, with increased emphasis being placed on the New Testament.[75] For example, the primitivist Christian movement that arose in the early part of the century focused almost exclusively on the New Testament; "no creed but the Bible," and "where the Scriptures speak, we speak; and where the Scriptures are silent, we are silent," were their creeds.[76] One effect was that the public religious discourse, including the political religious discourse, shifted from the eighteenth century's preference for the Old Testament to that of the New Testament. The evangelical perspective, coupled with a renewed belief in the millennial mission of the United States and its Manifest Destiny, led many to claim that America was a Christian nation, at times blurring the boundaries separating religious and political discourse.[77]

Because of the unique position of presidents in the nation's political structure and their ability to speak to and on behalf of the nation, historians have paid considerable attention to their religious beliefs. Beginning with Andrew Jackson and continuing for the next ninety years, a majority of presidents had some connection to evangelical Protestantism. James K. Polk converted to Methodism while attending a camp meeting revival; James Garfield was a lay preacher in the Disciples of Christ; Benjamin Harrison was a Presbyterian elder; Rutherford B. Hayes's temperance-wife Lucy famously served only lemonade at White House functions; and

---

75. William G. McLoughlin, *Revivals, Awakenings, and Reform* (Chicago, University of Chicago Press, 1978), 98–178; Winthrop S. Hudson, *Religion in America*, 3rd ed. (New York: Scribner's Sons, 1981), 134–58; Cushing Strout, *The New Heavens and New Earth: Political Religion in America* (New York: Harper & Row, 1974), 102–25; Nathan O. Hatch, *The Democratization of American Christianity* (New Haven: Yale University Press, 1989), 70–73; Robert S. Alley, *So Help Me God: Religion and the Presidency* (Richmond: Knox Press, 1972), 24–42.

76. Lester G. McAllister and William E. Tucker, *Journey in Faith* (St. Louis: Bethany Press, 1975), 110.

77. Robert T. Handy, *A Christian America*, 2nd ed. (New York: Oxford University Press, 1984), 24–56; Jon Butler, *Awash in a Sea of Faith* (Cambridge: Harvard University Press, 1990), 257–88.

Methodist William McKinley entertained guests on Sunday evenings with hymn singing. This meant that most presidents were familiar with the Bible and conversant in its language.[78] Probably the most devout president of the period was Woodrow Wilson who, as a son of a Presbyterian minister, read the Bible and prayed daily. A committed Calvinist, Wilson was prone to moralizing in his public statements, tying policy positions to notions of obligation, duty and service. But as scholars have commented, Wilson's religious concerns were chiefly moral rather than theological; as president, Wilson generally eschewed engaging in brash scriptural oratory like his political contemporary William Jennings Bryan. Yet in one famous address while serving as governor of New Jersey (and contemplating running for president), "The Bible and Progress" (1911), Wilson tied social reform and progress directly to biblical mandates. "We do not judge progress by material standards," he asserted. "Nothing makes America great ... except [for] her acceptance of the standards of judgment which are written large upon these pages of revelation." The "man whose faith is rooted in the Bible knows that reform cannot be stayed." Wilson concluded his speech with flourish: "America was born a Christian nation. America was born to exemplify that devotion to the elements of righteousness which are derived from the revelations of Holy Scripture."[79]

The enigma of the group is Abraham Lincoln, who abjured creeds and church membership but professed a personal spirituality. Even though Lincoln took a nontraditional religious path, he had a deep knowledge of the Bible, one that "far exceeded the content-grasp of most present-day clergymen," according to biographer William Wolf.[80] Wolf claims that no president prior to Lincoln possessed his detail for scripture, and none of them had "ever woven its thoughts and rhythms into the warp and woof of his state papers as he did."[81] Lincoln paraphrased the Bible regularly in his political statements; during the famous Lincoln-Douglas debates, he repeatedly corrected Douglas for the latter's inaccurate use of scripture. Upon receiving a ceremonial Bible by black residents of Baltimore

---

78. Richard V. Pierard and Robert D. Linder, *Civil Religion and the Presidency* (Grand Rapids: Academic Books, 1988), 114–60; Alley, *So Help Me God*, 32–42.

79. Woodrow Wilson, *The Bible and Progress* (New York: Globe Litho, 1911), 5, 7; John Morton Blum, *Woodrow Wilson and the Politics of Morality* (Boston: Little & Brown, 1956), 7–8.

80. William J. Wolf, *Lincoln's Religion* (Boston: Pilgrim, 1970), 39.

81. Wolf, *Lincoln's Religion*, 131.

during the war, Lincoln remarked that "in regard to this Great Book, I have but to say it is the best gift God has given to man."[82] Despite his religious nonconformity, Lincoln declared "I have never denied the truth of the Scriptures."[83] Likely his most famous allusion to the Bible was in his Second Inaugural Address where, quoting from the books of Matthew and Psalms, he declared that "Both [the North and the South] read the same Bible, and pray to the same God; and each invokes His aid against the other." As he continued, "let us judge not that we be not judged.... As was said three thousand years ago, so still it must be said 'the judgments of the Lord are true and righteous together.'"[84] Like many of those who have held that office, Lincoln understood the moral power of scriptural language; unlike some of his successors, Lincoln's use of scripture portrayed a level of sincerity that abjured any effort at political manipulation.[85]

In the modern era, the use of biblical rhetoric by presidents and other politicians has only increased. Franklin Roosevelt likely established the current practice, notwithstanding his own nominal religious faith. According to scholars, Roosevelt "had a rather simplistic approach to religion. He was not especially regular in church attendance, and he paid no attention to doctrine or theological questions."[86] Accordingly, Roosevelt's public statements about religion and the Bible took on a pragmatic quality, with him using them to inspire and motivate people in the great causes they faced: overcoming the Depression and fighting fascism. Although early manifestations of a civil religion can be seen in the statements of Lincoln—civil religion being the intertwining of America's democratic values with generic Judeo-Christian values, such that the celebration of the former takes on a religious dimension—Roosevelt created the modern notion of civil religion that presidents have employed ever since.[87] As he declared in a statement marking the four hundred anniversary of the first printing of an English Bible, "We cannot read the history of our rise and

---

82. Wolf, *Lincoln's Religion*, 135.
83. Wolf, *Lincoln's Religion*, 75.
84. Wolf, *Lincoln's Religion*, 182–83.
85. Pierard and Linder, *Civil Religion and the Presidency*, 91–113; Mark A. Noll, *One Nation under God? Christian Faith and Political Action in America* (San Francisco: Harper & Row, 1988), 90–104; Meacham, *American Gospel*, 114–23.
86. Pierard and Linder, *Civil Religion and the Presidency*, 169.
87. Pierard and Linder, *Civil Religion and the Presidency*, 161–83.

development as a Nation, without reckoning with the place the Bible has occupied in shaping the advances of the Republic."[88]

All of Roosevelt's successors, to one degree or another, have promoted aspects of a civil religion and a national public faith that proclaims scripture in a positive and politically reaffirming manner. Dwight Eisenhower became famous for his frequent innocuous (if not bland) endorsements of faith and civil religion: "our form of government has no sense unless it is founded in a deeply felt religious faith, and I don't care what it is."[89] Eisenhower's numerous religious statements led political commentator William Lee Miller to quip that the president was "a very fervent believer in a very vague religion."[90] The personal religious fealty of a president has never been a prerequisite to making generic affirmations of faith or scripture. Richard Nixon—not known as a particularly devout president—regularly endorsed the values contained in the Bible. In a statement commemorating National Bible Week in 1969, Nixon invited Americans to "pause[] to reflect on the meaning of the Bible in our lives" and "to express our thanks to God for strengthening our faith through Holy Writ."[91] Such uses of civil religion and expressions of public faith have commonly employed passages from the Bible that inspire and unify people and have eschewed passages that might be considered to be dogmatic or divisive.

Likely the most notable example of this approach occurred with the presidency of Jimmy Carter, who was the most religiously devout and biblically literate president since Wilson.[92] Despite his deep faith and mastery of scripture, Carter was generally cautious in his public statements about religion and scripture, particularly about tying policies to biblical dictates. During a town hall meeting in Elk City, Oklahoma, in 1979, Carter faced a hostile questioner who challenged him, as a professed born-again Christian, to reconcile his support for the Equal Rights Amendment (ERA) with the Bible. Carter first reaffirmed that he was "a believer in Jesus Christ

---

88. Franklin Roosevelt, "Statement on the Four Hundredth Anniversary of the Printing of the English Bible," 6 October 1935, Public Papers of the Presidents, American Presidency Project, http://www.presidency.ucsb.edu/ws/index.php.

89. Kevin M. Kruse, *One Nation Under God* (New York: Basic Books, 2015), 67.

90. William Lee Miller, *Piety along the Potomac* (Boston: Houghton Mifflin, 1964), 34.

91. Richard Nixon, "Statement about National Bible Week," 22 October 1969, Public Papers of the Presidents.

92. Pierard and Linder, *Civil Religion and the Presidency*, 238-239.

and a born-again Christian" who believed in the authority of scripture. Responding to the question, Carter stated:

> I don't predicate my support of the ERA on scriptural references. I think if one reads different parts of the Bible, you can find a good argument either way. I know that [the apostle] Paul felt very strongly that there ought to be a sharp distinction between men and women, and women's role ought to be minimal. But I have a feeling that Christ meant for all of us to be treated equally, and He demonstrated this in many ways. But I really don't think that it would be possible for me to prove all the arguments for or against ERA by reference to the Bible. I look to the Bible as a source for guidance and pray for God's guidance.[93]

Rather than exploiting scripture, Carter usually deferred on the side of humility and religious inclusion (although critics accused Carter of being a political moralizer, like Wilson, particularly for tying US foreign policies to human-rights issues). In his inaugural address, Carter quoted from the book of Micah: "He hath showed thee, O man, what is good; and what doth the Lord require of thee, but to do justly, and to love mercy, and to walk humbly with thy God."[94] This passage was emblematic of Carter's public religious persona.[95]

Despite Carter's cautious use of religious rhetoric, his presidency helped transform public expressions of scripture and faith by presidents and politicians in three ways. The first event, to Carter's chagrin, was that opposition to his presidency led to the rise of the evangelical Christian Right and to what many have claimed as the modern politicization of religion. Not only were religious conservatives now publicly aligned with conservative political policies, the tenor of public rhetoric about faith and scripture became more sectarian, intermixing with traditional expressions of civil religion.[96] The second, related development was that the number

---

93. Jimmy Carter, "Elk City, Oklahoma Remarks and a Question-and-Answer Session at a Town Meeting," 24 March 1979, Public Papers of the Presidents.

94. Jimmy Carter, "Inaugural Address," 20 January 1977, Public Papers of the Presidents (quoting Micah 6:8).

95. Pierard and Linder, *Civil Religion and the Presidency*, 231–56; Peter G. Bourne, *Jimmy Carter* (New York: Scribner, 1997), 170, 382, 466–68.

96. Garry Wills, *Under God: Religion and American Politics* (NY: Simon & Schuster, 1990), 119–21; Kenneth D. Wald and Allison Calhoun-Brown, *Religion and Politics in the United States*, 7th ed. (Lanham, MD: Rowman & Littlefield, 2014), 216–17.

of religious statements and affirmations of faith by public figures of both political parties significantly increased. Beginning with Ronald Reagan, the frequency and specificity of references to God, faith, and scripture in presidential statements skyrocketed. Political leaders became more comfortable with speaking publicly about their own religious faith and quoting from scripture, and they felt less constrained about what types of scriptural passages to use. In the words of Garry Wills, Reagan "spoke [evangelicals'] language of God and country, of finding the answer to all life's problems in the Bible."[97] Third, Reagan began a practice of using scripture to defend partisan and controversial policies. In 1983 Reagan proclaimed that year to be the "Year of the Bible" for its "unique contribution ... in shaping the history and character of this Nation."[98] Addressing a group of Christian women leaders several months later, Reagan defended that proclamation by quoting from the book of Isaiah, stating that the prophet "reminded us that 'The Lord opens His gates and keeps in peace the nation that trusts in Him'" (Isa 26:2). This meant "that preserving America must begin with faith in the God who has blessed our land." Using that as a segue, Reagan then declared that "I want to see the Congress act on our constitutional amendment permitting voluntary prayer in America's schoolrooms."[99] In another example of politicizing scripture, Reagan used the Bible in support of his opposition to abortion, telling the National Association of Religious Broadcasters in 1984 that "abortion has denied [helpless innocents] the first and most basic of human rights.... Without that right, no other rights have meaning. 'Suffer the little children to come unto me, and forbid them not, for such is the kingdom of God'" (Matt 19:14).[100] This is not to suggest Reagan crassly manipulated scripture for political ends; he reputedly had great faith in the Bible, telling one interviewer that "I have never had any doubts about [the Bible] being of divine origin."[101] Still, with the Reagan

---

97. Wills, *Under God*, 120.

98. Ronald Regan, "Presidential Proclamation 5018," 3 February 1983, Public Papers of the Presidents.

99. Ronald Reagan, "Remarks and a Question-and-Answer Session With Women Leaders of Christian Religious Organizations," 13 October 1983, Public Papers of the Presidents.

100. Ronald Reagan, "Remarks at the Annual Convention of the National Religious Broadcasters," 30 January 1984, Public Papers of the Presidents.

101. Pierard and Linder, *Civil Religion and the Presidency*, 257–83.

presidency, the political use of scripture seemed to shift qualitatively, as well as quantitatively.

Since Reagan, the use of scripture among presidents—at times to defend policies or agendas—has become commonplace, such that it is rarely questioned. Reagan's successor, George H. W. Bush, was elected in 1988 with widespread evangelical support, despite his own mainline religious leanings and apparent discomfort with employing evangelical rhetoric. As a result, Bush numerous references to faith and scripture—possibly employed to shore up his evangelical base—lacked the intensity of his predecessor and were more reminiscent of the generic statements from the Eisenhower era.[102] In contrast, his son George W. Bush was a born-again evangelical who was more comfortable using scripture and personalizing his affirmations of faith; at a 2003 observance of the National Day of Prayer, Bush II remarked: "The Scriptures say, 'The Lord is near to all who call on Him.' Calling on God in prayer brings us nearer to each other."[103] Like Reagan, Bush II was also more willing to employ religious rhetoric to defend administration policies. He defended his domestic Faith-Based Initiative (which provided funding to religious entities to perform social services) in part through scripture: "In the Book of James, we are reminded that faith without works is dead. By loving a neighbor as you'd like to be loved yourself, you prove every day that faith is alive. By your work and prayers, you have formed your own army, an army of compassion."[104] Finally, Bush II, a proponent of American exceptionalism, regularly equated the nation's values and mission with God's plan for humanity writ-large. As he remarked in his 2003 State of the Union Address to Congress, "The liberty we prize is not America's gift to the world, it is God's gift to humanity."[105]

---

102. See, for example, George H. W. Bush's statements and remarks at the Annual Southern Baptist Convention in Atlanta, Georgia, 6 June 1991; the Annual Convention of the National Religious Broadcasters, 27 January 1992, the National Prayer Breakfast, 30 January 1992, and the National Association of Evangelicals in Chicago, 3 March 1992, Public Papers of the Presidents.

103. George W. Bush, "Remarks on the National Day of Prayer," 1 May 2003, Public Papers of the Presidents. See also, Bush, "Remarks at the National Hispanic Prayer Breakfast," 15 May 2003, Public Papers of the Presidents.

104. George W. Bush, "Remarks at the White House National Conference on Faith-Based and Community Initiatives," 1 June 2004, Public Papers of the Presidents.

105. George W. Bush, "State of the Union Address, 2003," Public Papers of the

Lest anyone think that such use of scripture has been the sole purview of Republican presidents, Bill Clinton's references to the Bible in official statements outnumbered those of his successor. A Southerner with Baptist roots and regular church-goer, Clinton was comfortable speaking about matters of faith and quoting from scripture. Clinton regularly addressed religious audiences, going beyond the expected attendance at the annual National Prayer Breakfast to speaking frequently at black churches and Jewish groups.[106] Clinton referred to scripture in speeches and remarks concerning civil rights, international human rights, and his chief domestic policies, Charitable Choice, which partnered government with religious nonprofits and houses of worship to provide social services. On more than one occasion, Clinton applied the same biblical passage to these various issues (which he claimed was his favorite scriptural verse): "St. Paul's letter to the Galatians: 'Let us not grow weary in doing good, for in due season we shall reap if we do not lose heart'" (Gal 6:9).[107] Addressing another religious audience while he was under investigation by the special counsel, Clinton spoke about seeking humility. Quoting from 1 Kings, he remarked: "Your servant is here among people you have chosen, a great people, too numerous to count or number. So give your servant a discerning heart to govern your people and to distinguish between right and wrong, for who is able to govern this great people of yours" (1 Kgs 3:8). He asked the audience for their prayers so "that I, and we, might act justly and love mercy and walk humbly with our God."[108] Finally, issuing a statement on the International Day of Prayer for the Persecuted Church, Clinton remarked: "Today, in solidarity with millions of people at home and abroad, we pray for those who suffer for their beliefs—a suffering forewarned by Scripture: '... they shall lay their hands on you, and persecute you ... [you will be] brought before kings and rulers for my name's sake.'" Continuing with the quote from Luke 21:12–15, Clinton stated: "But with this warning comes the promise, 'I

Presidents. See also, Jillinda Weaver, "Civil Religion, George W. Bush's Divine Mission, and an Ethics of Mission," *Political Theology* 9 (2008): 9–26.

106. E.g., William J. Clinton, "Remarks at the Bethel A.M.E. Church in New York City," 25 September 1994, Public Papers of the Presidents.

107. E.g., William J. Clinton, "Remarks at the Ecumenical Breakfast," 20 November 1997, Public Papers of the Presidents.

108. William J. Clinton, "Remarks at the National Prayer Breakfast," 9 February 1998, Public Papers of the Presidents.

will give you a mouth and wisdom, which none of your adversaries will be able to deny or resist.'"[109]

Fellow Democratic President Barack Obama continued the pattern established by Clinton. According to two scholars: "Few presidents [spoke] about their faith as often or as eloquently as Obama as he explained the religious basis for his liberal, social justice orientation."[110] Addressing the National Prayer Breakfast in 2011, Obama noted that he often "petition[ed] God for a whole range of things" when he thought about policy.

> The first category of prayer comes out of the urgency of the Old Testament prophets and the Gospel itself. I pray for my ability to help those who are struggling. Christian tradition teaches that one day the world will be turned right side up and everything will return as it should be. But until that day, we're called to work on behalf of a God that chose justice and mercy and compassion to the most vulnerable.[111]

But like Clinton, Obama spoke to a wide variety of religious groups and gatherings, and he did not shy away from emphasizing the importance of faith and his reliance on scripture and prayer. Unlike Bush II, Obama did not intertwine religious rhetoric with claims of American exceptionalism; instead, he used it to comment on the nation's potential. Remarking on the nation's religious diversity, Obama told one religious audience that "I'm reminded of the power of faith in America; faith in God, and a faith in the promise of this great country.... So as we join in prayer, we remember that this is a nation of Christians and Muslims and Jews and Hindus and nonbelievers."[112] Ironically, despite his frequent references to faith and scripture, Obama was forced to publicly defend his personal religious beliefs against false claims he was a Muslim. Addressing a religious audience, Obama remarked: "My Christian faith, then, has been a sustaining force for me over these last few years. All the more so, when Michelle and I hear our faith questioned from time to time, we are reminded that, ultimately, what matters is not what other people say about us, but whether

---

109. William J. Clinton, "Statement on the International Day of Prayer for the Persecuted Church," 14 November 1998, Public Papers of the Presidents.

110. Wald and Calhoun-Brown, *Religion and Politics in the United States*, 157.

111. Barack Obama, "Remarks at the National Prayer Breakfast," 3 February 2011, Public Papers of the Presidents.

112. Barack Obama, "Remarks at the National Hispanic Prayer Breakfast," 19 June 2009, Public Papers of the Presidents.

we're being true to our conscience and true to our God. 'Seek first His kingdom and His righteousness and all these things will be given to you as well'" (Matt 6:33).[113]

At the time of writing this chapter, it is too early to assess the use of religious rhetoric by President Donald Trump. Trump gives few outward manifestations of the type of personal piety of his recent predecessors. Although raised Presbyterian, Trump is not a regular church-goer and appears uncomfortable speaking about faith or scripture (with him famously butchering a reference to 2 Corinthians during the 2016 campaign).[114] Trump's limited references to scripture have generally occurred at appearances before religiously conservative groups, such as the Values Voter Summit and the Faith and Freedom Coalition, and then in statements concerning mass shooting or other tragedies.[115] His administration has seemed more willing to allow Vice President Mike Pence, a born-again evangelical, to assume the role of the nation's pastor-in-chief, for as to date, Pence has made more than five times as many references to faith and scripture in public statements than has Trump.[116] There is some evidence that most Americans accept (or expect) public officials and politicians to use religious rhetoric, provided it is not sectarian or dogmatic. If approached adroitly, moderate religious rhetoric can be effective—the same statement can have multiple effects: religious moderates and liberals may consider it as either a rhetorical flourish or simply reflecting the personal faith of the speaker, while religious conservatives may interpret it as an affirmation of their religious values. Despite the willingness of the American public to allow their political leaders to acknowledge or even promote religious faith, the majority of Americans apparently do not vote for an elected official based on that candidate's announced faith. In 2012,

---

113. Barack Obama, "Remarks at the National Prayer Breakfast," 3 February 2011, Public Papers of the Presidents.

114. Daniel Burke, "The Guilt-Free Gospel of Donald Trump," CNN, 24 October 2016, https://tinyurl.com/SBL6704t1; Liz Hayes, "Hero Worship," *Church & State* (November 2017): 13–14.

115. Donald J. Trump, "Remarks at the Faith and Freedom Coalition's Road to Majority Conference," 8 June 2017, Public Papers of the Presidents; Trump, "Remarks on the Shootings in Las Vegas, Nevada," 2 October 2017, Public Papers of the Presidents; Trump, "Remarks at the Family Research Council's Values Voter Summit," 13 October 2017, Public Papers of the Presidents.

116. The comparison between Trump and Pence is based on the list provided in the Public Papers of the Presidents.

when the nation faced the prospect of electing the first Mormon president in Mitt Romney, 58 percent of voters indicated that the religious affiliation of a candidate was not important in determining their ultimate vote, as compared to 40 percent who indicated it was important in making their choice.[117] That data, however, may obscure the divisions that exist between Democrats and Republicans, as a candidate's profession of religious faith is more important to Republican voters and can be crucial for securing that party's nomination for political office.[118]

Most scholars predict that the political use of scripture will continue, if not increase, in the foreseeable future. The Bible is a source of comfort and inspiration, and many of its passages are familiar to a large number of people. While the majority of political references are no doubt heartfelt, there is also little doubt that the speakers are aware of the political advantages of such rhetoric. Political figures have little reason to feel constrained from relying on scripture to solemnize and legitimize their public statements or even policies, notwithstanding the potential downside of aligning controversial policies with "the word of God."[119] As a result, Noll has asked: "Has not the political use of the Bible in America amounted to a weary parade of misapplication, text mongering, self-serving interpretation, and (in general) abuse of Scripture?" Perhaps so, but as the political use of the Bible is such a large part of our political tradition, public appeals to its contents are likely to continue.[120]

Conclusion

Questions about the relationship between the Bible and American law and its political institutions present a paradox. The Bible has had an undeniable impact on the nation's history and culture, inspiring and motivating people in their social relationships and intellectual endeavors. Biblical mandates have dictated standards for personal and public behavior. Yet the Bible's influence on the development and maintenance of the nation's

---

117. First Amendment Center, *State of the First Amendment 2012* (Arlington, VA: Freedom Forum), 6.
118. Wald and Calhoun-Brown, *Religion and Politics in the United States*, 216–18.
119. Pierard and Linder, *Civil Religion and the Presidency*, 284–98; Jim Wallis, *God's Politics* (San Francisco: Harper San Francisco, 2005).
120. Noll, *One Nation Under God*, 166–76.

legal and political systems has been indirect and unofficial. Both systems operate at levels distinct from religion and base their legitimacy in secular rationales. Both systems presuppose a regime of separation of church and state. Yet, as discussed, neither system has operated completely free from scriptural influences. Because both systems are, at their core, institutions that reflect and reinforce the culture and because the Bible has had such an impact on the nation's history and cultural development, it should come as no surprise that some overlaps exist.

Bibliography

Adams Family Papers. Massachusetts Historical Society. www.masshist.org/digitaladame/archive.

Alley, Robert S. *So Help Me God: Religion and the Presidency*. Richmond: John Knox, 1972.

Bailyn, Bernard. *The Ideological Origins of the American Revolution*. Cambridge: Harvard University Press, 1967.

Balkin, Jack M. "Why Are Americans Originalists?" Yale Law School, Public Law Research Paper 492.

Barna Group. *State of the Bible 2017*. Philadelphia: American Bible Society, 2017.

Barton, David. *The Myth of Separation*. Aledo, TX: Wallbuilder, 1992.

Berman, Harold J. "The Interaction of Law and Religion." *Capital University Law Review* 8 (1979): 345–55.

———. *Law and Revolution: The Formation of the Western Legal Tradition*. Cambridge: Harvard University Press, 1983.

———. "Religion and Law: The First Amendment in Historical Perspective." *Emory Law Journal* 35 (1986): 777–93.

Blackstone, William. *Commentaries on the Laws of England—Book the First: Of the Rights of Persons*. Edited by Stanley N. Katz. Chicago: University of Chicago Press, 1979.

Blum, John Morton. *Woodrow Wilson and the Politics of Morality*. Boston: Little & Brown, 1956.

Bourne, Peter G. *Jimmy Carter*. New York: Scribner, 1997.

Burke, Daniel. "The Guilt-Free Gospel of Donald Trump." CNN. 24 October 2016. https://tinyurl.com/SBL6704t1.

Butler, Jon. *Awash in a Sea of Faith*. Cambridge: Harvard University Press, 1990.

Byrd, James P. *Sacred Scripture, Sacred War: The Bible and the American Revolution.* New York: Oxford University Press, 2013.
Cappon, Lester J., ed. *The Adams-Jefferson Letters.* Chapel Hill: University of North Carolina Press 1987.
Church, Forrest. *So Help Me God.* New York: Harcourt, 2007.
Conn, Joseph L. "Down for the Count." *Church & State* (December 2003): 2–4.
Corwin, Edward S. *The "Higher Law" Background of American Constitutional Law.* Ithaca, NY: Cornell University Press, 1955.
Davis, Derek H. *Religion and the Continental Congress, 1774–1789.* New York: Oxford University Press, 2002.
Dierenfield, Bruce J. *The Battle over School Prayer.* Lawrence, KA: University Press of Kansas, 2007.
Dreisbach, Daniel L. *Reading the Bible with the Founding Fathers.* New York: Oxford University Press, 2016.
Eidsmoe, John. *Christianity and the Constitution.* Grand Rapid, MI: Baker Book House, 1987.
Federer, William J. *The Ten Commandments and Their Influence on American Law.* Saint Louis: Amerisearch, 2003.
Finkelman, Paul. "The Ten Commandments on the Courthouse Lawn and Elsewhere." *Fordham Law Review* 73 (2005): 1477–1520.
First Amendment Center. *State of the First Amendment 2008.* Arlington, VA: Freedom Forum, 2008.
———. *State of the First Amendment 2012.* Arlington, VA: Freedom Forum, 2008.
Georgetown Law. "J.D. Program." Georgetown.edu. https://www.law.georgetown.edu/academics/jd-program/
Green, Steven K. *The Bible, the School, and the Constitution.* New York: Oxford University Press, 2012.
———. "The Fount of Everything Just and Right? The Ten Commandments as a Source of American Law." *Journal of Law and Religion* 14 (1999–2000): 525–58.
———. *Inventing a Christian America: The Myth of the Religious Founding.* New York: Oxford University Press, 2015.
———. *The Second Disestablishment: Church and State in Nineteenth-Century America.* New York: Oxford University Press, 2010.
———. *The Third Disestablishment: Church, State, and American Culture, 1940–1975.* New York: Oxford University Press, 2019.

Greene, Jamal, Nathaniel Persily, and Stephen Ansolabehere. "Profiling Originalism." *Columbia Law Review* 111 (2011): 356–418.

Hall, Kermit L. *The Magic Mirror: Law in American History.* New York: Oxford University Press, 1989.

Hall, Mark David. *Did America Have a Christian Founding?* Nashville: Nelson Books, 2019.

Handy, Robert T. *A Christian America.* 2nd ed. New York: Oxford University Press, 1984.

Hatch, Nathan O. *The Democratization of American Christianity.* New Haven: Yale University Press, 1989.

Hayes, Liz. "Hero Worship." *Church & State* (November 2017): 13–14.

Horwitz, Morton J. "The Meaning of the Bork Nomination in American Constitutional History." *University of Pittsburg Law Review* 50 (1989): 655–66.

———. *The Transformation of American Law, 1780–1860.* Cambridge: Harvard University Press, 1977.

Hudson, Winthrop S. *Religion in America.* 3rd ed. New York: Scribner's Sons, 1981.

Huston, James H., ed. *The Founders on Religion: A Book of Quotation.* Princeton: Princeton University Press, 2005.

Kidd, Thomas. *God of Liberty: A Religious History of the American Revolution.* New York: Basic Books, 2010.

Kramnick, Isaac, and R. Laurence Moore. *The Godless Constitution: The Case against Religious Correctness.* New York: Norton, 1996.

Kruse, Kevin M. *One Nation Under God.* New York: Basic Books, 2015.

Kutsko, John F. "The Curious Case of the Christian Bible and the U.S. Constitution." Pages 240–48 in *The Bible in American Life.* Edited by Philip Goff, Arthur E. Farnsley, and Peter J. Thuesen. New York: Oxford University Press, 2017.

Le Boutillier, Cornelia Geer. *American Democracy and Natural Law.* New York: Columbia University Press, 1950.

Locke, John. *Second Treatise of Government.* Edited by Mentor Book. New York: Cambridge University Press, 1963.

Lupu, Ira C., and Robert W. Tuttle. *Secular Government, Religious People.* Grand Rapids: Eerdmans, 2014.

Lutz, Donald S. *The Origins of American Constitutionalism.* Baton Rouge: Louisiana State University Press, 1988.

Mann, Horace. *Go Forth and Teach: An Oration Delivered before the Authorities of the City of Boston.* 4 July 1842. Repr. Washington, DC:

Committee on the Horace Mann Centennial, National Education, 1937.

———. *Twelfth Annual Report to the Board of Education*. Boston: Dutton & Wentworth, 1849.

McAllister, Lester G., and William E. Tucker. *Journey in Faith*. Saint Louis: Bethany Press, 1975.

McLoughlin, William G. *Revivals, Awakenings, and Reform*. Chicago: University of Chicago Press, 1978.

Meacham, John. *American Gospel: God, the Founding Fathers, and the Making of a Nation*. New York: Random House, 2006.

Miller, William Lee. *Piety along the Potomac*. Boston: Houghton Mifflin, 1964.

Morris, Richard B. *Studies in the History of American Law*. 2nd ed. New York: Octagon Books, 1974.

Munoz, Vincent Philip. *God and the Founders*. New York: Cambridge University Press, 2009.

Noll, Mark A. "The Bible in Revolutionary America." Pages 39–60 in *The Bible in American Law, Politics, and Political Rhetoric*. Edited by James Turner Johnson. Philadelphia: Fortress, 1985.

———. *In the Beginning Was the Word: The Bible in American Public Life, 1492–1783*. New York: Oxford University Press, 2016.

———. *One Nation Under God? Christian Faith and Political Action in America*. San Francisco: Harper & Row, 1988.

Paine, Thomas. "American Crisis X." Pages 189–207 in *The Life and Major Writings of Thomas Paine*. Edited by Philip S. Foner. New York: Citadel, 1993.

———. "Common Sense." Pages 3–46 in *The Life and Major Writings of Thomas Paine*. Edited by Philip S. Foner. New York: Citadel, 1993.

Pierard, Richard V., and Robert D. Linder. *Civil Religion and the Presidency*. Grand Rapids: Academic Books, 1988.

Powell, H. Jefferson. "Rules for Originalists." *Virginia Law Review* 73 (1987): 659–99.

Public Papers of the Presidents. American Presidency Project. http://www.presidency.ucsb.edu/ws/index.php.

Scalia, Antonin. "Originalism: The Lesser Evil." *University of Cincinnati Law Review* 57 (1989): 849–66.

Smith, Peter J., and Robert W. Tuttle. "Biblical Literalism and Constitutional Originalism." *Notre Dame Law Review* 86 (2011): 693–763.

Story, Joseph. "Natural Law." *Encyclopedia Americana* 9:150–58.

———. "Value and Importance of Legal Studies." Pages 503–48 in *The Miscellaneous Writings of Joseph Story*. Edited by William W. Story. Boston: Little & Brown, 1852.

Street, Nicholas. "The American States Acting over the Part of the Children of Israel in the Wilderness and Thereby Impeding their Entrance into Canaan's Rest." Pages 67–81 in *God's New Israel: Religious Interpretations of American Destiny*. Edited by Conrad Cherry. Englewood Cliffs, NJ: Prentis-Hall, 1971.

Strout, Cushing. *The New Heavens and New Earth: Political Religion in America*. New York: Harper & Row, 1974.

Sunstein, Cass R. *Radicals in Robes*. New York: Basic Books, 2005.

Thompson, Irving L. "Great Seal of the United States." *Encyclopedia Americana* 13:362.

Wald, Kenneth D., and Allison Calhoun-Brown. *Religion and Politics in the United States*. 7th ed. Lanham, MD: Rowman & Littlefield, 2014.

Wallis, Jim. *God's Politics*. San Francisco: Harper San Francisco, 2005.

Weaver, Jillinda. "Civil Religion, George W. Bush's Divine Mission, and an Ethics of Mission." *Political Theology* 9 (2008): 9–26.

Wills, Garry. *Under God: Religion and American Politics*. NY: Simon & Schuster, 1990.

Wilson, James. "Lectures on Law." Pages 100–126 in vol. 1 of *The Works of James Wilson*. Edited by James G. McCloskey. Cambridge: Harvard University Press, 1967.

Wilson, Woodrow. *The Bible and Progress*. New York: Globe Litho, 1911.

Wolf William J. *Lincoln's Religion*. Boston: Pilgrim, 1970.

Wright, Benjamin F. *American Interpretations of Natural Law*. New York: Russell & Russell, 1962.

8
THE BIBLE AND THE CURRICULUM OF AMERICAN PUBLIC SCHOOLS (K–12) IN THE TWENTY-FIRST CENTURY

MARK A. CHANCEY

When it comes to the Bible, educators have long faced a dilemma: knowledge of the Bible is important for cultural literacy in American contexts, but widely divergent views of the Bible and legal considerations often make teaching about it controversial. First Amendment jurisprudence cannot completely quell controversy, but it has provided some parameters for legality. According to the religion clauses of the First Amendment (at least as interpreted by the Supreme Court since the mid-twentieth century), public schools and other government agencies can neither create an establishment of religion by promoting religious viewpoints nor prohibit the free exercise of religion. But the extent to which schools succeed in implementing these requirements varies, as demonstrated by a review of places in the kindergarten through twelfth-grade curriculum that sometimes feature biblical material.

The best starting point for understanding the contemporary situation is the famous US Supreme Court case Abington Township School District v. Schempp (1963). The Schempp decision addressed school-sponsored Bible reading, a common (though not universal) practice that dated back to the Common School movement of the nineteenth century. In the mid-1900s, the custom's legality varied between states. Public school teachers or administrators might read a number of verses aloud, or they might ask a student to do so. The reading might occur in homeroom, morning assembly, over the intercom, or in other settings.

Two families filed suit to stop what they saw as an infringement of religious freedom, the Schempps in Pennsylvania and the Murrays in

Maryland. When their cases reached the Supreme Court, it combined them and ruled in the complainants' favor, declaring school-sponsored Bible reading a religious exercise. As such, it violated the First Amendment by constituting an establishment of religion. Despite initial resistance to the Court's ruling in some areas, school-sponsored Bible reading of the pre-Schempp variety faded away over time, though isolated examples may still occur under the radar of larger public attention. The ruling became infamous in some quarters as the case in which Madalyn Murray, who went on to become the famous atheist activist Madalyn Murray O'Hair, got the Bible banned from public schools.[1]

In reality, nothing of the sort happened. The Bible was never banned, just its school-sponsored ritualistic reading. The Court specifically acknowledged that another type of Bible reading was not only legal but also pedagogically desirable. Its majority opinion noted:

> It might well be said that one's education is not complete without a study of comparative religion or the history of religion and its relationship to the advancement of civilization. It certainly may be said that the Bible is worthy of study for its literary and historic qualities. Nothing we have said here indicates that such study of the Bible or of religion, when presented objectively as part of a secular program of education, may not be effected consistently with the First Amendment.[2]

According to this logic, school-sponsored study of the Bible and other aspects of religion are constitutional when done objectively for secular purposes such as cultural literacy. This short, three-sentence dictum has proven to be an important legal justification for subsequent attention to religion across the curriculum.

The Schempp decision prompted educators to devote new attention to identifying appropriate methods and resources for teaching about religion in a nonsectarian manner.[3] Though this movement enjoyed some

---

1. Abington Township School District v. Schempp, 374 U.S. 203 (1963); Joan DelFattore, *The Fourth R: Conflicts over Religion in America's Public Schools* (New Haven: Yale University Press, 2004), 82–105.

2. Abington Township School District v. Schempp at 225.

3. For overviews of the Bible and public education that include discussion of the pre-Schempp period, see DelFattore, *Fourth R*; Suzanne Rosenblith and Patrick Womac, "The Bible in American Public Schools," in *The Oxford Handbook of the Bible in America*, ed. Paul Gutjahr (New York: Oxford University Press, 2017), 263–75;

success, by the 1980s many of its advocates felt that progress had been insufficient. They argued that fear of controversy, lack of pertinent teacher training, and paucity of suitable resources had prevented schools from taking advantage of Schempp's endorsement of teaching about religion. The unfortunate result was a K–12 curriculum that was all too often religion-free, resulting in huge gaps in students' cultural literacy that left them unprepared for responsible citizenship in a religiously diverse society. In the 1980s and 1990s, scholars, teachers, educational organizations, civil libertarian groups, religious groups, and governmental offices renewed the call for greater attention to religion.[4] Most scholars who have studied the issue agree that the public schools of the 2000s have since made considerable strides in this area. Nonetheless, many argue that coverage of religion still remains spotty, incomplete, inconsistent, and insufficiently informed by scholarship.[5] Meanwhile, as America's population becomes more religiously diverse and globalization gives developments around the world

---

David L. Barr and Nicholas Piediscalzi, eds., *The Bible in American Education: From Source Book to Textbook* (Philadelphia: Fortress, 1982).

4. See especially First Amendment Center, *A Teacher's Guide to Religion in the Public Schools* (Nashville: First Amendment Center, 2008), and First Amendment Center, *The Bible and Public Schools: A First Amendment Guide* (Nashville: First Amendment Center, 1999), both available at the "National Consensus Documents" webpage of the Freedom Forum Institute's Religious Freedom Center, http://www.religiousfreedomcenter.org/grounding/consensus/. Other landmark publications include Association for Supervision and Curriculum Development, *Religion in the Curriculum* (Alexandria, VA: Association for Supervision and Curriculum Development, 1987); US Department of Education, "Religious Expression in Public Schools: A Statement of Principles" (1995), Educational Resource Information Center, https://tinyurl.com/SBL6704r2; C. Frederick Risinger, *Religion in the Social Studies Curriculum*, ERIC Digest (Bloomington, IN: ERIC Clearinghouse for Social Studies/Social Science Education, 1993), available at https://tinyurl.com/SBL6704v2; and Risinger, *Teaching about Religion in the Social Studies*, ERIC Digest (Bloomington, IN: ERIC Clearinghouse for Social Studies/Social Science Education, 1988), available at https://tinyurl.com/SBL6704w2.

5. Charles C. Haynes, "Battling over the Bible in Public Schools: Is Common Ground Possible?," in *The Bible in the Public Square: Its Enduring Influence in American Life*, ed. Mark A. Chancey, Carol Meyers, and Eric M. Meyers (Atlanta: Society of Biblical Literature, 2013), 181–91; Warren A. Nord, *Does God Make a Difference? Taking Religion Seriously in Our Schools and Universities* (New York: Oxford University Press, 2010); Warren A. Nord and Charles C. Haynes, *Taking Religion Seriously across the Curriculum* (Alexandria, VA: Association for Supervision and Curriculum Development; Nashville: First Amendment Center, 1998).

even more immediate relevance, the importance of religious literacy for civic formation is increasingly evident.⁶

Subsequent court decisions have expounded further on Schempp's affirmation of the study of the Bible for "its literary and historic qualities" and the "objective" study of religion as "part of a secular program of education." Lemon v. Kurtzman (1971), a US Supreme Court case that considered public reimbursement of parochial schools' expenses, is particularly important for its articulation of principles that became known as the Lemon Test. According to that test, a governmental entity violates the Establishment Clause if its actions were motivated by a religious purpose, have a primary effect of advancing or inhibiting religion, or result in excessive governmental entanglement with religion.⁷ A closely related principle from a later court decision is the Endorsement Test, articulated by Justice Sandra Day O'Connor in a concurring opinion in Lynch v. Donnelly (1984): "Endorsement sends a message to nonadherents that they are outsiders, not full members of the political community, and an accompanying message to adherents that they are insiders, favored members of the political community. Disapproval sends the opposite message."⁸ By this test, governmental entities should signal neither endorsement nor disapproval on matters of religion. For public schools, the legal and pedagogical goal is to teach about religion in ways that neither promote nor disparage religion in general, particular religions or religious views, or nonreligion. Though complete objectivity and neutrality are impossible, fair and evenhanded teaching that reflects the spirit of these legal principles is an achievable goal.⁹

---

6. Linda K. Wertheimer, *Faith Ed: Teaching about Religion in an Age of Intolerance* (Boston: Beacon, 2015); Walter Feinberg and Richard A. Layton, *For the Civic Good: The Liberal Case for Teaching Religion in the Public Schools* (Ann Arbor: University of Michigan Press, 2014); Emile Lester, *Teaching about Religions: A Democratic Approach for Public Schools* (Ann Arbor: University of Michigan Press, 2011); American Academy of Religion: Religion in the Schools Task Force, *Guidelines for Teaching about Religion in K–12 Public Schools in the United States* (Atlanta: American Academy of Religion, 2010), https://tinyurl.com/SBL6704c7; Diane L. Moore, *Overcoming Religious Illiteracy: A Cultural Studies Approach to the Study of Religion in Secondary Education* (New York: Palgrave Macmillan, 2007); Caroline Branch, "Unexcused Absence: Why Public Schools in Religiously Plural Society Must Save a Seat for Religion in the Curriculum," *Emory Law Journal* 56.5 (2007): 1431–74.

7. Lemon v. Kurtzman, 403 U.S. 602 (1971).

8. Lynch v. Donnelly, 465 U.S. 668 (1984) at 687.

9. Susan E. Eckes and Allison Fetter-Harrott, "Religion and the Public School Cur-

How does study of the Bible fit into the larger picture of public schools' study of religion? Trying to attain a comprehensive understanding of this issue is akin to looking through a glass dimly. Public school curricula and practices are constantly shifting. Standards for each subject vary between states, as does the degree of local control over the curriculum.[10] States routinely change their standards. Some favor highly detailed standards, while others do not. Textbook approval and selection processes diverge widely, and a single textbook can exist in different editions aimed at different states. Some districts allow students to take online courses from approved vendors. The success of the charter school movement has created further diversity. Charter schools must adhere to the same curricular and legal guidelines of regular public schools, but they operate outside the oversight of school districts.[11] For both regular schools and charter schools, details on what is taught at the classroom level are surprisingly difficult to come by. Nonetheless, the most likely places in the curriculum for K–12 students to encounter discussion of biblical material are easy to identify.

Bible Courses

In most states, at least a few schools offer Bible courses at either the junior high or high school level, and in some states (such as North Carolina) the number can be quite high. Such courses typically fall under the rubric of social studies or English language arts.[12] Occasionally schools incorporate Bible classes into even the elementary grades. When instruction about the

---

riculum," in *International Perspectives on Education, Religion and Law*, ed. Charles J. Russo (New York: Routledge, 2014), 28–41; Charles C. Haynes and Oliver Thomas, *Finding Common Ground: A First Amendment Guide to Religion and Public Schools* (Nashville: First Amendment Center, 2007); Kent Greenawalt, *Does God Belong in Public Schools?* (Princeton: Princeton University Press, 2005); First Amendment Center, *Teacher's Guide to Religion in the Public Schools* and *The Bible and Public Schools*.

10. A Christian group named Gateways to Better Education collated references to the Bible in standards across the country. See Gateways to Better Education, *The Bible in State Academic Standards: A Report on All Fifty States* (Lake Forest, CA: Gateways to Better Education, 2014).

11. National Alliance for Public Charter Schools, http://www.publiccharters.org/; National Charter Schools Resource Center. "What Is a Charter School?," https://tinyurl.com/SBL6704c9.

12. Marie Goughnour Wachlin, "The Place of Bible Literature in Public High School English Classes," *Research in the Teaching of English* 31.1 (1997): 7–49.

Bible is offered on-campus during school hours, it falls under the legal parameters described above. It is legal in many states, however, for students to receive overtly religious instruction off-campus during school hours from nonschool personnel in an arrangement known as "released time." In some states, religiously oriented released time courses can count for academic credit.[13]

Differences in contemporary configurations of Bible courses reflect their diverse historical origins. Beginning in the 1910s and 1920s, educators experimented with different ways to coordinate public and religious education. To preserve the separation of church and state, some opted for off-campus religious instruction, whether through released time plans, after school programs, or even arrangements in which students received credit for Sunday School. Others argued for religious education right in the classroom during the regular school day. In some states and localities, students received credit for these classes; in others, that option was not available. By the mid-century, programs of one type or another were common in many regions. Most were Protestant, but in some areas Jewish, Roman Catholic, and Latter-day Saints programs also existed.[14]

The survival of these courses faced a serious challenge when Vashti McCollum protested the plan utilized in Champaign, Illinois, in 1945. Students there were excused from their regular studies to get instruction on school premises from representatives of local houses of worship. The school placed enormous pressure on students to participate, and McCollum's decision to withdraw her child was met with harassment and ostracism. Her lawsuit eventually made its way all the way to the US Supreme Court,

---

13. James A. Swezey and Katherine G. Schultz, "Released Time Programs in Religion Education," in *Religion in the Public Schools: Negotiating the New Commons*, ed. Michael D. Waggoner (Lanham, MD: Rowman & Littlefield, 2013), 77–90; Released Time Bible Education, www.releasedtime.org.

14. On the history and different forms of Bible courses, see Jonathan Zimmerman, *Whose America? Culture Wars in the Public Schools* (Cambridge: Harvard University Press, 2002), 135–50; DelFattore, *Fourth R*; and Mark A. Chancey in the following: "The Bible and American Public Schools in Historical Perspective," in *The Oxford Handbook on Religion and American Education*, ed. Michael Waggoner and Nathan Walker (Oxford: Oxford University Press, 2018); Chancey, "Religious Instruction, Public Education, and the Dallas High Schools Bible Study Course (1923–1985)," *Church History* 86.1 (2017): 145–77; Chancey, "Public School Bible Courses in Historical Perspective: North Carolina as a Case Study," in Chancey, Meyers, and Meyers, *Bible in the Public Square*, 193–214.

which declared the program unconstitutional in McCollum v. Board of Education (1948). The Court faulted the program's coercive element, its use of "the State's tax-supported public school buildings for the dissemination of religious doctrines," and its use of "the State's compulsory public school machinery" to aid sectarian groups.[15] The Court later clarified in Zorach v. Clauson (1952) that noncompulsory, off-campus released time instruction was permissible.[16]

Responses to these rulings varied. Some districts dropped religious instruction entirely. Released-time proponents often benefited as some schools moved toward that less controversial option. Others continued to offer on-campus courses taught from a particular religious perspective (typically some version of Protestantism). Schools not offering religion courses found little encouragement to begin in what seemed like a shifting and unclear legal environment.

After the Schempp decision in 1963, educators and scholars began working on new materials that reflected more academic and less religiously biased approaches. Key books included *The Bible Reader: An Interfaith Interpretation*, which presented biblical excerpts alongside commentary written by a rabbi, a Catholic priest, and a Protestant minister, and *The Bible as/in Literature*, which focused on biblical themes and allusions in Western literature. Both of these works remain in use today.[17] Meanwhile, various federal courts weighed in on what was constitutionally permissible and what was not as complainants challenged courses they saw as devotional in nature.[18] A 1979 ruling noted that the central issue "is not the Bible itself, but rather the selectivity, emphasis, objectivity, and interpretive manner, or lack thereof, with which the Bible is taught."[19] It and other rulings have noted elements like the following as problematic: proselytiz-

---

15. McCollum v. Board of Education, 333 U.S. 203 (1948) at 212.
16. Zorach v. Clauson, 343 U.S. 306 (1952).
17. Arthur Gilbert, "Reactions and Resources," in *Religion and Public Education*, ed. Theodore R. Sizer (New York: Houghton Mifflin, 1967), 37–83; Peter S. Bracher and David L. Barr, "The Bible Is Worthy of Secular Study: The Bible in Public Education Today," in Barr and Piediscalzi, *Bible and American Education*, 165–97; Walter M. Abbott, Arthur Gilbert, Rolfe Lanier Hunt, and J. Carter Swaim, *The Bible Reader: An Interfaith Interpretation* (London: Chapman; New York: Bruce Books, 1969); James S. Ackerman and Thayer S. Warshaw, *The Bible as/in Literature*, 2nd ed. (Glennview, IL: ScottForesman, 1995).
18. DelFattore, *Fourth R*, 236–54.
19. Wiley v. Franklin, 468 F. Supp. 133 (E.D. Tenn. 1979) at 150.

ing by teachers, acts of worship, coerced participation, the promotion of theological claims and Bible-based life lessons, the depiction of stories of miracles or divine activity as accurate history, inattention to different biblical canons and the diversity of traditions they represent, and the selection of instructors on the basis of their religious views.[20]

Eager to address what she saw as an ongoing dearth of courses, in 1993 a real estate broker and paralegal named Elizabeth Ridenour started the National Council on Bible Curriculum in Public Schools in Greensboro, North Carolina. The National Council on Bible Curriculum in Public Schools created a curriculum, *The Bible in History and Literature*, for high schools that it portrayed as academically informed and legally sound.[21] According to the council, the curriculum spread to dozens of school districts across the country within just a few years. By 2017, it claimed that its course had "been voted into 1,280 school districts (2,900 high schools) in 39 states" and that over 650,000 students had taken it.[22]

Critics have charged that the council's numbers appear to be greatly exaggerated.[23] They also note that its board of directors and advisory board consist mostly of figures associated with the Christian Right—religious leaders, state and national legislators, donors, and the occasional celebrity—such as actor and martial arts expert Chuck Norris, who joined the board in 2006 and serves as its most prominent spokesman.[24] To address criticisms that input from biblical scholars was lacking, the council at some point began claiming the endorsement of an Austin, Texas-based evan-

---

20. Mark A. Chancey, "Sectarian Elements in Public School Bible Courses: Lessons from the Lone Star State," *Journal of Church and State* 49 (2007): 719–42.

21. National Council on Bible Curriculum in Public Schools, *The Bible in History and Literature*, rev. ed. (Ablu Publishing, 2007).

22. National Council on Bible Curriculum in Public Schools home page (http://bibleinschools.net/index.php).

23. Mark A. Chancey, "'Complete Victory Is Our Objective': National Council on Bible Curriculum in Public Schools," *Religion & Education* 35.1 (2008): 1–21; and Chancey, "A Textbook Example of the Christian Right: The National Council on Bible Curriculum in Public Schools," *JAAR* 75 (2007): 554–81.

24. National Council on Bible Curriculum in Public Schools, "Board of Directors and Advisors," http://bibleinschools.net/About-Us/Board-of-Directors-and-Advisors.php; "Actor Chuck Norris and Wife Gena Join National Council on Bible Curriculum in Public Schools Board of Directors," Standard Newswire, 31 August 2006, https://tinyurl.com/SBL6704u1.

gelical group named Bible Scholars, but even its leader has commented on problems with the council's curriculum.[25]

Thus far the different editions of the National Council on Bible Curriculum in Public Schools curriculum have fallen far short of the legal benchmarks. Its early versions promoted ideas such as the complete historical accuracy of the Bible, the near flawless preservation of the biblical text by scribes, and the Bible's scientific accuracy. One version taught students that NASA had discovered a missing day in time that corresponded to the story of the sun standing still in Josh 10, an urban legend. The council has since removed much of the more unambiguously sectarian content and corrected some factual errors, but its product retains its conservative Protestant flavor. It also retains an emphasis that has guided the project from the beginning: the belief that the Founding Fathers created the United States to be a distinctively Christian nation with the Bible as the foundation of its legal and governmental systems.[26]

The curriculum has been legally challenged twice. In 1998, a federal judge prohibited the Lee County, Florida, school district from offering the New Testament portion of the course because of sectarian bias. The judge allowed the district to teach the Hebrew Bible component because local educators had already made changes to it to address its shortcomings.[27] In 2008, a West Texas school district abandoned the course rather than defend it in court.[28] By the mid-2010s, the National Council on Bible Curriculum in Public Schools appeared to be somewhat in decline. Aside from occasional changes in the number of districts and schools supposedly teaching its course, its website was only occasionally maintained, still listing as advisors individuals who died years before (minister D. James Kennedy, d. 2007, and actress Jane Russell, d. 2011).

---

25. Bible Scholars, www.biblescholars.org; National Council on Bible Curriculum in Public Schools, "Bible Scholars Advisory Council," https://tinyurl.com/SBL6704n2; Katherine Stewart, *The Good News Club: The Religious Right's Stealth Assault on America's Children* (New York: Public Affairs, 2012), 179–80.

26. Feinberg and Layton, *For the Civic Good*, 62–64, 66–70; Brennan Breed and Kent Harold Richards, review of *The Bible in History and Literature*, *Religion & Education* 34.3 (2007): 94–102; Frances R. A. Paterson, "Anatomy of a Bible Course Curriculum," *Journal of Law and Education* 32.1 (2003): 41–65; Chancey, "Complete Victory Is Our Objective"; Chancey, "Textbook Example of the Christian Right."

27. Gibson v. Lee County School Board, 1 F. Supp. 2d 1426 (M.D. Fla. 1998).

28. Mark A. Chancey, "The Bible, the First Amendment, and the Public Schools in Odessa, Texas," *Religion and American Culture* 19.2 (2009): 169–205.

Much of this decline can be attributed to the success of a competing organization, the Bible Literacy Project, which began publishing a textbook titled *The Bible and Its Influence* in 2005. The book was authored by Chuck Stetson, a venture capitalist, and Cullen Schippe, an independent writer, but its list of reviewers and consultants includes numerous professors in pertinent fields, secondary school educators, and individuals from a variety of religious traditions.[29] The result is a project that shows much more effort than the National Council on Bible Curriculum in Public Schools to respect religious diversity and adhere to legal guidelines. The Bible Literacy Project's book is also often very successful in highlighting differences between traditional Jewish and Christian theological readings of key portions of scripture (for example, the prophetic literature of the Tanak). It often employs literary reading strategies and focuses on reception history, adopting an overall approach that Walter Feinberg and Richard A. Layton suggest "provides the basis on which a student might see the meaning of the Bible as mediated through different communities and times."[30]

Despite such strengths, religious studies scholars have also noted weaknesses in the Bible Literacy Project's textbook. It often accepts traditional authorship claims at face value, and its summaries of narrative content often veer close to a Bible-as-history approach. It tends to emphasize the ways in which the Bible has been used as a source for positive social and personal transformation while downplaying the ways in which it has been used to legitimize injustice or oppression. This tendency is perhaps most notable in the way it ignores how American slaveholders appealed to scripture while emphasizing how abolitionists did.[31]

A third high-visibility curriculum may be on its way via the Museum of the Bible (MOTB). Steve Green, president of the Hobby Lobby craft store chain, established this organization in 2010 to promote the ongoing cultural influence and relevance of the Bible.[32] The museum has generated no shortage of controversy, most notably for its acquisitions processes and

---

29. Cullen Schippe and Chuck Stetson, eds., *The Bible and Its Influence*, rev. ed. (Fairfax: BLP Publishing, 2006), iii–iv.

30. Feinberg and Layton, *For the Civic Good*, 64–66, 70–74, quote from 72.

31. Schippe and Stetson, *Bible and Its Influence*, 56–57, 80–81, 301, 302; Moore, "Teaching about the Bible in Public Schools: A Religious Studies Framework," in *Curriculum and the Culture Wars: Debating the Bible's Place in Public Schools*, ed. Melissa Deckman and Joseph Prud'homme (New York: Lang, 2014), 61–84.

32. Museum of the Bible, https://www.museumofthebible.org.

practices. In 2017, the US Department of Justice imposed a $3,000,000 payment on Hobby Lobby for receiving ancient artifacts that had been smuggled and lacked provenance.[33]

MOTB figures have discussed a public school curriculum for years and have already made one attempt to produce one. Speaking of this earlier effort, Green told the National Bible Association in April 2013, "We're working on a four-year, public school Bible curriculum." For Green, the stakes were high. He warned, "This nation is in danger because of its ignorance of what God has taught. There is [sic] lessons from the past that we can learn from, the dangers of ignorance of this book. We need to know it, and if we don't know it, our future is going to be very scary." Given that the Bible was "a book that's impacted our world unlike any other," it was essential in his eyes that students take a course on it. "Someday, I would argue, it should be mandated." Green made clear that the course would affirm the Bible's complete historical accuracy, but he insisted that it would do so in a constitutional manner.[34]

MOTB soon identified a school willing to try out a pilot version: Mustang High School, located just a few miles away from Hobby Lobby's Oklahoma City corporate headquarters. Its goal was to get the course into thousands of public schools within a few years.[35] Though the MOTB claimed that dozens of scholars had helped create the version it provided to Mustang for review, the curriculum was riddled with factual errors, such as the claim that the Bible is "the only book that has been studied, distributed, and interpreted continuously for more than 1,000 years." It often seemed to reflect the same sorts of religious claims that Green had

---

33. US Department of Justice, "United States Files Civil Action to Forfeit Thousands of Ancient Iraqi Artifacts Imported by Hobby Lobby," 5 July 2017, https://tinyurl.com/SBL6704s2; Candida Moss and Joel Baden, "Hobby Lobby's Black-Market Buys Did Real Damage," *New York Times*, 6 July 2017, https://tinyurl.com/SBL6704e2. For a broader examination of the museum's history, programming, collection, and acquisitions practices, see Candida R. Moss and Joel S. Baden, *Bible Nation: The United States of Hobby Lobby* (Princeton: Princeton University Press, 2017).

34. Steve Green, "Speech at the Templeton Awards 2013," YouTube, https://www.youtube.com/watch?v=hjjv9QVrCJU. For a transcript of portions of it, see Robert Cargill, "The Museum of the Bible: Why Are Archaeologists and Bible Scholars So Mad?," Robert Cargill Blog, 19 July 2017, https://tinyurl.com/SBL6704y1.

35. David Van Biema, "Hobby Lobby's Steve Green Launches a New Project: A Public School Bible Curriculum," Religion News Service, 15 April 2014, https://tinyurl.com/SBL6704u2.

expressed in his 2013 speech, encouraging students to think of individual Bible stories as parts of the larger traditional Christian metanarrative and urging them to read passages through the lenses of particular theological themes. One section summarized, "We can conclude that the Bible, especially when viewed alongside other historical information, is a reliable historical source." With the curriculum attracting criticism from scholars and church-state activists and the school district facing threats of a lawsuit, the Mustang board of education decided to shelve the course.[36]

MOTB initially indicated that it had dropped the idea of a public school curriculum altogether, but it reconsidered after finding a different partner: Israeli state schools. It gained access to this market through its connections with an Israeli technology company. The museum quickly revamped its curriculum by removing overtly Christian elements and in 2017 claimed that over 100,000 Israeli students had used the new version.[37]

The museum soon issued another revision, this one for American homeschoolers.[38] Accompanying resources make extensive use of "augmented reality (AR), animations, 3-D models, interactive maps, [and] gamified quizzes." An MOTB spokesman gushed that "the curriculum, with its carefully crafted lessons and technological elements, is without question the future of education."[39] He maintained that "all the educational material—from the representation to descriptions to texts to explanations—were developed in a straightforward and factual manner true to the original intent."[40] Candida R. Moss and Joel M. Baden, however, found that this curriculum bore a heavy Christian theological stamp.[41]

An overview of the museum written in 2017 a few weeks before it officially opened the doors to its Washington, DC, facility noted a "long-

---

36. Mark A. Chancey, *Can This Class Be Saved? The "Hobby Lobby" Bible Curriculum* (Austin: Texas Freedom Network Education Fund, 2014), http://tfn.org/resources/publications/; Moss and Baden, *Bible Nation*, 99–106, 117–136; Adelle M. Banks, "Hobby Lobby President's Bible Curriculum Shelved by Oklahoma School District," Religion News Service, 26 November 2014, https://tinyurl.com/SBL6704v1.

37. Cary L. Summers, *Lifting Up the Bible: The Story behind Museum of the Bible* (Washington, DC: Museum of the Bible; Franklin, TN: Worthy Books, 2017), 48.

38. Museum of the Bible, *Genesis to Ruth Teacher's Guide*, vol. 1 of *Home School Curriculum* (Washington, DC: Museum of the Bible & Compedia, 2016).

39. Summers, *Lifting Up the Bible*, 49.

40. Summers, *Lifting Up the Bible*, 47.

41. Moss and Baden, *Bible Nation*, 117–36.

term hope is to adapt the curriculum for use in American public schools."[42] Should the museum follow through on this goal, its high visibility in American public life guarantees that its product will be a popular choice. Whether its curriculum would satisfy the courts and gain the respect of biblical scholars across the religious spectrum is impossible to predict.

Studies of Bible courses in Florida, Texas, and elsewhere show that, while teachers often use older resources such as Warshaw and Ackerman's *The Bible as/in Literature* and national curricula like those produced by the National Council on Bible Curriculum in Public Schools or the Bible Literacy Project, they also incorporate a wide range of other materials into their classes. Online sources, videos, magazine articles, popular-level books, classic religious reference works, resources produced specifically for religious education—all make their way into the classroom. While some teachers succeed in creating academically sound, nonsectarian courses, others present the material in ways that reflect a particular religious viewpoint, typically one associated with Protestantism. Sometimes such bias appears to be intentional, but in many cases it is likely simply the result of inadequate resources and a lack of teacher preparation programs that provide specific training about religion.[43]

Such problems have not dampened enthusiasm for Bible courses among legislators. Since 2000, lawmakers have sponsored bills and resolutions promoting courses in over a third of the states.[44] Eight states have

---

42. Martyn Wendell Jones, "Inside the Museum of the Bible," *Christianity Today*, 20 October 2017, http://www.christianitytoday.com/ct/2017/november/inside-museum-of-bible.html.

43. Mark A. Chancey, *Reading, Writing and Religion II: Texas Public School Bible Courses in 2011–12* (Austin: Texas Freedom Network Education Fund, 2013); and Chancey, *Reading, Writing and Religion: Teaching the Bible in Texas Public Schools* (Austin: Texas Freedom Network Education Fund, 2006), both at http://tfn.org/resources/publications/; Feinberg and Layton, *For the Civic Good*; Judith E. Schaeffer, *The Good Book Taught Wrong: Bible History Classes in Florida Public Schools* (Washington, DC: People for the American Way, 2000); David Levenson, "University Religion Departments and Teaching about the Bible in Public High Schools: A Report from Florida," *Religious Studies News: AAR Edition* 17 (2002): 3, 7, 10.

44. Bret Lewis and Crystal Lopez, "Politics and Perceptions of Religious Studies: The Arizona Legislature and the Teaching of Religion," *Religion & Education* 42.2 (2015): 147–64; Melissa Deckman, "Religious Literacy in Public Schools: Teaching the Bible in America's Classrooms," in *Curriculum and the Culture Wars: Debating the Bible's Place in Public Schools*, ed. Melissa Deckman and Prud'homme (New York: Lang, 2014), 31–48; Mark A. Chancey, "Bible Bills, Bible Curricula, and Controver-

passed laws that encourage schools to offer them by outlining course content, ensuring the courses count toward state requirements for graduation, and providing legal guidelines (Arizona, Arkansas, Georgia, Kentucky, South Carolina, Tennessee, Texas, and West Virginia). Louisiana and South Dakota approved resolutions encouraging them, and five states passed laws authorizing credit for released time courses taken off campus (Alabama, Indiana, Ohio, South Carolina, and Tennessee).[45] Democrats and Republicans alike have authored and sponsored these measures, but the issue took a new partisan twist in 2016 with the national GOP Platform. It declared, "A good understanding of the Bible being indispensable for the development of an educated citizenry, we encourage state legislatures to offer the Bible in a literature curriculum as an elective in America's high schools."[46] In 2017, the Congressional Prayer Caucus and allied Christian Right organizations released a playbook of model state bills that includes a Bible Literacy Act promoting Bible electives. The courses, in the eyes of those groups, would strengthen recognition of "the place of Christian principles in our nation's history and heritage." New state laws, whether passed for these or other reasons, might boost the number of Bible courses, but whether any such increases will be long-term is unpredictable.[47]

The Society of Biblical Literature has acknowledged the educational and civic value of carefully designed, well-taught Bible electives. Its 2008 *Bible Electives in Public Schools: A Guide* discusses issues of legality (draw-

---

sies of Biblical Proportions: Legislative Efforts to Promote Bible Courses in Public Schools," *Religion & Education* 34.1 (2007): 28–47.

45. Details for laws and resolutions are available at the states' legislative websites. For Bible course laws, see Arizona (2012), Arkansas (2013), Georgia (2006), Kentucky (2017), South Carolina (2007), Tennessee (2008), Texas (2007), and West Virginia (2020). For resolutions, see Louisiana (2008 in the House) and South Dakota (2012). For released time credit laws, see Alabama (2019), Indiana (2019), Ohio (2014), South Carolina (2006), and Tennessee (2019).

46. *The Republican Platform 2016* (Republican National Convention, 2016), 33, available at https://www.gop.com/platform/.

47. Congressional Prayer Caucus, National Legal Foundation, and WallBuilders ProFamily Legislative Network, *Report and Analysis of Religious Freedom Measures Impacting Prayer and Faith in America* (Chesapeake, VA: Congressional Prayer Caucus Foundation, 2017), 4, https://tinyurl.com/SBL6704c4; Frederick Clarkson, "'Project Blitz' Seeks to Do for Christian Nationalism What ALEC Does for Big Business," *Religion Dispatches*, 27 April 2018, http://religiondispatches.org/project-blitz-seeks-to-do-for-christian-nationalism-what-alec-does-for-big-business/.

ing on the resources of the First Amendment Center), academic quality, and sensitivity to religious diversity. Thus, for example, it emphasizes the distinctively Christian nature of the term *Old Testament*, briefly explains differences between canons, advises against the use of a Bible-as-history approach, and notes the challenge of teaching about New Testament passages that disparage Jewish religious leaders.[48]

The American Academy of Religion's 2010 *Guidelines for Teaching about Religion in K–12 Public Schools in the United States* is another strong resource. Their summary of different methods used in religious studies observes, "When the focus is on religious texts themselves, students learn to appreciate their literary value and how religious texts influence literary styles." A Frequently Asked Questions section includes thoughtful responses to questions like. "Does the Bible say that homosexuality is wrong?," "Do Jews believe in heaven?," and "Did the Jews kill Jesus?"[49]

The General Social-Studies Curriculum

Bible courses are not the only type of religion course offered by public schools. Some states (how many is unclear) have formally approved courses on the so-called world religions as social-studies electives.[50] Even where there is no state-recognized elective, some districts may offer such courses as special topics classes or for local credit (meaning that they count toward local graduation requirements even if they do not count toward state requirements). Students taking these courses presumably learn at least basic facts about the Bible and perhaps read selected passages and books.

In 2011, the International Baccalaureate (IB) Programme added a world religions elective to the course roster for its Diploma Programme. The IB class is intended to provide students in upper grades a "systematic, analyti-

---

48. Society of Biblical Literature, *Bible Electives in Public Schools: A Guide*, sbl-site.org, https://tinyurl.com/SBL6704m3.

49. American Academy of Religion: Religion in the Schools Task Force, *Guidelines for Teaching about Religion in K–12 Public Schools in the United States*, 10, 15–16.

50. By far the most famous and best studied of these courses is that of Modesto, California. See Lester, *Teaching about Religions*, 105–48; Emile Lester and Patrick S. Roberts, *Learning about World Religions in Public Schools: The Impact on Student Attitudes and Community Acceptance in Modesto, California* (Nashville: First Amendment Center, 2006).

cal yet empathetic study of the variety of beliefs and practices encountered in nine main religions of the world." Teachers choose five religious traditions out of nine options to study in depth, at least one of which must be Judaism, Christianity, or Islam. Sacred texts are a major theme, along with rituals, doctrines/beliefs, religious experience, and ethics and moral conduct. Courses in which Judaism or Christianity are focal points are thus explicitly required to include study of the Bible. A sample IB essay question asks: "With reference to both creed and scripture, evaluate two different interpretations of the resurrection of Jesus Christ."[51] Only a relatively small number of American public schools offer the IB curriculum (802 as of 2017), however, and presumably only a fraction of those offer this course.[52]

Most students take neither Bible nor world religions courses, but they typically encounter discussion of biblical material elsewhere in the social-studies curriculum in classes on history, geography, and perhaps social sciences.[53] Indeed, the field of social studies has figured prominently in calls for more in-depth instruction about religion, with the National Council for the Social Studies issuing multiple statements on the matter over the decades. Its 2014 statement notes that, despite progress since the 1980s, "religious illiteracy remains wide spread in the United States."[54] In 2017, the council added a new section on religious studies to its College, Career, and Civic Life (C3) Framework for state standards.[55] It developed

---

51. International Baccalaureate Organization, "International Baccalaureate Diploma Programme Subject Brief: Individuals and Societies: World Religions—Standard Level," Ibo.org. https://tinyurl.com/SBL6704b2; see also International Baccalaureate Organization, "Studying World Religions," Ibo.org. https://tinyurl.com/SBL6704c2.

52. International Baccalaureate Organization, "Find an IB World School," Ibo.org, http://www.ibo.org/programmes/find-an-ib-school/?SearchFields.Country=US.

53. Susan L. Douglass, *Teaching about Religion in National and State Social Studies Standards* (Fountain Valley, CA: Council on Islamic Education and Nashville: First Amendment Center, 2000); executive summary at the ERIC website, https://tinyurl.com/SBL6704x2.

54. National Council for the Social Studies, "Study about Religions in the Social Studies Curriculum: A Position Statement of National Council for the Social Studies (NCSS) 2014," socialstudies.org, https://tinyurl.com/SBL6704k2. For a historical overview of its statements, see National Council for the Social Studies, "Supplement on the Academic Study of Religion Added to C3 Framework," socialstudies.org, 2017, https://tinyurl.com/SBL6704m2.

55. National Council for the Social Studies, "Religious Studies Companion Document for the C3 Framework," in *College, Career, and Civic Life (C3) Framework for*

this supplement in collaboration with the Religious Freedom Center of the Freedom Forum Institute and the American Academy of Religion, building on earlier materials by the First Amendment Center and American Academy of Religion's *Guidelines for Teaching about Religion in K–12 Public Schools in the United States*. The section included student learning objectives reflecting religious studies methods and a nonsectarian approach. Sacred texts are one of several types of evidence it identifies for students to study. It specifies that "college, career, and civic ready students ... [can] collect and analyze the meaning and significance of primary and secondary religious sources in their particular social, historical, and political context, including statements of theology and doctrine, sacred texts, depictions of rites and rituals, biographies, histories, ethnography, art and architecture, and demographic data."[56]

The places in the social-studies curriculum where most students learn about religion are in treatments of world history, world geography, and US history. Though states vary in how they align these subjects with grade levels, they typically include them in the elementary school curriculum and then provide opportunities for more in-depth courses at higher grades. They usually require an upper-level US history course, but whether the other courses are mandatory or optional varies.[57]

World history and (to a lesser extent) world geography courses typically include study of Judaism, Christianity, Islam, Buddhism, Hinduism, and sometimes other traditions such as Sikhism or categories such as animism. Because they place considerable emphasis on origins, formative figures and concepts, and sources of authority, their treatments of Judaism and Christianity inevitably include at least some discussion of the Bible. These courses might teach about traditional claims regarding Abraham, Moses, David, Jesus, and Paul and discuss the Ten Commandments, ancient Israelite monarchies, the First and Second Temple, the teachings of Jesus,

---

Social Studies State Standards: Guidance for Enhancing the Rigor of K–12 Civics, Economics, Geography, and History, rev. ed. (Silver Spring, MD: National Council for the Social Studies, 2017), 92–97, available at https://www.socialstudies.org/c3; National Council for the Social Studies, "Supplement on the Academic Study of Religion Added to C3 Framework"; Valerie Strauss, "What Should Students Know about Religion? New Guidance on Teaching It in Public Schools," Washington Post, 1 July 2017, https://tinyurl.com/SBL6704q2.

56. National Council for the Social Studies, "Religious Studies Companion Document for the C3 Framework," 94–95.

57. Douglass, *Teaching about Religion in National and State Social Studies Standards*.

and the spread of Christianity in the Roman world. Explicit attention to ancient history might reappear in discussions of the roots of conflict in the modern Middle East. Most of the course content in this regard probably consists of broad summaries of biblical stories rather than direct engagement with biblical texts, but data proving this for certain one way or the other is unavailable. Biblical scholars might laud attention to Jewish and Christian scriptures where it occurs while also noting the academic (and potentially legal) problems created if and when courses present biblical history uncritically.[58]

Religion also often makes an appearance at several points in standard US history courses. It is prominent in presentations of European exploration and colonization and in considerations of immigration and diversity throughout American history. Other frequently discussed topics include the First Amendment and religious freedom; the two Great Awakenings; religion, slavery, and abolition; the clash between fundamentalism and science in the early twentieth century; the Social Gospel; the Civil Rights movement; and the rise of the Religious Right. Theoretically, exploration of these subjects could easily incorporate academic study of the Bible. Students might read key biblical passages alongside slave narratives or while comparing the dueling hermeneutical strategies of slaveholders and abolitionists. In practice, it is not at all clear how often this happens, and one suspects that most of the time discussions of these subjects refer to biblical content and influential interpretations in only a general way.[59]

---

58. This overview is based on Douglass, *Teaching about Religion in National and State Social Studies Standards*; College Board, *AP World History Course and Exam Description* (New York: College Board, 2017) and *AP Human Geography Course Description* (New York: College Board, 2015), both available at "AP Courses," https://apstudent.collegeboard.org/apcourse; and examination of the standards of California, Georgia, Indiana, Massachusetts, New York, Tennessee, Texas, and Wisconsin. The author would like to thank Moira Bucciarelli, Steve Friesen, Gary Herion, Richard Layton, David Levenson, Carleen Mandolfo, and Kent Richards for their help in examining state standards. See also Dennis R. Ybarra and Gary A. Tobin's *The Trouble with Textbooks: Distorting History and Religion* (Lanham, MD: Lexington, 2008), which is helpful for its compilation of details regarding textbooks' depictions of Jewish history, though occasionally uncritical in its own assumptions about ancient sources.

59. Detailed insights about US history at all grade levels are found in Sheldon M. Stern and Jeremy A. Stern, *The State of State U.S. History Standards 2011* (Washington, DC: Thomas B. Fordham Institute, 2011), https://tinyurl.com/SBL6704r9. For the framework used in both 2014 and 1998 to assess eighth-grade history by the National

One state that has tried to increase attention to the Bible in its social-studies curriculum is Texas.[60] The sheer size of the Texas market makes many publishers eager to please its state board of education, and content developed for Lone Star schools often finds its way into textbooks for other states. In 2009–2010, a faction of the school board aligned with the Christian Right succeeded in steering the social-studies standards more toward their understanding of American history. In their view, the nation's founders intended it to be a (conservative) Christian country, and the Bible was the philosophical and theological basis for the Declaration of Independence and the Constitution. For the high-school US government course, they added a standard on the "major intellectual, philosophical, political, and religious traditions that informed the American founding" that listed "Judeo-Christian (especially biblical law)" first among those traditions. Another new standard that identified individuals whose thought "informed the American founding documents" began with Moses. For high-school US History, they modified a standard about influences on the development of modern political systems by adding "the Jewish Ten Commandments" to a list of documents that ranged from the Code of Hammurabi to the Declaration of the Rights of Man and of the Citizen.[61] Whether other states will follow Texas's lead by highlighting the Bible in this way remains to be seen.

Assessment Governing Board, a federal department, see National Assessment Governing Board, *U.S. History Framework for the 2014 National Assessment of Educational Progress* (Washington, DC: National Assessment Governing Board, 2014). Other works consulted include College Board, *AP United States History Course and Exam Description* (New York: College Board, 2017), and standards of the states mentioned in the previous note.

60. David R. Brockman, *Religious Imbalance in the Texas Social Studies Curriculum: Analysis and Recommendations* (Houston: James A. Baker III Institute for Public Policy of Rice University, 2016), https://tinyurl.com/SBL6704c6; Mark A. Chancey, "Rewriting History for a Christian America: Religion and the Texas Social Studies Controversy of 2009–2010," *JR* 94.3 (2014): 325–53; Keith A. Erekson, ed., *Politics and the History Curriculum: The Struggle over Standards in Texas and the Nation* (New York: Palgrave Macmillan, 2012), especially Richard T. Hughes, "Why Do We Think of America as a Christian Nation?," 127–47.

61. Texas Education Agency, Texas Essential Knowledge and Skills (TEKS) §113.44.c.1.B, §113.44.c.1.C.F, and §113.42.c.20.C.

The General English Language Arts Curriculum

Acknowledging the presence of biblical quotations, allusions, themes, and character types in literature, whether *The Canterbury Tales* or *The Color Purple*, has long been a standard practice of English language arts courses. The Common Core standards, published in 2010, illustrate this point. The standards focus on reading, writing, oral communication, and arithmetic skills across the curriculum and were developed at the request of the Council of Chief State School Officers and the National Governors Association Center for Best Practices. Most states (forty-two as of 2017) have adopted them, though because of their lack of detail in terms of course content individual states continue to maintain their own distinctive standards as well.[62] For a variety of reasons, the Common Core standards have proven controversial and their longevity is by no means assured, but in any case they are useful as a window into current thinking in the field.[63]

References to the Bible in Common Core standards for grades 6–12 focus primarily on its value as source material for later writers and for traditional figures of speech. Students in grades 9 and 10 are expected to "analyze how an author draws on and transforms source material in a specific work (e.g., how Shakespeare treats a theme or topic from Ovid or the Bible or how a later author draws on a play by Shakespeare)." Similarly, students in eighth grade must "analyze how a modern work of fiction draws on themes, patterns of events, or character types from myths, traditional stories, or religious works such as the Bible, including describing how the material is rendered new." A seventh-grade standard on word meanings requires pupils to "interpret figures of speech (e.g., literary, biblical, and mythological allusions) in context."[64]

The Advanced Placement English Literature and Composition course for high schoolers acknowledges a similar appreciation for the Bible's liter-

---

62. Common Core State Standards Initiative, "Standards in Your State," 2017, http://www.corestandards.org/standards-in-your-state/.

63. Joy Resmovits, "The Other Big Debate: What Is the Common Core, Anyway?," *Los Angeles Times*, 16 September 2015, https://tinyurl.com/SBL6704p2. Three states that had initially adopted the standards have since dropped them (see the references to forty-five states for 2013 and forty-two for 2017 at Common Core State Standards Initiative, "Development Process," https://tinyurl.com/SBL6704a2).

64. Common Core State Standards Initiative, *Common Core State Standards for Language Arts and Literacy in History/Social Studies, Science, and Technical Subjects*, 2010, 38, 37, 53, https://tinyurl.com/SBL6704z1.

ary legacy. It notes, "Because the Bible and Greek and Roman mythology are central to much Western literature, students should have some familiarity with them. These religious concepts and stories have influenced and informed Western literary creation since the Middle Ages, and they continue to provide material for modern writers in their attempts to give literary form to human experience."[65]

Yet more information is needed on how teachers handle this material, as an impressively thorough analysis by Robert Todd Bruce and Beatrice Bailey demonstrates.[66] Bruce and Bailey explored the general treatment of religion in K–12 English courses by reviewing the Common Core standards, a 1996 set of guidelines by the International Reading Association and the National Council of Teachers of English, state standards, the most pertinent scholarly journals, materials of a sample of teacher education programs, and several anthologies often used for a specific course, high school-level American literature.[67] They concluded that although "religion, religious beliefs and values, and religious texts" all affect English language arts curricula, "the frequent invisibility of religion in documents related to teacher preparation, teacher development, and research suggest that teacher candidates may not be well prepared for dealing with these particular issues."[68]

From a constitutional perspective, classes can certainly go beyond studying biblical allusions to studying the Bible itself as literature.[69] Yet no comprehensive data exists for how often schools do this or at what grade levels. One longs for detail on which biblical books they most frequently select, which passages they highlight, which genres they favor, and how they address issues of authorship, dates of composition, historical accuracy, and the interpretation of troubling passages.

---

65. College Board, *AP English Literature and Composition* (New York: College Board, 2014), 9.

66. Robert Todd Bruce and Beatrice Bailey, "Religious Issues in English Education: An Examination of the Field," *Religion & Education* 41.3 (2014): 310–28.

67. International Reading Association and the National Council of Teachers of English, *Standards for the English Language Arts* (Newark, DE: International Reading Association and Urbana, IL: National Council of Teachers of English, 1996).

68. Bruce and Bailey, "Religious Issues in English Education," 326.

69. Wachlin, "Place of Bible Literature in Public High School English Classes."

The Arts Curriculum

Courses in visual arts, art history, music, dance, media arts, and other arts provide natural contexts in which students might explore different interpretations of biblical characters, stories, and imagery. These classes are typically designed to cultivate sensitivity to the social and historical contexts of artists and their works, the inseparability of cultural context and reception history, and the significance of the social location of students as they interpret art. The National Core Arts Standards, created in 2014 as a resource for states and other entities, exemplify these values, noting that "artistically literate citizens know and understand artwork from varied historical periods and cultures, and actively seek and appreciate diverse forms and genres of artwork of enduring quality/significance."[70]

The College Board's 2011 review of art standards from several states found such emphases to be common.[71] It is thus no surprise that when the College Board released its new Advanced Placement art history course description in 2015 its learning objectives emphasized the crucial nature of cultural context for both creation and reception of art.[72] Religious content from multiple traditions is well represented in the image set of 250 artistic works that AP students must know. Works that explicitly feature biblical imagery include a Byzantine encaustic of the Theotokos and Child between Saints Theodore and George; the portrait page of Saint Luke from the famous Lindisfaren Gospels, an illuminated manuscript (ca. 700 CE); and the images associated with the exodus story in the Golden Haggadah, also an illuminated manuscript (ca. 1320 CE).[73]

Band, orchestra, chorus, and other music classes often learn about sacred music, much of which references the Bible. To foster understanding of the influence and prevalence of religious music, standards often emphasize the importance of historical and cultural context in regard to

---

70. National Coalition for Core Arts Standards, "National Core Arts Standards: A Conceptual Framework for Arts Learning," nationalartsstandards.org, 2014, p. 10, https://tinyurl.com/SBL6704c8.

71. College Board, *A Review of Selected State Art Standards* (New York: College Board, 2011).

72. College Board, *AP Art History: Course and Exam Description Effective Fall 2015* (New York: College Board, 2015), 13, 14, 19.

73. College Board, *AP Art History*, 62, 70.

the composition, performance, and interpretation of musical works.[74] Yet music educators have recognized the delicacy of the task of teaching about religion without promoting it. A 2006 position statement by the National Association for Music Education (NAfME) stresses that when teachers select sacred works for teaching or performance, they must do so on the basis of their "educational value" and "musical and artistic considerations." It stresses the emphasis of respecting "traditions of different people" and showing "sensitivity to the various religious beliefs represented by the students and parents." It urges care in avoiding performance in "devotional settings" or those with "religious symbols and scenery."[75]

Music classes are inherently different from most others: they are performative. The fact that students play or sing songs with religious content or origins, often in front of public audiences and sometimes in off-campus venues, complicates questions of secular purpose, secular effect, and entanglement with religion. This performative aspect raises the possibility that students might find themselves in the position of singing or playing songs with themes that offend them religiously. Music educators face the need to consider how other students, fellow school employees, and public audiences will respond to performances of sacred music. In these circumstances, the line between teaching about the intersection of music and religion, on the one hand, and promoting religion, on the other, can become blurry.

Two court cases from the late twentieth century show the potential for controversy. Both resulted in rulings that affirmed the legality of school groups' performance of sacred music. In both cases, however, observers have criticized those rulings for insufficient consideration of rights of conscience, inattention to how such performances might relate to other issues of religion in particular school environments, and insensitivity to religious minorities.[76] In the first case, a Jewish high school

---

74. See the definitions of "Context, Cultural," "Context, Historical," and "Culture" at National Core Arts Standards, "Music Glossary," nationalartsstandards.org, https://tinyurl.com/SBL6704j2, and National Association for Music Education, "Music Glossary," nafme.org, https://tinyurl.com/SBL6704f2.

75. National Association for Music Education, "Sacred Music In Schools (Position Statement)," nafme.org, 1996, https://tinyurl.com/SBL6704g2.

76. William Michael Perrine, "*Bauchman v. West High School* Revisited: Religious Text and Context in Music Education," *Philosophy of Music Education Review* 25.2 (2017): 192–213; Tim Drummond, "Singing over the Wall: Legal and Ethical Considerations for Sacred Music in the Public Schools," *Music Educators Journal* 101.2

student in Salt Lake City protested her choral director's music selection for the graduation ceremony. In her view, the teacher had already used his position earlier in the year to promote Christianity. When he announced that the choir would sing two religious pieces at graduation, she was disturbed.[77] The first song was "The Lord Bless You and Keep You," by the influential contemporary composer John Rutter. Its lyrics are a slightly modified version of the priestly benediction in Num 6:24–26, with the prayer's scope universalized by the omission of the pronouncement in 6:27 that the Lord's name and blessing would be on the children of Israel.[78] The second piece was Michael W. Smith's 1983 Christian pop song "Friends," the lyrics of which promise that "friends are friends forever if the Lord's the Lord of them."[79] A federal court issued an injunction that directed the school to drop the songs from the graduation ceremony and more broadly prohibited it from performing music with religious content. The court order was only partly successful; an unauthorized student ended up seizing the microphone and leading the crowd of two thousand in singing "Friends" nonetheless.

An appellate court later upheld the constitutionality of the music director's selections. It determined that the primary purpose of choosing Rutter's "The Lord Bless You and Keep You" was "teaching broad musical appreciation and increasing awareness of culture and diversity," a secular reason. Given the premise that singing choral music with religious lyrics inevitably results in at least some entanglement with religion, the entan-

---

(2014): 27–31; Richard Collins Mangrum, "Shall We Sing? Shall We Sing Religious Music in Public Schools," *Creighton Law Review* 38 (2005): 815–70; Faith D. Kasparian, "The Constitutionality of Teaching and Performing Sacred Choral Music in Public Schools," *Duke Law Journal* 46 (1997): 1111–68; Lisa Ness Seidman, "Religious Music in the Public Schools: Music to Establishment Clause Ears?," *George Washington Law Review* 65 (1996–1997): 466–505.

77. Bauchman v. West High School, 132 F. 3d 542, Court of Appeals, 10th Circuit (1997); Rachel Bauchman, "Rachel Bauchman Versus Utah," Freethought Today, October 1996, https://tinyurl.com/SBL6704w1.

78. John Rutter, "The Lord Bless You and Keep You," in *Oxford Easy Anthems*, ed. David Willcocks (Oxford: Oxford University Press, 1981); Siobhán Dowling Long and John F. A. Sawyer, "The Lord Bless You and Keep You," in *The Bible in Music: A Dictionary of Songs, Works, and More* (Lanham, MD: Rowman & Littlefield, 2015), 237. For the lyrics, see SongLyrics.com, https://tinyurl.com/SBL6704y2.

79. Michael W. Smith, "Friends," *Michael W. Smith Project*, Reunion Records, 1983; lyrics available at Google Play Music, https://tinyurl.com/SBL6704z2.

glement in this particular situation had not been excessive. Public school music groups could continue to perform pieces of sacred music as long as they did so for secular purposes.[80]

"The Lord Bless You and Keep You" also figured in an earlier case, which involved the school system of Duncanville, Texas. A student who enrolled in the district in 1988 noticed pervasive religious elements in her new environment, such as school-sponsored prayer at various events. In the early 1990s, she and her family took the district to court. Among their complaints, they cited the use by the high school choir of "The Lord Bless You and Keep You" as a theme song. As it turned out, the song had served that function for at least twenty years. For the seventh and eighth grade chorus, the theme song was "Go Ye Now in Peace," the opening and closing lines of which echo Judg 18:6 and other verses.[81] The court determined that "given the dominance of religious music in this field," the school district could "hardly be presumed to be advancing or endorsing religion by allowing its choirs to sing a religious theme song." Such choices might be defensible on secular grounds, it reasoned, such as the general pervasiveness of sacred music and the usefulness of particular songs for teaching a capella music.[82]

The Science Curriculum

Given the high public visibility of controversies over creation science, the Bible itself probably appears less often in science classrooms than might be supposed. This is because the principles articulated in Schempp and subsequent cases make it difficult for schools to justify explicit discussion of scripture in that context.[83] In 1968, the US Supreme Court declared unconstitutional a 1928 Arkansas law that prohibited public schools from using textbooks that taught that "mankind ascended or descended from

---

80. Bauchman v. West High School.
81. Joyce Eilers, "Go Ye Now In Peace," Unichappell Music, 2001; cf. Exod 4:18, 1 Sam 20:42, Acts 16:36, Mark 5:34, Luke 7:50, and James 2:16.
82. Doe v. Duncanville Independent School District, United States Court of Appeals for the Fifth Circuit 70 F.3d 402 (1995) at 407.
83. Randy Moore, "The History of the Evolution/Creationism Controversy and Likely Future Developments," in *Teaching about Scientific Origins: Taking Account of Creationism*, ed. Leslie S. Jones and Michael J. Reiss (New York: Lang, 2007), 11–29; Edward John Larson, *Trial and Error: The American Controversy over Creation and Evolution*, 3rd. ed. (New York: Oxford University Press, 2003).

a lower order of animals," arguing that the law existed solely for religious purposes.[84] Henceforth, state and local governments could not prevent the teaching of evolution in public schools. In 1987, a lower federal court ruled against a 1980 Arkansas law that called for "balanced treatment of creation-science and evolution-science in public schools." Citing references in that law to *creatio ex nihilo*, a young earth, and a worldwide flood, the court decided that it was "simply and purely an effort to introduce the biblical version of creation into the public school curricula."[85] In 1987 the Supreme Court rejected a similar "balanced treatment" law in Louisiana.[86]

Creation science supporters have since employed other strategies to get their ideas into public schools, such as advocating Intelligent Design.[87] Intelligent Design attempts to circumvent charges of religious motivation by asserting that the claim that the universe bears the marks of intentional design does not necessitate the conclusion that the designer was divine—an argument that fell flat in the famous 2005 Dover, Pennsylvania, case.[88] Whether Intelligent Design proponents, young earth creationists, or other types of creation scientists, members of this movement usually eschew explicit references to scripture and religion. Instead, they argue that academic freedom requires that teachers be allowed to explore alternative theories and identify both the strengths and weaknesses of scientific views that they regard as incompatible with creationism. This particular notion of academic freedom and the discourse of strengths and weaknesses have made considerable headway into the science standards of many states. Some schools have regarded such language as opening the door to teach that many scientists believe that the fossil record has insurmountable gaps, the processes of evolution are unobservable, and the theory of natural selection is wholly illogical—even though none of those claims has any currency within mainstream scientific circles.[89] Though explicit appeals to

---

84. Epperson v. Arkansas, 393 U.S. 97 (1968) at 97.

85. McLean v. Arkansas Board of Education, 529 F. Supp. 1255, 1258–1264 (E.D. Ark. 1982) at 1264.

86. Edwards v. Aguillard, 482 U.S. 578 (1987).

87. On varieties of creation science, see Susan L. Trollinger and William Vance Trollinger Jr., "The Bible and Creationism," in *The Oxford Handbook of the Bible in America*, ed. Paul Gutjahr (New York: Oxford University Press, 2017), 216–28; Ronald L. Numbers, *The Creationists: From Scientific Creationism to Intelligent Design*, exp. ed. (Cambridge: Harvard University Press, 2006).

88. Kitzmiller v. Dover Area School District, 400 F. Supp. 2d 707 (W.D. Pa. 2005).

89. Adam Laats and Harvey Siegel, *Teaching Evolution in a Creation Nation*

the Bible usually play little role in such debates, occasional episodes show that they have definitely not completely disappeared.[90]

Health and Sexuality Education

Not all states require schools to offer sex education, and, even in those that do, students (or rather, their parents) can often opt out. What states prescribe or prohibit regarding instruction about the relation of sex to marriage, gender identity, LGBTQ relationships, contraception, abortion, HIV/AIDS, and sexually transmitted diseases varies. Many states have based their schools' approaches to sexuality education on traditional assumptions that heterosexual marriage is the ideal and normative context for sexual relations. Beginning with the Reagan presidency in 1981 and continuing with every subsequent administration, the federal government has provided significant financial support for the development of sex education programs that promote abstinence until marriage. Religious agencies that advocate socially conservative positions on sexuality (and obviously, not all religious groups do) have often availed themselves of federal funding to create abstinence-centered curricula that they market to both private and public schools. These curricula sometimes present the issues in terms of maintaining purity, a concept that in much American culture is on some level related to interpretive traditions of biblical passages, even if the passages themselves go unmentioned.[91]

(Chicago: University of Chicago Press, 2016); National Center for Science Education (https://ncse.com/).

90. Christine Lagorio, "School to Stop Teaching 'Design' Class," CBSNews.com, 17 January 2006, https://tinyurl.com/SBL6704d2; Ian Urbina, "Teacher with Bible Divides Ohio Town," *New York Times*, 19 January 2010, https://tinyurl.com/SBL6704t2; Associated Press, "Settlement in Suit Involving La. Buddhist Student," *USA Today*, 14 March 2014, https://www.usatoday.com/story/news/nation/2014/03/14/buddhist-student-louisiana-settlement/6440001/.

91. Zimmerman, *Whose America?*, 186–211; Matthew Lashof-Sullivan, "Sex Education in Schools," *Georgetown Journal of Gender and the Law* 16.1 (2015): 263–94; Nancy Kendall, *The Sex Education Debates* (Chicago: University of Chicago Press, 2012); Jean Calterone Williams, "Battling a 'Sex-Saturated Society': The Abstinence Movement and the Politics of Sex Education," *Sexualities* 14.4 (2011): 416–43; and the Sexuality Information and Education Council of the United States (SIECUS), http://www.siecus.org/. On the purity movement, see Sara Moslener, *Virgin Nation: Sexual Purity and American Adolescence* (New York: Oxford University Press, 2015).

In some cases—no doubt relatively few—curricula and other resources cite scripture as an authority. Clear examples come from Texas. A 2009 study of sex education materials there found "inappropriate religious content" in 9.5 percent of school districts for which curricula were examined. One district's handout on "Things to look for in a mate" asked, "Is Jesus their first love?" It directed students to look for potential partners who displayed "humility—willing to accept correction, put others first—Phil. 2:3" and who were "industrious—Proverbs 31:17." Materials used in three districts near Fort Worth went so far as to present what many evangelicals regard as the "plan of salvation." Given the prevalence nationwide of religiously motivated abstinence-based programs, Texas is unlikely to be unique in having schools that teach sex education this way. It is a method that would not pass court muster.[92]

Although the Obama administration did not eliminate support for abstinence-based education, it did begin providing funds in its first term to encourage the creation and adoption of more comprehensive programs of sex education.[93] The Trump administration reversed this approach and is instead prioritizing abstinence-centered efforts to reduce teen pregnancy.[94] Exactly how its policies will affect public schools remains to be seen. If increased federal funding flows to socially conservative religious organizations that produce sex education curricula, then it is imaginable that resources with biblical content will make their way into classrooms more frequently.

Schools and Scholars

For every classroom controversy that makes its way into media reports or courtrooms, there are numerous examples of teachers who incorporate attention to the Bible in ways that are academically informed, pedagogically appropriate, and legally permissible. Ideally, they do so while also devoting similar attention to teaching about other expressions of religion

---

92. Ryan Valentine, "Finding 6: Some Texas Classrooms Mix Religious Instruction and Bible Study into Sexuality Education Programs," in *Just Say Don't Know: Sexuality Education in Texas Public Schools*, ed. David Wiley and Kelly Wilson, (Austin: Texas Freedom Network Education Fund, 2009), 39–46, http://tfn.org/resources/publications/.

93. Lashof-Sullivan, "Sex Education in Schools," 289.

94. Pam Belluck, "Trump Administration Pushes Abstinence in Teen Pregnancy Programs," *New York Times*, 23 April 2018, https://tinyurl.com/SBL6704x1.

than sacred texts and other traditions than Judaism and Christianity. These teachers have developed voices that are both true to their own beliefs, whatever they may be, and sensitive to the diverse views of their students and larger community.

The Freedom Forum Institute's Religious Freedom Center emphasizes a framework of rights, responsibility, and respect (the 3 Rs) for living out American notions of religious freedom.[95] Recognizing the wisdom of that framework, the Society of Biblical Literature is partnering with the Religious Freedom Center's Georgia 3 Rs project to create high school lesson plans for world history, US history, and English language arts that incorporate academic, nonsectarian study of the Bible.[96] Harvard University's Pluralism Project is similarly developing lesson plans for the Georgia 3 Rs project on a broad range of religious traditions.[97] Though initially intended for Georgia, these lessons will eventually serve as resources for schools nationwide. Over a half century after Schempp, the project of K–12 teachers and scholars of religion finding ways to strengthen how public schools teach about religion "objectively as part of a secular program of education" continues.

Bibliography

"Actor Chuck Norris and Wife Gena Join National Council on Bible Curriculum in Public Schools Board of Directors." Standard Newswire. 31 August 2006. https://tinyurl.com/SBL6704u1.

Abbott, Walter M., Arthur Gilbert, Rolfe Lanier Hunt, and J. Carter Swaim. *The Bible Reader: An Interfaith Interpretation*. London: Chapman; New York: Bruce Books, 1969.

Ackerman, James S., and Thayer S. Warshaw. *The Bible As/In Literature*. 2nd ed. Glennview, IL: ScottForesman, 1995.

---

95. Religious Freedom Center of the Freedom Forum Institute, "Framework," https://tinyurl.com/SBL6704a3.

96. http://www.religiousfreedomcenter.org/schools/ga3rs/.

97. http://pluralism.org/. In addition, Harvard Divinity School's Religious Literacy Project is also doing ground-breaking work in developing resources to foster greater religious literacy (https://rlp.hds.harvard.edu/), and the American Academy of Religion and Religious Freedom Center continue to sponsor the Public Scholars Project, which "equips scholars of religion to effectively communicate in the public sphere and foster religious literacy" (http://www.religiousfreedomcenter.org/resources/psp/).

American Academy of Religion: Religion in the Schools Task Force. *Guidelines for Teaching about Religion in K–12 Public Schools in the United States.* Atlanta: American Academy of Religion, 2010. https://tinyurl.com/SBL6704c7.

American Academy of Religion and Religious Freedom Center of the Freedom Forum Institute. Public Scholars Project. http://www.religiousfreedomcenter.org/resources/psp/.

Associated Press. "Settlement in Suit Involving La. Buddhist Student." *USA Today.* 14 March 2014. https://www.usatoday.com/story/news/nation/2014/03/14/buddhist-student-louisiana-settlement/6440001/.

Association for Supervision and Curriculum Development. *Religion in the Curriculum.* Alexandria, VA: Association for Supervision and Curriculum Development, 1987.

Banks, Adelle M. "Hobby Lobby President's Bible Curriculum Shelved by Oklahoma School District." Religion News Service. 26 November 2014. https://tinyurl.com/SBL6704v1.

Barr, David L., and Nicholas Piediscalzi, eds. *The Bible in American Education: From Source Book to Textbook.* Philadelphia: Fortress, 1982.

Bauchman, Rachel. "Rachel Bauchman versus Utah." Freethought Today. October 1996. https://tinyurl.com/SBL6704w1.

Belluck, Pam. "Trump Administration Pushes Abstinence in Teen Pregnancy Programs." *New York Times.* 23 April 2018. https://tinyurl.com/SBL6704x1.

Bible Scholars. www.biblescholars.org.

Bracher, Peter S., and David L. Barr. "The Bible Is Worthy of Secular Study: The Bible in Public Education Today." Pages 165–97 in *The Bible and American Education: From Source Book to Textbook.* Edited by David L. Barr and Nicholas Piediscalzi. Philadelphia: Fortress, 1982.

Branch, Caroline. "Unexcused Absence: Why Public Schools in Religiously Plural Society Must Save a Seat for Religion in the Curriculum." *Emory Law Journal* 56.5 (2007): 1431–74.

Breed, Brennan, and Kent Harold Richards. Review of *The Bible in History and Literature. Religion & Education* 34.3 (2007): 94–102.

Brockman, David R. *Religious Imbalance in the Texas Social Studies Curriculum: Analysis and Recommendations.* Houston: James A. Baker III Institute for Public Policy of Rice University, 2016. https://tinyurl.com/SBL6704c6.

Bruce, Robert Todd, and Beatrice Bailey. "Religious Issues in English

Education: An Examination of the Field." *Religion & Education* 41.3 (2014): 310–28.

Cargill, Robert. "The Museum of the Bible: Why Are Archaeologists and Bible Scholars So Mad?" Robert Cargill Blog. 19 July 2017. https://tinyurl.com/SBL6704y1.

Chancey, Mark A. "The Bible and American Public Schools in Historical Perspective." Pages 271–82 in *The Oxford Handbook on Religion and American Education*. Edited by Michael Waggoner and Nathan Walker. Oxford: Oxford University Press, 2018.

———. "Bible Bills, Bible Curricula, and Controversies of Biblical Proportions: Legislative Efforts to Promote Bible Courses in Public Schools." *Religion & Education* 34.1 (2007): 28–47.

———. "The Bible, the First Amendment, and the Public Schools in Odessa, Texas." *Religion and American Culture* 19.2 (2009): 169–205.

———. *Can This Class Be Saved? The "Hobby Lobby" Bible Curriculum*. Austin: Texas Freedom Network Education Fund, 2014. http://tfn.org/resources/publications/.

———. "'Complete Victory Is Our Objective': National Council on Bible Curriculum in Public Schools." *Religion & Education* 35.1 (2008): 1–21.

———. "Public School Bible Courses in Historical Perspective: North Carolina as a Case Study." Pages 193–214 in *The Bible in the Public Square: Its Enduring Influence in American Life*. Edited by Mark A. Chancey, Carol Meyers, and Eric M. Meyers. Atlanta: Society of Biblical Literature, 2013.

———. *Reading, Writing and Religion: Teaching the Bible in Texas Public Schools*. Austin: Texas Freedom Network Education Fund, 2006. http://tfn.org/resources/publications/.

———. *Reading, Writing and Religion II: Texas Public School Bible Courses in 2011-12*. Austin: Texas Freedom Network Education Fund, 2013. http://tfn.org/resources/publications/.

———. "Religious Instruction, Public Education, and the Dallas High Schools Bible Study Course (1923–1985)." *Church History* 86.1 (2017): 145–77.

———. "Rewriting History for a Christian America: Religion and the Texas Social Studies Controversy of 2009–2010." *JR* 94 (2014): 325–53.

———. "Sectarian Elements in Public School Bible Courses: Lessons from the Lone Star State." *Journal of Church and State* 49 (2007): 719–42.

———. "A Textbook Example of the Christian Right: The National Council on Bible Curriculum in Public Schools." *JAAR* 75 (2007): 554–81.

Clarkson, Frederick. "'Project Blitz' Seeks to Do for Christian Nationalism What ALEC Does for Big Business." *Religion Dispatches*. 27 April 2018. http://religiondispatches.org/project-blitz-seeks-to-do-for-christian-nationalism-what-alec-does-for-big-business/.

College Board. *AP Art History: Course and Exam Description Effective Fall 2015*. New York: College Board, 2015.

———. *AP English Literature and Composition*. New York: College Board, 2014.

———. *AP Human Geography Course Description*. New York: College Board, 2015.

———. *AP United States History Course and Exam Description*. New York: College Board, 2017.

———. *AP World History Course and Exam Description*. New York: College Board, 2017.

———. *A Review of Selected State Art Standards*. New York: College Board, 2011.

Common Core State Standards Initiative. *Common Core State Standards for Language Arts and Literacy in History/Social Studies, Science, and Technical Subjects*. 2010. https://tinyurl.com/SBL6704z1.

———. "Development Process." https://tinyurl.com/SBL6704a2.

———. "Standards in Your State." 2017. http://www.corestandards.org/standards-in-your-state/.

Congressional Prayer Caucus, National Legal Foundation, and WallBuilders ProFamily Legislative Network. *Report and Analysis of Religious Freedom Measures Impacting Prayer and Faith in America*. Chesapeake, VA: Congressional Prayer Caucus Foundation, 2017. https://tinyurl.com/SBL6704c4.

Deckman, Melissa. "Religious Literacy in Public Schools: Teaching the Bible in America's Classrooms." Pages 31–48 in *Curriculum and the Culture Wars: Debating the Bible's Place in Public Schools*. Edited by Melissa Deckman and Prud'homme. New York: Lang, 2014.

DelFattore, Joan. *The Fourth R: Conflicts over Religion in America's Public Schools*. New Haven: Yale University Press, 2004.

Douglass, Susan L. *Teaching about Religion in National and State Social Studies Standards*. Fountain Valley, CA: Council on Islamic Education; Nashville: First Amendment Center, 2000.

Drummond, Tim. "Singing over the Wall: Legal and Ethical Considerations for Sacred Music in the Public Schools." *Music Educators Journal* 101.2 (2014): 27–31.

Eckes, Susan E., and Allison Fetter-Harrott. "Religion and the Public School Curriculum." Pages 28–41 in *International Perspectives on Education, Religion and Law*. Edited by Charles J. Russo. New York: Routledge, 2014.

Eilers, Joyce. "Go Ye Now in Peace." Unichappell Music, 2001.

Erekson, Keith A., ed. *Politics and the History Curriculum: The Struggle over Standards in Texas and the Nation*. New York: Palgrave Macmillan, 2012.

Feinberg, Walter, and Richard A. Layton. *For the Civic Good: The Liberal Case for Teaching Religion in the Public Schools*. Ann Arbor: University of Michigan Press, 2014.

First Amendment Center. *The Bible and Public Schools: A First Amendment Guide*. Nashville: First Amendment Center, 1999.

———. *A Teacher's Guide to Religion in the Public Schools*. Nashville: First Amendment Center, 2008.

Gateways to Better Education. *The Bible in State Academic Standards: A Report on All Fifty States*. Lake Forest, CA: Gateways to Better Education, 2014.

Gilbert, Arthur. "Reactions and Resources." Pages 37–83 in *Religion and Public Education*. Edited by Theodore R. Sizer. New York: Houghton Mifflin, 1967.

Green, Steve. "Speech at the Templeton Awards 2013." YouTube. https://www.youtube.com/watch?v=hjjv9QVrCJU.

Greenawalt, Kent. *Does God Belong in Public Schools?* Princeton: Princeton University Press, 2005.

Harvard Divinity School. Religious Literacy Project. https://rlp.hds.harvard.edu/.

Haynes, Charles C. "Battling over the Bible in Public Schools: Is Common Ground Possible?" Pages 181–91 in *The Bible in the Public Square: Its Enduring Influence in American Life*. Edited by Mark A. Chancey, Carol Meyers, and Eric M. Meyers. Atlanta: Society of Biblical Literature, 2013.

Haynes, Charles C., and Oliver Thomas. *Finding Common Ground: A First Amendment Guide to Religion and Public Schools*. Nashville: First Amendment Center, 2007.

Hughes, Richard T. "Why Do We Think of America as a Christian Nation?" Pages 127–47 in *Politics and the History Curriculum: The Struggle over*

Standards in Texas and the Nation. Edited by Keith A. Erekson. New York: Palgrave Macmillan, 2012.

International Baccalaureate Organization. "Find an IB World School." Ibo.org. http://www.ibo.org/programmes/find-an-ib-school/?Search Fields.Country=US.

———. "International Baccalaureate Diploma Programme Subject Brief: Individuals and Societies: World Religions—Standard Level." Ibo.org. https://tinyurl.com/SBL6704b2.

———. "Studying World Religions." Ibo.org. https://tinyurl.com/SBL6704c2.

International Reading Association and the National Council of Teachers of English. *Standards for the English Language Arts*. Newark, DE: International Reading Association and Urbana, IL: National Council of Teachers of English, 1996.

Jones, Martyn Wendell. "Inside the Museum of the Bible." *Christianity Today*. 20 October 2017. http://www.christianitytoday.com/ct/2017/november/inside-museum-of-bible.html.

Kasparian, Faith D. "The Constitutionality of Teaching and Performing Sacred Choral Music in Public Schools." *Duke Law Journal* 46 (1997): 1111–68.

Kendall, Nancy. *The Sex Education Debates*. Chicago: University of Chicago Press, 2012.

Laats, Adam, and Harvey Siegel. *Teaching Evolution in a Creation Nation*. Chicago: University of Chicago Press, 2016.

Lagorio, Christine. "School to Stop Teaching 'Design' Class." CBSNews.com. 17 January 2006. https://tinyurl.com/SBL6704d2.

Larson, Edward John. *Trial and Error: The American Controversy over Creation and Evolution*. 3rd ed. New York: Oxford University Press, 2003.

Lashof-Sullivan, Matthew. "Sex Education in Schools." *Georgetown Journal of Gender and the Law* 16.1 (2015): 263–94.

Lester, Emile. *Teaching about Religions: A Democratic Approach for Public Schools*. Ann Arbor: University of Michigan Press, 2011.

Lester, Emile, and Patrick S. Roberts. *Learning about World Religions in Public Schools: The Impact on Student Attitudes and Community Acceptance in Modesto, California*. Nashville: First Amendment Center, 2006.

Levenson, David. "University Religion Departments and Teaching about the Bible in Public High Schools: A Report from Florida." *Religious Studies News: AAR Edition* 17 (2002): 3, 7, 10.

Lewis, Bret, and Crystal Lopez. "Politics and Perceptions of Religious Studies: The Arizona Legislature and the Teaching of Religion." *Religion & Education* 42.2 (2015): 147–64.

Long, Siobhán Dowling, and John F. A. Sawyer. "The Lord Bless You and Keep You." Page 237 in *The Bible in Music: A Dictionary of Songs, Works, and More*. Lanham, MD: Rowman & Littlefield, 2015.

Mangrum, Richard Collins. "Shall We Sing? Shall We Sing Religious Music in Public Schools." *Creighton Law Review* 38 (2005): 815–70.

Moore, Diane L. *Overcoming Religious Illiteracy: A Cultural Studies Approach to the Study of Religion in Secondary Education*. New York: Palgrave Macmillan, 2007.

———. "Teaching about the Bible in Public Schools: A Religious Studies Framework." Pages 61–84 in *Curriculum and the Culture Wars: Debating the Biblels Place in Public Schools*.Edited Melissa Deckman and Joseph Prud'homme. New York: Lang, 2014.

Moore, Randy. "The History of the Evolution/Creationism Controversy and Likely Future Developments." Pages 11–29 in *Teaching about Scientific Origins: Taking Account of Creationism*. Edited by Leslie S. Jones and Michael J. Reiss. New York: Lang, 2007.

Moslener, Sara. *Virgin Nation: Sexual Purity and American Adolescence*. New York: Oxford University Press, 2015.

Moss, Candida R., and Joel S. Baden. *Bible Nation: The United States of Hobby Lobby*. Princeton: Princeton University Press, 2017.

———. "Hobby Lobby's Black-Market Buys Did Real Damage." *New York Times*. 6. July 2017. https://tinyurl.com/SBL6704e2.

Museum of the Bible. *Genesis to Ruth Teacher's Guide*. Vol. 1 of *Home School Curriculum*. Washington, DC: Museum of the Bible & Compedia, 2016.

———. https://museumofthebible.org.

National Alliance for Public Charter Schools. http://www.publiccharters.org/.

National Assessment Governing Board. *U.S. History Framework for the 2014 National Assessment of Educational Progress*. Washington, DC: National Assessment Governing Board, 2014.

National Association for Music Education. "Music Glossary." nafme.org. https://tinyurl.com/SBL6704f2.

———. "Sacred Music in Schools (Position Statement)." nafme.org. 1996. https://tinyurl.com/SBL6704g2.

National Center for Science Education. https://ncse.com/.

National Charter Schools Resource Center. "What Is a Charter School?" https://tinyurl.com/SBL6704c9.

National Coalition for Core Arts Standards. "National Core Arts Standards: A Conceptual Framework for Arts Learning." nationalartsstandards.org. 2014. https://tinyurl.com/SBL6704r8.

National Core Arts Standards. "Music Glossary." nationalartsstandards.org. https://tinyurl.com/SBL6704j2.

National Council for the Social Studies. "Religious Studies Companion Document for the C3 Framework." Pages 92–97 in *College, Career, and Civic Life (C3) Framework for Social Studies State Standards: Guidance for Enhancing the Rigor of K–12 Civics, Economics, Geography, and History*. Rev. ed. Silver Spring, MD: National Council for the Social Studies, 2017.

———. "Study about Religions in the Social Studies Curriculum: A Position Statement of National Council for the Social Studies (NCSS) 2014." socialstudies.org. 2014. https://tinyurl.com/SBL6704k2.

———. "Supplement on the Academic Study of Religion Added to C3 Framework." socialstudies.org. 2017. https://tinyurl.com/SBL6704m2.

National Council on Bible Curriculum in Public Schools. http://bibleinschools.net/index.php.

———. *The Bible in History and Literature*. Rev. ed. Ablu Publishing, 2007.

———. "Bible Scholars Advisory Council." https://tinyurl.com/SBL6704n2.

———. "Board of Directors and Advisors." http://bibleinschools.net/About-Us/Board-of-Directors-and-Advisors.php.

Nord, Warren A. *Does God Make a Difference? Taking Religion Seriously in Our Schools and Universities*. New York: Oxford University Press, 2010.

Nord, Warren A., and Charles C. Haynes. *Taking Religion Seriously across the Curriculum*. Alexandria, VA: Association for Supervision and Curriculum Development; Nashville: First Amendment Center, 1998.

Numbers, Ronald L. *The Creationists: From Scientific Creationism to Intelligent Design*. Exp. ed. Cambridge: Harvard University Press, 2006.

Paterson, Frances R. A. "Anatomy of a Bible Course Curriculum." *Journal of Law and Education* 32.1 (2003): 41–65.

Perrine, William Michael. "*Bauchman v. West High School* Revisited: Religious Text and Context in Music Education." *Philosophy of Music Education Review* 25.2 (2017): 192–213.

Released Time Bible Education. www.releasedtime.org.

Religious Freedom Center of the Freedom Forum Institute. "Framework." https://tinyurl.com/SBL6704a3.

The Republican Platform 2016. Republican National Convention, 2016.
Resmovits, Joy. "The Other Big Debate: What Is the Common Core, Anyway?" *Los Angeles Times*. 16 September 2015. https://tinyurl.com/SBL6704p2.
Risinger, C. Frederick. *Religion in the Social Studies Curriculum*. ERIC Digest. Bloomington, IN: ERIC Clearinghouse for Social Studies/Social Science Education, 1993. https://tinyurl.com/SBL6704v2.
———. *Teaching about Religion in the Social Studies*. ERIC Digest. Bloomington, IN: ERIC Clearinghouse for Social Studies/Social Science Education, 1988. https://tinyurl.com/SBL6704w2.
Rosenblith, Suzanne, and Patrick Womac. "The Bible in American Public Schools." Pages 263–75 in *The Oxford Handbook of the Bible in America*. Edited by Paul Gutjahr. New York: Oxford University Press, 2017.
Rutter, John. "The Lord Bless You and Keep You." In *Oxford Easy Anthems*. Edited by David Willcocks. Oxford: Oxford University Press, 1981.
Schaeffer, Judith E. *The Good Book Taught Wrong: Bible History Classes in Florida Public Schools*. Washington, DC: People for the American Way, 2000.
Schippe, Cullen, and Chuck Stetson, eds. *The Bible and Its Influence*. Rev. ed. Fairfax: BLP Publishing, 2006.
Seidman, Lisa Ness. "Religious Music in the Public Schools: Music to Establishment Clause Ears?" *George Washington Law Review* 65 (1996–1997): 466–505.
Sexuality Information and Education Council of the United States. http://www.siecus.org/.
Smith, Michael W. "Friends." *Michael W. Smith Project*. Reunion Records, 1983.
Society of Biblical Literature. *Bible Electives in Public Schools: A Guide*. sbl-site.org. https://tinyurl.com/SBL6704m3.
Stern, Sheldon M., and Jeremy A. Stern. *The State of State U.S. History Standards 2011*. Washington, DC: Thomas B. Fordham Institute, 2011. https://tinyurl.com/SBL6704r9.
Stewart, Katherine. *The Good News Club: The Religious Right's Stealth Assault on America's Children*. New York: Public Affairs, 2012.
Strauss, Valerie. "What Should Students Know about Religion? New Guidance on Teaching It in Public Schools." *Washington Post*. 1 July 2017. https://tinyurl.com/SBL6704q2.
Summers, Cary L. *Lifting Up the Bible: The Story behind Museum of the*

Bible. Washington, DC: Museum of the Bible; Franklin, TN: Worthy Books, 2017.

Swezey, James A., and Katherine G. Schultz. "Released Time Programs in Religion Education." Pages 77–90 in *Religion in the Public Schools: Negotiating the New Commons*. Edited by Michael D. Waggoner. Lanham, MD: Rowman & Littlefield, 2013.

Trollinger, Susan L., and William Vance Trollinger Jr. "The Bible and Creationism." Pages 216–28 in *The Oxford Handbook of the Bible in America*. Edited by Paul Gutjahr. New York: Oxford University Press, 2017.

US Department of Education. "Religious Expression in Public Schools: A Statement of Principles." 1995. Educational Resource Information Center. https://tinyurl.com/SBL6704r2.

US Department of Justice. "United States Files Civil Action to Forfeit Thousands of Ancient Iraqi Artifacts Imported by Hobby Lobby." 5 July 2017. https://tinyurl.com/SBL6704s2.

Urbina, Ian. "Teacher with Bible Divides Ohio Town." *New York Times*. 19 January 2010. https://tinyurl.com/SBL6704t2.

Valentine, Ryan. "Finding 6: Some Texas Classrooms Mix Religious Instruction and Bible Study into Sexuality Education Programs." Pages 39–46 in *Just Say Don't Know: Sexuality Education in Texas Public Schools*. Edited by David Wiley and Kelly Wilson. Austin: Texas Freedom Network Education Fund, 2009. http://tfn.org/resources/publications/.

Van Biema, David. "Hobby Lobby's Steve Green Launches a New Project: A Public School Bible Curriculum." Religion News Service. 15 April 2014. https://tinyurl.com/SBL6704u2.

Wachlin, Marie Goughnour. "The Place of Bible Literature in Public High School English Classes." *Research in the Teaching of English* 31.1 (1997): 7–49.

Wertheimer, Linda K. *Faith Ed: Teaching about Religion in an Age of Intolerance*. Boston: Beacon, 2015.

Williams, Jean Calterone. "Battling a 'Sex-Saturated Society': The Abstinence Movement and the Politics of Sex Education." *Sexualities* 14.4 (2011): 416–43.

Ybarra, Dennis R., and Gary A. Tobin. *The Trouble with Textbooks: Distorting History and Religion*. Lanham, MD: Lexington, 2008.

Zimmerman, Jonathan. *Whose America? Culture Wars in the Public Schools*. Cambridge: Harvard University Press, 2002.

9
But Is It Useful?
The Perennial Problem of American Biblical Scholarship and Higher Education

Davina C. Lopez

The Bible is omnipresent in American higher education—in seminaries and divinity schools, in university religion departments, and in liberal arts colleges. American educators and administrators have long debated the Bible's fundamental importance in the formation of young adults.[1]

I thank Claudia Setzer and David Shefferman for their generous invitation to contribute to this important and timely volume. Research for this essay was enhanced by project grants on the Bible, biblical scholarship, and the American liberal arts tradition from the Wabash Center for Teaching and Learning in Theology and Religion (2013–2014, 2015–2016), the Louisville Institute (2013–2014), and the Lloyd W. Chapin Faculty Development Program at Eckerd College (2017).

1. Although there is an abundance of scholarly (and nonscholarly) literature on the roles that the Bible has played in American higher education from the last five decades, as well as a growing body of literature on teaching the Bible in college settings, more scarce is literature by biblical scholars about the contours of biblical scholarship and higher education. For contributions by biblical scholars, see especially the volume commissioned for the Society of Biblical Literature's 1980 centennial, David Barr and Nicholas Piediscalzi, eds., *The Bible in American Education* (Philadelphia: Fortress; Chico, CA: Scholars Press, 1982). For a set of views that traces the Bible's journey through Christian higher education, see David Lyle Jeffrey and C. Stephen Evans, eds., *The Bible and the University*, Scripture and Hermeneutics 8 (Grand Rapids: Zondervan, 2007). Much of the recent literature on the Bible and higher education focuses on specific teaching strategies and classroom contexts; see, for example, Mark Roncace and Patrick Gray, eds., *Teaching the Bible: Practical Strategies for Classroom Instruction*, RBS 49 (Atlanta: Society of Biblical Literature, 2005); Roncace and Gray, eds., *Teaching the Bible through Popular Culture and the Arts*, RBS 53 (Atlanta:

As well, aspects of biblical reception history—how the stories have been used in culture across time and space—are significant in conversations about the Bible and American higher education. As a canonical literary work, as a resource for understanding histories of art, literature, and law, as a foil for claims about evolutionary theory, and as a template for personal character orientation, moral formation, and theological affiliation, there is much to be said about the perennial place of the Bible in higher-educational contexts.

The Bible has endured as a presence in American higher education not only because of its contents, but also because it functions as a lightning rod for curricular controversies, disciplinary and community identities, and institutional power relationships. Debates about whether the Bible should be taught as part of a religion department's offerings, how it might appear on the common syllabus for a core curriculum or other general education course, and what its inclusion in any course might represent to students and other stakeholders are ongoing among faculty members and administrators. Constitutional issues color perceptions about the teaching of biblical literature at public institutions; these are well-documented, and their contours are often privileged in discussions about the Bible and American education.[2] Private American colleges and universities with

---

Society of Biblical Literature, 2007); Jane Webster and Glen Holland, eds., *Teaching the Bible in the Liberal Arts Classroom* (Sheffield: Sheffield Phoenix, 2012); and Webster and Holland, eds., *Teaching the Bible in the Liberal Arts Classroom*, vol. 2 (Sheffield: Sheffield Phoenix, 2015). For a series of perspectives on graduate education in biblical studies, see Elisabeth Schüssler Fiorenza and Kent Harold Richards, eds., *Transforming Graduate Biblical Education: Ethos and Discipline*, GPBS 10 (Atlanta: Society of Biblical Literature, 2010). For earlier commentary on the Bible in higher educational settings, see Margaret Crook and the Bible Faculty at Smith College, *The Bible and Its Literary Associations* (New York: Abingdon, 1937), a book of essays compiled out of a team-taught class on Bible and literature at Smith; and James Muilenburg, *Specimens of Biblical Literature* (New York: Crowell, 1923), which was written for a nonsectarian high school or college course focused on biblical literature.

2. In fact, most of the questions about whether and how the Bible ought to be taught concern public K–12 educational contexts, and analysis about pedagogies of the Bible tend to dwell in the same area. See, for example, Charles C. Haynes, "Battling over the Bible in Public Schools: Is Common Ground Possible?," in *The Bible in the Public Square: Its Enduring Influence in American Life*, ed. Mark A. Chancey, Carol Meyers, and Eric M. Meyers, BSNA 27 (Atlanta: SBL Press, 2014), 181–92; and Mark A. Chancey, "Public School Bible Courses in Historical Perspective: North Carolina as a Case Study," in Chancey, Meyers, and Meyers, *Bible in the Public Square*, 193–214.

denominational affiliation, however nominal, deliberate whether to teach the Bible in alignment with doctrinal allegiances. Also, those who teach Bible in paid faculty positions, regardless of institution type, are under pressure to maintain enrollments so that their faculty line is secure or at least not under threat of competition for resources with other, more popular, departments or programs. That said, if and when college students enroll in a course in religious studies, there is an above-average chance that course will include attention to the Bible.

I observe that conversations about the role of *the Bible* in American higher education are, for better or for worse, often linked to the role of *biblical scholarship* in American higher education. While the history of such entanglements is too vast to comprehensively consider here, it is safe to say that it is not possible to articulate a history of American higher education without including some attention to the role of biblical scholarship, nor is it possible to articulate a historical understanding of American biblical scholarship that does not attend to its embeddedness in higher education. Given this relationship, which arguably frames the historical trajectory of the field, in this essay I will think conceptually about the longstanding and intimate relationship between American biblical scholarship and American higher education. To this end, I will explore the rhetoric of utility and inutility in our field and in the humanities more broadly. Discourses about usefulness comprise a common defensive characterization of biblical scholarship—and the humanities as a whole—in the neoliberal, largely anti-intellectual, capitalist landscape that houses American higher education. The question "But is it useful?" haunts many of us working in the humanities. However, attending to the history of American biblical scholarship as it has negotiated higher education reveals that the rhetoric of uselessness is not at all new or specific to our current moment.

Narrating the Landscape of Uselessness

As the essays in this collection demonstrate, it is difficult to find places in American society where the Bible does not make at least a passing appearance; simply examining *current* (not to mention historical!) American political discourses while alert to biblical allusions, references, and deployments can be overwhelming. *Bible* here does not necessarily refer to a specific translation or type—this kind of specificity is relatively unimportant in American public displays—but rather a shorthand way of saying "this important sacred book." The larger cultural situation obviously informs educational contexts. Teaching biblical literature in an American higher educational setting occurs at an electric intersection where social location, sophisticated technological embraces, a longing for belonging in a world far from home, the special kind of hostility that stems from the trauma of learning that one does not know what they thought they did, and persistent anxiety about material circumstances and future prospects are foregrounded. Even if college students disavow any personal allegiance to the Bible, they always bring some kind of relationship with it to the classroom. That said, college students' mileage with biblical literacy and their awareness of biblical saturation varies. This compounds the difficulties of encountering the Bible in the college classroom.

Among American institutions of higher education, there are distinctive views of both the Bible and biblical scholarship that are relevant for this discussion of the rhetoric of uselessness and utility. In liberal arts college contexts, the Bible is not just the property of biblical scholars or religious studies courses but serves as a battleground whose presence in general education curricula signifies a commitment to some articulation of the so-called great books and whose absence can indicate a decline of moral character and amnesiac orientation to literature, history, and culture. As Jonathan Z. Smith has observed, maintaining a relationship with biblical literature in general education symbolizes not expertise in teaching the Bible or that the texts have intrinsic value, but rather a position that the faculty has taken regarding canons and character development as befits the term *generalizing*.[3] An assumption that Bible visibility on college campuses indicates an expectation of adherence to particular religious or theological positions is a largely sidestepped pedagogical issue. In general education curricula, the Bible is especially difficult to teach in part because of students' assumptions that to read it is to declare doctrinal allegiance and in part because teachers of those courses have little training in how to teach such texts—or think that the Bible is the pedagogical responsibility of religious authorities. To be fair, where to start when one has the task of teaching the Bible from a nonsectarian perspective, without training in

---

3. Jonathan Z. Smith, "Teaching the Bible in the Context of General Education," *TTR* 1.2 (1998): 73–78; see also Christopher I. Lehrich, ed., *On Teaching Religion: Essays by Jonathan Z. Smith* (New York: Oxford University Press, 2012); and the essays in Webster and Holland, *Teaching the Bible in the Liberal Arts Classroom* (2012).

biblical studies, is not always obvious. To be truly fair, it is not always obvious to biblical scholars either!

While it can be taken for granted that the Bible is a great book and its meaning is consistent across time and cultures, biblical scholars tend to take the position that the Bible, as a collection of books composed and canonized across two millennia and multiple cultural settings, is at least inconsistent and at times contradictory. As Tim Beal states, the Bible is "a library of questions, not a book of answers,"[4] and we would do well to teach this literature with that in mind regardless of our own commitments and baggage. However, some of the more enjoyable (at least to me) aspects of our field—including that the Bible is a site where great conversations take place, often on account of its inconsistencies and contradictions—rarely translate successfully in American higher education contexts. Herein a pedagogical challenge for biblical scholars resides in contestations over content, method, and interpretive authority, alongside students' biblical illiteracy and the Bible's elevated position in American culture. When and if biblical scholars are consulted to weigh in on such matters in the context of nonreligion courses that might include biblical literature, it may be because of assumptions that we function as religious authorities who will readily provide answers to questions like whether the exodus or Jesus's crucifixion actually happened. Insisting that texts do not do anything outside of what people do with them is not received well either, especially among proponents of the *sui generis* power that great books have to change lives upon contact. Biblical scholarship here is likened to Sunday school teaching or moral development work, on one hand, and the destroyer of the capacity of canonically anointed texts to work magic on readers, on the other.

In university-based religion programs, the link between Bible reading and doctrinal affinity can be used as a wedge in departmental identity conversations. This is complicated and often politicized by the relationship of many universities to state funding and oversight. Ideologically, the presence of the Bible in the curriculum can serve as a signifier for older paradigms of studying religion that are implicated in colonializing, mainline Protestant projects. Attempts to diversify the faculty and offerings of such departments, often along what I would consider to be

---

4. Timothy K. Beal, *The Rise and Fall of the Bible: The Unexpected History of an Accidental Book* (New York: Mariner, 2011), 5.

fairly traditional lines—that is, faculty members with special interests and expertise in a tradition—have largely been (at least rhetorically) in response to a perceived predominance of biblical piety among scholars of religion. The Bible, as emblem of (mostly Christian) singularity and supersessionism, must move over to make room for the diversity of the others. Biblical scholarship here is couched as the domain of what Russell McCutcheon has termed "caretakers" of the study of religion, rather than "critics."[5] In a cafeteria model of curricular arrangement, students may avoid taking courses in biblical literature altogether, thus avoiding a major element of the history of theorizing about religion.[6]

For many theological schools, the Bible still serves as the subject of a foundational course of study that informs subsequent historical, theological, and practical fields. Yet how the Bible is pedagogically encountered in seminary—that is, through learning the discipline of exegesis—is often the locus of animus from aspiring ministers not on account of biblical contents or its authoritative status, but because of the perceived irrelevance of biblical scholarship for the day-to-day concerns of a contemporary religiously affiliated public or the assumption that biblical scholarship's primary audience should be the church.[7] Who cares about JEDP or the Synoptic problem when there are more pressing questions on the minds of the public, when the Bible continues to be embedded in modern American life, deployed in consequential scenarios ranging from

---

5. Russell McCutcheon, *Critics not Caretakers: Redescribing the Public Study of Religion* (Albany, NY: SUNY Press, 2001), which takes a rhetorical approach to reframing the study of religion. For a different view that still ascribes belief to the majority of biblical scholars, see Jacques Berlinerblau, *The Secular Bible: Why Nonbelievers Must Take Religion Seriously* (New York: Cambridge University Press, 2005).

6. For an overview of the consequences of overlooking this history in the recent past, I refer to Jonathan Z. Smith's 2008 Society of Biblical Literature presidential address, delivered at an Annual Meeting of the Society of Biblical Literature that was not concurrent with the American Academy of Religion. Published as Smith, "Religion and Bible," *JBL* 128 (2009): 5–27.

7. This has long been the struggle in seminary contexts and in the United States perhaps was most obvious around the edges of the fundamentalist-modernist debate of the early twentieth century. The history of American biblical scholarship is in fact plagued by the notion that biblical scholars are not doing enough for the church, theology, and ordinary readers. For an outline of how this problem presents itself in contemporary seminary classrooms, see Dale B. Martin, *Pedagogy of the Bible* (Louisville: Westminster John Knox, 2008).

war to immigration to what happens in people's bedrooms? For the more traditionally minded, there is little about biblical scholarship that helps seminarians understand denominational doctrines and theologies. Biblical scholarship here is characterized as that which is useless unless it is directly tied to the immediate needs and desires of church communities.

The rhetoric of uselessness may arise from misunderstandings of biblical scholarship among disciplinary outsiders in various higher educational contexts. Even among scholars of religion more broadly, biblical scholarship can often be framed as a suspect field or carrier of retrogressive values and hegemonic impulses. However, we biblical scholars also contribute to discourses concerning our own uselessness. Even if these are insider conversations, one does not have to search too far into contemporary biblical scholarship to locate such accusations. These are often articulated in terms of the antiquarianism or scientific-positivism of the discipline. A special target is traditional biblical scholarship, which is cast as useless to those who propose innovative methods. Most often linked to traditional is the range of approaches that fall under the umbrella of historical criticism. To be clear, criticism is not the same as wholesale dismissal, although the two can be conflated in argumentative strategies. The task of the critic is methodological in nature. It is to expose the hands at work, to test claims, and to ask probing questions.[8] As A. O. Scott notes, we are all critics, as critical thinking informs virtually every aspect of personal creativity and common life.[9]

---

8. Criticism of the field is not the problem per se, as criticism from within the ranks of biblical scholarship is one way to move methodological issues forward and promote best practices. Feminist appraisals of the field as androcentric, for example, serve as reminders that there is always work to be done to create as big a tent as possible. However, facile claims that historical criticism—a signifier for what we might call prelinguistic-turn methodological approaches—is outdated and therefore useless do not quite qualify, in my view, as an exposure of hands, an appraisal of labor, a testing of claims, or a programmatic inquiry. See Davina C. Lopez, "Curatorial Reflections: On Rhetorics of Tradition and Innovation in Biblical Scholarship," in *Present and Future of Biblical Studies: Celebrating Twenty-Five Years of Brill's Biblical Interpretation*, ed. Tat-siong Benny Liew (Leiden: Brill, 2018), 68–92.

9. A. O. Scott, *Better Living through Criticism: How to Think about Art, Pleasure, Beauty, and Truth* (New York: Penguin, 2016). I should note that Scott's exploration of the task of the critic, framed as expository essays and dialogues, is a response in part to the charge of uselessness leveled at his professional film criticism. For a discussion of the task of the critic in biblical scholarship, see Todd Penner and Davina C.

Within the field, charges of uselessness also come from those who are wary of theological claims made by other biblical scholars, lest such claims indicate a religionist investment that indicates bias and, as far as teaching is concerned, the specter of indoctrination.[10] In this frame, an objectivist view, or at least one wherein theological inclinations are not immediately visible, is privileged. Discourses about the uselessness of the field come from the opposite direction as well, as biblical scholars who openly claim particular theological positioning or religious affiliation tend to regard as useless more theoretically inclined, atheistic/agnostic, or science-based approaches.[11] It is perfectly legitimate to disagree—multiplicity of perspectives have, in my estimation, long been the reality of the field. Using the rhetoric of uselessness about one's own discipline, though, can serve to flatten out ideological diversity and hide the processes of productive disagreement. Such rhetoric also has the potential effect of hiding disparate historical threads and reaffirming dominant narratives about the field.

Biblical scholars did not invent the rhetoric of uselessness, of course. This characterization has plagued the humanities, particularly in American higher education. As Helen Small has posited in her appraisal of arguments for the humanities, the "spectre of trial by proven utility" has been central to discussions about the role and function of higher education since the foundation of the modern university and especially since the popularization of the capitalist opposition between "economic usefulness and cultured uselessness." This is traceable to Adam Smith's statement, in *The Wealth of Nations*, that higher education should be subject to free-market forces.[12] Whether one claims that the humanities contribute to

---

Lopez, *De-introducing the New Testament: Texts, Worlds, Methods, Stories* (Hoboken, NJ: Wiley Blackwell, 2015), 215–35.

10. See, for example, Hector Avalos, *The End of Biblical Studies* (Amherst, NY: Prometheus, 2007); Berlinerblau, *Secular Bible*; and the essays in Roland Boer, ed., *Secularism and Biblical Studies*, BibleWorld (London: Equinox, 2010).

11. Especially popular in methodological debates about critical theory and biblical studies; see, for example John J. Collins, *The Bible after Babel: Historical Criticism in a Postmodern Age* (Grand Rapids: Eerdmans, 2005); Stephen D. Moore and Yvonne Sherwood, *The Invention of the Biblical Scholar: A Critical Manifesto* (Minneapolis: Fortress, 2011). For an appraisal of the rhetoric of academic legitimacy among theologically-inclined scholars, see Stephen Young, "Protective Strategies and the Prestige of the 'Academic,'" *BibInt* 23 (2015): 1–35.

12. Helen Small, *The Value of the Humanities* (New York: Oxford University Press, 2013), 59.

overall personal happiness, that these disciplines are necessary for a functioning American democracy,[13] or that the humanities are useful for their own sake, all of these arguments are made in response to a repeated call to give an account of one's self in an economic context and cultural moment where the humanities are already ideologically linked to uselessness and idleness. It is admittedly difficult to move out of such a defensive position.

In this rhetorical context, the humanities are useful for providing productions such as novels, plays, and visual arts that can be pleasurably consumed on occasion but are not necessary for everyday living, "like a delightful dessert" as Michael Bérubé observes.[14] The rhetoric of uselessness in the United States has been especially, well, useful in moments when the public is invoked as being left out of academic conversations when they should be at the center, which renders such conversations irrelevant on account of exclusion. Biblical scholars might detect a similarity in our own discourses, where we use ordinary (Bible) readers—those who do not know the intricacies of exegesis and yet still engage biblical literature—as examples of why our professional jargon-filled writings are useless. Such discourses not only downplay the intellectual acuity of ordinary people, they also weaponize conceptual binaries such as specialist/nonspecialist, intellectual/nonintellectual, and reason/emotion. When the intrinsic value of the humanities is promoted via arguments insisting that educated goodness trumps vulgar uneducated utilitarianism, it is an act of defiance against the charge of uselessness. However, aside from reinscribing a class-infused semiotic relation between elitism and education, such defenses may actually affirm that utility is the main question, rather than change the conversation.

The rhetoric of uselessness has a lot of traction in characterizations of what is at stake in the purpose of an American higher education: job preparedness (economic usefulness) or personal growth (cultured uselessness).[15] In fact, usefulness appears to be an organizing principle in

---

13. See also Martha Nussbaum, *Not for Profit: Why Democracy Needs the Humanities*, The Public Square (Princeton: Princeton University Press, 2010); and Geoffrey Galt Harpham, *The Humanities and the Dream of America* (Chicago: University of Chicago Press, 2011).

14. Michael Bérubé, *Rhetorical Occasions: Essays on Humans and the Humanities* (Chapel Hill: University of North Carolina Press, 2006), 71.

15. For more on the useful/useless binary in American higher education, see Jennifer Summit and Blakey Vermeule, *Action versus Contemplation: Why an Ancient Debate Still Matters* (Chicago: University of Chicago Press, 2018).

the history of American higher education.[16] The stakes are significant in the American cultural context, where the sentiment that access to higher education should result in jobs and economic mobility runs deep. That students who otherwise could not afford college are willing to shoulder substantial student-loan debt reflects the pervasive notion that higher education is an investment that guarantees economic prosperity as its return. The development of the major as a rubric of organizing undergraduate courses has exacerbated the question of utility, as such a designation is shorthand for promoting job training and professional school readiness.[17] This opens the rhetorical option of associating majors with careers and salary expectations, as well as ranking them hierarchically according to perceptions of usefulness. Here the purported congruency of curricular nomenclature with the title of an undergraduate's first postcollege job is an interesting indicator: since no one majors in barista studies, that one would get that job is linked to a major's uselessness. In a context where the religious studies major consistently ranks near the bottom of such lists,[18] the rhetoric of uselessness should be on the radar of scholars of religion contending with declining enrollments, conversations with students that feature the reasons they cannot take multiple courses in our field, and demands to produce tangible and marketable job-related outcomes.

Similarly, controversies over the great books in American higher education have opened the door to reconsidering the Bible's role in general education curricula, as it is thought to be largely incoherent and useless for contemporary students. The tension between the major, as stand-in for useful specialization, and general education, as stand-in for useless cultural competence, is palpable in this respect. This is especially ironic since

---

16. The most thorough examination of utility as a rubric in American higher education remains Lawrence R. Veysey, *The Emergence of the American University* (Chicago: University of Chicago Press, 1970), 57–120.

17. For an example of emergent literature that aims to combat the rhetoric of uselessness and stereotypes about the college major and appropriate employment, see George Anders, *You Can Do Anything: The Surprising Power of a 'Useless' Liberal Arts Education* (New York: Little, Brown, 2017).

18. One can easily search online for college majors and starting salaries and learn which majors lead to the highest and lowest starting salaries. Religion is almost never in the highest-salary list. For a representative list, see Delece Smith-Barrow and Josh Moody, "Ten College Majors with the Lowest Starting Salaries," *US News and World Report*, 2019, 2020, https://www.usnews.com/education/best-colleges/slideshows/10-college-majors-with-the-lowest-starting-salaries (accessed 23 June 2020).

the history of general education programs is more recent, and the content less traditional, than one might expect. Despite assumptions that general education was the original liberal arts program (for elite gentlemen and/or aspiring ministers) that eventually made room for specialized knowledge and other kinds of bodies in the classroom, the idea of a core curriculum is a distinctly American phenomenon that rose to prominence on account of efforts to provide a common reference point for a postwar influx of college students from social locations other than moneyed and northeastern.[19] Colleges and universities implemented general education in part to mitigate against the drive toward specialization and job preparedness—a German import that took hold in the United States as the research university model.[20] Thus, while the major and general education might seem to be opposites, it is the case that these two modes of classifying knowledge have a more complicated, even symbiotic, relationship. The idea of American cultural literacy being central to the formation of citizens receded as American students and faculty became disillusioned with the idea of attaining competence in a fundamentally corrupt and exclusionary culture where great books also signified dominant culture. The Bible, as great book, is caught in the fray here. How, then, to negotiate student lack of interest in, and abundance of hostility toward, traditional religion and a lack of faculty preparedness to deal with students' religion issues is a persistently undertheorized question.

---

19. Richard Hofstadter, *Anti-intellectualism in American Life* (New York: Knopf, 1963); Andrew Delbanco, *College: What it Was, Is, and Should Be* (Princeton: Princeton University Press, 2011); Derek Bok, *Higher Education in America* (Princeton: Princeton University Press, 2013). On the importance of a general education in this postwar period, see the still-referenced Harvard University, *General Education in a Free Society: Report of the Harvard Committee* (Cambridge: Harvard University Press, 1945); this study notes that, on the one hand, biblical literature is not simple and should be studied in the context of general education at a higher literary level, and, on the other hand, a semester-long general education course that only has a certain amount of time for the largest number of books should include selections from the Bible (113, 207).

20. See Frederick Rudolph, *The American College and University: A History* (Athens: University of Georgia Press, 1962); John Thelin, *History of American Higher Education*, 2nd ed. (Baltimore: Johns Hopkins University Press, 2011). For more on the Germanness of this model, see Jurgen Herbst, *The German Historical School in American Scholarship: A Study in the Transfer of Culture* (Ithaca, NY: Cornell University Press, 1965); and Peter Watson, *The German Genius: Europe's Third Renaissance, the Second Scientific Revolution, and the Twentieth Century* (New York: Harper, 2010).

The rhetoric of uselessness appears in various ways in conversations about biblical scholarship as a part of the humanities in American higher education. Such rhetoric appears from multiple directions: on the ground, through decline in enrollments and uptick in student anxiety about the economic future; among faculty curricular deliberations, through a perceived decline in religious interest or affiliation; in American culture more broadly, through a perceived dichotomy between job readiness and cultured idleness as questions about the purpose of higher education (re)surface; and in our guild, through dismissal of traditional biblical scholarship as a means to expose bias or position innovative methods as better. What we face as biblical scholars is, in my view, a distinctly American problem because of the entanglements of American economic and religious life and higher education. In the current higher-educational landscape, usefulness is a loaded characterization. It is also a defensive term, deployed against the charge—at times warranted, at times imagined—that whatever we are doing is useless. It is tempting to blame the recent past for this conundrum—as if there was a golden age of teaching in biblical scholarship and/or the humanities where our utility was celebrated. As David Labaree has noted, though, since the nineteenth century American higher education has emphasized an intimate economic relationship between students and institutions based on negotiating a balance between populism, usefulness, and elitism that shaped curricula and ideological orientations.[21]

It might be comforting to assume that the rhetoric of uselessness about biblical scholarship is new. However, a cursory examination of the historical interactions between the Bible, biblical scholarship, and American higher education reveals that the rhetoric of uselessness has in fact been a perennial concern of American biblical scholars, particularly those who have taken up the challenge of how, on what terms, and to what ends the Bible and biblical scholarship are taught in American colleges and universities. In what follows I will briefly explore this history and its embeddedness in a narrative about the role of the Bible and biblical scholarship in American higher education, focusing on the late nineteenth century through the end of the Second World War, or the heyday of historical criticism.

---

21. See David Labaree, *A Perfect Mess: The Unlikely Ascendancy of American Higher Education* (Chicago: University of Chicago Press, 2017).

Narrating the History of Uselessness

A popular narrative about the Bible and American education over time provides a background for debates about biblical scholarship and higher education. This narrative, couched in some version of a secularization thesis, often proceeds thus: the founding generations of the United States were deeply entrenched in their Protestant piety and the Bible reading that came along with it. The Bible was not only an inspired book; it was also a textbook for children and adults that was useful for learning the English alphabet, how to read, and learning about history. This order of things was challenged as America became more religiously diverse, at least in part through waves of immigration and migration, first among European Catholics and then among others. The rise of modern science—especially Darwinian notions of evolution—and the industrial revolution, along with the introduction of rationalism and historical-critical biblical scholarship into the American mix, produced a situation where people were not reading their Bibles with as much piety or passion as previously, even as more Americans were becoming literate and more citizens were leaving farm and factory jobs for college and university programs. The last few decades have seen a serious drop in mainline Protestant church membership and attendance.

According to this narrative, the decline of religious affiliation and the secularization of American society and institutions over the last century has engendered a decline in biblical readership and, as Stephen Prothero has noted, a pervasive religious illiteracy.[22] Major court cases in the twentieth century about the Bible in public schools complicated the landscape further, the story goes, and now we live in a time of unprecedented religious diversity and disenchantment. In the midst of this decrease in religious interest and increase in secularism, along with the rise of the so-called nones,[23] the Bible's place in higher education has suffered. If we cannot

---

22. Stephen Prothero, *Religious Literacy: What Every American Should Know—and Doesn't* (New York: HarperCollins, 2008). Prothero's argument rests somewhat on a narrative about the history of American biblical literacy.

23. Linda Mercadante has argued that, while the none identification, or "spiritual but not religious," has experienced an increase in numbers over the last two decades, such categories are erroneously identified solely with very recent developments in religious identification among the millennial generation of Americans. She indicates that disidentification with established religious institutions is a feature of multiple

assume that college students have had an upbringing that includes being steeped in the contents of the Bible and if they are (probably) not going to concentrate their studies in religion or the humanities, then how does that change our orientation to how a course in Bible is taught, if it indeed needs to be taught at all?

This narrative is alluring for several reasons. It features a golden age of true piety and biblical literacy that is a major characteristic of early (Euro-) American life and from which we have departed. It assumes an original consistency, singularity, and homogeneity in terms of people's relationship with their scriptures way back when. It enables the rendering of a complex history into a linear narrative of decline that fronts a directly proportional relationship between church affiliation and Bible fluency that has affected educational practices. Moreover, it offers a useful aetiology that allows us to contrast the present situation with that of an increasingly distant time and either mourn or celebrate the loss of a common biblical piety and literacy as a precursor for engaging the Bible in higher education. It links Bible reading to religious knowledge and commitment.

This narrative also rhetorically positions American biblical scholarship as that which, in its early stages, was largely opposed to, and corrosive of, church authority and Sunday school Bible instruction. Herein the field is framed as a mostly German invention, aligned with European post-Enlightenment philology, philosophy of history, and archaeology. It is easy to characterize this history as one that has privileged disinterested exegesis and positivistic historical reconstruction, whose dead white (mostly) European male proponents strived for objectivity but reproduced oppression and orientalism. The rhetoric of uselessness leaves this narrative largely unchallenged, glosses over regional epistemological trajectories, and obscures a long history of efforts among American biblical scholars to make their own ideological space.

A different narrative, more useful for this discussion, casts the history of American biblical scholarship as the history of struggles over how knowledge is produced, disseminated, *and taught* in higher educational settings. Herein historical criticism developed as a means to conduct independent inquiry about biblical literature—the most unquestionable of literatures—without regard for the predeterminations of ecclesiastical hierarchies.

---

generations and is an important part of American religious history. See Linda Mercadante, *Belief without Borders: Inside the Minds of the Spiritual but not Religious* (New York: Oxford University Press, 2014).

Historical criticism emphasized the difference between the present and the past, which intervened in popular narratives of continuity and inevitability. Developments in historical science, and particularly tools that could help support inquiry into how people and institutions changed over time, were important for such scholars—especially in the college classroom.

Early American biblical scholars traveled to Europe to learn new methods and upon their return attempted to make those methods work in an unfriendly American situation. American scholars encountered hostility due to a chronic lack of funding, hospitality, and understanding. They also endured a lack of job security on account of heresy trials that were tied not only to what offended denominational bodies on doctrinal grounds, but also what was threatening in college and seminary classrooms. The two famous Presbyterian heresy trials of Charles Augustus Briggs in the 1890s, for example, were initiated in part because denominational leaders disapproved of his teaching such outlandish ideas as rationalism and critical thinking about what he called "bibliolatry," or the uncritical veneration of the Bible. Although Union Theological Seminary rebuffed the ecclesial recommendation to remove Briggs from his teaching post and supported the academic freedom of its faculty to profess to the best of their ability regardless of creedal fidelity, a line in the sand about the inappropriateness of teaching critical biblical scholarship was publicly drawn. Briggs's trial and others like it shaped the material conditions under which biblical scholarship was taught and charted a course for the relationship between biblical scholarship and American higher education that we are now still negotiating.

Far from simply imitating their German masters, earlier American biblical scholars attempted to set an agenda that was germane to their time and place. This was not just about research, as conversations about the Bible and higher education appear to have been somewhat pressing and a source of conflict between scholars, pastors, and other parties. We can see evidence of these attempts at agenda-setting particularly in times of crisis such as debates about science and the two world wars. Three themes emerge here. First, it appears that the cultural sentiment that the Bible was to be taught as a useful source to be mined for public morality and conduct was an irritant and challenge to American biblical scholars, who saw such a task as antithetical to their methods. Second, American biblical scholars were concerned with how to claim a robust position in the academy that was less dependent on German scholarship and more attentive to the specific needs of the American situation, particularly during times of international political upheaval. Third, American biblical scholars were concerned with how to address the biblical illiteracy of college and seminary students, as it was frustrating to teach different ways of critically appraising the Bible with students who were unfamiliar with its contents.

In a series of writings that gained notoriety through his 1891 inaugural address and heresy trials, Briggs challenged his colleagues to not sacrifice intellectual rigor in the face of public pressure to treat students and other bible readers as illiterate infants and blind adherents to church doctrines.[24] For Briggs, American college and seminary students were best served if introduced to the capacity to think independently and pose their own questions. He maintained that American biblical scholars had a responsibility to ensure that pastors were the best-educated members of their congregations since they, too, served a teaching function in a democratic society.[25] Several decades later, in his 1919 Society of Biblical Literature presidential address, James Montgomery warned of two issues facing American scholars. He posited that, should they uncritically imitate German science and its capacity to subsume other disciplines, the result would be a decline in curricular attention to biblical scholarship and the humanities in American colleges and seminaries, which would lead to less demand for biblical scholars to hold faculty positions and secure research funding. He opined that a cleavage between scientific and popular research was too severe in the American context, that while attention to producing scholarship for the public was the "line of greatest demand and also of profit,"[26] such attention was also a deflection from research that would move the field forward. On the other hand, Montgomery noted, the public's refusal to understand American biblical scholarship resulted in charges of uselessness. For him, there needed to be a balance between depth and breadth that could be achieved and taught in the college classroom, even as there might never be much financial support for American biblical scholars.[27]

---

24. Charles Augustus Briggs, *The Authority of Holy Scripture: An Inaugural Address* (New York: Scribners, 1891).

25. Charles Augustus Briggs, "A Plea for the Higher Study of Theology," *The American Journal of Theology* 8 (1904): 433–51. In this essay Briggs argues that ministers in his time were no longer the most educated people in the congregation, so they needed a more critical, rigorous, and thoroughgoing education than the useful one offered by seminaries. To Briggs, American biblical scholarship was leading the way in critical thought.

26. James Montgomery, "Present Tasks of Biblical Scholarship," *JBL* 38 (1919): 5.

27. Montgomery, "Present Tasks of Biblical Scholarship," 5–6.

Almost forty years and another world war after Montgomery, Morton Enslin commented on the specter of the practical and its effects on American biblical scholarship. In his 1945 Society of Biblical Literature presidential address, Enslin put the matter bluntly. Drawing the comparison with Nazi co-optation of biblical scholarship in Germany, he states, "I see a similar peril here, and it is even more forbidding and ominous because it appears so innocent and virtuous. It is the demand that our researches strengthen faith and provide blueprints for modern conduct."[28] Enslin called the demand to conduct biblical scholarship that is useful to institutional leaders and the public a "virus" that had plagued scholars in Germany and was threatening American scholars, too:

> At first it was so obvious as to constitute no especial danger ... when he [the biblical scholar] becomes more concerned in the practical availability and moralistic application of his findings than he is in discovering facts, it is time to sound the tocsin. And this situation seems to me to have been reached today and to be tincturing our whole discipline.... Repeatedly we have been told that we owe it to our students to aid them to a warm religious attitude to life, to a deeper and more satisfying faith; that we lay too great emphasis on the critical and analytical—I have heard it styled, the minutiae—that we need a new and more positive technique; that we should realize that scholarly reserve and dispassionate appraisal are out of place in our field. We are dealing with "words of life," with materials of divine revelation, with materials vastly different from those in other disciplines. Above all we are ministers before we are scholars. To me this emphasis is utterly false and vicious.[29]

For Enslin, American biblical scholars should not be obligated to conduct their work—because it is about the Bible and not the classics, mathematics, or chemistry—toward a warm, practical purpose among students. To be sure, it is not the drive for an outmoded scientific positivism that is at issue here—rather, it is how to combat the demand that biblical scholars should do something special to build up faith in the classroom because that is what institutional leaders (and students!) think they ought to be doing. Refusing to capitulate would, Enslin continued, result in the kind of American college and seminary teaching where students would hopefully learn

---

28. Morton Enslin, "The Future of Biblical Studies," *JBL* 65 (1946): 6.
29. Enslin, "Future of Biblical Studies," 7.

to be dissatisfied with anything save the most honest and unbiased work they are capable of, to refuse to take the short cuts, to assume the answers, to discover what they want to discover, to prefer the neat and brisk encyclopaedia articles to the labor of discovering the facts themselves; above all, to rid their minds utterly of the notion that the literature which they are examining is of a different sort from that under scrutiny by their brothers, the classical students and Assyriologists; in short, to encourage them to let their findings determine their feelings, not their feelings their findings; to keep their hands off the scales when weighing evidence, even if it concerns the validity of the faith of their fathers (or pastors); to make them realize that it is the one unforgivable sin against the deities of learning to make the one pan of the balance go down because they want it to go down, even if they are convinced that their own soul's salvation is hanging in the balance.[30]

While some contemporary readers may bristle or scoff at the idea that biblical scholars, American or otherwise, can ever achieve unbiased work or keep their hands off the scales, the critical impulse in Enslin's address is worth considering as an enduring feature and challenge of American biblical scholarship. That is, in the face of suggestions to teach toward useful ends by affirming dominant pieties and/or assumptions about the specialness of biblical literature, biblical scholars stay closer to the field's primary orientation by developing the tools for critical thinking, studying biblical literature as a human product, and not letting preconceived notions or the desires of religious or political (or parental) authority figures dictate the outcome of educational pursuits or intellectual development.

At the turn of the twentieth century, coterminous with significant institutional reforms, American biblical scholars prioritized thinking about the intersection of the Bible and higher education. A decade before Montgomery's 1919 address, four American scholars—Ismar Peritz, Irving Wood, Raymond Knox, and Olive Dutcher—met after a Society of Biblical Literature and Exegesis meeting in New York City and outlined the need to regularly gather and discuss the role of biblical scholarship in teaching. The story of the founding of the National Association of Biblical Instructors (NABI) is better known as the founding of the American Academy of Religion (AAR). These scholars were interested in organized professional deliberations about teaching the Bible in colleges and secondary schools. One of their main concerns was to apply critical biblical

---

30. Enslin, "Future of Biblical Studies," 7–8.

scholarship to the classroom and help move students beyond a Sunday-school relationship with the Bible. They were also concerned about raising biblical literacy rates among entering college students by organizing biblical studies courses for high schools.[31] The capacity to think critically, in the eyes of these biblical scholars, would make students into more thoughtful American citizens. Although early documents from the National Association of Biblical Instructors seem to be lost, their journal (now the *Journal of the American Academy of Religion*) records long-standing conversations about their challenges. It appears that this guild dropped a secondary-school focus to concentrate efforts on higher education, where the gravest area of concern was registered.

Alongside bemoaning the implications of declining college enrollments (an eternal problem, it seems) and pressures from various sources to make their work practical, these biblical scholars were also negotiating the charge of uselessness. As Chester Quimby laments in his 1932 National Association of Biblical Instructors address,

> It is no fault of ours that Sunday School teaching sends youth to college scorning any thought of Bible study. We are hardly to blame that many preachers are openly hostile to us and most of the rest quite indifferent. We cannot help it that even the best of the church-going parents have so thoroughly neglected the Bible that their children consider it of no account. *It is not chargeable to us that college executives and faculties generally do not see that Bible has any place in modern education. Ours is not the blame that Bible is not needed in making a living. One may need chemistry or English or pedagogy, but not Bible.*[32]

Quimby states that there are aspects of this situation for which biblical scholars are responsible, namely, ineffectively bridging the pedagogical divide between Sunday school and college and becoming too beholden to European scientific methods instead of configuring a mutual relationship between science and American biblical scholarship. However, it is the uselessness of the Bible in American colleges, and the idea that biblical scholars

---

31. This was the recommendation of a National Association of Biblical Instructors committee in 1917; see "Bible Study in Secondary Schools: A Committee Report" and "Standardization of Biblical Departments in Colleges: A Committee Report," *Religious Education* 12 (1917): 136–39 and 139–45.

32. Chester Warren Quimby, "The Word of God: Presidential Address," *JNABI* 1.1 (1933): 1, emphasis added.

ought to engage that rhetoric, that concerns Quimby. Hugh Hartshorne echoes this concern when he notes that students' precollege encounters with the Bible may be the reason that they do not enroll in biblical studies in college, that in Sunday schools the Bible is not used in a dignified manner: "either it is broken up into unrelated passages of supposedly inspirational value, or it is dealt with as a glorified prooftext for the solution of all human ills. Fortunately neither method is common in college teaching."[33] College, Hartshorne proposes, is the appropriate, natural place to teach an adult book like the Bible. He acknowledges that transitioning from seeing the Bible as a moral guide to seeing it as a human work of literature is difficult for college students, who may turn away from such courses to avoid questioning their faith.[34]

Other biblical scholars affirmed these challenges and shared resources. James Muilenburg, for example, argued for teaching ancient mythology alongside biblical literature to help generate student interest and depth of understanding,[35] and Eliza Hall Kendrick published a history of approaches used in teaching the Bible at Wellesley College.[36] Taking a more optimistic stance on teaching the Bible with historical criticism, Florence Fitch outlined the problem of student resistance and the promise that historical criticism held for teaching:

> A student enters his first college class in Bible with a different attitude from that with which he begins a course in Chemistry or Sociology. He has some definite theory about this Book; he believes that it is the inspired Word of God, or a repository of outworn superstition, or a collection of charming myths and fairy tales and exquisite poems of naïve idealism, or he holds some less extreme view. Every teacher knows the difficulty of working with a group representing such variety of opinion, and of helping each one to make the transition to an open-minded attitude and a scientifically tenable position.... By his own discovery, rather than by the iconoclastic dogmatism of teacher or text, he finds reconstruction necessary; often he finds it alluring; and sometimes he is almost unconscious

---

33. Hugh Hartshorne, "The Future of the Bible in the American College," *JNABI* 1.1 (1933): 10.

34. Hartshorne, "Future of the Bible in the American College," 10.

35. James Muilenburg, "The Literary Approach: The Old Testament as Hebrew Literature," *JNABI* 1.2 (1933): 14–22.

36. Eliza Hall Kendrick, *A History of Bible Teaching at Wellesley College, 1875–1950*, edited by her colleagues (Wellesley, MA: Wellesley College, 1932, 1950).

of the processes by which he has passed from childish literalism to maturity of thought, from supercilious skepticism to profound appreciation.[37]

For Fitch, students of historical criticism have an opportunity to learn an invaluable intellectual discipline: through understanding historical distance and the ultimate inaccessibility of another time and place, through discerning the difference between history and historical source material, through understanding one's own assumptions about the material at hand, and through coming to realize the vast array of uses that biblical literature endures. Fitch and other members of the National Association of Biblical Instructors—many of whom were women faculty members at liberal arts colleges—developed defenses against the charge of uselessness, using their understanding of the material realities of American higher education in their time. These concerns were pondered amid declining enrollments in Bible courses, lack of student and faculty preparation for rigorous historical analysis, perceived lack of interest in religion, and assumptions that students were only interested in new the array of new technologies brought by rapid industrialization and developments in science (!).

Even as they shared a commitment to historical criticism as a meaningful orientation to teaching the Bible, not all American biblical scholars of this earlier era eschewed the general public or practical application of their academic training. The Religious Education Association (REA), for example, was founded in 1903 by William Rainey Harper, a biblical scholar perhaps better known as the first president of the University of Chicago. The purpose of this guild, different than the National Association of Biblical Instructors, was to provide resources for the American public to learn about religion and the Bible, as well as to encourage scholars of religion and scholars of education to interact with one another and with the public. In so doing, perhaps the usefulness of modern biblical scholarship for broad audiences would be realized. John Dewey, one of the founding members of the Religious Education Association, was concerned with the connection between rigorous historical analysis and the professorial freedom to inquire.

The role of American biblical scholarship, and particularly historical criticism, was emphasized from the Religious Education Association's inaugural gathering. Herein, commenting on the power of historical criticism

---

37. Florence Mary Fitch, "The Historical Approach to the Study of the Bible," *JNABI* 1.2 (1933): 12.

for teaching college-level biblical literature courses, Chester Willett quipped that, for the average student, the Bible is a self-evident document. However, what historical criticism can help students realize is that "ideas are seen to have a history, as well as institutions; philosophies have their genealogy as well as individuals. Nothing is stationary. All things are changing. Constitutions, beliefs, habits, systems, all are in a state of flux."[38] Rush Rhees shared Willett's characterization, adding that historical-critical biblical scholarship had vast potential for American higher education, since

> criticism is the modern effort to answer certain questions which are forced upon readers of the Bible by traditional views. It is most natural to ask who wrote certain books, when they were written, and why they were written; and criticism is simply the modern, fearlessly honest, effort to answer these questions with a, perhaps bold, disregard of the answers that have been handed down by the tradition which furnishes the questions.[39]

These biblical scholars emphasized the notion that ideas, institutions, and individuals changed over time and according to environmental influences, over and against doctrinal insistence to the contrary. They also emphasized the power of asking questions freely and without restraint, as opposed to the predetermined answers that their students associated with church settings. In the context of the fundamentalist-modernist debates of the early twentieth century—in which American biblical scholarship played no small role—this kind of position-taking in terms of teaching practices among biblical scholars is important to consider, even a century later.

It is common to narrate the history of biblical scholarship in a homogenous manner. The historical foundations of American biblical scholarship are more distinct and contentious than such a narrative suggests. From this very brief survey, it appears that what was (and is) at stake in teaching biblical literature from the standpoint of historical criticism as it was practiced at educational institutions in the United States were several key

---

38. Chester Willett, "Address: Religious Education as Affected by the Historical Study of the Bible," in *The Religious Education Association: Proceedings of the First Annual Convention, Chicago, February 10–12, 1903* (Chicago: Executive Office of the Religious Education Association, 1903), 91–92.

39. Rush Rhees, "Address: Religious Education as Affected by the Historical Study of the Bible," in *The Religious Education Association*, 80.

issues: cultural literacy, freedom of inquiry, subjection of everything held dear to critical analysis, resistance to dogmatism, and a transdisciplinary orientation. These are the issues—issues that are about authority at their root—that put earlier American biblical scholars at risk for heresy trials and removal from their teaching posts. American higher education has long been ideally concerned with democratic aims, the question of scientism and progress, and the production of cultivated citizens. These ideal concerns, however, have been fraught with controversy. Moreover, conversations about the utility of higher education are longstanding. American biblical scholars stepped into these conflicts more emphatically than most. It would be easy to dismiss this propensity as that which is overly concerned with morality and missionary zeal, but that would obscure an important two-pronged part of our intellectual history: the fight, as it were, with dogmatism was fought on that terrain, with the tools of history, and the concern with higher education as a critical arena for the performance of modern biblical scholarship.

Rhetoric and Reality

Debates about the usefulness of a higher education have only intensified in the United States—among pundits, politicians, and the public. At the same time, the consequences of the rhetoric of uselessness are material, as institutions are downsizing and eliminating humanities programs in the name of preparing for the future and job readiness. Casualties like this have contributed to a situation where explaining the usefulness of a disciplinary framework is necessary for surviving, not to mention thriving. For some in the humanities, this is thought to be a new problem. However, American biblical scholarship has always been linked to the demand and capacity to explain the usefulness of our work—to theologians, to ethicists, to church people, to scholars in other disciplines, to the public, to pretty much *everyone but ourselves*. The rhetoric of uselessness has long been steeped in a skepticism about biblical scholarship as a distinctive means of engaging biblical literature, which, if pressed, is also a skepticism about modernism and ways of ordering data and knowledge that are not predetermined by doctrinal dedication or ecclesiastical domination. In this way, American biblical scholarship, the humanities, and higher education are linked in intellectual and educational history in terms of methods, disciplinary formation, and academic freedom.

Attending to the rhetoric of uselessness and its history at the intersection of biblical scholarship and higher education shows that these conversations are not part of a new phenomenon or epoch in American educational history, nor are they unique to this particular cultural moment. Moreover, current debates about utility of the humanities in American higher education—an important occasion for any thought experiments about the Bible and higher education—are rooted in conversations about the Bible and higher education among earlier American biblical scholars. It is the case that American biblical scholars have historically had an intimate relationship with research and the production of knowledge, and the tensions about that knowledge with the public. However, they (we) have also been wrestling with the connections between knowledge production and the practices of teaching in higher-educational settings for some time. To be sure, any argument for the humanities should fold in the study of the Bible and religion. The history of American biblical scholarship, then, at least as far as higher education is concerned, is tied to the history of the humanities.

Examining historical discourses at the intersection of American biblical scholarship and higher education reveals a key methodological component of the discipline: the propensity to question assumptions and authority. This critical part of the intellectual legacy of biblical scholarship can get lost in intramural debates over reading strategies. It might be the case that some research in biblical studies is not quite fit for public consumption. However, the question of principles and methods is definitely relevant for various publics. As far as the history of teaching historical criticism is concerned, it is difficult to underestimate just how powerful an ideological intervention it was (and is) to ask, in a classroom situation, whether the way things are now are the same as they were in the ancient past, especially when narratives about that ancient past have been expedient as a means to attempt to control the present, and particularly when posing difficult questions about what we take for granted carries considerable risk beyond the charge of uselessness. Every engagement with the past is ultimately done through the lens of contemporary concerns; this is not a recent innovation. The disconnect settles in when one realizes that vast diachronic differences can be interrogated toward understanding various aspects of human experience. To this end, identifying assumptions is the first step of critical thinking and of ideological analysis and intervention. While the scholarship of every historical moment is highly occasional, struggles over the utility and authority of the educational enterprise of

American biblical scholarship comprise a thread that is difficult to ignore, particularly in our own context. Behind such struggles lie unsettled (and unsettling) questions about knowledge and power, then and now.

Bibliography

Anders, George. *You Can Do Anything: The Surprising Power of a 'Useless' Liberal Arts Education.* New York: Little, Brown, 2017.

Avalos, Hector. *The End of Biblical Studies.* Amherst, NY: Prometheus, 2007.

Barr, David, and Nicholas Piediscalzi, eds. *The Bible in American Education.* Philadelphia: Fortress; Chico, CA: Scholars Press, 1982.

Beal, Timothy K. *The Rise and Fall of the Bible: The Unexpected History of an Accidental Book.* New York: Mariner, 2011.

Berlinerblau, Jacques. *The Secular Bible: Why Nonbelievers Must Take Religion Seriously.* New York: Cambridge University Press, 2005.

Bérubé, Michael. *Rhetorical Occasions: Essays on Humans and the Humanities.* Chapel Hill: University of North Carolina Press, 2006.

Boer, Roland, ed. *Secularism and Biblical Studies.* BibleWorld. London: Equinox, 2010.

Bok, Derek. *Higher Education in America.* Princeton: Princeton University Press, 2013.

Briggs, Charles Augustus. *The Authority of Holy Scripture: An Inaugural Address.* New York: Scribners, 1891.

———. "A Plea for the Higher Study of Theology." *The American Journal of Theology* 8 (1904): 433–51.

Chancey, Mark A. "Public School Bible Courses in Historical Perspective: North Carolina as a Case Study." Pages 193–214 in *The Bible in the Public Square: Its Enduring Influence in American Life.* Edited by Mark A. Chancey, Carol Meyers, and Eric M. Meyers. BSNA 27. Atlanta: SBL Press, 2014.

Collins, John J. *The Bible after Babel: Historical Criticism in a Postmodern Age.* Grand Rapids: Eerdmans, 2005.

Crook, Margaret, and the Bible Faculty at Smith College. *The Bible and Its Literary Associations.* New York: Abingdon, 1937.

Delbanco, Andrew. *College: What it Was, Is, and Should Be.* Princeton: Princeton University Press, 2011.

Enslin, Morton. "The Future of Biblical Studies." *JBL* 65 (1946): 1–12.

Fitch, Florence Mary. "The Historical Approach to the Study of the Bible." *JNABI* 1.2 (1933): 11–14.

Harpham, Geoffrey Galt. *The Humanities and the Dream of America*. Chicago: University of Chicago Press, 2011.

Hartshorne, Hugh. "The Future of the Bible in the American College." *JNABI* 1.1 (1933): 9–10.

Harvard University. *General Education in a Free Society: Report of the Harvard Committee*. Cambridge: Harvard University Press, 1945.

Haynes, Charles C. "Battling over the Bible in Public Schools: Is Common Ground Possible?" Pages 181–92 in *The Bible in the Public Square: Its Enduring Influence in American Life*. Edited by Mark A. Chancey, Carol Meyers, and Eric M. Meyers. BSNA 27. Atlanta: SBL Press, 2014.

Herbst, Jurgen. *The German Historical School in American Scholarship: A Study in the Transfer of Culture*. Ithaca: Cornell University Press, 1965.

Hofstadter, Richard. *Anti-intellectualism in American Life*. New York: Knopf, 1963.

Jeffrey, David Lyle, and C. Stephen Evans, eds. *The Bible and the University*. Scripture and Hermeneutics 8. Grand Rapids: Zondervan, 2007.

Kendrick, Eliza Hall. *A History of Bible Teaching at Wellesley College, 1875–1950*. Edited by her colleagues. Wellesley, MA: Wellesley College, 1932, 1950.

Labaree, David. *A Perfect Mess: The Unlikely Ascendancy of American Higher Education*. Chicago: University of Chicago Press, 2017.

Lehrich, Christopher I., ed. *On Teaching Religion: Essays by Jonathan Z. Smith*. New York: Oxford University Press, 2012.

Lopez, Davina C. "Curational Reflections: On Rhetorics of Tradition and Innovation in Biblical Scholarship." Pages 68–92 in *Present and Future of Biblical Studies: Celebrating Twenty-Five Years of Brill's* Biblical Interpretation. Edited by Tat-Siong Benny Liew. Leiden: Brill, 2018.

Martin, Dale B. *Pedagogy of the Bible*. Louisville: Westminster John Knox, 2008.

McCutcheon, Russell. *Critics not Caretakers: Redescribing the Public Study of Religion*. Albany, NY: SUNY Press, 2001.

Mercadante, Linda. *Belief without Borders: Inside the Minds of the Spiritual but not Religious*. New York: Oxford University Press, 2014.

Montgomery, James. "Present Tasks of Biblical Scholarship." *JBL* 38 (1919): 1–14.

Moore, Stephen D., and Yvonne Sherwood. *The Invention of the Biblical Scholar: A Critical Manifesto*. Minneapolis: Fortress, 2011.

Muilenburg, James. "The Literary Approach: The Old Testament as Hebrew Literature." *JNABI* 1.2 (1933): 14–22.

———. *Specimens of Biblical Literature*. New York: Crowell, 1923.

National Association of Biblical Instructors. "Bible Study in Secondary Schools: A Committee Report." *Religious Education* 12 (1917): 136–39.

———. "Standardization of Biblical Departments in Colleges: A Committee Report." *Religious Education* 12 (1917): 139–45.

Nussbaum, Martha. *Not for Profit: Why Democracy Needs the Humanities*. The Public Square. Princeton: Princeton University Press, 2010.

Penner, Todd, and Davina C. Lopez. *De-introducing the New Testament: Texts, Worlds, Methods, Stories*. Hoboken, NJ: Wiley-Blackwell, 2015.

Prothero, Stephen. *Religious Literacy: What Every American Should Know—and Doesn't*. New York: HarperCollins, 2008.

Quimby, Chester Warren. "The Word of God: Presidential Address." *JNABI* 1.1 (1933): 1–6.

Rhees, Rush. "Address: Religious Education as Affected by the Historical Study of the Bible." Pages 80–87 in *The Religious Education Association: Proceedings of the First Annual Convention, Chicago, February 10–12, 1903*. Chicago: Executive Office of the Religious Education Association, 1903.

Roncace, Mark, and Patrick Gray, eds. *Teaching the Bible: Practical Strategies for Classroom Instruction*. RBS 49. Atlanta: Society of Biblical Literature, 2005.

———, eds. *Teaching the Bible through Popular Culture and the Arts*. RBS 53. Atlanta: Society of Biblical Literature, 2007.

Rudolph, Frederick. *The American College and University: A History*. Athens: University of Georgia Press, 1962.

Schüssler Fiorenza, Elisabeth, and Kent Harold Richards, eds. *Transforming Graduate Biblical Education: Ethos and Discipline*. GPBS 10. Atlanta: Society of Biblical Literature, 2010.

Scott, A. O. *Better Living through Criticism: How to Think about Art, Pleasure, Beauty, and Truth*. New York: Penguin, 2016.

Small, Helen. *The Value of the Humanities*. New York: Oxford University Press, 2013.

Smith, Jonathan Z. "Religion and Bible." *JBL* 128 (2009): 5–27.

———. "Teaching the Bible in the Context of General Education." *TTR* 1.2 (1998): 73–78.

Smith-Barrow, Delece, and Josh Moody. "Ten College Majors with the Lowest Starting Salaries." *US News and World Report*. 2019, updated

2020. https://www.usnews.com/education/best-colleges/slideshows/10-college-majors-with-the-lowest-starting-salaries (last accessed 23 June 2020).

Summit, Jennifer, and Blakey Vermeule. *Action versus Contemplation: Why an Ancient Debate Still Matters*. Chicago: University of Chicago Press, 2018.

Thelin, John. *History of American Higher Education*. 2nd ed. Baltimore: Johns Hopkins University Press, 2011.

Veysey, Lawrence R. *The Emergence of the American University*. Chicago: University of Chicago Press, 1970.

Watson, Peter. *The German Genius: Europe's Third Renaissance, the Second Scientific Revolution, and the Twentieth Century*. New York: Harper, 2010.

Webster, Jane, and Glen Holland, eds. *Teaching the Bible in the Liberal Arts Classroom*. Sheffield: Sheffield Phoenix, 2012.

———, eds. *Teaching the Bible in the Liberal Arts Classroom*. Vol. 2. Sheffield: Sheffield Phoenix, 2015.

Willett, Chester. "Address: Religious Education as Affected by the Historical Study of the Bible." Pages 88–98 in *The Religious Education Association: Proceedings of the First Annual Convention, Chicago, February 10–12, 1903*. Chicago: Executive Office of the Religious Education Association, 1903.

Young, Stephen. "Protective Strategies and the Prestige of the 'Academic.'" *BibInt* 23 (2015): 1–35.

10
THE BIBLE AND SOCIAL REFORM: MUSINGS OF A BIBLICAL SCHOLAR

EMERSON B. POWERY

I teach biblical studies, early Christianity, and hermeneutics to undergraduates at a religiously affiliated college a few miles from Harrisburg, the state capitol of Pennsylvania. In 2012, the state of Pennsylvania passed a resolution to declare 2012 the Year of the Bible. This resolution had a deeply profound effect on my courses that year as every student engaged more carefully the study of the Bible more than in any other year in my decade of teaching here. Not! In fact, the undergraduates I encounter rarely read the Bible any longer. The resolution gained national attention when American Atheists—an organization committed to the separation of church and state—sponsored a billboard in the heart of Harrisburg that read "Slaves Obey Your Masters." In protest of the political resolution, the billboard message backfired, however, when they depicted an image of a person of African descent in bondage to accompany the posted biblical text (Col 3:22). This image created much more controversy within the city of Harrisburg than the American Atheists's desire to mobilize a protest against a violent Bible.[1]

With or without reference to this state resolution, I remind my students why they should develop critical awareness about the use of the Bible (and

---

I am grateful to Michael E. Fuller for reading an earlier version of this draft and making helpful recommendations. Also, I wish to thank the editors of this volume for suggesting a beneficial structure for the essay.

1. Diana Fishlock, "Atheists 'Slaves Obey Your Masters' Billboard Raises Temper in Pennsylvania," *Huffington Post*, 13 March 2012, https://tinyurl.com/SBL6704e3. African Americans represent the largest racial group—approximately 50 percent—within city limits.

other sacred texts, for that matter) and public life, especially when public figures appropriate the Bible in areas of nationalistic speech and political identity. Rather than assume that individuals interpret biblical passages in a historical, political, and religious vacuum, I wish to situate the classroom conversation in our shared public US history. I remind them that if the year were 1800, because of my skin complexion, I would not be able to secure an advanced degree in religion in order to stand in front of them. If the year were 1830, the female students who constitute the majority of this college (61 percent) would not be among us. If the year were 1850, a public, collegiate space for our gathering would be very difficult to locate (Oberlin College would be one of the few exceptions). If the year were 1966, the year I was born, your intimate, interracial relationships could not be sanctioned in marriage, as such unions were illegal.[2] If the year were 2014, your intimate, same-sex relationships could not be realized in state-recognized marriages, since these relationships would be outlawed. For these laws, many proponents would draw on the Bible to support their claims.

Of course, the state house of Pennsylvania has not been alone in the symbolic (mis)appropriation of the Bible. Most recently, the governor of Kentucky, Matt Bevin, upped the ante by declaring two consecutive years—2016 and, again, 2017—The Year of the Bible. These declarations followed the national attention given to Kim Davis, the county clerk, when she denied marriage licenses in 2015 to same-sex couples based on her religious convictions. Later that year, Bevin issued the executive order removing county clerks' names from marriage licenses.[3]

The Bible also recently made the news in another controversial manner. In spring 2017, a thirty-five-year-old man, a former Army medic, threw rocks and a Bible through the front glass doors of a local mosque.[4] The man's violent and public use of the Bible made headline news across the United States.[5] The following day, a local rabbi led an interreligious gathering in support of the mosque's positive presence in the community.

---

2. See Loving v. Virginia, 388 U.S. 1 (1967).

3. None of these resolutions received the national attention of former President Ronald Reagan's declaration of 1983 as the Year of the Bible.

4. Alicia Stice and Cassa Niedringhaus, "Suspect Arrested in Islamic Center Attack," *The Coloradoan*, 27 March 2017, https://www.coloradoan.com/story/news/2017/03/27/breaking-suspect-arrested-islamic-center-attack/99716732/.

5. When compared to the following day's interreligious gathering to support the mosque, the man's violent action epitomizes a distinction Frederick Douglass made,

These symbolic activities surrounding the Bible pale in comparison to the way in which the Bible informed supporters of preceding social reform movements within the United States. In the nineteenth and early twentieth centuries, advocates for abolition, women's suffrage (linked with women in ministry), peace, and temperance utilized the resources of the Bible as frequently as proponents of the status quo appropriated their own hermeneutical strategies in their use of the ancient texts of the Jewish and Christian traditions.[6]

Since the major accomplishments of the Civil Rights era in the 1960s when sacred texts were utilized in a more generative way, the Bible has largely functioned more as a tool for societal control than a useful guide for social change. There are exceptions to this claim, for example, in the work of the Moral Monday movement led by Rev. William Barber. Social reform movements seem less interested in securing assistance from the Bible than previous centuries.[7] This may have less to do with dropping levels of biblical literacy than with other reasons associated with reading the Bible. In a recent study organized by the Center for the Study of Religion and American Culture at Indiana University–Purdue University Indianapolis, several organizers of a project called "The Bible in American Life" concluded from the survey that "individuals are actually far more likely to read the Bible for personal edification and growth than to shape their views of culture war issues."[8] Many readers engage the Bible primarily on an individual, spiritual level. This is not the case for all Bible interpreters. What seems to be the case—among more conservative readers—is an increasing appropriation of biblical themes from those who desire less reform in the social practices of

---

in a different context, between the "Christianity of the land" and the "Christianity of Christ," in the appendix to his 1845 *Narrative of the Life of Frederick Douglass* (Boston: Anti-Slavery Office, 1845).

6. Jonathan Sarna has recently summed up well, with the use of two appropriate metaphors, the understanding of the Bible in Jewish circles, "the Bible served both as a bridge and a boundary marker between Jews and Christians in America." See Jonathan Sarna, "The Bible and Judaism in America," in *The Oxford Handbook of the Bible in America*, ed. Paul C. Gutjahr (Oxford: Oxford University Press, 2017), 506.

7. Even as I write this essay, tens of thousands of high school teenagers are leading the March for Our Lives protest in Washington, DC, calling for gun reform. The Bible, apparently, offers little to no support for this movement.

8. Philip Goff, Arthur E. Farnsley II, and Peter J. Thuesen, "The Bible in American Life Today," in *The Bible in American Life*, ed. Philip Goff, Arthur E. Farnsley II, and Peter J. Thuesen (Oxford: Oxford University Press, 2017), 16.

contemporary culture.⁹ The tension between social reform and social control—and the Bible's role within each—remains an ongoing conversation among religious interpreters.

The Use of the Bible in (Two) Significant Reform Movements

Historically, the Bible has played a crucial role in the rhetorical shaping—and, to some extent, the ideological shaping—of a larger, bonded community and mission in the history of the United States. From the early stages of the developing nation, many national myths (myths = stories that the nation attempted to live into) took shape, which were often buttressed by biblical themes. Richard Hughes defines the nation's myths—including the "myth of the chosen people" and the "myth of the Christian nation"—as "the stories that explain why we love our country and why we have faith in the nation's purposes ... the means by which we affirm the meaning of the United States."¹⁰ Of course, biblical rhetoric informed many public speeches in their shaping of these public myths for the emerging country. Without awareness of the hermeneutical irony, Americans read their (nation's) story into Israel's story—a story that included within its origins the bondage of Israel in Egypt—and found within the biblical theme of chosenness their own sense of exceptionalism. United States citizens did not create the myth but inherited it from English forebears.¹¹ Although there were various critical uses of this myth, the popular (and political) presentation of it rarely allowed nonwhite populations into their communal narrative. Hughes provides numerous examples to show that "if one imagines one's tribe or clan or nation a chosen people, then it is also clear that others are not."¹²

---

9. Former judge Roy Moore (of Alabama) is one example of those who attempt to maintain biblical principles for social order, with his promotion of the (symbolic) plaque of the Ten Commandments on the county courthouse premises and his consistent opposition to same-sex relationships.

10. Richard Hughes, *Myths America Lives By* (Urbana: University of Illinois Press, 2003). See also Paul Hanson, *A Political History of the Bible in America* (Louisville: Westminster John Knox, 2015).

11. Hughes, *Myths America Lives By*, 19–28.

12. Hughes, *Myths America Lives By*, 30.

10. THE BIBLE AND SOCIAL REFORM

Of particular interest, though perhaps not always directly related to the public articulation of these constructive narratives, many public figures attempted to determine the racial identities and explore the cultural disparities in the contemporary setting by postulating a so-called origins of human history with a belief that the biblical accounts of Genesis could inform such histories.[13] The so-called curse of Ham myth, the so-called Table of Nations chapter, and the destruction of the lands of Canaan were utilized as supporting narratives that played out politically in the displacement of Native Americans and the (mis)appropriation of Africans as an unpaid labor force.[14] Imposing ancient ethnic identity markers onto the contemporary world informed the shaping of national identities, and scholarship developed around identity mapping. A review of nineteenth-century dictionaries on the Bible will reveal racialized biases in entries on almost any ethnic group in the Bible. Many nineteenth-century biblical scholars also participated in explicit exploration of coloration.[15] This racialized discourse magnifies what Edward Said described as the Western gaze on the so-called Orient with its fierce (and usually distorted) description of the Other.[16]

Interweaving coloration, the US slave institution, and "slaves obey your masters" passages was common practice. The debates surrounding the Fugitive Slave Laws (of 1793 and 1850) informed by Paul's Letter to Philemon was just one such specific example of the Bible's public life.[17] Approximately two years *after* the formal announcement of the "Emancipation Proclamation," President Abraham Lincoln gave the Second Inaugural Address (March 4, 1865) as the war approached its end: "Both

---

13. Not too long ago, these were public conversations. Now many of those holding onto this approach to the Bible—the mapping of (ethnic) identity—generally operate only within private, religious domains. The myths of superior racial groups, however, still permeate pockets of society that have consequences for nonwhite populations in various regions of the country.

14. See Sylvester Johnson, *Myth of Ham in Nineteenth-Century American Christianity: Race, Heathens, and the People of God* (New York: Palgrave MacMillan, 2004).

15. Emerson B. Powery and Rodney S. Sadler Jr., *The Genesis of Liberation: Biblical Interpretation in the Antebellum Narratives of the Enslaved* (Louisville: Westminster John Knox, 2016), 106–9.

16. Edward Said, *Orientalism* (New York: Vintage Books, 1979).

17. J. Albert Harrill, "The Use of the New Testament in the American Slave Controversy: A Case History in the Hermeneutical Tension between Biblical Interpretation and Christian Moral Debate," *Religion and American Culture* 10 (2000): 149–86.

[North and South] read the same Bible, and pray to the same God; and each invokes (God's) aid against the other." Nothing shaped American biblical interpretation more than the slave debate and the ensuing war.[18] During this time period, it was primarily a crisis in the United States. By the nineteenth century, as Mark Noll shows, the international Protestant community generally opposed the bondage of other humans.[19]

Fast forward 150 years after Lincoln's speech, and many social issues still divide the country; chief among them is the debate over marriage equality. On June 26, 2015, the Supreme Court ruled (5 to 4) that states cannot ban same-sex marriage, only two decades after Congress passed and President Bill Clinton signed into law the Defense of Marriage Act (1996), which defined marriage as a legal union (only) between a male and a female. No Bible passages appear in the four individually written dissents nor in the majority position (written by Anthony Kennedy).[20] As expected, they discussed the issue as a matter of civil life in light of rising tensions between federal and states' rights within US society. Yet, because of the influence of the Bible on the religious traditions of American life, justices of the highest court in the land are often aware of its influence, and there are hints to that effect within the written dissents.

Some justices explicitly affirmed that religion played no role in the decision. For example, in an attempt to support that the primary concern was states' rights, Justice Roberts concluded,

> Marriage did not come about as a result of a political movement, discovery, disease, war, religious doctrine, or any other moving force of world history—and certainly not as a result of a prehistoric decision to exclude gays and lesbians. It arose in the nature of things to meet a vital need: ensuring that children are conceived by a mother and father committed to raising them in the stable conditions of a lifelong relationship.[21]

Roberts cites Cicero to support the claim that marriage originated as part of the natural order.

---

18. See also Mark Noll, "Nineteenth-Century American Biblical Interpretation," in Gutjahr, *The Oxford Handbook of the Bible in America*, 123.

19. Mark Noll, *The Civil War as a Theological Crisis* (Chapel Hill: University of North Carolina Press, 2006).

20. Anthony Kennedy voted with the four progressive judges. The four conservative opponents each wrote his own separate dissent.

21. Obergefell v. Hodges, 135 S. Ct. 2584 (2015).

Others, in the minority opinion, were less inclined to follow Roberts's lead, preferring instead to acknowledge the absence of certain religious arguments that should have been available (and influential?) to their colleagues. Indeed, religion subtly lay behind the objections of some of these dissents. Justice Scalia bemoaned the lack of representation of an evangelical voice on the court, to provide, in his opinion, a more fair representation of the American populace: "Not a single evangelical Christian (a group that comprises about one quarter of Americans), or even a Protestant of any denomination" sits on the Court.[22] His assumption is that an evangelical would interpret life and religion—and, presumably, his or her Bible—in a way that would have influenced this hypothetical justice's decision to vote along with (and tip the balance in favor of) the minority position.[23]

In Justice Thomas's dissent, the institution of marriage is a religious institution—an idea Roberts specifically and initially omitted—and "the majority's decision threatens the religious liberty our Nation has long sought to protect." A paragraph later, he continues: "In our society, marriage is not simply a governmental institution; it is a religious institution as well.... It appears all but inevitable that the two will come into conflict, particularly as individuals and churches are confronted with demands to participate in and endorse civil marriages between same-sex couples."[24]

Drawing near the end of his own written dissent, Roberts turns to remarks on the freedom of religion, a right, he exhorts, explicitly guaranteed in the Constitution, even if marriage equality, he claims, is not, and shares Thomas's sentiment:

> Hard questions arise when people of faith exercise religion in ways that may be seen to conflict with the new right to same-sex marriage—when, for example, a religious college provides married student housing only to opposite-sex married couples, or a religious adoption agency declines to place children with same-sex married couples.[25]

---

22. Obergefell v. Hodges, 135 S. Ct. 2584 (2015), 73–74*.
23. Presumably, Scalia's evangelical representative would be unpersuaded by David Gushee's *Changing Our Mind* (Canton: Read the Spirit Books, 2017). Gushee expresses his concern over the contemporary use of the label evangelical to describe his own religious faith (see 173–75).
24. Obergefell v. Hodges, 135 S. Ct. 2584 (2015), 91–92*.
25. Obergefell v. Hodges, 135 S. Ct. 2584 (2015), 66–67*.

Justice Samuel Alito wrote the fourth and final dissent in which he recognizes distinct hermeneutical approaches to the Constitution as the rationale for the two opposing sides: "I do not doubt that my colleagues in the majority sincerely see in the Constitution a vision of liberty that happens to coincide with their own.... What it evidences is the deep and perhaps irremediable corruption of our legal culture's conception of constitutional interpretation."[26] Along with the other three judges in the minority opinion, Alito interprets the Constitution in such a manner as to consider legal only those practices for which the Constitution allowed *in its original setting*.[27] Alito's hermeneutical observation may provide an imperfect, nonetheless useful, analogy to how many conservative interpreters construe the Bible on same-sex relationships. As John Kutsko aptly puts it, "Popular biblical and constitutional hermeneutics are a match made in heaven."[28]

The absence of religious influence is viewed favorably in an increasingly secular society. But religious convictions also shape many social progressives. Religion does not belong to one camp. Representative of many progressive thinkers, Justice Ruth Bader Ginsburg believes her Jewish faith encourages her to empathize with marginalized groups.[29]

But what does the Bible have to do with this debate? Contemporary discussions surrounding sexual orientation and sexual preference far outweigh their importance in specific passages in the Bible. The four canonical gospels do not explicitly address the issue at all. Of course, Jesus's position on same-sex relationships requires other assumptions about ancient world communities and their ideologies surrounding sexuality that Jesus's silence on the matter simply obfuscates. More than likely, Jesus shared the sexual-ethical concerns of many of his Jewish contemporaries. Accepting this assumption, however, may hinder questions interpreters bring to other passages. For example, was the centurion's slave (in Luke 7) sexually available to the master as some have argued? If so, was Jesus aware of this possibility, ignored the relationship, and healed the slave anyway?

---

26. Obergefell v. Hodges, 135 S. Ct. 2584 (2015), 103*.

27. Obergefell v. Hodges, 135 S. Ct. 2584 (2015), 101*.

28. John F. Kutsko, "The Curious Case of the Christian Bible and the U.S. Constitution: Challenges for Educators Teaching the Bible in a Multireligious Context," in Goff, Farnsley, and Thuesen, *Bible in American Life*, 244.

29. "Justice Ruth Bader Ginsburg Surprises Synagogue as Rosh Hashanah Guest Speaker," *Haaretz*, 21 September 2017, https://tinyurl.com/SBL6704j3.

Nonetheless, despite the omission of biblical references in the justices' opinions, such references appear frequently in the national debates surrounding marriage equality. Many prominent religious (and, political) figures will use the Bible in order to *oppose* same-sex relationships. Despite the insistence of many that the Bible opposes any same-sex *attraction*, social reformers have been able to shift the conversation to attend to a debate on same-sex *relationships*, more formally speaking within civil society. This focus on formal, legal relationships between persons of the same sex is more recent.

In both cases, interpreters assume that they are, first, interpreting the Bible in its cultural context and, secondarily, transferring that meaning into the contemporary setting. Putting the meaning of an ancient biblical document into an applicable form for a new, contemporary context is certainly more complex than what many popular interpreters assume. Contemporary gay life is a complicated life, and, as Jonathan Jackson has recently examined, it refers to more than sexual activity. The Bible, as Jackson argues, deals primarily with sexual acts and not complicated identities: "it bans certain sex acts in a very specific and explicit manner."[30] This may explain why many Catholics (and some Evangelicals, for that matter) do not consider LGBTQ orientation a sin unless acted upon.[31]

Ken Stone wisely turns the question on its head in an essay entitled "What the Homosexuality Debates Really Say about the Bible." As he puts it, "The study of 'Bible and homosexuality' therefore is not only a matter of getting some perspective on the topic of homosexuality. It is also, significantly, a matter of getting some perspective on the Bible and on biblical interpretation."[32] As Stone implies, these interpretive debates reveal much more about contemporary people—and the assumptions we have—than what the ancients thought. As Ernest Sandeen recognized twenty-five years ago (I will explore further below), "it is also clear that the Bible cannot be defined simply as either a conservative or progressive force in social reform."[33]

---

30. Jonathan Jackson, "Culture Wars, Homosexuality, and the Bible," in *The Bible and Political Debate*, ed. Frances Flannery and Rodney A. Werline (London: Bloomsbury T&T Clark, 2016), 96.

31. Jackson, "Culture Wars," 88–89.

32. Ken Stone, "What the Homosexuality Debates Really Say about the Bible," in *Out of the Shadows into the Light: Christianity and Homosexuality*, ed. Miguel A. de la Torre (St. Louis: Chalice, 2009), 23.

33. Ernest Sandeen, introduction to *The Bible and Social Reform*, ed. Ernest R. Sandeen (Philadelphia: Fortress; Chico, CA: Scholars Press, 1982), 7.

The Impact of Social Movements on Biblical Studies

There have always been scholars within the larger field of biblical studies who have attempted to enter into more public spaces with the intent of influencing public discourse around a number of themes.[34] A significant turning point came in 1988 with Elisabeth Schüssler Fiorenza's presidential address. She took this opportunity to use the Society address (or, the Society of Biblical Literature's state of the union, if you will) to call on its members "to consider the political context of their scholarship and to reflect on its public accountability."[35] Other Society of Biblical Literature presidents have also raised issues directly as general statements about (or, even, general critiques of) the affairs of the society. The talks of Schüssler Fiorenza, Vincent Wimbush, and Fernando Segovia have been the most forthright.[36]

Thirty years ago, Schüssler Fiorenza called for a "responsible scholarly citizenship" that would "engage in a disciplined reflection on the public dimensions and ethical implications of our scholarly work."[37] She called for a "decentering" of the Bible that would allow scholars to recognize their own contemporary situatedness. She encouraged research that includes a sensitivity toward the implications of the outcomes because it may not be easy to say after the fact that our conclusions stand on their own since we are *only* reflecting on the ancient world. Schüssler Fiorenza appropriately challenged a professional naiveté that assumes that our work could not be used for ill. If it is, we are partly responsible for our historical conclusions. That is the rhetorical nature of interpreting the Bible—even with a

---

34. E.g., Martti Nissinen, *Homoeroticism in the Biblical World: A Historical Perspective* (Minneapolis: Augsburg Fortress, 1998). Along these lines, academic journals in biblical studies are becoming less reluctant to tackle sexuality. See Megan Warner, "'Therefore a Man Leaves His Father and His Mother and Clings to His Wife': Marriage and Intermarriage in Genesis 2:24," *JBL* 136 (2017): 269–88. Also, George M. Hollenback, "Who Is Doing What to Whom Revisited: Another Look at Leviticus 18:22 and 20:13," *JBL* 136 (2017): 529–37.

35. Elisabeth Schüssler Fiorenza, "The Ethics of Biblical Interpretation: Decentering Biblical Scholarship," *JBL* 107 (1988): 8.

36. Other addresses that tackle broader concerns have more indirectly heeded Schüssler Fiorenza's charge: e.g., Gene Tucker, "Rain on a Land Where No One Lives: The Hebrew Bible on the Environment," *JBL* 116 (1997): 3–17; John J. Collins, "The Zeal of Phinehas: The Bible and the Legitimation of Violence," *JBL* 122 (2003): 3–21.

37. Schüssler Fiorenza, "Ethics of Biblical Interpretation," 16.

goal of exploring its historical setting—from within a contemporary culture that has its own dilemmas, social categories, and social obligations. Nineteenth-century hermeneutical debates investigating the biblical passages on slaves, in light of legalized enslavement of black bodies, is a case in point. It is a fitting irony that the democratic, hermeneutical practices of Bible readers in the United States would become a juggernaut in dismantling the indignities of human bondage in a developing democracy.[38]

A number of years later (in 2011), Wimbush wondered aloud,

> How can we be students of Scriptures in this century at this moment without making our agenda a radically humanistic science or art, excavating human politics, discourse, performances, power relations, the mimetic systems of knowing we may call scripturalization?... How exciting and compelling and renegade would be a Society of interpreters that excavates all representations of Scriptures in terms of discourse and power![39]

Interpretation of the Bible—especially on themes that are more pertinent to present-day affairs like economic systems—reveal much about contemporary interpreters (as Ken Stone acknowledges). Shortly thereafter, Segovia (in 2014) called for (what he has labeled) a "global-systemic" orientation, so that the guild of the Society could develop discourses and analyses to speak to a post–Cold War global community.[40]

In a brief exposé on the history of the "critical investigation of the Bible," a recent editor of the *Journal of Biblical Literature* (Adele Reinhartz) announced her vision for what the journal might become, a written forum that might allow for a broadening of "the range of critical approaches and perspectives at the same time as continuing to welcome more 'traditional'

---

38. Along these lines, Noll explains, "As much as abolitionist overreach and the ability of pro-slavery advocates to quote chapter and verse strengthened the antiabolitionist cause, hermeneutical conventions that functioned more powerfully in the United States than anywhere else in the world also played their part: democratic empowerment of ordinary people able to read the Bible for themselves, distrust of biblical interpretations from intellectual authorities, and common sense confidence that one's own reading of experience represented universally valid truths" ("Nineteenth-Century American Biblical Interpretation," 120).

39. Vincent L. Wimbush, "Interpreters—Enslaving/Enslaved/Runagate," *JBL* 130 (2011): 5–24.

40. Fernando Segovia, "Criticism in Critical Times: Reflections on Vision and Task," *JBL* 134 (2015): 6–29.

research."[41] As one example of this endeavor (which will be discussed below), Reinhartz opened up the journal to provide a brief collection of critical reflections wrestling with the Black Lives Matter movement and the (potential?) impact it might have on biblical studies.

Recently, the Society has made more formal efforts along these lines to situate the Bible in various public settings in three *distinct* directions, some of these areas sponsored by the Society and other areas instigated by members without the Society's explicit support.

One direction has been the Society's attempt to make the scholar available to the inquiring public. Accessibly available online, the Bible Odyssey website allows readers to explore the ancient world—that is, the origins of the Bible and its history—from the perspective of scholars of the Bible.[42] On one occasion when I checked the home page of the Bible Odyssey site, the highlighted links included information about "conversion and identity in the Hebrew Bible," "Baal," "immigrants and foreigners in the Bible," and "the Parable of the Good Samaritan." This venue beckons the public's questions about the past with an available tab labeled Ask A Scholar, as long as the inquisitor remembers "that this site is focused on the historical, social, literary, and cultural contexts of the Bible, rather than on theology, spirituality or personal religious beliefs." This is a natural outgrowth of the Society's traditional priorities in light of its commitment to the critical investigation of the Bible,[43] even if the instructions express a reluctance to engage concerns of social reform.

More directly, in the public sphere, is a second trend when biblical scholars engage the public in ways that affect the role of the Bible in the development of its citizenry. Here the scholar must venture into the public square. A recent example of this effort can be seen in the debates surrounding the teaching of the Bible in public educational institutions. The conversations in Texas—whether and how to teach the Bible in the public school—have wide-ranging consequences for other states, as some state governments attempt to advocate for more faith-based curriculums with respect to the Bible (and its world), rather than assist students to gain wide-ranging knowledge about the Bible and its ongoing cultural

---

41. Adele Reinhartz, "The *Journal of Biblical Literature* and the Critical Investigation of the Bible," *JBL* 134 (2015): 457–70.

42. The Bible Odyssey site receives ten thousand uses a day.

43. See the Society of Biblical Literature's mission statement: https://tinyurl.com/SBL6704k3.

relevance in a nonsectarian manner. The work of Mark Chancey encourages public school teachers (1) to recognize that the Bible is not a science book, (2) to acknowledge that Judaism is a religion in itself and not only background material for understanding Christianity, and (3) to provide various interpretations of a biblical passage rather than highlight one position as normative.[44] His research is included in this present volume as well. The Society is interested in assisting secondary educators in the process of educating the young (e.g., *Bible Electives in Public Schools* or their sponsored newsletter, *Teaching the Bible*).[45]

A global example may also be apropos here. One fine example is the productive work of Gerald West's contextual Bible studies, especially the recent activist work on "Leadership and Land" in which intellectuals and local communities of the poor, working-class, and marginalized discuss biblical passages as a way to develop their thinking and strategy for the work of land restructuring.[46]

A third direction takes up the activist life by placing the sacred text in alternative public spaces. What I have in mind is, for example, Rodney Sadler's blog-talk radio show in North Carolina. On his show ("The Politics of Faith"), Sadler—professor of Bible at Union Presbyterian Seminary in Charlotte, North Carolina, and an active organizer of religious leaders for the Moral Mondays movement—regularly interviews biblical scholars (e.g., Brian Blount, Obery Hendricks, Diana Swancutt) who discuss broad issues of concern for the public, such as poverty, voting rights, racial tension, and violence.[47]

Of course, it is easier to describe the status of the conversation in biblical scholarship than it is to recognize (and examine) the public

---

44. For a short statement on Chancey's position, see his "How Should We Teach the Bible in Public Schools?," *Religion & Politics*, 7 January 2014, https://tinyurl.com/SBL6704b3. See, also, John Kutsko, "Curious Case of the Christian Bible and the U.S. Constitution," 244–48.

45. See Society of Biblical Literature, "Bible Electives in Public Schools: A Guide," sbl-site.org, https://tinyurl.com/SBL6704m3; Society of Biblical Literature, "Teaching the Bible," sbl-site.org, https://tinyurl.com/SBL6704n3..

46. Gerald West, "'Leadership and Land': A Very Contextual Interpretation of Genesis 37–50 in KwaZulu-Natal, South Africa," in *Genesis: Texts@Contexts*, ed. Athalya Brenner, Archie Chi-Chung Lee, and Gale Yee (Minneapolis: Fortress, 2010), 175–90.

47. I am grateful to my former research assistant, Leslie Giboyeaux, who tracked down most of the iPod/blog sites.

conversation with respect to issues of the Bible—race relations, LGBTQ concerns, immigration policies, environmental issues, et cetera—that draws on the fruits of this type of scholarship or operates quite happily without cognizance of biblical scholarship at all.[48]

Most of us in the Society are interested in studying the past; fewer of us are interested in interrogating our access to that past. For many of us, the graduate education we received came from the tradition of biblical scholarship that was derived from methods of inquiry from the nineteenth century and its European influences. Have we worked so hard in the history of the Society and in investigations of the past in order to create a *distance* from contemporary life? If so, should that not be interrogated as well? There is little that is objective about this approach that many within the guild recognize nowadays. In his own 1991 presidential address, Walter Brueggeman, reflecting on Schüssler Fiorenza's previous challenge to the Society, signaled that so-called "'objective' and 'neutral' readings are themselves political acts in the service of entrenched and 'safe' interpretation."[49] After a long day of working with biblical texts in the academic office, do we only wish to cultivate our homegrown gardens rather than cultivate thriving communities around us? Can we do both? Not only should we determine what the present political issues are surrounding sacred texts but also discover whether our scholarship has any ethical and public impact. Furthermore, if we determine that our scholarship has no contemporary (ethical?) value, should that matter?

Many biblical scholars may find the topic of the Bible's use in contemporary social reform movements ancillary, at best. Some researchers, however, recognize that interpreters are located within historical moments and that situatededness may affect the questions that guide scholars and may impact the conclusions they draw. The recent Black Lives Matter movement may provide one noteworthy example.

"Black lives matter," as a public declaration, belies the reality of contemporary black bodies in present-day spaces. It is spoken as a challenge to the pervasive nature of antiblackness that exists. Despite how some opponents interpret it, the claim is not an assertion about other lives; rather, it is a prophetic outcry against those empowered to cause good or

---

48. Flannery and Werline, *Bible in Political Debate*, offers a corrective to this manner of popular interpretation.

49. Brueggemann, "At the Mercy of Babylon: A Subversive Rereading of the Empire," *JBL* 110 (1991): 20.

harm—especially those entrusted to protect life and community—who do not recognize black life as deserving of the basic civil and human dignities given to others. As Angela Davis articulated in a speech in Ferguson, Missouri, "More often than not universal categories have been clandestinely racialized. Any critical engagement with racism requires us to understand the tyranny of the universal."[50] "Black lives matter" has become an acknowledgement of the necessity of a social reform movement to continue to uncover and recover the ideologies of US history that have led us to this moment and to uphold the American myth espoused in the Declaration of Independence that all may pursue "life, liberty, and happiness." "Black lives matter" is an affirmation, still (unfortunately) necessary, well into the first quarter of the twenty-first century.

In 2017, as mentioned earlier, Reinhartz took the unprecedented action of devoting forty-one pages of one issue of *Journal of Biblical Literature* to the impact of this moment in history. Reinhartz wished to explore the intersectionality of violence upon black bodies and biblical scholarship in order to understand "how racial violence and the movements that attempt to eradicate such violence intersect with the field of biblical studies, both as an area of research and teaching and as an academic guild."[51] Six authors—Wil Gafney, Nyasha Junior, Kenneth Ngwa, Richard Newton, Bernadette Brooten, and Tat-siong Benny Liew—provided brief, meaningful reflections on the intersectional nature of the discipline of biblical studies and black identity within this violent period in US history. These essays explore and advocate for a social reform *within* the guild more than they reflect on the nature of the discipline (and the Bible in particular) as useful for a social reform *outside* the guild. The title and proposed theme of this essay—"the Bible and Social Reform"—is interpreted as an investigation into how the Bible may have functioned to bring about reform within contemporary society. These essays, wisely, reverse that approach, by assuming that a reform within society should

---

50. Angela Y. Davis, *Freedom Is a Constant Struggle: Ferguson, Palestine, and the Foundations of a Movement*, ed. Frank Barat (Chicago: Haymarket, 2016), 87.

51. Adele Reinhartz, introduction to "Black Lives Matter for Critical Biblical Scholarship," *JBL* 136 (2017): 203. Reinhartz's awareness of her identity as a child of Holocaust survivors allows her to wrestle with issues of identity, interpretation, and (linguistic) violence and discover an invaluable opportunity to broach this topic for readers of the journal. See Reinhartz, "The Vanishing Jews of Antiquity," *Marginalia*, 24 June 2014, https://tinyurl.com/SBL6704f3.

have critical bearing on how interpreters approach their task(s), their source(s), their discipline(s), their pedadogy(ies), and their professional lives. A few examples are instructive.

Informed by what she calls a Black Lives Matter hermeneutic, Gafney's teaching has facilitated her students' recognition of how Israelite lives matter in the Bible's narrative. Gafney concludes the following: "It cannot be said that all lives matter in the Bible, nor can it be said that, of those lives that do matter, they matter equally."[52] Furthermore, she continues, "While racism does not exist in the Hebrew Scriptures, there is vicious ethnic conflict that can function as an analogue for contemporary race-based conflict." Along these lines, this Black Lives Matter hermeneutic allows Gafney to "look for those lives that are at risk, subject to oppression, relegated to the margins of the text, and/or discounted as disposable, particularly as a result of an intersecting element of identity."[53]

Junior's essay takes the discussion in a different direction. The Black Lives Matter movement has not had a direct impact on her scholarship, yet it has contributed to her ongoing "motivation and efforts to support black and other underrepresented scholars through networking and social media."[54] It has provoked a more conscious awareness of the professional guild in which we labor. For example, she contacted The Wabash Center for Teaching and Learning to encourage them to initiate an educational response immediately following the murder of Michael Brown in Ferguson, Missouri.[55] To their credit, Wabash organized the "Race Matters in the Classroom" blog.

Ngwa attempts to utilize this particular moment of tension (in a longer history of US aggression against black and brown bodies) as a reflective resource for understanding the book of Exodus: "How do violence and communal responses to violence shape the narrative content and significance of Exodus and exodus storytelling? Which bodies are dying, and how are they dying, and where are they dying—dying as a result of official discourse,

---

52. Wil Gafney, "A Reflection on the Black Lives Matter Movement and Its Impact on My Scholarship," *JBL* 136 (2017): 206.

53. Gafney, "Reflection on the Black Lives Matter Movement and Its Impact on My Scholarship," 206.

54. Nyasha Junior, "The Scholarly Network," *JBL* 136 (2017): 210.

55. Junior, "Scholarly Network," 211. My own coauthored work (e.g., Powery and Sadler, *The Genesis of Liberation*) has benefited from Junior's social media network.

policy, and practice?"⁵⁶ Ngwa offers a reflection of what he calls "trauma-hope" in an attempt to hold this dialectical tension in his scholarship.

Newton recognizes how the Bible is bound up in this so-called Christian Nation, as he is "theorizing about an African American Bible," which leads him to suggest that members of the academic guild "might re-cognize the category of Scriptures as indicative of the stories not only that we read but also read us back."⁵⁷ Often, what interpreters claim to read in ancient texts reveals as much about the present (and contemporary readers) as it does about the past. Newton emphasizes that readers do not only deal with ancient written sources "but with the social forces with which Americans must reckon—regardless of one's relationship to the color line."⁵⁸ The present violence has brought what Newton calls a "'scriptural economy,' wherein we use texts to imprint values on our bodies."⁵⁹ Bible interpretation matters because of its potential impact on real bodies.

Brooten, informed by her mentor Krister Stendahl's "concept of the 'public health' aspect of New Testament studies," shares this concern with others, "to undertake research that may limit harm caused to marginalized persons through specific uses of the New Testament and further the values of human dignity and equality as these interact with the Bible."⁶⁰ In this vein, she has organized and participated in collaborative projects, such as *Beyond Slavery: Overcoming Its Religious and Sexual Legacies*, as well as become the driving force and cochair of the Slavery, Resistance, and Freedom section of the Society of Biblical Literature.⁶¹ Her efforts have shown how the "ancient sources burst the mold of early Christian slavery as a benign institution and of female slaveholders as kinder and gentler than their male counterparts."⁶²

The final essay comes from Liew, who strategically moves from Black Lives Matter within the larger society to the significance of black scholarship matters within the Society of Biblical Literature despite its general

---

56. Kenneth Ngwa, "At Exodus as the Door of [No] Return," *JBL* 136 (2017): 220.

57. Richard Newton, "The African American Bible: Bound in a Christian Nation," *JBL* 136 (2017): 222.

58. Newton, "African American Bible," 226.

59. Newton, "African American Bible," 227.

60. Bernadette Brooten, "Research on the New Testament and Early Christian Literature May Assist the Churches in Setting Ethical Priorities," *JBL* 136 (2017): 229.

61. Brooten, "Research on the New Testament and Early Christian Literature," 230.

62. Brooten, "Research on the New Testament and Early Christian Literature," 231.

absence from the wider research projects and classrooms of many (most?) interpreters of the Bible. As he states, "it is one thing to have black bodies showing up at the annual SBL meeting or even joining SBL committees and council and serving as SBL presidents. It is quite another to acknowledge and integrate black scholarship into our disciplinary discourse."[63] He traces his own educational journey, assisted by the black voices that guided his thinking and encouraged his own hermeneutical ownership of an identity politics that enhanced his research agenda. Liew clearly calls for a social reform *within* the larger academy of our discipline.

The Malleable Bible and Social Reform

In an introduction to a collection of essays published as *The Bible and Social Reform*, Ernest Sandeen concluded the following (a generation ago) on the effectiveness of the Bible as a social-change resource: "its effect is not predictable, one-dimensional, certainly not magical."[64] In the edited volume on such topics ranging from "American Indian Missions" to "Dorothy Day and the Bible," Sandeen surmises that it "is also clear that the Bible cannot be defined simply as either a conservative or progressive force in social reform."[65] This claim still holds true. The Bible takes no sides, or, some may claim, the Bible seems to take both sides.

Among the seven essays included in Sandeen's volume are ones on such traditional topics as slavery/abolition, women's roles in ministry (or, other public spaces), and war/peace.[66] For example, Charles Chatfield's

---

63. Tat-siong Benny Liew, "Black Scholarship Matters," *JBL* 136 (2017): 243.

64. Sandeen, introduction, 6. There has been a growing interest in this area in recent years. See Nathan O. Hatch and Mark A. Noll, eds., *The Bible in America: Essays in Cultural History* (Oxford: Oxford University Press, 1982); Vincent L. Wimbush, ed., *African Americans and the Bible: Sacred Texts and Social Textures* (London: Continuum, 2000); Claudia Setzer and David Shefferman, eds., *The Bible and American Culture: A Sourcebook* (New York: Routledge, 2011); Mark A. Chancey, Carol Meyers, and Eric M. Meyers, eds., *The Bible and the Public Square: Its Enduring Influence in American Life*, BSNA 27 (Atlanta: SBL Press, 2014); Flannery and Werline, *Bible in Political Debate*; Goff, Farnsley, and Thuesen, *Bible in American Life*; and Gutjahr, *Oxford Handbook of the Bible in America*.

65. Sandeen, introduction, 7.

66. See James Brewer Stewart, "Abolitionists, the Bible, and the Challenge of Slavery," in Sandeen, *Bible and Social Reform*, 31–57; Barbara Brown Zikmund, "Biblical Arguments and Women's Place in the Church," in Sandeen, *Bible and Social Reform*,

claim about peace movements is worth mentioning: "Peace movements in all their diversity have been grounded in some measure upon the Bible and upon the richness of its interpretation."[67] This has not been the case with the Black Lives Matter movement, technically speaking. Even the recent essays in the *Journal of Biblical Literature* address what biblical scholars should take away from the movement rather than how the Bible has shaped the movement.

While the 1982 chapters address topics related to reforms within society, other chapters within the collection are less obvious examples of societal reforms (e.g., Native American missions; the black church's use of the Bible). In Sandeen's words, the intent of the collection was not to assess "whether the Bible was properly appropriated." As historians, they "wondered whether reform itself was not tainted—whether all attempts to improve the condition of the poor or provide for the unfortunate have not also been, consciously or unconsciously, attempts to control society." To further this point, Sandeen suggests a few sentences later, "there is an inescapable element of manipulation in all reform movements." In the editor's appropriate example, "The abolitionists were not attempting to reform the slave, of course, but the slave owner."[68] To be fair, the present author is more of a student of the Bible in the ancient world than an historian of contemporary movements (as most of the authors in Sandeen's collection were).[69] Yet, as I assume Sandeen would acknowledge, manipulation is also part of the rhetorical strategy for maintaining the status quo as well.

85–104; Charles Chatfield, "The Bible and American Peace Movements," in Sandeen, *Bible and Social Reform*, 105–31.

67. Chatfield, "Bible and American Peace Movements," 105. Although there is little interaction with the Bible in Chatfield's essay (in terms of understanding the function of the Bible in the hands of peace thinkers), the author concludes the chapter as he began: "Outstanding peace advocates almost without exception have been motivated by values rooted more or less consciously in Scripture. As they have clarified their values and applied them, many peace advocates have refined their understanding of the Bible" (127).

68. Sandeen, introduction, 2–5.

69. Other essays included James P. Ronda, "The Bible and Early American Indian Missions," in Sandeen, *Bible and Social Reform*, 9–30; William McGuire King, "The Biblical Base of the Social Gospel," in Sandeen, *Bible and Social Reform*, 59–84; Peter J. Paris, "The Bible and Black Churches," in Sandeen, *Bible and Social Reform*, 133–54; and William D. Miller, "Dorothy Day and the Bible," in Sandeen, *Bible and Social Reform*, 155–77.

A collective desire to witness society's progress on a given social issue, one that affects all, is central to social reform. As Sandeen briefly discussed in 1982, there is a fine line between social reform and social control.[70] Lincoln historian Allen Guelzo summed up President Lincoln's Enlightenment belief in a manner that helpfully explores the thinking on the principle of social reform: "the idea of a mechanically predictable universe ... thought that progress, improvement, and invention were written into the script of human affairs beyond the power of human effacement."[71] The inevitable belief in society's progress has been fundamental to enlightenment thinking. More provocatively and recently, Martin Luther King Jr. would make his version of the nineteenth-century abolitionist Theodore Parker's saying famous in our day, "The arc of the moral universe is long, but it bends towards justice."

Because of the history of the Bible in America's life and in the contemporary political scene, the Bible may be called upon to support any number of causes. The great length to which Donald Trump's supporters in the 2016 election—especially his evangelical, white Christian base—attempted to emphasize Trump's link to Christian faith, the Bible, and Christian morality expresses the extent to which individuals may go to establish a presidential candidate as Christian.[72] As it appears, Trump has been difficult to define, without pretense, as a true Christian candidate. On the other hand, Bernie Sanders—a Jewish candidate reluctant to stress this distinction publicly[73]—provided a formidable challenge to Hillary Clinton. Since he did not win, we have no way to judge what difference his religion (or lack thereof) might have meant nationally. Although this expectation is not new, it is clear candidates running for the highest office must find appropriate ways to introduce, even minimally (with Trump as a prime example), some sensitivity and awareness of biblical language and,

---

70. A good example of this tension is in the essay on Indian missions, in which conversion leads to a loss of Indian identity; see Ronda, "Bible and Early American Indian Missions," 23.

71. Allen C. Guelzo, *Lincoln's Emancipation Proclamation: The End of Slavery in America* (New York: Simon & Schuster, 2004), 7.

72. As Flannery and Werline recognize, "Showing dedication to the Bible is often a prerequisite for successful political life in the United States, and some cultural critics wonder whether anyone could now be president without claiming to be Christian" (introduction to Flannery and Werline, *Bible in Political Debate*, 5).

73. Asher Schechter, "Bernie Sanders Isn't Flaunting His Jewishness, and That's OK," *Haaretz*, 25 February 2016, https://tinyurl.com/SBL6704g3.

possibly, themes in their public rhetoric. Again, Sanders provides an interesting example, since it has not been uncommon to view him through a Christian lens, as Peter Weber's aptly titled opinion piece suggests, "Bernie Sanders is Jewish. He also might be the most Christian candidate in the 2016 race."[74] With respect to potential Christian principles that may assist a governing candidate, as Weber reasons, "Sanders is talking the Jesus talk better than his Christian rivals."[75] The irony of Jesus's Jewishness is lost on many church-going Christians.

Numerous examples flood the airwaves and social media, as contemporary political figures make use of biblical verses as soundbites (outside of their immediate context) to bolster their points with respect to a given political policy or, less directly, to express something about one's religious character:

- The media's desire to ascertain and his refusal to reveal what was so personal: Trump's favorite Bible verse.
- Ben Carson's (flippant?) desire to advocate a tax plan modeled on the tithing practice of the Bible. As Adam Chodorow (a law professor) has suggested in a recent *Slate* article, which biblical tithing practice Carson has in mind is complicated by the various practices espoused throughout various biblical texts.[76]
- Sanders's attempt to appeal to and connect with his college age audience at Jerry Falwell's Liberty University, by citing Matt 7:12 ("do unto others as you would have them do unto you") and Amos 5:24 ("let justice roll down like water") in order to support his policies that would aid the poor.
- Obama appealed to Exod 23 when he explained his position on immigration: "Scripture tells us that we shall not oppress a stranger, for we know the heart of a stranger—we were once strangers too."[77]

---

74. Weber, "Bernie Sanders Is Jewish. He Also Might Be the Most Christian Candidate in the 2016 Race," *The Week*, 11 April 2016, https://tinyurl.com/SBL6704h3.

75. Weber refers to Sanders's policies on "helping the poor, the sick, and the needy." Of course, these concerns are central to the Hebrew Bible as well (Exod 22:21; Ps 82:3; Prov 23:10; Isa 58:7).

76. Chodorow, "Holy Crap," *Slate*, 30 October 2015, https://tinyurl.com/SBL6704c3.

77. Cited by Hector Avalos, "Diasporas 'R' Us: Attitudes toward Immigrants in the Bible," in Flannery and Werline, *Bible in Political Debate*, 35.

- Obama drew on John 15:13, when discussing his executive action on gun control: "Greater love hath no man than this that a man lay down his life for his friends."[78]
- Senator James Inhofe, Chair of the Senate Environment and Public Works Committee, called on Gen 22:8 to provide some heavy (Bible) lifting for him to propose any legislation that would suggest that environmental changes are human-made; "as long as the earth remains, there will be springtime, harvest, cold and heat, winter and summer, day and night."[79]
- Rep. Stephen Fincher utilized 2 Thess 3:10 ("Anyone unwilling to work should not eat") as support for cutting governmental assistance programs for impoverished people.[80]
- In a 2002 interview with the *Congressional Quarterly*, Mike Pence explained, "My support for Israel stems largely from my personal faith. In the Bible, God promises Abraham, 'Those who bless you I will bless, and those who curse you I will curse.'"[81]

Jacques Berlinerblau's 2014 assessment, however, may be vindicated by the rise of Trump: "it is important to recall that elections are never won by Scripture alone." Undoubtedly, this has always been the case. Nonetheless, the examples above point to an expectation of biblical rhetoric on the campaign trail and while holding office, even if its usefulness (in the minds of policy makers) is minimal. Indeed, if the race were determined by Scripture alone, the irony of the 2016 election could not be missed. As Berlinerblau continues, "Countless other policies, ads, political positions, and backroom compromises seal a politician's electoral fate. Thus it is hard to discern metrics for gauging effective and ineffective biblical citation."[82]

Yet there are politicians—on the left and on the right of the political spectrum—who would claim that their faith provides a deep sense of

---

78. Cited by Flannery and Werline, introduction, 4.

79. Cited by Frances Flannery, "Senators, Snowballs, and Scripture: The Bible and Climate Change," in Flannery and Werline, *Bible in Political Debate*, 62.

80. Cited by Rodney Werline, "Work, Poverty, and Welfare," in Flannery and Werline, *Bible in Political Debate*, 75.

81. Cited by McKay Coppins, "God's Plan for Mike Pence," *The Atlantic*, January-February 2018, https://tinyurl.com/SBL6704d3.

82. Jacques Berlinerblau, "The Bible in the Presidential Elections of 2012, 2008, 2004, and the Collapse of American Secularism," in Chancey, Meyers, and Meyers, *Bible in the Public Square*, 30.

who they are and why they make the political and moral decisions they make. So, it may be important, in this particular age, to allow opportunities for these public figures to provide their understanding of their sacred texts, whatever their religious commitments, and to give more thorough (and, hopefully, more contextual) responses to questions that matter.[83] In the spring of 2008, there was such an attempt. The Compassion Forum was coordinated by "Faith in Public Life," a national nonpartisan center for faith leaders in Washington, DC.[84] Messiah College in Mechanicsburg, Pennsylvania, hosted the event. Senators Hillary Clinton and Barack Obama attended; Senator John McCain declined the invitation due to another commitment. The overall goal of the event was to give these public officials an opportunity to discuss how their faith (or religion) affected their political decision making. Each senator took the stage separately, as moderators Campbell Brown (of CNN) and Jon Meacham (of Newsweek) posed questions. Also, there were other prepared questions that came from prominent religious US leaders from across the spectrum.[85]

In a question raised about the issue of theodicy to which Meacham added sarcastically, "and we just have 30 seconds," Clinton made her first specific reference to the Bible to support her action, whatever God's activity might mean (which she wisely avoided), on how the Bible calls for people of faith to commit themselves on behalf of the poor. Since Clinton addressed the Bible specifically, Brown then immediately followed up with the popular (and usually inconsequential), "Do you have a favorite Bible story?" Clinton responded with the story of Esther, because "there weren't too many models of women [in the Bible] who had the opportunity to make a decision, to take a chance, a risk that, you know, was very courageous." Clinton displayed her contemporary religious knowledge as

---

83. Admittedly, the American Academy of Religion seems more prone to offer these public opportunities than the Society of Biblical Literature. In Boston in 2017, the American Academy of Religion invited former governor of Massachusetts, Deval Patrick, to discuss "religion and the most vulnerable." In 2014, they invited former President Jimmy Carter to address religion scholars with his talk, "*The Role of Religion in Mediating Conflicts and Imagining Futures: The Cases of Climate Change and Equality for Women.*"

84. Other organizational sponsors of the event included the Council of Christian Colleges and Universities, the ONE campaign, and Oxfam America. Cable News Network (CNN) broadcasted the event.

85. See the entire transcript of the interviews at https://www.messiah.edu/compassion_forum/pdf/transcript.pdf.

well when she acknowledged this story's function during the Jewish holiday of Purim. Finally, Meacham asked the final question of the interview with Clinton: "To return to faith, do you believe God wants you to be president?" It is worth recording a fuller response, even if not all of the particulars, as she alludes to her understanding of the role of the Bible:[86]

> I don't presume anything about God. I believe, you know, Abraham Lincoln was right in admonishing us not to act as though we knew God was on our side. In fact, our mission should be on God's side....
>
> And I wouldn't presume to even imagine that God is going to tell me what I should do. I think that he has given me enough guidance, you know, through how I have been raised and how I have been, thankfully, given access to the Bible over so many years, commentary and the like. So I just get up and try to do the best I can. And I think that I see through a glass darkly. I don't believe that any of us know it all and can with any confidence say that we are going to, you know, be doing God's will unless, you know, we are just out there doing our very best, hoping that we make a difference in people's lives....
>
> I really worry when people become very complacent in their faith, when they do believe they have all the answers, because I just don't think it's humanly possible for any of us to know God's mind. I think we are just searching.... But whatever happens, I will get up the next day and try to continue on my journey to do what I can to try to fulfill what I believe to be God's expectations of us.

Then Obama took the stage. Before moderator Brown directed his attention to the creation account of Genesis, Obama offered an allusion to a biblical theme that he finds to be central to his understanding of making moral decisions: "if I'm acting in an ethical way, if I am working to make sure that I am applying what I consider to be a core value of Christianity, but also a core value of all great religions, and that is that I am my brother's keeper and I am my sister's keeper, then I will be doing my part to move his agenda forward."[87] Attempting to make the question more personal, Brown asked, "Senator, if one of your daughters asked you—and maybe

---

86. Hillary Rodham Clinton, interview by Campbell Brown and Jon Meacham, Compassion Forum, CNN, 13 April 2008, 12–13*.

87. Barack Obama, interview by Campbell Brown and Jon Meacham, Compassion Forum, CNN, 13 April 2008, 15*. While Obama extended the biblical theme to be more inclusive, he did not offer gender inclusive language for God.

they already have—'Daddy, did God really create the world in six days?' What would you say?" Again, a fuller response from Obama is worthwhile:

> You know, what I've said to them is that I believe that God created the universe and that the six days in the Bible may not be six days as we understand it. It may not be 24-hour days. And that's what I believe. I know there's always a debate between those who read the Bible literally and those who don't. And, you know, that, I think, is a legitimate debate within the Christian community of which I am a part. You know, my belief is, is that the story that the Bible tells about God creating this magnificent Earth … that is essentially true. That is fundamentally true. Now whether it happened exactly as we might understand it reading the text of the Bible, that, you know, I don't presume to know.

Before they were able to move in a different direction, Obama continued, "But let me just make one last point on this. I do believe in evolution. I don't think that is incompatible with Christian faith. Just as I don't think science generally is incompatible with Christian faith."[88]

Finally, Brown asked the same question she asked Clinton, about those who think too much religion is already involved in American politics, to which Obama responded with these words: "What religious language can often do is allow us to get outside of ourselves and mobilize around a common good." He acknowledged that people of religious faith must translate the language of their faith into a universal language that others can understand. Locating successful examples in Lincoln and King, Obama confessed that "we are not just a Christian nation. We are a Jewish nation; we are a Buddhist nation; we are a Muslim nation; Hindu nation; and we are a nation of atheists and nonbelievers."[89] Obama is a child of the Civil Rights era.[90]

When given the opportunity, some public officials are able to articulate a more carefully nuanced opinion on their understandings of biblical passages and themes and how those themes impact their faith, in particular, and their political policies more generally. In many ways, the snippets that are usually posted in the thirty-second clips on evening news outlets—and even more so in the age of Twitter—provide little insight into how these

---

88. Obama, interview by Brown and Meacham, 19*.
89. Obama, interview by Brown and Meacham, 26*.
90. TaNehisi Coates, *We Were Eight Years in Power: An American Tragedy* (New York: One World, 2017).

public figures really think about the connections between their political choices, their ethical practices, and the way in which they understand their religious commitments (including the use of their sacred texts). [It is hard to imagine whether such an event as The Compassion Forum would have even been possible in 2016!]

Conclusion

The Bible is unable to reform society for the good on its own. Neither is Scripture able to maintain the status quo of thriving communities by posting up biblical passages on billboards or cementing plaques of the Ten Commandments within courtyards. Proponents for and against social change must take up their causes and activities and, if they so choose, speak on behalf of a particular interpretation of the Bible. The Bible, itself, reforms nothing. As US history has shown with respect to abolition, women's suffrage (and the ministerial roles of women), and, now, marriage equality, the Bible is unable to speak for itself; it has no voice except through those who choose to speak on its behalf. The Bible's interpreters, then, must bring those ancient words into contemporary discourse—if they so choose—and should attempt to make a case, also, for why they would choose to do so.

Social reforms may occur without the assistance of the Bible, but many American people (Jews, Christians, Muslims, and those of other faiths) still have religious motivations and those who do wish to engage in social reform movements that are compatible with their religious lives. They hope that the way they practice their religion is harmonious with the progress they attempt to participate in within the larger society. Whenever people assume that religion is a motivating factor in the position they hold and the actions they take, the Bible (or the Qur'an or other sacred texts) will offer those with religious sensibilities ways of navigating the developing horizon and the interpretation of those sacred writings will always appeal to their socially reforming (or, for those who defend the status quo, the socially preserving) stance they choose to take. Their sacred texts, their Bible, will speak with *their* voice.[91] That has always been the American way.

---

91. Perhaps Obama's words from the 2008 Compassion Forum are worth repeating: "what those of us of religious faith have to do when we're in the public square is to translate our language into a universal language that can appeal to everybody....

Bibliography

Avalos, Hector. "Diasporas 'R' Us: Attitudes toward Immigrants in the Bible." Pages 33–46 in *The Bible in Political Debate*. Edited by Frances Flannery and Rodney A. Werline. London: Bloomsbury T&T Clark, 2016.

Berlinerblau, Jacques. "The Bible in the Presidential Elections of 2012, 2008, 2004, and the Collapse of American Secularism." Pages 15–36 in *The Bible in the Public Square*. Edited by Mark A. Chancey, Carol Meyers, and Eric M. Meyers. BSNA 27. Atlanta: SBL Press, 2014.

Brooten, Bernadette. "Research on the New Testament and Early Christian Literature May Assist the Churches in Setting Ethical Priorities." *JBL* 136 (2017): 229–36.

Brueggemann, Walter. "At the Mercy of Babylon: A Subversive Rereading of the Empire." *JBL* 110 (1991): 3–22.

Chancey, Mark. "How Should We Teach the Bible in Public Schools?" Religion & Politics. 7 January 2014. https://tinyurl.com/SBL6704b3.

Chancey, Mark A., Carol Meyers, and Eric M. Meyers, eds. *The Bible and the Public Square: Its Enduring Influence in American Life*. BSNA 27. Atlanta: SBL Press, 2014.

Chatfield, Charles. "The Bible and American Peace Movements." Pages 105–31 in *The Bible and Social Reform*. Edited by Ernest Sandeen. Philadelphia: Fortress; Chico, CA: Scholars Press, 1982.

Chodorow, Adam. "Holy Crap." *Slate*. 30 October 2015. https://tinyurl.com/SBL6704c3.

Clinton, Hillary Rodham. Interview by Campbell Brown and Jon Meacham. Compassion Forum. CNN. 13 April 2008.

Coates, TaNehisi. *We Were Eight Years in Power: An American Tragedy*. New York: One World, 2017.

Collins, John. "The Zeal of Phinehas: The Bible and the Legitimation of Violence." *JBL* 122 (2003): 3–21.

Coppins, McKay. "God's Plan for Mike Pence." *The Atlantic*. January–February 2018. https://tinyurl.com/SBL6704d3.

Because we are not just a Christian nation. We are a Jewish nation; we are a Buddhist nation; we are a Muslim nation; Hindu nation; and we are a nation of atheists and nonbelievers" (Obama, interview by Brown and Meacham, 26*).

Davis, Angela Y. *Freedom Is a Constant Struggle: Ferguson, Palestine, and the Foundations of a Movement*. Edited by Frank Barat. Chicago: Haymarket, 2016.

Douglass, Frederick. *Narrative of the Life of Frederick Douglass*. Boston: Anti-Slavery Office, 1845.

Fishlock, Diana. "Atheists 'Slaves Obey Your Masters' Billboard Raises Temper in Pennsylvania." *Huffington Post*. 13 March 2012. https://tinyurl.com/SBL6704e3.

Flannery, Frances. "Senators, Snowballs, and Scripture: The Bible and Climate Change." Pages 61–73 in *The Bible in Political Debate*. Edited by Frances Flannery and Rodney A. Werline. London: Bloomsbury T&T Clark, 2016.

Flannery, Frances, and Rodney A. Werline, eds. *The Bible and Political Debate*. London: Bloomsbury T&T Clark, 2016.

———. Introduction to *The Bible and Political Debate*. Edited by Frances Flannery and Rodney A. Werline. London: Bloomsbury T&T Clark, 2016.

Gafney, Wil. "A Reflection on the Black Lives Matter Movement and Its Impact on My Scholarship." *JBL* 136 (2017): 204–7.

Goff, Philip, Arthur E. Farnsley II, and Peter J. Thuesen. "The Bible in American Life Today." Pages 5–32 in *The Bible in American Life*. Edited by Philip Goff, Arthur E. Farnsley II, and Peter J. Thuesen. Oxford: Oxford University Press, 2017.

Goff, Philip, Arthur E. Farnsley II, and Peter J. Thuesen, eds. *The Bible in American Life*. Oxford: Oxford University Press, 2017.

Guelzo, Allen C. *Lincoln's Emancipation Proclamation: The End of Slavery in America*. New York: Simon & Schuster, 2004.

Gushee, David. *Changing Our Mind*. Canton: Read the Spirit Books, 2017.

Gutjahr, Paul C, ed. *The Oxford Handbook of the Bible in America*. Oxford: Oxford University Press, 2017.

Hanson, Paul. *A Political History of the Bible in America*. Louisville: Westminster John Knox, 2015.

Harrill, J. Albert. "The Use of the New Testament in the American Slave Controversy: A Case History in the Hermeneutical Tension between Biblical Interpretation and Christian Moral Debate." *Religion and American Culture* 10 (2000): 149–86.

Hatch, Nathan O., and Mark A. Noll, eds. *The Bible in America: Essays in Cultural History*. Oxford: Oxford University Press, 1982.

Hollenback, George M. "Who Is Doing What to Whom Revisited: Another Look at Leviticus 18:22 and 20:13." *JBL* 136 (2017): 529–37.
Hughes, Richard. *Myths America Lives By*. Urbana: University of Illinois Press, 2003.
Jackson, Jonathan. "Culture Wars, Homosexuality, and the Bible." Pages 87–99 in *The Bible and Political Debate*. Edited by Frances Flannery and Rodney A. Werline. London: Bloomsbury T&T Clark, 2016.
Johnson, Sylvester. *Myth of Ham in Nineteenth-Century American Christianity: Race, Heathens, and the People of God*. New York: Palgrave MacMillan, 2004.
Junior, Nyasha. "The Scholarly Network." *JBL* 136 (2017): 208–12.
"Justice Ruth Bader Ginsburg Surprises Synagogue as Rosh Hashanah Guest Speaker." *Haaretz*. 21 September 2017. https://tinyurl.com/SBL6704j3.
King, William McGuire. "The Biblical Base of the Social Gospel." Pages 59–84 in *The Bible and Social Reform*. Edited by Ernest Sandeen. Philadelphia: Fortress; Chico, CA: Scholars Press, 1982.
Kutsko, John F. "The Curious Case of the Christian Bible and the U.S. Constitution: Challenges for Educators Teaching the Bible in a Multireligious Context." Pages 240–48 in *The Bible in American Life*. Edited by Philip Goff, Arthur E. Farnsley II, and Peter J. Thuesen. Oxford: Oxford University Press, 2017.
Liew, Tat-siong Benny. "Black Scholarship Matters." *JBL* 136 (2017): 237–44.
Miller, William D. "Dorothy Day and the Bible." Pages 155–77 in *The Bible and Social Reform*. Edited by Ernest Sandeen. Philadelphia: Fortress; Chico, CA: Scholars Press, 1982.
Newton, Richard. "The African American Bible: Bound in a Christian Nation." *JBL* 136 (2017): 221–28.
Ngwa, Kenneth. "At Exodus as the Door of [No] Return." *JBL* 136 (2017): 213–20.
Nissinen, Martti. *Homoeroticism in the Biblical World: A Historical Perspective*. Minneapolis: Augsburg Fortress, 1998.
Noll, Mark. "Nineteenth-Century American Biblical Interpretation." Pages 115–28 in *The Oxford Handbook of the Bible in America*. Edited by Paul C. Gutjahr. Oxford: Oxford University Press, 2017.
———. *The Civil War as a Theological Crisis*. Chapel Hill: University of North Carolina Press, 2006.

Obama, Barack. Interview by Campbell Brown and Jon Meacham. Compassion Forum. CNN. 13 April 2008.

Paris, Peter J. "The Bible and Black Churches." Pages 133–54 in *The Bible and Social Reform*. Edited by Ernest Sandeen. Philadelphia: Fortress; Chico, CA: Scholars Press, 1982.

Powery, Emerson B., and Rodney S. Sadler Jr. *The Genesis of Liberation: Biblical Interpretation in the Antebellum Narratives of the Enslaved*. Louisville: Westminster John Knox, 2016.

Reinhartz, Adele. "The *Journal of Biblical Literature* and the Critical Investigation of the Bible." *JBL* 134 (2015): 457–70.

———. Introduction to "Black Lives Matter for Critical Scholarship." *JBL* 136 (2017): 203.

———. "The Vanishing Jews of Antiquity." *Marginalia*. 24 June 2014. https://tinyurl.com/SBL6704f3.

Ronda, James P. "The Bible and Early American Indian Missions." Pages 9–30 in *The Bible and Social Reform*. Edited by Ernest Sandeen. Philadelphia: Fortress; Chico, CA: Scholars Press, 1982.

Said, Edward. *Orientalism*. New York: Vintage, 1979.

Sandeen, Ernest. Introduction to *The Bible and Social Reform*. Edited by Ernest Sandeen. Philadelphia: Fortress; Chico, CA: Scholars Press, 1982.

Sarna, Jonathan. "The Bible and Judaism in America." Pages 505–16 in *The Oxford Handbook of the Bible in America*. Edited by Paul C. Gutjahr. Oxford: Oxford University Press, 2017.

Schechter, Asher. "Bernie Sanders Isn't Flaunting His Jewishness, and That's OK." *Haaretz* 25. February 2016. https://tinyurl.com/SBL6704g3.

Schüssler Fiorenza, Elisabeth. "The Ethics of Biblical Interpretation: Decentering Biblical Scholarship." *JBL* 107 (1988): 3–17.

Segovia, Fernando. "Criticism in Critical Times: Reflections on Vision and Task." *JBL* 134 (2015): 6–29.

Setzer, Claudia, and David Shefferman, eds. *The Bible and American Culture: A Sourcebook*. New York: Routledge, 2011.

Society of Biblical Literature. *Bible Electives in Public Schools: A Guide*. sbl-site.org. https://tinyurl.com/SBL6704m3.

———. "Mission Statement." sbl-site.org. https://tinyurl.com/SBL6704k3.

———. "Teaching the Bible." sbl-site.org. https://tinyurl.com/SBL6704n3.

Stewart, James Brewer. "Abolitionists, the Bible, and the Challenge of Slavery." Pages 31–57 in *The Bible and Social Reform*. Edited by Ernest Sandeen. Philadelphia: Fortress; Chico, CA: Scholars Press, 1982.

Stice, Alicia, and Cassa Niedringhaus. "Suspect Arrested in Islamic Center Attack." *The Coloradoan*. 27 March 2017. https://www.coloradoan.com/story/news/2017/03/27/breaking-suspect-arrested-islamic-center-attack/99716732/.

Stone, Ken. "What the Homosexuality Debates Really Say about the Bible." Pages 19–38 in *Out of the Shadows into the Light: Christianity and Homosexuality*. Edited by Miquel A. de la Torre. Saint Louis: Chalice, 2009.

Tucker, Gene. "Rain on a Land Where No One Lives: The Hebrew Bible on the Environment." *JBL* 116 (1997): 3–17.

Warner, Megan. "'Therefore a Man Leaves His Father and His Mother and Clings to His Wife': Marriage and Intermarriage in Genesis 2:24." *JBL* 136 (2017): 269–88.

Weber, Peter. "Bernie Sanders Is Jewish. He Also Might Be the Most Christian Candidate in the 2016 Race." *The Week*. 11 April 2016. https://tinyurl.com/SBL6704h3.

Werline, Rodney. "Work, Poverty, and Welfare." Pages 75–86 in *The Bible in Political Debate*. Edited by Frances Flannery and Rodney A. Werline. London: Bloomsbury T&T Clark, 2016.

West, Gerald. "'Leadership and Land': A Very Contextual Interpretation of Genesis 37–50 in KwaZulu-Natal, South Africa." Pages 175–90 in *Genesis: Texts@Contexts*. Edited by Athalya Brenner, Archie Chi-Chung Lee, and Gale Yee. Minneapolis: Fortress, 2010.

Wimbush, Vincent L., ed. *African Americans and the Bible: Sacred Texts and Social Textures*. London: Continuum, 2000.

Wimbush, Vincent L. "Interpreters—Enslaving/Enslaved/Runagate." *JBL* 130 (2011): 5–24.

Zikmund, Barbara Brown. "Biblical Arguments and Women's Place in the Church." Pages 85–104 in *The Bible and Social Reform*. Edited by Ernest Sandeen. Philadelphia: Fortress; Chico, CA: Scholars Press, 1982.

Contributors

Mark A. Chancey is Professor of Religious Studies in Dedman College of Humanities and Sciences at Southern Methodist University. His research interests range from archaeology to American public life. He has published widely on political, constitutional, and historical aspects of Bible courses in American K–12 public schools. Chancey's books include *The Bible in the Public Square: Its Enduring Influence in American Life* (SBL Press, 2014) (coedited with Carol Meyers and Eric M. Meyers); *Alexander to Constantine: Archaeology of the Land of the Bible* (Yale University Press, 2012) (with Eric M. Meyers); *Greco-Roman Culture and the Galilee of Jesus* (Cambridge University Press, 2005); and *The Myth of a Gentile Galilee* (Cambridge University Press, 2002). He serves as chair of the Society of Biblical Literature's Educational Resources and Review Committee and on the editorial boards of *Journal of the American Academy of Religion* and *Religion & Education*.

Lori Anne Ferrell is Dean of the School of Arts and Humanities and John D. and Lillian Maguire Distinguished Professor in Humanities at Claremont Graduate University. She is a Fellow of the Royal Historical Society. Her research interests include Renaissance and Reformation literature and history, the history of the English-language Bible, and sermon literature as both historical evidence and political discourse. Her many publications include: *Government by Polemic: James I and the King's Preachers* (Stanford University Press, 1998); *The Bible and the People* (Yale University Press, 2004); and volume 11 of *The Oxford Edition of the Sermons of John Donne: Sermons Preached at St Paul's Cathedral* (Oxford University Press, forthcoming).

Steven K. Green is the Fred H. Paulus Professor of Law and Affiliated Professor of History and Religious Studies at Willamette University in Salem, Oregon. He is the author of *The Third Disestablishment: Church, State and*

American Culture, 1940–1975 (Oxford University Press, 2019); *Inventing a Christian America* (Oxford University Press, 2015); *The Bible, the School, and the Constitution: The Clash That Shaped Modern Church-State Doctrine* (Oxford University Press, 2012); *The Second Disestablishment: Church and State in the Nineteenth Century* (Oxford University Press, 2010); coauthor of *Religious Freedom and the Supreme Court* (Baylor University Press, 2008); a casebook in church-state law; and more than forty scholarly articles and book chapters on religion, history, and the law. Green has also participated in numerous church-state cases before the US Supreme Court, including serving as cocounsel in Zelman v. Simmons-Harris, the Cleveland voucher case, and has authored or collaborated on more than twenty-five *amicus curiae* briefs in the US Supreme Court.

M. Cooper Harriss is Assistant Professor in the Department of Religious Studies at Indiana University, Bloomington, where he teaches courses on American religion, literature, and culture. He is the author of *Ralph Ellison's Invisible Theology* (NYU Press, 2017) and is working on a book *Muhammad Ali and the Irony of American Religion*. His writing has appeared in *African American Review*, *Biblical Interpretation*, *The Immanent Frame*, *The Journal of Africana Religions*, *The Journal of Religion*, *Soundings*, and *Literature and Theology*. Harriss is a founding coeditor of the journal *American Religion*, published by Indiana University Press, and serves on the editorial board of *Literature and Theology* (Oxford University Press).

Davina C. Lopez is Professor of Religious Studies and core faculty in Women's and Gender Studies at Eckerd College. Her research interests include Pauline studies and the study of the New Testament and Christian origins, histories of American biblical scholarship, theory and method in the study of religion, discourses of religious innovation, visual rhetoric, and gender studies. She is the author of *Apostle to the Conquered: Reimagining Paul's Mission* (Fortress, 2008); senior editor of the Greek, Roman, New Testament, and Early Christian worlds for *The Oxford Encyclopedia of the Bible and Gender Studies* (Oxford University Press, 2014); and the coauthor (with Todd Penner) of *De-introducing the New Testament: Texts, Worlds, Methods, Stories* (Wiley, 2015).

Joseph Orchard is a Senior Editor at Répertoire International de Littérature Musicale. He earned a BA at the University of Dallas, an MA at NYU, and a PhD at Rutgers, the State University of New Jersey, writing his dissertation on rhetoric in the string quartets of W. A. Mozart. He has taught at Rutgers, Seton Hall University, and Caldwell University, creating a course for the last institution on the subject of music and contemplation from the perspective of the Dominican and Catholic traditions. Besides some managerial duties at Répertoire International de Littérature Musicale, he focuses on topics related to music history and to liturgy, mostly in relation to Catholic and Protestant churches. He has written program notes for the Aston Magna Festival for the past two decades. He also contributes to the music scene in New Jersey through his activities as a Catholic scholar and playing violoncello.

Emerson B. Powery is Professor of Biblical Studies and former Coordinator of Ethnic and Area Studies at Messiah College. He is the author of *Jesus Reads Scripture: The Function of Jesus' Use of Scripture in the Synoptic Gospels* (Brill, 2002); "Philemon" for *The New Interpreter's One-Volume Commentary* (Abingdon, 2010); and coauthor of *The Genesis of Liberation: Biblical Interpretation in the Antebellum Narratives of the Enslaved* (Westminster John Knox, 2016), which wrestles with the function of the Bible in the nineteenth-century African American slave-narrative tradition. He was one of the editors of *True to Our Native Land: An African American NT Commentary* (Fortress Augsburg, 2007) and has served on the editorial boards of the *Journal of Biblical Literature* (2005–2013) and *The Common English Bible*. He presently cochairs (with Bernadette Brooten) the Slavery, Resistance, and Freedom section within the Society of Biblical Literature, was president of the Society of Biblical Literature's Southeast region (2006–2007), and serves on the Board of Trustees at Lancaster Theological Seminary.

Aaron Rosen is Professor of Religion and Visual Culture and Director of the Henry Luce III Center for the Arts and Religion at Wesley Theological Seminary in Washington, DC, and Visiting Professor at King's College London, where he taught previously. He began his career at Yale, Oxford, and Columbia, after receiving his PhD from Cambridge. He has curated exhibitions around the world and written widely for scholarly and popular publications. Rosen is the author of several books: *Imagining Jewish Art* (Routledge, 2009); *Art and Religion in the Twenty-First Century* (Thames & Hudson, 2015); and *Brushes with Faith* (Cascade, 2019). His edited books include: *Religion and Art in the Heart of Modern Manhattan* (Ashgate, 2015); *Visualising a Sacred City* (Tauris, 2016); *Encounters: The Art* *of Interfaith Dialogue* (Brepols, 2018); and *Religion and Sight* (Equinox, forthcoming). He is currently working on a monograph entitled *The Hospitality of Images: Modern Art, Architecture, and Interfaith Dialogue* for Cambridge University Press.

Claudia Setzer is Professor of Religious Studies at Manhattan College in Riverdale, New York. Her books include *The Bible and American Culture: A Sourcebook* (Routledge, 2011, with David Shefferman); *Resurrection of the Body in Early Judaism and Early Christianity* (Brill, 2004); and *Jewish Responses to Early Christians* (Augsburg Fortress, 1994). She studies early Jewish-Christian relations, the development of belief in resurrection, women in the Greco-Roman era, nineteenth-century women interpreters of scripture, and the Bible in American culture. She served on the editorial board of the *Journal of Biblical Literature* and on the steering committee for the Recovering Women Interpreters of Scripture group at the Society of Biblical Literature. In 2006 she founded the Columbia University Seminar on the New Testament and has chaired the Early Jewish-Christian Relations group and the Bible in America section at the Society of Biblical Literature. She is currently writing a book on the use of the Bible in progressive movements.

David Shefferman is Associate Professor of Religious Studies at Manhattan College in Riverdale, New York. His research and teaching explore intersections of religion and culture, with particular focus on North America and the Hispanic world. His publications include *The Bible and American Culture: A Sourcebook* (Routledge, 2011, with Claudia Setzer); "Rhetorical Conflicts" (on public debates surrounding Spain's Festivals of Moors and Christians for the journal *Religions*); and a number of articles about the emergence of Afro-Cuban studies. He is currently working on a book *Fictions of Santeria*, a comparison of notions of narrative truthfulness in African-inflected Caribbean practices and in representations of them in popular literature, music, film, and ethnography. He has also presented widely on theory and method in the study of religion, religious tourism, and religion and environmentalism.

Jeffrey S. Siker is Professor of New Testament and Early Christianity, Emeritus, at Loyola Marymount University, where he taught for thirty-two years. He has written in the areas of early Jewish-Christian relations (*Disinheriting the Jews: Abraham in Early Christian Controversy*, Westminster

John Knox, 1991); the use of the Bible in contemporary theological ethics (*Scripture and Ethics: Twentieth Century Portraits*, Oxford University Press, 1996); debates over the inclusion of LGBT individuals within the church (ed., *Homosexuality and the Church: Both Sides of the Debate*, Westminster John Knox, 1994); the status of LGBT individuals within various religious traditions (ed., *Homosexuality and Religion: An Encyclopedia*, Greenwood, 2007); how Jesus came to be viewed as perfectly sinless in early Christianity (*Jesus, Sin, and Perfection in Early Christianity*, Cambridge University Press, 2015); what difference it makes to read the Bible in print form or on digital screens (*Liquid Scriptures: The Bible in a Digital World*, Fortress, 2017); and how the different writings of the New Testament approach the topic of sin (*Sin in the New Testament*, Oxford University Press, 2019). In addition, he has published over two dozen articles on areas related to these books. Siker is also an ordained minister in the Presbyterian Church (PCUSA).

Jason A. Wyman Jr. received his PhD from Union Theological Seminary in the City of New York. His first book, *Constructing Constructive Theology: An Introductory Sketch* (Fortress, 2017), looks at the history and method of constructive theology as a coherent tradition. He has also published articles in *Black Theology: An International Journal* and *Theology Today*. Wyman teaches classes on theology, social ethics, and religion in New York.

Biblical Index

Hebrew Bible/Old Testament		1 Samuel	
		20:42	213
Genesis			
1	140	2 Samuel	
1:28–30	122	18:33	141
2:24	264		
6:14	83	1 Kings	
6:19–7:3	122	3:8	180
7:4	122	12: 27–32	17
8:20	122		
9:2–4	86	Psalms	
9:20–27	98, 122, 259	17	141
12:3	276	18	142
15:6	60	19	142
16:8	99	34	142
22:8	276	39	142
		40	142
Exodus		42	143
4:18	213	96	142
15	149	102	149
23	275	126	142
		150	142
Leviticus			
18:22	264	Proverbs	
19:18	148	30:18–19	144
20:13	264	31:17	216
Numbers		Song of Songs	
6:24–26		2:16	101
		8:6–7	143, 145
Joshua			
10	197	Isaiah	
		1:3	136
Judges		26:2	178
18:6	213	61:1	98

BIBLICAL INDEX

Jeremiah
20 — 144

Lamentations
1:12 — 144

Amos
5:24 — 275

New Tetament

Matthew
3:13–23 — 136
7:12 — 275
19:14 — 178

Mark
5:34 — 213

Luke
2 — 149
2:34 — 146
4:18 — 98
7:1–10 — 262
7:36–50 — 137
7:50 — 213
8:2 — 137
21:12–15 — 180

John
5 — 149
8:2–11 — 137
15:13 — 276

Acts
2 — 146
16:32 — 213

Romans
4:3 — 60
9:25 — 101

1 Corinthians
6:9–10 — 47–48

Galatians
6:9 — 180

Ephesians
3 — 142

Philippians
2:3 — 216

Colossians
3:22 — 98, 255

2 Thessalonians
3:10 — 276

James
2:16 — 213

Revelation
15:3–4 — 149
21:1–5 — 148

GENERAL INDEX

Abington v. Schempp (1963)   9, 163–65, 189–90, 213
Ackerman, James S.   195, 201
Adamo, Mark   138–39
Adams, John (composer)   134, 136–38
Adams, John (president)   169–71
African American interpretation   3, 12, 14, 27, 97–98, 110
Aken, Sam van   122–23
Alden, John   15–16
Alley, Robert S.   173–74
American Academy of Religion (AAR) origins   244–47
American Bible Society   21–22, 28, 39, 128, 171
Anders, George   236
Anderson, Laurie   140–41
Anderson, Porter   39
Ansolabehere, Stephen   167
anti-Semitism   4
Argento, Dominick   149
Avalos, Hector   234, 275
Babbitt, Milton   133, 140
Baden, Joel S.   4, 11, 87–88, 199–200
Bailey, Beatrice   209
Bailey, Randall C.   3
Bailyn, Bernard   168
Balkin, Jack M.   167
Barber, Samuel   133
Barr, David   1, 191, 195, 227
Bartkowski, John P.   135
Barton, David   154
Beal, Timothy K.   231
Benedict XVI, Pope   148
Benjamin, Siona   126–27
Bérubé, Michael   235
Berlinerblau, Jacques   232, 234, 276
Berlinkski, Herman   149
Berman, Harold J.   155–56, 161
Bernstein, Leonard   133
Bibb, Bryan   40
Bible Literacy Project   9, 198, 201
biblical literacy/illiteracy   4, 10, 94, 101, 107, 109, 168, 230–31, 239–40, 242, 245, 257
Bible Odyssey website   266
Black, Hugo   153
Black Lives Matter   4, 11, 80, 266–73, 282, 284
Blackstone, William, 8, 157. *See also* common law
Bland, Kalman   125
Blount, Brian K.   3, 11, 266
Blum, John Morton   174
Bok, Derek   237
Borysewicz, Alfonse   124
Bottigheimer, Ruth   49
Bourne, Peter   177
Boylan, Alexis   116
Bracher, Peter S.   195
Branch, Caroline   192
Breed, Brennan   197
Breslin, James   114
Brettler, Marc   4
Bridgman, Valerie   3
Briggs, Charles Augustus   241–42
Brockman, David R.   207
Brooten, Bernadette   269, 271
Bruce, Robert Todd   209
Brueggemann, Walter   268

GENERAL INDEX

Bush, George H. W. 179
Bush, George W. 179–81
Butler, Jon 173
Butler, Octavia 7, 95–109
Byrd, James P. 170, 172
Calhoun-Brown, Allison 177, 181, 183
Callahan, Allen 3, 98–101
Campbell, Colin 118
Cargill, Robert 199
Carter, Elliott 133
Carter, Jimmy 9, 176–77, 277
Castellanos, Rosario 136, 137
Catholic League 117–18
Chancey, Mark A. 2, 9, 194–97, 200, 201, 207, 228, 267, 272
Chatfield, Charles 272–73
Cheong, Pauline 59
Childs, Brevard 96
Church, Forrest 156
Clausen, René 145, 148
Cleage, Albert 77, 80
Clinton, Bill 180–81, 260
Clinton, Hillary Rodham 274, 277–79
Coates, Ta-Nehisi 279
Coke, Sir Edward, 157. *See also* common law
Collins, John J.
common law. *See* legal traditions
Concannon, Cavan 4
Cone, James 77–81, 99
Conn, Joseph L. 156
Constitution, 4, 8–11, 95, 97, 117, 155–56. 165–68, 262
    First Amendment (Free Exercise and Establishment Clauses), 9, 153–54, 164, 189, 192, 206
    separation of church and state, 153–54, 163–65, 189–90, 194, 197, 200, 211–13, 228, 239, 255, 279
Copland, Aaron 133
Corbett, Sidney 139
Corigliano, John 141, 143, 144
Corwin, Edward S. 156, 158
creationism. *See* science and religion debates

Crenshaw, Dave 46
Crumb, R. 119
Danielpour, Richard 142
David, Angela Y. 269
Davis, Derek H. 169
Deckman, Melissa 201
Dehaene, Stanislas 41–42
Delbanco, Andrew 237
DelFattore, Joan 190, 194–95
Dewey, John 247
Diamond, David 134, 141
Dierenfield, Bruce J. 163, 165
Dixon, John 7, 15, 113–16, 125
Douglass, Frederick 256–57
Douglass, Susan L. 204–6
Dreisbach, Daniel 2, 171–72
Drummond, Tim 211
Eckes, Susan E. 192
Eidsmoe, John 154
Eisenhower, Dwight D. 176
Ellison, Ralph 95
Enslin, Morton 243–44
environmentalism 4–5, 73, 84–87, 105, 114, 119, 122–23, 135
Eskenazi, Tamara Cohn 3
Establishment Clause. *See* Constitution
Evans, C. Stephen 227
evolution. *See* science and religion debates
exceptionalism 6–7, 93–95, 99, 101, 106–9, 179, 181, 258
Farnsley, Arthur E. 2, 27, 257, 272, 282
Federer, William 162
Feinberg, Walter 192, 197–98, 201
Felder, Cain Hope 3, 97
Ferrell, Lori Anne 5–6, 16
feminist interpretation 2–3, 233
Fetter-Harrott, Allison 192
film 73, 82–90, 117
Finkelman, Paul 163
First Amendment. *See* Constitution
Fitch, Florence 246–47
Flannery, Frances 2, 268, 272, 274, 276, 282
Forbes, Bruce 69

formats 30–33, 36–40, 50–52, 119–20
Free Exercise Clause. *See* Constitution
Freeman, Bernard "Bun B" 72
Frerichs, Ernest 1, 16
Gafney, Wil 4, 11, 269, 270, 282
Gaustad, Edwin S. 1
Gazzaley, Adam 46
Geer Le Boutillier, Cornelia 156
gender 2, 95, 99, 109, 215, 278
Gibbs, Christopher 134
Gilbert, Arthur 195
Ginsburg, Ruth Bader 262
Glass, Philip 134, 142. 143
Glassroth v. Moore 8
Goff, Philip 2, 27, 256–57, 272, 282
Good, Edwin 133
Gould, Morton 134
Gray, Patrick 227
Green, Steven K.8, 157, 160–62 164, 169, 171
Greenberg, Clement 114
Greene, Jamal 167
Greenawalt, Kent 193
Griffiths, Paul 134
Grotenhuis, Dale (Jack) 149
Gryboski, Michael 44
Guelzo, Allen C. 274
Gunn, Giles 1, 6, 93–99, 104–5
Gushee, David 261
Gutjahr, Paul 2, 13, 21, 22, 272
Hagar 99–100, 103, 139
Hall, Kermit L. 155, 157, 161
Hall, Mark David 168
Hailstork, Adolphus 143
Handy, Robert T. 173
Hanson, Howard 133
Hanson, Paul D. 2, 258, 282
Harbison, John 8, 135–36, 141
Harper, William Rainey 247
Harpham, Geoffrey Galt 235
Harrelson, Walter 1
Harrill, Albert 259
Harriss, M. Cooper 6–7
Hartshorne, Hugh 246
Hartley, John 37
Hatch, Nathan O. 173, 272
Hawkins, Peter 94
Haynes, Charles C. 191, 193, 228
Herbst, Jurgen 237
Hicks-Keeton, Jill 4
Higdon, Jennifer 137
higher law. *See* legal traditions
hip hop 72–79, 81–82, 89–90
Hodge, Daniel White 73, 78–81
Hofstadter, Richard 237
Holland, Glen 228, 230
Hollenbock, George M. 264
homosexuality 260–64
Horrell, David G. 4
Horwitz, Morton J. 157, 167
Hudson, Winthrop S. 173
Hughes, Richard T. 207, 258
Hungerford, Amy 100–1, 106–7
intelligent design. *See* science and religion debates
IUPUI study 27, 39–40, 257
Jackson, Jonathan 263
Jefferson, Thomas 169–70
Jeffery, David Lyle 227
Johnson, James Turner 1
Johnson, Sylvester 98, 259
Junior, Nyasha 269–70
Kahn, Tobi 125–27
Kasparian, Faith D. 212
Kendall, Nancy 215
Kendrick, Eliza Hall 246
Kent, Orit 62
Kidd, Thomas 168
Kim, Byong-kon 145–46
King, Martin Luther 274, 279
King, William McGuire 273
Kinkade, Thomas 116–18
Knehans, Douglas 145
Knight, Edward 144
Kokalitcheva, Kia 40
Kramnick, Isaac 156
Kruse, Kevin M. 176
Kutsko, John F. 11, 167, 262, 267
Laats, Adam 214
Labaree, David 238

Lang, David 146
Lapsley, Jacqueline 3
Larsen, Libby 142–43
Larson, Edward John 213
Lashof-Sullivan, Matthew 215–16
Lauridsen, Morten 136
Layton, Richard A. 192, 197–98. 201, 206
legal traditions
    biblical influence on, 154–68. *See also* Ten Commandments
    common law, 157
    higher law, 157
    natural law, 157–60
Lemon v. Kurtzman (1971) 9, 192
Lester, Emile 192, 203
Levenson, David 201, 206
Levin, Martin 135
Levine, Amy-Jill 4
Levine, Gilbert 141
Lewis, Bret 201
liberation theology 75–81, 89–90, 99
Liew, Tat-siong Benny 269, 271–72
Lincoln, Abraham 9, 174–75, 259–60, 274, 278–79
Linder, Robert D. 174–78, 183
Locke, John 8, 158
Lopez, Crystal 201
Lopez, Davina C. 10–11, 233–34
Lupu, Ira C. 154
Lutz, Donald S. 170
Magruder, Michael Takeo 120–21
Mahler, Gustav 141
Mangrum, Richard Collins 212
Mann, Horace 163–64
marriage equality, 215, 256, 260–63, 280. *See also* Obergefell v. Hodges
Martin, Clarice J. 3
Martin, Dale B. 232
Mather, Cotton 93
May, Thomas 138
McAllister, Lester G. 173
McBride, James 106,
McClary, Susan 141
McCarthy, Cormac 107

McCutcheon, Russell 232
McDannell, Colleen 23
McFague, Sallie 74, 89
McLoughlin, William G. 173
McNaughton, Jon 117–18
Meacham, Jon 2, 156, 175, 277–79, 281
Mercadante, Linda 239–40
Mermerstein, David 138
Meyers, Carol 2, 272
Meyers, Eric 2, 272
Miller, Monica R. 72
Miller, William D. 273
Miller, William Lee 176, 273
Mitchell, W.J.T. 129
Moneo, Rafael 124
Montgomery, James 242
Moore, Diane 192, 198
Moore, R. Laurence 156
Moore, Randy 213
Moore, Roy 8, 156, 258
Moore, Stephen 234
Moral Monday movement 257, 267
Moravec, Paul 145
Morgan, C. E. 108
Morgan, David 115–17
Moring, Mark 84
Morris, Richard B. 158
Morrison, Toni 7, 95–109
Moslener, Sara 215
Moss, Candida 4, 11, 199–200, 223
Muhly, Nico 143
Munoz, Vincent Philip 168
Muilenburg, James 228, 246
museums 4, 9, 115–16, 127–29
Museum of Biblical Art 127–28
Museum of the Bible 4, 9, 127–29, 198–201
National Association of Biblical Instructors (NABI). *See* American Academy of Religion
National Council on Bible Curriculum in Public Schools 9, 196–98, 201
National Endowment for the Arts 117
natural law. *See* legal traditions
Newman, Barnett 114–15, 127

GENERAL INDEX

Newsom, Carol 3
Newton, Richard 11, 269–71
Ngwa, Kenneth 269–71
Nicolás, Adolfo 61
Nissinen, Martti 264
Nixon, Richard 176
Noah story 82–88, 122
Noll, Mark A., 1–4, 97, 171–75, 183, 260, 265, 272, 282–83
Nord, David Paul 25
Nord, Warren 191
Numbers, Ronald L. 214
Nussbaum, Martha 236
Obama, Barack 117–18, 181–82, 216, 275–81
Obergefell v. Hodges (2015) 11, 260–62
O'Brien, Julia 2
Olin, Margaret 125
Ong, Walter 37
Orchard, Joseph 7
Page, Hugh 3
Paine, Thomas 169, 171
Panter, Gary 120
Paris, Peter J. 273
Paterson, Frances R. 197
Paulus, Stephen 148
Penner, Todd 233
Perle, George 133
Perrin, Andrew 38
Perrine, William Micahael 211
Persily, Nathaniel 167
Petre, Jonathan 74
Peursen, Wido van 49
Phy, Allene Stuart 1
Piediscalzi, Nicholas 1, 191, 195, 227
Pierard, Richard V. 174–78, 183
Pinn, Anthony 6, 72, 75–76, 90
political rhetoric 168–83, 256, 258–63, 275–80
Powell, H. Jefferson 166
Powell, Rosephayne 144
Powery, Emerson 3, 10–11, 259, 270, 284
Prothero, Stephen 239
Putnam, Robert D. 135
Pyper, Hugh 50
Quimby, Chester 245–46
racialization 97–98, 109, 259–60, 269
reading, print versus digital 41–45
Rakow, Katja 45
Rand, Archie 125
rap 6, 75–76
Reagan, Ronald 8, 165, 178–79, 215, 256
Reich, Steve 139–42
Reinhartz, Adele 265–66, 269
Religious Education Association 247–48
Residents (musical group) 146–47
revivalism 172–74
Rhees, Rush 248
rhetoric, 264–65, 273. *See also* political rhetoric
on biblical scholarship 249–51
Richards, Kent Harold 197, 206, 228
Ringe, Sharon 3
Robinson, Marilynne 107–8
Roncane, Mark 227
Ronda, James P. 273–74
Roosevelt, Franklin 8, 175–76
Rosen, Aaron 7, 113, 128
Rosen, Larry D. 46
Rosenblith, Suzanne 190
Ross, Bobby 40
Ross, Steve 120
Rothko, Mark 114
Rouse, Christopher 143
Rudolph, Frederick 237
Rushkoff, Douglas 119–20
"sacred gaze" 115–16
Ruffin, Kimberly 104
Sadler, Rodney 3, 11, 259, 267, 270, 284
Said, Edward 259
Sandeen, Ernest 1, 11, 263, 272–74, 281, 284
Sanders, Bernie 274–75
Sarna, Jonathan 257
Schaeffer, Judith E. 201
Schultz, Katherine G. 194
Schüssler Fiorenza, Elisabeth 228, 264, 268
science and religion debates 2, 213–15, 228, 239, 279

Scott, A. O. 233
Second Vatican Council 28, 147
Segovia, Fernando 264–65
Seidman, Lisa Ness 212
Sellars, Peter 136
separation of church and state. *See* Constitution
Serrano, Andres 117–18
Setzer, Claudia 2, 3, 14, 21, 272, 284
Sharp, Liam 119–20
Shefferman, David A. 2, 14, 272, 284
Sherwood, Yvonne 234
Siegel, Harvey 214
Siker, Jeffrey 5–6, 38
Small, Helen 234
Smith, Jonathan Z. 230, 232
Smith, Peter J. 166
Smith, Ted A. 106
social media 57–61, 74, 120, 270, 275
Stahlberg, Lesleigh Cushing 94
Stern, Jeremy A. 206
Stern, Sheldon M. 206
Stewart, James Brewer 272
Still, William Grant 134, 144
Stokes, Harvey 146
Story, Joseph 159–60
Street, Nicholas 169
Stewart, Katherine 197
Stone, Ken 263, 265
Strout, Cushing 173
Summers, Cary L. 200
Summit, Jennifer 235
Sunstein, Cass 167
Sussman, Lance 20–21
Swancutt, Diana 11, 267
Swezey, James A. 194
Taruskin, Richard 134
Taylor, Marion Ann 2
Ten Commandments 8, 156, 161–62, 205, 207, 258, 280
Thelin, John 237
Thomas, Oliver 193
Thompson, Craig 120
Thuesen, Peter 2, 27, 257, 272, 282
Tobin, Gary A. 206
Torke, Michael 143–44
Trollinger, Susan L. 214
Trollinger, William Vance 214
Trotta, Michael J. 145
translation(s) 5, 18–21, 24–32, 40, 47–48
Trump, Donald J. 108, 129, 182, 216, 274–76
Tucker, Gene 264
Tucker, Jeffrey 147–48
Tucker, William E. 173
Tuttle, Robert W. 154, 166
Tyndale, William 16
Valentine, Ryan 216
Vander Stichele, Caroline 50
Vermeule, Blakey 235
versions
    American Revised 25–26
    Eliot's "Indian Bible" 18, 20
    English Revised 25
    Catholic 20, 26, 49
    children's 49–51, 29
    Geneva 16–18, 32
    Gideon 24, 71
    Jewish 20–21, 43, 49, 198, 257
    King James 17, 19, 23, 25, 27–29, 37, 52, 61, 71, 106, 164, 171
    New Century 5, 29
    New Jerusalem 5, 28
    New King James 5, 28, 37
    New Revised Standard 5, 28, 47
Veysey, Lawrence R. 236
Wachlin, Marie Goughnour 193, 209
Wald, Kenneth D. 177, 181, 183
Waldman, J. T. 119–20
Warner, Megan 264
Warshaw, Thayer S. 195, 201
Watson, Peter 237
Weaver, John 40
Weber, Peter 275
Webster, Jane 228, 230
Weiss, Andrea 3
Werline, Rodney A. 2, 268, 272, 274, 276, 282, 285
Wertheimer, Linda K. 191

West, Gerald	267
Whitacre, Eric	141
Willet, Chester	248
Williams, Delores	99
Williams, Jean Calterone	215
Wills, Garry	177–78
Wilson, James	158–59
Wilson, Woodrow	174
Wimbush, Vincent	3, 97–98, 264–65, 272
Wojnarowicz, David	117–18
Wolf, Maryanne	41–42
Wolf, William	174
Womac, Patrick	190
Womanist interpretation	2, 97, 99
Wright, Benjamin F.	158
Wuorinen, Charles	133, 140
Wyman, Jason	6
X, Malcolm	97
Xu, Xiaohe	135
Ybarra, Dennis R.	206
Young, Stephen	234
Zikmund, Barbara	272
Zimmerman, Jonathan	194, 215
Zorn, John	144–45

www.ingramcontent.com/pod-product-compliance
Lightning Source LLC
Chambersburg PA
CBHW030817230426
43667CB00008B/1259